VOID

The Unpublished Lectures
of Gilbert Highet

Hawaii Classical Studies

Robert J. Ball and J. D. Ellsworth
General Editors

Vol. 2

PETER LANG
New York • Washington, D.C./Baltimore • Boston
Bern • Frankfurt am Main • Berlin • Vienna • Paris

The Unpublished Lectures of Gilbert Highet

Edited by
Robert J. Ball

PETER LANG
New York • Washington, D.C./Baltimore • Boston
Bern • Frankfurt am Main • Berlin • Vienna • Paris

Library of Congress Cataloging-in-Publication Data

Highet, Gilbert, 1906–1978.
The unpublished lectures of Gilbert Highet / edited by Robert J. Ball.
p. cm. — (Hawaii classical studies; vol. 2)
Includes bibliographical references and index.
1. Classical literature—History and criticism. 2. Civilization, Modern—
Classical influences. 3. Literature, Modern—Classical influences.
I. Ball, Robert J. II. Title. III. Series.
PA3003.54   880'.09—dc21   98-10552
ISBN 0-8204-3824-3
ISSN 1073-6050

Die Deutsche Bibliothek-CIP-Einheitsaufnahme

Highet, Gilbert:
The unpublished lectures of Gilbert Highet / ed. by Robert J. Ball.
–New York; Washington, D.C./Baltimore; Boston; Bern;
Frankfurt am Main; Berlin; Vienna; Paris: Lang.
(Hawaii classical studies; Vol. 2)
ISBN 0-8204-3824-3

Back cover photo of Gilbert Highet by Antony Di Gesú.
Back cover photo of Robert J. Ball by Dwight Okumoto.

The paper in this book meets the guidelines for permanence and durability
of the Committee on Production Guidelines for Book Longevity
of the Council of Library Resources.

Printed in the United States of America.

PERMISSIONS

GILBERT HIGHET

1906–1978

And gladly wolde he lerne and gladly teche

CONTENTS*

---

*In some instances, the titles of the lectures (as they appear in the original typescripts) have been modified in order to provide the reader with a more accurate idea of their contents.

PREFACE

Gilbert Arthur Highet, Anthon Professor of Latin at Columbia University, was one of the twentieth century's most erudite and distinguished classicists. In 1983 I edited (in memory of this great teacher and scholar) a volume of his classical papers for Columbia University Press—a volume that included a biographical essay about his career and a bibliography of his publications.[*] As contrasted with the first volume, containing in the main papers that he had published in professional journals, the current volume consists almost entirely of unpublished lectures that he presented on a variety of occasions. The lectures included in this volume consist of scholarly essays and those less technical, some directed to the professional classicist and others to the educated lay person—the two different audiences whom he addressed.

This volume contains virtually all Dr. Highet's unpublished classical lectures—lectures that he presented during the 1950s, 1960s, and 1970s. These lectures have been arranged in three groups—Greek Literature, Latin Literature, and the Classical Tradition—corresponding to the three central interests to which he devoted himself in his research on classical subjects. Within each group the lectures have been arranged chronologically by the authors considered, in order to demonstrate in the clearest manner the vast period of time and large number of writers contained in the collection. Some of the lectures exist in more than one version, in different stages of development; in those instances where multiple versions of a manuscript exist, the most recent version of that manuscript has been reproduced. Several of the listings, although not actually lectures or not strictly classical, have been included in

---

[*]See R. J. Ball, ed., *The Classical Papers of Gilbert Highet* (New York, 1983) 1–14, for the biographical essay and list of publications about Highet, and 349–78, for the bibliography of his publications—a bibliography spanning a period of fifty years and consisting of approximately one thousand items. See also R. J. Ball, "Gilbert Highet and the Augustan Poets," in C. Deroux, ed., *Studies in Latin Literature and Roman History* 7 (1994) 310–26, for a survey of Highet's publications in Augustan poetry—an aspect of classical literature to which he devoted considerable attention throughout his career.

this volume, inasmuch as they demonstrate how Dr. Highet's love of classical literature influenced other aspects of his research.

With respect to the text of each lecture, Dr. Highet's words have been reproduced for the most part exactly as they appear in his typescripts. However, because of variations in spelling involving American versus British usage, the American practice has been adopted uniformly, from one lecture to another, in order to provide the volume with internal consistency. Furthermore, in the course of verifying the literary references (ancient and modern), I have occasionally inserted missing references without notice and corrected those in the text—this mostly having to do with line numbers. In addition, I have occasionally softened certain words and phrases that are found in the typescripts but are not appropriate today, in accordance with the conventions that currently govern the standard of public discourse. Now and then I have translated a non-English word or phrase directly after its occurrence, as did Dr. Highet in many instances, in accordance with his desire to make the classical subject more accessible to the general reader.

Regarding the footnotes in each lecture, two different kinds have been employed—those written by Dr. Highet and those that I have introduced. Those written by Dr. Highet have been reproduced for the most part exactly as he printed them, but occasionally with minor corrective refinements, usually involving a more complete bibliographical citation for a book or article. Those that I have introduced as the editor, which identify or elaborate on the different source materials referred to or alluded to in the lecture, have uniformly been enclosed in brackets with the standard abbreviation 'Ed.' Just as I have verified the literary references in the text, so I have also verified the bibliographical information in the footnotes, which have been presented as accurately as possible in accordance with traditional philological procedure. I have occasionally introduced footnotes for the general reader clarifying items in the text that may seem obscure today, and footnotes referring to other publications by Dr. Highet that deal with items appearing in the text.

One finds in these lectures a celebration of classical literature that made Gilbert Highet one of the most well-known classicists in America in his day. In these lectures, as in his numerous publications, one observes the entire classical world through the perspective of one man's powerful mind, with emphasis on those aspects of great writing that make the classical authors worth reading. In them one also observes an endless enthusiasm for classical literature, which pervades his rich and detailed studies of the ancient masterpieces and their enormous influence on the modern world and on modern literature. His research demonstrates a humane form of scholarship, which may well differ from the sort of literary criticism cultivated today, but which earned for this remarkable man an enduring place in the history of his profession.

Honolulu, Hawaii   ROBERT J. BALL

ACKNOWLEDGEMENTS

I wish to thank the following individuals and organizations for helping me bring this project to a successful conclusion:

Keith Highet, Co-Trustee of the Helen Highet Trust, for allowing me to honor his father with this volume and for providing me with useful comments regarding several of the lectures;

Andrew Boose, Co-Trustee of the Helen Highet Trust, for officially authorizing me to undertake this project and for providing me with his legal expertise in the appropriate matters;

J. D. Ellsworth, Professor of Classics at the University of Hawaii, for answering my numerous questions about the lectures and about their systematic reproduction on the computer;

The University of Hawaii Research Council, for awarding me a travel grant at the inception of this project to conduct research on Gilbert Highet's papers at Columbia University;

The Columbia University Rare Book and Manuscript Library, for enabling me to examine Gilbert Highet's papers and for supporting my plans to publish this collection of his lectures;

The Hawaii Committee for the Humanities—an affiliate of the National Endowment for the Humanities—for awarding me a publication grant toward the completion of this project.

ABBREVIATIONS

AFSS *Audio-Forum Sound Seminar*

AJA *American Journal of Archaeology*

AJPh *American Journal of Philology*

BMCT *Book-of-the-Month Club Transcripts*

CPh *Classical Philology*

CQ *Classical Quarterly*

CW *Classical World*

GRBS *Greek, Roman, and Byzantine Studies*

HSPh *Harvard Studies in Classical Philology*

JHS *Journal of Hellenic Studies*

RE *Real-Encyclopädie der klassischen Altertumswissenschaft*

TAPhA *Transactions of the American Philological Association*

GREEK LITERATURE

Pandora's Box[*]

I expect we all know the story of Pandora and her box, at least in outline. It is beautiful and rather horrible, and (like most of the old stories) rather confused and silly here and there. It comes down to us from early Greek legend. Pandora was the first woman. Her name means "All Gifts." She was specially made by the gods, who each contributed some quality to make her a perfect woman; and she was sent down to her husband, who received her with delight. His name was Epimetheus, which means "Afterthought."

And then she had a box. Was it her dowry, and did she know what was in it? It is hard to be sure. Anyhow, the story is one of those typical Greek tales of cunning and entrapment and disillusion, like the Trojan horse. She opened the mysterious box, and at once out there flew all the troubles of the whole world, all the sins and diseases, all the hideous inventions and perversions which now plague mankind. Before then, they had been imprisoned; but then they escaped, and (so the story goes) they have been out wandering ever since, and the earth is full of evils, and full is the sea.

Yet there is a touching and charming end to the story, the kind of thing which very few nations except the Greeks could have created. After the box of Pandora had been emptied of all its vile contents, she and her husband looked inside to see if there was anything left. There remained one single being, perhaps caught under the lid, perhaps reluctant to go out into the world among the crowd of foul invaders. It was one of the rare spirits which console human beings in the midst of their suffering in this world. It was Hope.

That is the story as it has passed into the popular imagination. Confused it may be; pessimistic it certainly is; but like most of the Greek myths, it penetrates the imagination and lingers in it. Recently I have seen several newspaper cartoons printed both in the United States and in Europe showing a modern Pandora

---

[*]Presented in 1956 on Highet's radio program (= *BMCT* 75). [See R. J. Ball, ed., *The Classical Papers of Gilbert Highet* (New York, 1983) 9, for information on Highet's radio program of the 1950s, and 361–68, for a complete list of his radio talks and the articles developed from them. Ed.]

opening her box. Nearly always the box was the atom, and the powers that flew out of it shocked the modern Pandora as much as the more normal and accustomed human evils shocked the mythical Greek Pandora. Evidently this a fundamental, an archetypal story.

After years of research, two experts in symbolism have produced a delightful book on the myth. They are Dora and Erwin Panofsky, of Princeton; the book is called simply *Pandora's Box* (although the authors know the title is a misnomer).[1] Their purpose is to tell how the myth has been transformed, both by the fantasy and by the mistakes of modern artists and writers from the Renaissance to the present day. Not only do they do so, vividly and sometimes wittily, but they give us sixty pictures ranging all the way from an exquisite Benvenuto Cellini sculpture to a percipient but loathsome Paul Klee still life.

There are certain fascinations about studying mythology as the Panofskys do. There is the obvious but delicious experience of seeing how a single story inspires so many different artists to different types of creation. For instance, Pandora, prototype of womanhood, is a fine subject for painters. It is wonderful to watch how the Renaissance French painter Jean Cousin made her into a beautiful reclining nude with one arm resting on a skull, while Dante Gabriel Rossetti, the Pre-Raphaelite, conceived her as a fully clothed woman with dark, voluptuous, fateful eyes, a sensuous mouth, and a mass of dark hair hovering like a stormcloud behind her head; the English artist John Flaxman took another moment of her story and produced an elegant piece of almost-Greek sculpture, showing Pandora, half-naked with draperies streaming out behind her, being carried down to earth by Hermes, the messenger of heaven; Nathaniel Hawthorne's illustrator, Hammatt Billings, turned Pandora into a little girl looking rather like Alice in Wonderland, starting back from the open box as a child starts back if it comes too close to a wasp's nest.

Another fascination, which goes deeper, is to examine the visual symbols which artists develop in order to convey spiritual meanings without the use of language. This is one of the specialties of Mr. Panofsky: he can take a single page of one of those books of allegorical illustration called emblem books, or a single picture such as Albrecht Dürer's *The Knight, Death, and the Devil,* interpret every image in it, and relate them all to the central conception with such depth and subtlety that we realize once more the shal-

---

[1][See D. and E. Panofsky, *Pandora's Box* (New York, 1956[1] and 1962[2]). Ed.]

lowness of modern art—which is usually a collection of purely visual effects, as contrasted with the art of our forefathers, where one picture could contain as much meaning as a long poem.

For instance, in a painting of Pandora opening the box, how should that important figure Hope be portrayed? The evils—well, they can be made into monstrous figures, diseased, overdeveloped and distorted, and a skeleton will depict the final evil, Death. But Hope? Early in the sixteenth century a book of allegorical pictures came out which presented Hope as a female spirit accompanied by a crow. And why a crow? Because a crow, when it opens its beak, says *cras, cras*—which is Latin for "tomorrow, tomorrow"—and therefore its call is the utterance of hope, or if you prefer, pro*cras*-tination.

Sometimes the symbols get mixed up. The Panofskys stress the fact that the most important symbol of the entire myth has gone wrong. In the original story, Pandora had no box. She came down from heaven perfectly equipped with her own gifts—the gifts of perfect womanhood, which the Greek poet Hesiod, writing in the seventh century B.C. or so, cynically lists as beauty, skill in weaving and needlework, lovely clothes and jewelry, plus a deceitful character and a shameless mind. This, it is implied, was quite enough trouble for her poor husband Afterthought; but then she started interfering with his domestic arrangements. She found not a box but an enormous jar; apparently it was sitting peacefully on or in the earth, imprisoning the troubles destined for man, in the same way as the bottle sealed by King Solomon imprisoned the evil genie in the *Arabian Nights*. She opened this jar. Out flew the troubles. Hope alone remained.

There are at least two different stories here. One is the tale which everyone now accepts instinctively, that a beautiful woman was sent down from heaven with a gift-casket which, when opened, proved to be full of evil. The other is the earlier myth told by Hesiod, or rather handed down to him, that a beautiful woman was sent down from heaven, and when she got to earth, she opened a great jar which until then had been the prison for all the troubles of earth. The first is a story of treachery. The second is a story of prying curiosity. One reason they have been mixed up is that the Greeks, and later the men of the Renaissance, thought that women were both inquisitive and deceitful. But there is another reason, which through some detective work the Panofskys revealed. This is that the first writer to tell the story in modern times was the Dutch scholar Erasmus of Rotterdam. He put it into "one

of the world's most popular and influential books,"[2] his collection of
Adages or *Wise Sayings,* with running commentaries. He told it to
illustrate the proverb that fools never learn until they are hurt;
and he told it wrongly. It was he who changed what had been a
large immovable storage jar on earth into a small portable casket
brought down from heaven; and Mr. Panofsky suggests that he
confused the story of Pandora with another beautiful myth—the
tale of the princess Psyche, who was sent down to the underworld
to bring back some of the beauty of the queen of the dead and who,
when she opened the casket that contained it, was nearly killed by
the deadly vapor that emerged.

Still, even when we look at the original story, which is told twice
(*Theogony* 562–616 and *Works and Days* 42–105) by the Greek
poet Hesiod, that prehistoric successor of Homer, we see that it also
is mixed up. Its central purpose is clear. It is meant to be an explanation of one of the central problems of human life—namely, what
is the origin of evil? We surely cannot believe that the world was
created utterly evil. We find it very hard to believe that it was created by pure chance, without any good or evil significance. We are
unwilling to believe that it was created imperfect, partly good and
partly evil. We want to believe that it was intended to be perfectly
good and somehow went wrong. There was at one time—very early and before recorded history—a period when men and women
were happy; and then there was a disaster. Ever since then we
have been trying to recover from it. Now, if so, what was the nature of the disaster?

The old Greek poet Hesiod, in his story about Pandora, gives two
different explanations. In one place he confuses them. His first explanation is simply that all the trouble in the world is caused by
women. There were (he says) two brothers, a wise one and a foolish one: the wise one superhuman, the foolish one, Afterthought,
just like you and me. The king of heaven was angry at mankind,
and so he created and sent down woman, to be the mate of the
foolish brother Afterthought. He was warned by his wise brother,
Forethought, not to accept any gift from heaven in case it might be
harmful; but Pandora was so beautiful that he took her; she was
lovely and lying and shameless, and she was the mother of all
other women and thus the origin of all our troubles.

Then, mixed up with this, there is a second explanation of the
origin of evil. This is that men had always been quite happy, because all the evils possible for humanity were imprisoned in a

---

[2][See Panofsky (above, note 1) 15 in 1956 edition and 15 in 1962 edition. Ed.]

great jar. But when Pandora came to earth, she opened the prison of the evils and let them out. Her motive, apparently, was merely curiosity, to see what was inside; or else sheer interference, the mischievous passion for touching what should not be touched.

Do these stories not remind you of other primitive explanations of the origin of evil? In particular, do they not sound like the first chapters of the Book of Genesis? Of course they do—so closely that they make us reread and analyze the story as told in Genesis. There we are informed that the first man and the first woman were perfectly happy together in Paradise, so long as they did not eat the fruit of the tree of the knowledge of good and evil. Adam (such is the implication) would never have touched it if it had not been that his wife was curious and that he loved his wife. She was tempted by the serpent; she saw that it was "a tree to be desired to make one wise" (Gen. 3.6), and she broke the command and ate its fruit. Then she gave the fruit to her husband, and he too ate. Her first motive apparently was pure curiosity, not unmingled with sheer mischief, and it corresponds to Pandora's opening the box of evils out of sheer curiosity, not unmingled with pure mischief.

But once Adam and Eve ate the fruit, surely they acquired the knowledge of good and evil? If so, what did it amount to? We are told in only one sentence, the only sentence which says how their nature was changed. "The eyes of them both were opened, and they knew that they were naked, and they sewed fig leaves together, and made themselves aprons" (Gen. 3.7). It is implied that God knew they had eaten of the tree of knowledge primarily because they had put on clothes; and later he himself made them suits of animal skin. Finally, it was apparently only after they had been driven out of Paradise that Adam and Eve became man and wife. If so, this answer to the problem of evil would correspond to the first of the tales told by the Greek philosophical poet: that man was perfectly happy and good until he was given a wife, whose nature, combining great physical attraction with irresponsible naughtiness, became the cause of all subsequent human trouble. Of course there are important differences. Eve was created to be a "helpmeet" for Adam (Gen. 2.18), and they were happy together until she was tempted; while Pandora was created to be a trap and a disillusionment for her husband Afterthought, and (it is implied) they were never happy together at all. But the core of the two explanations of evil is very similar. This has been obvious for centuries. John Milton compared Pandora to Eve (*Paradise Lost* 4.714–15); the painter Cousin called his reclining nude Eva Prima

Pandora ("Eve the first Pandora"), and in the eighteenth century a German scholar tried to prove that the pagans had a faint notion of the fall of man and tried to symbolize it in the tale of Pandora, with her descent from heaven to torment the world.[3]

Astonishing, these two explanations of the origin of evil, one given in the Hebrew scriptures and the other in the poems of an ancient Greek, Hesiod. Ultimately, it seems, they can be reduced to two of the most powerful forces that still dominate human life. One is sex; and the other is intellectual curiosity. The fig leaf of Genesis has become a very famous sexual symbol; but surely, even before the revelations of Freud, our ancestors recognized Pandora's box as another such symbol. As for the constant pressure of intellectual curiosity, that needs no comment. Now that we are no longer in Paradise, we need not be ashamed of the expanding power of the mind. But it is a little sad to think that we men should be blaming our attractive helpmeets, women, not only for being attractive, as they are, but for being inquisitive in a scientific way. If they, the women, invented the myths, I wonder where they would place the origin of evil?

---

[3][See N. E. Zobel, *Dissertatio inauguralis de lapsu primorum humani generis parentum a paganis adumbrato* (Altdorf, 1723)—indexed along with other dissertations under the name of C. G. Schwarz, the person who apparently directed and/or approved these dissertations. Ed.]

Aristophanes[*]

Let us get into the mood. It is a big public holiday. No one in all Athens is working. It is the festival of the wine-god Dionysus; the god himself has made an epiphany in the city, and his gift of wine is everywhere. The heart of his feast is the drama: this morning we began with the tragedies; now we can relax. It is the afternoon. We have all had a good lunch and several drinks and several more, and we are back in the theater. Men only. Women went to the tragedies, but this afternoon we have the comedies, and the audience is strictly stag. We are all looking forward to the first one, for it is by Aristophanes, who has already won the prize for comedy several times, although he is only a youngster in his twenties. The war, the long war with the Spartans and their allies, has been dragging on for over ten mortal years now; but Aristophanes will be able to make us forget it, or at least laugh at it. His comedy is called the *Peace*.

There is a gay flourish of music, and the play begins. The scene shows us an ordinary house, and a courtyard, and outside the courtyard two servants, working hard on an enormous pile of crap. They are busy cutting out lumps of it, and kneading them, and rolling them out flat, and shaping them into—crapburgers; and as fast as they cut them out, they take them into the courtyard, one after another, and feed them to an enormous beetle which is stabled there. It is a dung-beetle. It lives on crap. Once upon a time, so the fable goes, the dung-beetle flew up to heaven and broke the eagle's eggs; so now the master of the house, called Trygaeus, is fattening it up for a long journey into outer space. If it could fly in an Aesop fable, it can fly now with Trygaeus on its back, and so he can get to heaven and ask the Father Almighty, Zeus, whether he cannot stop the awful war in Greece. Meanwhile, it has to be fed, and so the two servants mash up one dung-cake after another, complaining all the time. To tempt the beetle's appetite, they give him different flavors and consistencies: big round pieces of donkey-dung, and then later an elegant morsel obtained from a young homosexual.

---

[*]Presented in 1963 at Columbia University (= Humanities public lecture).

By this time the whole theater is shouting with laughter. And the
laughter grows even stronger, when Trygaeus himself, singing a
cheerful song, appears on the back of the dung-beetle, flying up to
the top of the theater to interview Father Zeus. He waves to all of
us in the audience and asks us not to crap on any account for the
next three days, in case his mount is attracted and wanders out of
orbit. And then, far below, he sees someone actually doing it. He
cries (164–69)[1]:

> Man! Man in Piraeus! You'll kill me, I swear,
> Committing a nuisance! Good fellow, forbear!
> Dig it down in the ground, scatter perfumes around,
> Heap, heap up the earth on the top,
> Plant sweet-smelling thyme to encircle the mound,
> And bring myrrh on its summit to drop!

But in spite of this, he reaches heaven safely. And there, buried in a
prison, he finds the goddess who has been lost to the world for so
long, the lovely goddess Peace. With the help of the chorus, he res-
cues her and brings her back to earth; and at last things begin to go
right again. Helmets are much reduced in price and are sold as
bowls to hold laxatives; breastplates are converted into metal
chamber-pots. And the play ends with singing and dancing, and a
feast to celebrate the wedding of Trygaeus to the beautiful attendant of Peace, the maiden Harvest.

There then is Aristophanes—or rather, one aspect of his work. It
is gay fantastic comedy on a deadly serious subject. For what could
be more serious than the war—almost a civil war—which was
devastating Greece and wrecking her prosperity and ruining her
morale, the war that (seventeen years later) was to break the back
of Athens in a blow from which she never fully recovered? And
what could be sadder than the notion that it would need a miracle
to bring peace back to earth? And what more fantastic than the
rescue-flight of an Athenian farmer from earth to heaven? And
what could be dirtier than the opening idea—the gigantic dung-
beetle fed on a huge pile of variegated raw sewage? Aristophanes is
one of the dirtiest *good* authors who ever wrote. There are plenty of
dirty *bad* authors, who, as Swinburne said of journalists, "make the
filth they feed on";[2] but Aristophanes is one of the few really distin-

---

[1][Highet's slightly modified version of the B. B. Rogers translation (London,
1924), quoted here and elsewhere in this lecture. Ed.]
[2][See C. Y. Lang, ed., *The Swinburne Letters,* 6 vols. (New Haven, 1959–62)
vol. 2, pp. 274–75, for Swinburne's letter of January 30, 1874, referring to his
critics as "autocoprophagous baboons who make the filth they feed on." Ed.]

guished poets and thinkers who is exultantly and successfully obscene. In this he is more like François Rabelais than any other extant author. Both Rabelais and Aristophanes thought that sexual
activity, and the processes of digestion and elimination, and several
other phenomena of ordinary life, could not be ignored, and could
not be disguised, and could not be idealized, and were by their very
nature extremely and irresistibly funny.

Dirt, dirt of all kinds, is inseparable from Aristophanes' work.
But there is much more than that in him. Suppose we go to the
Athenian theater seven years after the *Peace*. This time we see a
comedy called the *Birds*. As it opens, we find two Athenian citizens
like ourselves on stage, wandering through a rocky wilderness.
They are sick to death of life in Athens and are trying to find
somewhere quiet to settle. They reach the land where the birds all
live; and there, between earth and heaven, they found a new state,
the republic of Nephelococcygia ("Cloud-cuckoo-land"). Some of
the characters and all the chorus of this dream-comedy are birds;
and with the nightingale piping sweetly to them, they sing a marvelous song declaring that not men but birds are the senior race
and the rulers of the universe (685–730):

> Ye men who are dimly existing below, who perish and fade as the
> leaf,
> Pale, woebegone, shadowlike, spiritless folk, life feeble and wing-
> less and brief,
> Frail castings in clay, who are gone in a day, like a dream full of
> sorrow and sighing,
> Come listen with care to the Birds of the air, the ageless, the
> deathless, who flying
> In the joy and the freshness of Ether, are wont to muse upon wis-
> dom undying.
>
> . . . .
> There was Chaos at first, and Darkness and Night, and Tartarus
> vasty and dismal;
> But the Earth was not there, nor the Sky, nor the Air, till at length
> in the bosom abysmal
> Of Darkness, an egg, from the whirlwind conceived, was laid by
> the sable-plumed Night.
> And out of that egg, as the seasons revolved, sprang Love, the en-
> trancing, the bright,
> Love brilliant and bold with his pinions of gold, like a whirlwind,
> refulgent and sparkling!
> Love hatched us, commingling in Tartarus wide, with Chaos, the
> murky, the darkling,
> And brought us above, as the firstlings of Love, and first to the
> light we ascended.
> There was never a race of Immortals at all till Love had the uni-
> verse blended;

Then all things commingling together in love, there arose the fair
    Earth and the Sky,
And the limitless Sea; and the race of the Gods, the Blessed, who
    never shall die.
So we than the Blessed are older by far.
. . . .
Then take us for gods, as is proper and fit,
And Muses prophetic you'll have at your call,
Spring, winter, and summer, and autumn, and all
. . . .
Health and wealth we'll bestow, as the formula runs,
On yourselves and your sons, and the sons of your sons.

And then off they go into a song in which (as in Respighi's *Pines of Rome*) we can actually hear the bird-notes (737–43):

Μοῦσα λοχμαία,
τιὸ τιὸ τιὸ τιοτίγξ,
ποικίλη, μεθ' ἧς ἐγὼ
νάπαισι καὶ κορυφαῖς ἐν ὀρείαις,
τιὸ τιὸ τιὸ τιοτίγξ,
ἱζόμενος μελίας ἐπὶ φυλλοκόμου,
τιὸ τιὸ τιὸ τιοτίγξ . . .

O woodland Muse,
tio, tio, tio, tiotinx,
Of varied plume, with whose dear aid
On the mountaintop and the sylvan glade,
tio, tio, tio, tiotinx,
I, sitting up aloft on a leafy ash, full oft,
tio, tio, tio, tiotinx . . .

This is something quite different from the horrible insect and his disgusting food. Aristophanes had an imagination that really soared in the air; only, sometimes it was a flying dung-beetle and sometimes it was a nightingale. You will remember that this beautiful poetry was not simply recited. It was sung to music which Aristophanes composed, and sometimes it was accompanied by dancing which Aristophanes himself planned and staged. This is another aspect of his work altogether. It makes us think of Shakespeare's fairy chorus in *A Midsummer Night's Dream,* and of the musical setting which Berlioz wrote for Mercutio's evocation of Queen Mab in *Romeo and Juliet.*

But there is a little more solid substance in this lyric. It is not mere fancy. It is a cosmogony.

There was Chaos at first, and Darkness and Night, and Tartarus
    vasty and dismal;
But the Earth was not there, nor the Sky, nor the Air, till at length
    in the bosom abysmal

> Of Darkness, an egg, from the whirlwind conceived, was laid by
> the sable-plumed Night.
> And out of that egg, as the seasons revolved, sprang Love, the en-
> trancing, the bright.

This description of the origin of the universe is a poetic version of the mystical genesis given in the religion of Orpheus and is in fact a useful piece of evidence for the knowledge of that remarkable creed. At the same time, you notice that Aristophanes has translated it into the right terms for birds: the *egg* which is *laid* by Night with her black *wings*. In this, then, there is a depth of poetic and religious feeling which prevents us from calling Aristophanes a mere clown, a dirt-loving satirist. He is a poet and sometimes almost a mystic. This side of him was seen by Plato, who brought him in rather drunk to the Symposium to tell a beautiful myth about the origin of love.

However, he wrote plays, and plays are drama, action, conflict. If poetry can be combined with the action, so much the better; but action comes first. And action does not necessarily mean the clash of wills between two or three individuals—although the modern stage is usually forced to limit itself to that. Action also means the clash of groups, of classes, of armies, and is often displayed in physical terms, by actual fighting. Aristophanes never (as far as I know) put on the stage the conflict which dominated his city of Athens throughout much of his life—the war between Athens and the Spartans with their allies. It was too grim, too immediate. But in his comedies there are other splendid scenes of suspense and conflict. The most famous suspense scene is the postponed embrace in the *Lysistrata*. Lysistrata—the word means "Discharge the Army"—is the heroine's name. She stops the war by persuading the women on both sides to go on strike and deny their husbands the pleasure of their company until peace is achieved, thus using one of the two most powerful masculine impulses to nullify the other. The scene (829–953)—you all know it, or you should—in which poor Cinesias brings his baby up to the fortress held by the women, so as to entice his wife Myrrhina to slip out and come to his arms, while she increases the sense of crisis by pretending to be willing, but inventing new excuses for postponement—a mattress ("not on the bare ground"), a pillow ("just lift your head a minute"), a blanket, a little perfume . . . and finally runs back into the stronghold leaving her husband in a state of permanent tension—this is one of the simplest and strongest suspense scenes ever played. But the central conflict of the comedy begins when the women, instead of being isolated each in her own home, seize power and take over the Acropolis itself. The men, with flaming torches, approach the citadel to burn the women out; the women—and remember that one of the main tasks of every woman in ancient Athens, as in the 'undeveloped' countries today, was to draw water from the well and carry it home—the women drench them and souse them until their fire has gone completely out. And when finally the Athenian police approach, the women sally out and put them to flight, after a marvelous summons by Lysistrata herself, in which two words fill almost the whole length of two big iambic lines (457–58):

ὦ σπερμαγοραιολεκιθολαχανοπώλιδες,
ὦ σκοροδοπανδοκευτριαρτοπώλιδες!

O egg-and-seed-and-potherb-market-girls,
O garlic-selling-barmaid-bakery-girls!

Such a battle is comic action on a large scale—a thing one seldom sees nowadays on the legitimate stage, although it happens frequently on the motion-picture screen. Aristophanes has many dramatic scenes of this kind; he liked crowd effects and must have been a skillful producer. In this his work lies somewhere between comic operettas such as Gilbert and Sullivan's *Pirates of Penzance* and more important works such as Rossini's *Barber of Seville* and Richard Wagner's *Mastersingers*.

In drama, conflict need not mean physical action. Conflict is the clash of wills, however that clash may be expressed: in blows, in colliding emotions, or in intellectual fencing, the crossing and clashing of ideas as keen as rapier-blades. And here is one of the true strengths of Aristophanes. Clown, foul-mouth, mountebank, fantast—call him what you like—he is still a man deeply interested in important ideas, surprisingly skillful at seizing vital issues and dramatizing them. What could be more imaginative and daring than his staging a debate between two great Athenian tragic poets—both dead, but alive in the world of death, and claiming immortality, with Dionysus himself, the god of drama, as the judge? In the *Frogs,* the two match their work on high moral grounds: Aeschylus, the old conservative, and Euripides, the new existentialist. Aeschylus begins (1008):

> Come tell me, what are the points for which a noble poet our
> praise obtains?

Euripides answers (1009–10):

For his ready wit and his counsels sage, and because the citizen
     folk he trains
To be better townsmen and worthier men.

His opponent says (1010–12):

If then you have done the very reverse,
Found noblehearted and virtuous men, and altered them, each
     and all, for the worse,
What is the reward you deserve to get?

Yet, asks Euripides in return (1052):

Was then the tale I told of Phaedra's passionate love untrue?

His opponent replies (1053–55):

Not so: but tales of incestuous vice the sacred poet should hide
     from view,
Nor ever exhibit and blazon forth on the public stage to the public
     ken.
For boys a teacher at school is found, but we the poets are teachers
     of men.

There is another fine debate like this in the *Clouds,* the comedy
about Socrates and the contemporary intellectuals. The boast of the
sophists was that, by the power of intellectual manipulation and
rhetorical obfuscation, they could "make the worse cause appear
the better"; and so Aristophanes brings the two Causes on to the
stage in person, the Right Cause and the Wrong Cause. They debate in a struggle for the soul of the modern youth. "You therefore," says the Right Cause (990–96),

You therefore, young man, choose me while you can; cast in with
     my Method your lot;
And then you shall learn the market to shun and from dissolute
     baths to abstain,
And fashions impure and shameful abjure, and scorners repel
     with disdain;
And rise from your chair if an elder be there, and respectfully
     give him your place,
And with love and with fear your parents revere, and shrink from
     the brand of Disgrace;
And deep in your breast be the image impressed of Modesty, sim-
     ple and true,
Nor resort even once to a dancing-girl's door, nor glance at the
     prostitute crew.

The Wrong Cause now replies with a warm encouragement to a
free sexual life and bases it on the myths of the gods (1071–82):

Just take this chastity, young man; sift it inside and out;
Count all the pleasures, all the joys, it bids you live without:
No kind of dames, no kind of games, no laughing, feasting, drink-
    ing—
Why, life itself is little worth without these joys, I'm thinking.
Well, I must notice now the wants by Nature's self implanted.
You love, seduce (you can't help that), you're caught, convicted.
    Granted!
You're done for; you can't say one word; while if you follow me,
Indulge your genius, laugh and booze, hold nothing base to be.
Why, if you're in adultery caught, your pleas will still be ample:
You've done no wrong, you say, and then bring Zeus as your ex-
    ample.
He fell before the wondrous powers by Love and Beauty wielded;
And how can you, the mortal, stand, where he, the Immortal,
    yielded?

These are only two of the many debates in Aristophanes, half-serious and half-comic and wholly dramatic. And, mark you, the right side (or the side which Aristophanes favors) does not always win. Although Aeschylus beats Euripides in the *Frogs* and is brought back to the upper world as an inspiration for Athens, the Right Cause is beaten in the *Clouds*. He looks round the theater, sees that the seats are full of woman-chasers and bottom-wigglers, and gives up and runs off to join the majority.

In this Aristophanes is more like George Bernard Shaw than any other modern dramatist; perhaps Jean Giraudoux also; but he is also like an earlier English poet who greatly admired him and had much in common with him. Robert Browning wrote a superb characterization of Aristophanes in a poem called *The Last Adventure of Balaustion*. And now that I think of it, he is like Rabelais here too. François Rabelais had a keen mind, which loved to take big problems and play with them. Sometimes he gave his readers a serious debate on a comic subject, sometimes a comic debate on a serious subject, and sometimes a ridiculous debate on a perfectly absurd subject. Both Rabelais and Aristophanes realized—what some philosophers shrink from admitting—that although men may expend a formidable amount of energy on discussing a problem, the problem itself may not be important. Here is a potentially comic disparity, and Aristophanes made excellent comedy out of it.

To contemporary satirists I should like to recommend the later works of Ludwig Wittgenstein—himself, like the sophists whom Aristophanes knew, a very impressive character, but addicted to constructing multidimensional puzzles out of spider-webs and tissue-paper. Here is an extract from his *Blue Book*[3] (in his own broken syntax):

> Suppose I pointed to a piece of paper and said, to someone: "this colour I call 'red.' " Afterwards I give him the order: "now paint me a red patch." I then ask him: "why, in carrying out my order, did you paint just this colour?" His answer could then be: "This colour (pointing to the sample which I have given him) was called red; and the patch I have painted has, as you see, the colour of the sample." He has now given me a reason for carrying out the order in the way he did . . .

This goes on for almost an entire page. It is customary now in higher intellectual circles to show vast respect for the late Ludwig Wittgenstein, respect almost amounting to awe. Aristophanes, who felt respect for very few men, presented Socrates as theorizing in the field of natural history (a field Socrates never cared much about) and explaining the process by which a mosquito buzzes (it evacuates wind through a very narrow channel in its hinder parts, said the Master). Now Aristophanes would have been delighted to present a dialogue between Wittgenstein and a house-painter; and I think I can imagine how he would have made it end, with a large brush and a bucket of red paint.

Talking about Socrates reminds me of one problem. Now we all know who Socrates was; but how many of you knew the name of Ludwig Wittgenstein? And if some modern comedian working like Aristophanes were to write a funny scene or a whole comedy involving Wittgenstein, how many would appreciate it today? And in a hundred years, or a thousand, how many would still enjoy it? Surely after some generations Wittgenstein will be a subject only for specialists to understand, and any jokes about him in a play will have to be explained in printed footnotes, and on the stage, unless they are very skillfully produced, will be dull and unfunny. Take someone more famous: take Jean-Paul Sartre. He would be almost perfect for a comedy in the manner of Aristophanes. His appearance is almost as striking as that of Socrates; his relationship with the formidable Simone de Beauvoir is rich in comic possibilities; there are some exquisite episodes in his life, as she records it, for instance a period when he believed he was being followed around by gigantic crayfish; and he is the author of an almost wholly opaque philosophical treatise called *Being and Nothingness*. Yet how long will his reputation last? How long will his eccentricities be

---

[3]See L. Wittgenstein, *The Blue and Brown Books* (New York, 1958) 14.

remembered? A funny scene written about him tomorrow—will it still be funny in thirty years, or in a century?

This is one reason why some parts of Aristophanes fall flat today, whether they are read or seen on the stage. He was not a universal comedian like his successor Menander, or like Molière, or like Shakespeare at Shakespeare's best. He was a satirical comedian, and he was an intensely topical playwright. He loved making fun of his own Athenian contemporaries for their own weaknesses and follies, for tiny scandals, recent fluffs and booboos which were sometimes forgotten a year later. It would be possible to go through his eleven plays and compile a sort of Walter Winchell gossip column of trivial happenings in late fifth-century Athens, things which were notorious and funny at the time and have now become unintelligible without footnotes. The playwright Carcinus had three ugly sons who did modernistic dances: bring them on and make them dance so that everyone will laugh (*Peace* 781–96). Cleonymus was a fat and greedy man who dropped his shield and ran away at the Battle of Delium: whenever a joke is needed, bring in Cleonymus (*Acharnians* 844). Someone called Diopeithes, with a deformed hand, used to peddle oracles forecasting the future: in a scene about oracles, allude to him (*Knights* 1085). The mother of the playwright Euripides—there was some joke about her selling vegetables from her farm: when in doubt, that will always raise a laugh; and so on. The plays of Euripides are immortal; and so we enjoy Aristophanes' comedy the *Frogs*, which shows Euripides trying to defend their merit. And if we know the plays well, we shall enjoy Aristophanes' other comedy the *Thesmophoriazusae,* which parodies them and brings Euripides on stage as several of his own characters. But the joke about Euripides' mother and her vegetables is dead now and has been dead for thousands of years. It was too topical to live, too trivial to deserve immortality.

This is a built-in weakness of much satire, whether it is satire on the stage like the work of Aristophanes (notice the recent failure of Bertolt Brecht's pathetic attempt to present Adolf Hitler as a Chicago gangster called Arturo Ui),[4] or satire in poetic and prose narrative and description. Open one of the most famous English nondramatic satires, Alexander Pope's *Dunciad:* in Book 2 you will find the goddess Dulness presiding over games which parody those of the *Iliad* and *Aeneid*. To make the publishers—those vile "book-

---

[4][A reference to George Tabori's adaptation of Brecht's *The Resistible Rise of Arturo Ui*—starring Christopher Plummer—which had its première in New York two weeks before Highet delivered this lecture at Columbia. Ed.]

sellers" whom Pope detested—run as fast as possible in the races, she disguises some of her own subjects as eminent authors and sends the publishers to chase them (2.123–30):

> Three wicked imps of her own Grubstreet choir,
> She deck'd like Congreve, Addison, and Prior;
> Mears, Warner, Wilkins, run: delusive thought!
> Breval, Bond, Bezaleel, the varlets caught.
> Curll stretches after Gay, but Gay is gone,
> He grasps an empty Joseph for a John:
> So Proteus, hunted in a nobler shape,
> Became, when seized, a puppy or an ape.

It is a fairly funny idea; and we know Congreve and Addison, perhaps Prior and Gay too; but who on earth are Mears, Warner, Wilkins, Breval, Bond, and Bezaleel? Long forgotten. Known now only to specialists in the eighteenth century; and when a joke becomes a subject for a Ph.D. dissertation, it has ceased to be funny.

Shakespeare himself fell into this fault sometimes, to please the groundlings. There is a particularly ugly example which mars one of the finest moments in the tragedy of *Macbeth*. Just after the murder of Duncan, when Lady Macbeth is smearing the faces of Duncan's attendants with blood and Macbeth himself is standing aghast waiting for her, there is a formidable knocking at the castle door. Macbeth and his guilty wife rush off to their room. A drunken porter enters, and instead of opening the door, he produces a string of jokes so miserable that they would disgrace Jerry Lewis or Henny Youngman—contemporary Elizabethan jokes which immediately take the hearer or the reader right out of a Scottish castle in the eleventh century and smash the great dramatic illusion into fragments (*Macbeth* 2.3.1–20). "Faith, here's an English tailor," he says, "come hither for stealing out of a French hose: come in, tailor; here you may roast your goose." (Yet notice, Shakespeare was such a marvelous poet, in spite of his frequent flashes of bad taste, that even here he produces one truly immortal phrase: "I had thought," the porter goes on, "to have let in some of all professions that go the primrose way to the everlasting bonfire.")

This then is the most serious obstacle to anyone who tries to produce Aristophanes today or to read him with unbroken enjoyment: the trivial contemporary allusions and topical gags. If they are left in unexplained, they sound flat and unintelligible; if we try to substitute modern gags for them, the result is incongruous; the best way is to skip them, to leave them out altogether—as a sensible producer will cut the porter's drunken droolings in the second act of Shakespeare's *Macbeth.*

Another aspect of this is seen in the fact that Aristophanes could not create a great comic character. He was quite unable to draw someone like Sir John Falstaff with his absurd attendants, Bardolph and Nym and Pistol; or Malvolio; or Molière's Arnolphe. At his best, he was able to create someone equal to Nick Bottom in *A Midsummer Night's Dream,* or to Monsieur Jourdain in *Le Bourgeois Gentilhomme;* but beyond that his gift was not for creative portrait-painting but rather for outrageously comic caricature. Satiric caricature is another kind of humor, with a great deal of cruelty in it. It is possible to laugh at Falstaff and yet to love him in the end; it is difficult not to laugh at the Socrates or Cleon or Euripides drawn by Aristophanes, but we cannot love them; we are meant to despise them and to enjoy their ridiculous behavior and the outrageous disasters that eventually fall upon them.

What he could do was, not like Shakespeare the comedian, create life, but create comical and imaginative distortions of life. So the chorus in his comedy about Socrates is made not of men and women, but of Clouds, the drifting clouds of the air (*Clouds* 316), who provide Socrates and his thinkers with all their ideas and their impalpable dialectic and their misty metaphysic. So the old farmer in the *Acharnians* who is disgusted with the pointless war sends a messenger to Sparta to bring him back a private treaty of peace. The messenger returns with sample treaties, in the form of bottles of wine; and Dicaeopolis tastes them. The five-year treaty tastes of tar (because a five-year treaty would have meant building a vast fleet against its expiration); the ten-year treaty smells of secret negotiations; but the thirty-year treaty—ah, that smells of nectar and ambrosia, and at once he starts to hold a private festival of the god of wine (*Acharnians* 186–203). If you know that the Greek word σπονδαί ("treaty") also means "libation of wine"— because when a treaty was concluded, both parties poured out wine for the gods—then this is a little funnier; but the knowledge is not needed for the real joke. In the *Wasps,* another delightful comedy, Aristophanes satirizes the Athenians who had a passion for serving on juries and always stinging the rich. Instead of bringing on a chorus of jurymen, he brings on a chorus of giant wasps brandishing their stings. The hero has gone crazy and thinks about nothing except lawsuits and trials; so to keep him happy his son stages a prosecution. The family dog Pincher is accused of stealing a cheese from the kitchen and prosecuted. He is likely to be found guilty, but his defense produces witnesses to character: the sauce-pan, the cheese-grater, the water-jug, and other honest utensils from the kitchen. This very comedy was produced at Cambridge University in 1909, and Ralph Vaughan Williams wrote admirable comic music for it, including a buzzing stinging chorus for the wasps, and a march for the pots and pans.[5]

That reminds me. You and I think of Aristophanes as a playwright. Just see one of his comedies properly produced—they do them very well in modern Greek in the theater at Athens—and you will realize that he was something more. He was a musician and a choreographer. His plays are rich in music and dancing; in most of them the chorus occupies a great deal of the action and dances to complicated rhythms. Lyric poetry, for the Greeks, meant poetry which was designed for music; and Aristophanes was one of the finest lyricists in the whole of Greek literature. This makes his comedies far more varied and brilliant than those of Shakespeare and Molière. Most of *A Midsummer Night's Dream* is blank verse, and the rest prose; with only a few intercalated songs. But a large part of almost every comedy by Aristophanes is delightfully complicated singing often mingled with dancing or gay processional movements. There are war dances, hymns, festival dances, wedding dances, clean dances, and dirty dances, all with words in complex lyric measures; and with what words! The words dance too, in coiling processions and quick kicking prancing steps. The longest word in any Western language is the word that Aristophanes invented to describe a delicious savory stew of many ingredients at the end of his *Ecclesiazusae;* in English it is a dish "brimming with game and with fowl and with fish" (1169–75):

plattero-filleto-mulleto-turboto-
cranio-morselo-pickleo-acido-
silphio-honeyo-pouredonthe-topothe-
ouzelo-throstleo-cushato-culvero-
cutleto-roastingo-marrowo-dippero-
leveret-syrupo-gibleto-wings

This verbal masterpiece contains no less than 170 letters, over thirty laughing tripping syllables, and there was music to go with it. So then, when you read Aristophanes, improvise music in your head and feel the rhythms of the dance: music more sophisticated than Sullivan's music for Gilbert's comedies—except perhaps the

[5][See M. Kennedy, *The Works of Ralph Vaughan Williams* (London, 1964) 439–42, for a detailed description of the music composed for the *Wasps*—a description not fully preserved in the 1980 edition of Kennedy's volume. Ed.]

patter-songs; music as melodious and gay as the finest Offenbach, Rossini, and even Mozart.

Very clever, you will say. Technically brilliant. Very funny too. But is there any meaning in it? Is there any social or spiritual significance, anything to make Aristophanes' plays worth reading and producing again after twenty-four centuries? Well, in the first place, many critics would say that there need be no special significance in a comedy and that if a comic drama is wholly or largely given up to conveying some message to the public, then it is apt to fail. *Wholly,* yes; and *largely,* yes. But surely a great playwright must be more than a mere entertainer. The old Keystone comedies are very funny, but at their best they are merely folk art like the work of the clowns in the circus—episodic, absurd, and simply monotonous in form. Athenian comedy had grown out of that kind of folk art. This is one reason why it is so dirty and one reason why it is so topical. But by the time of Aristophanes it had higher standards. Aristophanes himself could make one of his own characters ask:

> Come tell me, what are the points for which a noble poet our
> praise obtains?

and another reply:

> For his ready wit and his counsels sage, and because the citizen
> folk he trains
> To be better townsmen and worthier men.

And he himself was devoted to social reform. Throughout his long life as a playwright—remember, he began writing when he was about twenty and was still producing plays nearly forty years later; he wrote forty-four plays altogether, of which we still have eleven—throughout his long life as a playwright he kept commenting on social problems. One of the most interesting parts of an Aristophanic comedy is the parabasis. At this point, after the main conflict of the comedy has been resolved in laughter, the individual characters usually leave the stage. The chorus—of wasps or cavalry captains or women or old countrymen—fans out over the stage and speaks, or rather sings, directly at the audience. Paced by the chorus leader and using the pronoun "I", they give the Athenian citizenry serious advice in a genial but far from extravagant vein. So in the *Frogs,* he thought back to the days of Pericles, and accused his countrymen of giving way to demagogues with no real sense of the grandeur of Athens, and compared them to the cheap modern coins issued during the inflation (718–33):

> Often it has crossed my fancy that the city loves to deal
> With the very best and noblest members of her commonweal,
> Just as with her ancient coinage, and the newly minted gold.
> Yes, for these our sterling pieces, all of pure Athenian mould,
> All of perfect die and metal, all the fairest of the fair,
> All of workmanship unequalled, proved and valued everywhere,
> Both amongst our own Hellenes and barbarians far away,
> These we used not; but the worthless pinchbeck coins of yesterday,
> Vilest die and basest metal, now we always use instead.
> Even so, our sterling townsmen, nobly born and nobly bred,
> Men of worth and rank and mettle, men of honorable fame,
> Trained in every liberal science, choral dance, and manly game,
> These we treat with scorn and insult; but the strangers newliest come,
> Worthless sons of worthless fathers, pinchbeck townsmen, yellowy scum,
> Whom in earlier days the city hardly would have stopped to use
> Even for her scapegoat victims, these for every task we choose.

No doubt it sounds reactionary. It *was* reactionary. It was also correct in fact. Just a year later, Athens was defeated and compelled to surrender, largely because of the criminal folly of the new demagogues whom Aristophanes compared to worthless new coins. And this is not *my* opinion. Not only was the *Frogs* given the first prize when it was produced, but also a second performance was commanded, and at the second performance Aristophanes was given the crown reserved for great patriots, the crown made from the sacred olive-tree of Athena herself. There could be no better proof that Aristophanes was not only a great comedian but a wise playwright and a thoughtful teacher. Behind all the absurd foolery and high above all the obscene piles of manure and far beyond the temporary jokes, we can see over these twenty-four centuries the soul of a man worthy to stand beside the tragedian Aeschylus and the statesman Pericles.

Aristophanes' *Frogs*[*]

Old Comedy, as we see it in Aristophanes, is not a presentation of real life. It is much more like a fantastic dream, in which the impossible constantly happens, magical transformations take place, wrongs are miraculously righted, and agonizing problems are solved almost without any practical difficulty whatever. One of the principal motives which (according to modern psychologists) cause us to dream appears to be central in Old Comedy. This is wish-fulfillment: the desire to alter reality without trouble to ourselves and remold it nearer to the heart's desire.

Furthermore, Old Comedy was part of a religious festival. Now two of the chief elements in Greek religion were prayer and orgy. Both of these are allied to wish-fulfillment. Prayer is the act of asking a divine power for a benefit which (the worshiper thinks) cannot be secured without supernatural help, and an orgy is the act of rejoicing in a manner quite unlike the usual behavior of workaday mortals, throwing aside normal modes of conduct and accepted inhibitions, and surrendering oneself to unbridled merriment and license, not as mere bestiality but as service to a divinity. Both these elements appear very clearly in the *Frogs:* for the main plot is that a god performs a miracle to help his worshipers and the principal chorus is a procession of holy revelers.

Since it is so like a dream, Old Comedy makes frequent use of symbols, which are the language of the subconscious mind. Many of the most effective creations of Aristophanes are symbolic incidents and figures—often quaint and even grotesque, but always meaningful and memorable. This can well be illustrated from the *Frogs,* where the principal symbols are grouped in conflicting pairs of opposites.

(1) *Death and Life.* The play ends with the death of the unworthy Euripides. His very last word is "dead" (τεθνηκότα 1476), which is answered by a quotation of his own paradox about the identification of life with death. His reputation also is sentenced to death in the cruel words of Aeschylus, which serve as his final dismissal (1515–23); and Aristophanes hopes that his plays, which

---

[*]Presented in 1956 for the American Philological Association.

he himself has mocked and parodied so often, are now so dead that they will never be revived. At the same time the play asserts the immortality of Aeschylus and concludes with his resurrection and return to the life of the upper world.

Lighthearted and inventive though it is, there is still something sad and terrible about the *Frogs:* for it was produced when Athens was dying and when all thoughtful men knew that she was dying, and yet it takes place almost entirely in the world of the dead and is filled with symbols of death. Not only that: the audience was full of men who had fought at Arginusae and had lost friends or kinsmen in that disastrous victory. Aristophanes refers to it several times in the play (48–50, 190–91, and 693–94); it must have been in everyone's mind; and jokes about death would be uncommonly hard to make before spectators who had all faced it and seen it so recently. Yet Aristophanes contrives to do so, successfully. Even more, he ventures to imply that the present Athenians are all dead without knowing it (419–20) and that the only good Athenians are those who have died and been resurrected—the initiates!

Symbols of death recur again and again as the play proceeds. In a very early scene Heracles answers Dionysus's question about the quickest way to the underworld by describing three methods of suicide (117–35). Shortly afterward Dionysus and Xanthias meet a corpse being carried to burial in the cemetery near the house of Heracles: the corpse not only speaks to them but says it would rather be restored to life than accept less than two drachmae for carrying their baggage down to the underworld. Meeting the grim ferryman Charon, Dionysus greets him with a line which contains a pun on his name (χαῖρ' ὦ Χάρων 184) but which also involves a reminiscence of the practice of calling a dead man's name three times; and a little later (271) we hear him calling the lost servant Xanthias three times. The dead politicians Cleon and Hyperbolus are evoked (569–70), and the king of the dead, Pluto himself, sends various drastic instruments of death to certain living racketeers with the ominous words "tell them to come to me quickly, or else" (1504–14). Finally, even the amusing scene in which lines by Aeschylus and Euripides are weighed against each other (1365–1410) would remind many of Aristophanes' hearers of the scene in the *Iliad* where Zeus weighs the fates of Hector and Achilles against each other, to show that Hector is irrevocably doomed to perish (22.208–13).

(2) *Descent and Ascent.* The play opens with the descent of Dionysus through darkness and danger to the underworld, and

closes with the ascent of Dionysus and Aeschylus to the world of the living in a blaze of torchlight. Dionysus explicitly says that his descent is modeled on the journey of Heracles, the hero who won his way to immortality by conquering death. Now C. G. Jung explains that a journey down into darkness and the depths followed by an ascent into the light symbolizes the confrontation and conquest of a dangerous spiritual crisis.[1] Both Odysseus and Aeneas descended to the world of the dead during a crisis of their lives, and both gained new wisdom and new strength from their experience; and in medieval legend the conquest of sin and death by Jesus was symbolized in the doctrine that he had gone down to hell and 'harrowed' it before his resurrection. Dionysus makes the perilous descent in order to surmount a crisis which directly affects him—the threatened disappearance of good dramatic poetry—and while in the underworld, he realizes that this crisis is merely part of a larger and graver crisis, the spiritual impoverishment of Athenian culture; and to defeat this threat, he changes his original intention and causes Aeschylus to ascend along with him. Translated from symbolic terms, this means that only a miracle can save Athens from spiritual death.

Jung also tells us that the journey down into darkness followed by an ascent into the light symbolizes the acquisition of new wisdom through the exploration of the subconscious mind.[2] Not all wisdom, not all truth, can be consciously reasoned out and expressed in cool clear logical terms—as Plato admits when he closes an intellectual discussion with an imaginative myth. In the *Frogs* the different phases of this journey are made visible and audible in the two different choruses who meet Dionysus. The first is a group of frogs, creatures of earth and water, and yet somehow under divine patronage (229–34), who are themselves constantly engaged in descents and ascents (241–49). They sing to Dionysus more and more loudly, and perhaps faster and faster, until Dionysus silences them by taking up their song and outsinging them. This must mean that he has at last listened to the promptings of his own subconscious mind. Immediately after this he passes through a terrifying ordeal among darkness and monsters, and then he is welcomed by the lights borne by the happy initiates, men and women

---

[1][See B. Forryan and J. M. Glover, comps., *General Index to the Collected Works of C. G. Jung* (Princeton, 1979) 91 and 207, for citations to passages on the motif of 'descent and ascent'—any number of which Highet may have seen before making this statement. Ed.]

[2][See Forryan and Glover (above, note 1). Ed.]

who were formerly mortal but who, after passing through an ordeal not unlike his, have acquired new wisdom and have become immortal. Not only does Dionysus end by bringing back the personification of wisdom to Athens but he himself becomes wiser as the play proceeds. In the early scenes he is often little more than a coward and a buffoon, and his spiritual inadequacy is shown by the fact that he dresses now as the hero Heracles—although retaining some of his own effeminate costume (45–47)—and now as the slave Xanthias (494–97). In the latter part of the play there are no further allusions to his costume, but surely when he presides over the contest of the poets and is entertained at a banquet by Pluto, he would have resumed his normal costume as the god of poetry, and thus by a final change symbolized his recovery of true wisdom after the long infection of Euripidean intellectualism.

(3) *Weight and Lightness.* The gigantic scales which ascend and descend in the climactic scene of the play are highly important, for they make visible another of the chief symbolic conflicts of the *Frogs*—the contrast of weight and lightness. Aeschylus is represented as heavy and solid, Euripides as light and flimsy. This is because Aeschylus embodies the wisdom which is largely unconscious and instinctive (even his silences are not empty but heavy with brooding), while Euripides represents airy reason and weightless words. Rational, logical discussion, which Euripides loves, is always called light and subtle, and is referred to in terms of fragmentation ("hairsplitting", "splintering", etc., 826–29). On the other hand, he dislikes music and gymnastics (1491–99, cf. 1087–98) because they train the body, which is heavy, and the emotions, which are rooted in the deep subconscious. Euripides even prefers light superficial animals: the halcyons, which skim above the water (1309–12), spiders hanging high beneath the ceiling (1313–16), dolphins which do not swim deep like other fish but on the surface, sometimes leaping into the air (1317–19), and the cock which takes wings and flies away (1351–52). Aeschylus on the other hand prefers monsters, massive and terrifying creatures which symbolize the union of the conscious with the subconscious mind.

This will help to explain the change in the meaning of σοφός and σοφία throughout the play. At first these words are applied to the merely intellectual subtlety and "cleverness" of Euripides, but after the play has developed and the distinction has been made clear, they signify the true "wisdom" of Aeschylus, which comes not from glib talk but from brooding silence, not from chop-logic but from majestic imagery.

Perhaps Aristophanes prepares his audience for the contrast of heaviness and lightness by his early references to the burdens of Xanthias, which begin in the first ten lines of the play and culminate in the notable phrase ὄνος ἄγω μυστήρια, "a donkey celebrating the mysteries" (159). Certainly he intends it to be one of the final impressions left on his audience, for at the end of the weighing scene Aeschylus says (and his claim is left undisputed) that two lines from his work will outweigh Euripides, his children, his wife, his assistant Cephisophon, and all his books (1407–10). Some at least of his audience would have remembered the scenes of the *Clouds* in which the intellectual activity of Socrates is symbolized by his being suspended above the heavy earth in a basket and measuring the leap of a flea, and then imaged in the chorus of aerial transient weightless Clouds.

(4) *Darkness and Light.* After the preliminary scenes, the play takes us into the darkness of the underworld. This is made audible (if not perhaps visible) in the chorus of frogs, creatures who live in the dark mud and are constantly disappearing into the marshy water. After this ordeal has ended, the theater is filled with a blaze of light from the torches of the initiates. They sing a hymn to Iacchus, calling him a lightbringing star (342, cf. 455–56), and they speak as though they were clearly calmer and wiser than Dionysus; in fact, he joins their procession, although not for very exalted motives (417–19). At the end of the play the initiates rekindle their torches (1524–26) and move out in a solemn procession to escort Aeschylus to the upper world. The play thus ends with a dead man, escorted by a dead man, bringing wisdom to the living (Aeschylus had died before many of the audience were born). The light of the initiates' torches symbolizes true wisdom, the wisdom which flows from the subconscious. Strangely enough, the final procession looks like a counterpart to the procession found at the end of Aeschylus's *Eumenides.* There a procession of living Athenians escorts chthonic powers who had until then been too powerful and too dangerous, but had been controlled and converted by Athena and Apollo, down into the dark cave where they were thenceforward to live. Here a procession of dead but immortal Athenians escorts a poet resurrected from the underworld on his way up into the sunlight of contemporary Athens, in the hope that by restoring the balance between the intellect and the emotions, he may save his city from disintegration and destruction.

There are other symbols in the *Frogs,* but even these are enough to show the imaginative depth of Aristophanes' apparently gay and superficial dramas. He was a great poet; and in this play about life and death, performed before an audience which was poised between life and death, he used symbols of intense power and dignity to convey a meaning which was almost too terrible to be confronted face to face.

Plato's *Phaedrus*[*]

One of the strangest of Plato's dialogues takes us outside the city of Athens, to what was then a charming country landscape and is now a dismal little urban eyesore. It is a hot summer forenoon. Socrates meets his friend Phaedrus, who is going out for a walk in the country, and accompanies him. They stroll down the little stream Ilissus, with their bare feet in the cool water, until they reach a sanctuary of the water spirits, a spring bubbling out below a great plane tree hung with little images; and there, in its kindly shade, they make themselves comfortable on the rich soft grass, with the summer-intoxicated crickets choiring around them. Even Socrates, who never leaves the crowded walls of Athens, speaks eloquently of the beauty of the scene.

In this idyllic setting, Phaedrus, full of happy excitement, reads aloud a speech which he says he has just heard delivered by its author, Lysias, son of Cephalus, "the cleverest of the modern writers" (228a1–2) and which he has borrowed in order to get it by heart. He wished to be alone in order to go over it, but after some coquetry Socrates persuades him to share it with a friend who truly loves speeches.

The speech is a curious and in some ways a disquieting performance. It is not an oration intended for a group audience. It is a formal address made by one individual to another, presumably in private. In fact, it is only because the Athenians regarded the living voice as superior to writing on a dead page, that it can be called a speech at all (cf. 274c5–275b2). It is rather difficult for us to picture a private interview in which one party sits silent while the other utters nearly five pages of continuous prose. Nowadays it would not be conceived as a speech, but as a letter, to be read and meditated in silence by its recipient. Nevertheless, it is clearly conceived as being *spoken* (ἀκήκοας 230e7 and εἰρημένα 234c4). So is its counterpart (ἔλεγέν τε ὧδε 237b6).

Furthermore, it is not a complete speech. Its first sentence is: "You know my situation, and you have heard how I believe this course will benefit us" (230e6–7). Vague as this is—deliberately

---

[*]Presented in 1960 for the American Philological Association.

vague—it implies that the speaker has already explained something about himself and has then made a proposal which he asserts will bring advantages to both himself and the addressee. In a personal interview where one man makes a long address urging some action upon another, we expect the address to open with a description of the state of affairs and to proceed to recommendations which will somehow improve the prevailing situation. But here there is no such opening—although the speech has a neat little formal ending: "I believe that what I have said is enough; if you think anything has been omitted and wish for more, ask" (234c4–5).

The author does not refer to the fact that the speech is incomplete. There are two possible explanations for this. The first is that the speech is the final phase of an interview which is imagined as taking place over several days or weeks. If so, the speaker has explained his "situation" some time previously and has made his proposal, which the other party has been thinking over; and now he comes forward with a set of arguments to clinch it. This is acceptable—although it is still surprising to hear this truncated fragment called a λόγος ("speech") and admired by Phaedrus its reader as though it were perfectly shaped and proportioned. There is another explanation. The first part of the speech is tacitly suppressed because it is too repulsive to read, too brutal and revolting to discuss. As we go through the section which Phaedrus actually rehearses, it is only slowly that its impact comes through to us. By the time he reaches the end, we understand, and if we have normal feelings, we are disgusted; but because the language of the speech is so quiet, its phrasing so cool and impersonal, the full effect is delayed and accumulates its force only toward the end. If the first part had been read, we should perhaps be too disgusted to maintain our attention throughout.

The speech is addressed by a man to a boy whom he is trying to seduce. The "situation" which he mentions in the first sentence is not described, but clearly it is the fact that he is attracted by the boy's handsome face and figure. The "course" which he says will benefit them both is that he should be permitted to have habitual sexual (or, more accurately, homosexual) intercourse with the boy. These two aspects of the affair are concealed under the flat phrases τῶν ἐμῶν πραγμάτων (230e6) and γενομένων τούτων (230e7). But in the first part of the speech, whether it was imagined as having been delivered in the course of the same interview, or at one or several previous interviews, the speaker would surely be compelled to state the facts and his desires more frankly. No

doubt many good-looking Athenian boys were accustomed to receive indecent proposals from men, and perhaps this one would not
require to have the situation and the course spelled out in detail.
Still, the seducer would have to be forced at some point to be fairly
explicit. There is a special reason for this. In Athens men sometimes fell in love with boys and expressed themselves with real
passion, and all its symptoms—utter devotion, self-forgetfulness,
rapturous admiration, agonizing despair, and furious jealousy.
Such a lover would scarcely need to say much in declaring his love
and pressing his desire. But the speaker of this particular speech is
quite different. He is not in love with the boy. Not only does he not
try to conceal this (and indeed genuine love is difficult to feign), but
he explains it with cynical frankness. The fact that his desire is *not*
true love is (he suggests for five pages) really an advantage for the
boy. He himself merely wants to use the boy for a while without
emotional involvement, as he would eat a well-cooked dinner
without weeping on the shoulder of the chef, or drink a cup of fine
wine without writing poetry to the vintner. In this unusual situation, he would necessarily be forced to make his proposal fairly
explicit; and apparently Plato felt that not even the agile Greek
language and not even the intellectual subtlety of its putative author would be capable of putting it in terms which were not repellent. Therefore the man's avowal and his request are both omitted.
When Phaedrus begins to read, he is at least halfway through the
original speech. The most important part of it is over.

The speech is a λόγος συμβουλευτικός ("deliberative speech"), in
which the speaker describes a situation, suggests a policy to cope
with it, and then gives arguments to support his suggestion. The
section which Phaedrus reads contains the πίστεις ("arguments").
Now we have seen that the problem described was the man's desire for the boy; and the policy recommended for solving it was the
boy's surrender to the man. However, there is a particular quirk in
this situation. A lover would scarcely require to buttress his passionate pleadings by a long series of practical, logical arguments.
But this man is not a lover. Therefore his logical arguments have
to be designed to support his peculiar request. In fact, he is asking
the boy to behave like a male prostitute, giving his body to someone
who has no emotional interest in him whatever. This outrageous
suggestion he tries to make palatable by detailing a number of general arguments. The best that can be said of them is that they are
not vulgar bribes; he could obviously have offered the boy money,
or expensive presents, or cheap flattery; he could have tried to turn

the boy's head with compliments. No, they are cool general arguments on one single paradoxical theme. The theme is that it is more advantageous, more profitable, for a boy to be seduced by a man who confessedly does not love him than by a man who does.

The arguments which may be used to support any policy recommended in a deliberative speech amount to variations on three or at most four main ideas: that the policy is honorable, that it is pleasant, that it is advantageous, and occasionally that it is necessary. The speaker of this speech is clearly limited in his scope. He cannot possibly argue that his proposal will bring either honor or pleasure to the boy, nor that it must be accepted from necessity. Therefore he has to confine himself to variations on the least elevated of all the motives, χρήσιμον ("advantage"). The variations are ingenious—some of them to the point of being wire-drawn and artificial, one or two of them blatantly insincere; and it is difficult to imagine any but the most cold-hearted boy being genuinely impressed by them, although some might be dazzled by their smooth fluency and sinuous elaboration. Something of their quality may be judged from the fifth argument, which is that it is more advantageous to yield to a man who does not love you, because he will not bring unwelcome publicity on you by following you about, as a passionate adorer would (231e3–232b5). By the way, we are often told, even by those who ought to know better, that homosexual love affairs were regarded as perfectly normal and blameless in Athens. This is directly contradicted by the fifth argument of this speech, which states with considerable emphasis that any boy who yields to any male lover will suffer ὄνειδός ("shame"), if people learn about it, because he has broken τὸν νόμον τὸν καθεστηκότα (231e3–4). However, Plato makes Socrates contradict this later in the dialogue, at the opening of the climactic paragraph in Socrates' speech about homosexual passion (255a1–b1).

The various arguments based on advantage come, by my count, to nine: (1) non-lovers do not change with time, (2) or ruin their household, (3) or pretend to prize the beloved and then forget him; (4) they are many and not few, (5) conceal the affair, (6) do not drive away friends of the boy through jealousy, (7) have real affection and not physical desire only, (8) aim at permanent improvement of the boy, (9) and are not to be denied merely because they do not plead with passion. Three of them really state the same point—that passionate lovers are apt to cool off and their passion to change into neglect or even hatred—but the emphasis is a little different each time. The speaker punctuates his arguments with introductory particles such as τοίνυν and transitional phrases such as ἔτι δέ and καὶ μὲν δή. Yet it is noticeable that the speech has no truly tight structure. One argument succeeds another, and is followed by a third and that by a fourth, but there is no link between them; they do not grow out of one another or form any logical pattern. We receive the impression that the speaker offers no single compellingly persuasive argument but is merely heaping one point upon another as fast as his dexterous mind can think of them.

In style, the speech is a fairly close parody of the speeches of Lysias. Plato had a marvelous ear, which enabled him to reproduce the manner of any author he chose; he had a strong sense of humor and a cruel desire to wound those whom he disliked and distrusted. This is only one of the many parodies in Plato's works which reproduce minute details of their victims' speech, and reveal and emphasize salient weaknesses in their victims' thought.[1]

To begin with the trifles, the connective phrase καὶ μὲν δή occurs five times, and the lighter connective ἔτι δέ four times within less than five pages. The former, καὶ μὲν δή, is an odd combination, which is a specialty of Lysias and is far less common in all other Attic writers.[2] However, in this little speech it occurs far more frequently than it does in Lysias's acknowledged works. The latter, ἔτι δέ, is a weak little connection, which implies that its speaker cannot forge a real link between one section of his speech and the next, so that he merely tacks on a paragraph with "and further." These two connective phrases occur far less often than once a page in the genuine works of Lysias. Plato has apparently increased the frequency of their appearance in this erotic speech in order to make Lysias's style seem thinner and more monotonous than it is—a favorite device of parodists, the exaggeration of caricature.[3]

---

[1][See G. Highet, *The Anatomy of Satire* (Princeton, 1962) 136–38, for Plato as a parodist, with reference to the *Phaedrus* and other dialogues. Ed.]

[2]P. Shorey, "On the *Erotikos* of Lysias in Plato's *Phaedrus*," *CPh* 28 (1933) 131–32, counts about twenty in all Plato's works. This is confirmed by J. D. Denniston, *The Greek Particles* (Oxford, 1954[2]) 395–97, who says it is "notably common" (twenty-one times) in Lysias, not infrequent in Plato and in Isocrates (eleven times), and very rare elsewhere (twice each in Antiphon and Andocides, once in Thucydides).

[3]So also G. E. Dimock, "ΑΛΛΑ in Lysias and Plato's *Phaedrus*," *AJPh* 73 (1952) 381–96, shows that "eliminative" ἀλλά (οὐ ... ἀλλά ...) appears thirteen times per hundred lines in the *Erotikos* (the word sometimes used to identify the erotic speech recited by Phaedrus) but only five and one-half times per hundred lines in the regular speeches of Lysias (this is the usage which Socrates criticizes in 235a6–8).

One of Lysias's commonest patterns of argument is the argument ἀπὸ τοῦ εἰκότος ("from probability"): he frequently asks or suggests what is likely to happen, what it was reasonable to assume happened in the past, and he often tells his audience to draw conclusions or infer from the facts stated. This method is imitated and reproduced in the erotic speech: ἐνθυμεῖσθαι occurs twice, εἰκός three times, and its variant εἰκότως once.

Habitually moderate and mellifluous, Lysias seldom builds up powerful complex paragraphs or elaborate resounding climaxes. The sentence-structure of Plato's parody is therefore suitably quiet. But toward the end comes a more closely wrought paragraph which is the crown of the speech. And here we find two devices which Lysias himself used with great effect: a single sentence containing six verbs linked by the conjunction καί six times (233e2–5)—a polysyndeton, like that in one of the main climaxes of Lysias's great democratic speech against Eratosthenes (12.78); and then a paragraph of eleven lines in which the pattern of contrast οὐ . . . ἀλλά is repeated six times (233e5–234b1)—as in Lysias 12.56 and 21.24.

In Lysias's own speeches, one of the most typical and at first one of the most baffling tricks of style is understatement, achieved by the use of neutral or quiet-toned words to denote facts which, if fully and accurately described, might be shocking or exciting to the audience. Thus the most painful events of recent Athenian history—the defeat of Athens by the Peloponnesians, the revolutionary regime of the Thirty Tyrants installed by the victors, and the civil war in which it was overthrown—are often described only in mild periphrases or colorless abstract words. The young knight Mantitheus, wishing to say that he is loyal to the restored democracy, says only εὔνους εἰμὶ τοῖς καθεστηκόσι πράγμασι (16.3, cf. 25.3). Theramenes' impassioned speech against Critias in the Council is summarized by Lysias in a single sentence, whose heart is this (12.77):

> ὀνειδίζων δὲ τοῖς τῆς πολιτείας μετέχουσιν, ὅτι πάντων τῶν πεπραγμένων τοῖς εἰρημένοις τρόποις ὑπ' ἐμοῦ αὐτὸς αἴτιος γεγενημένος τοιούτων τυγχάνοι.

> reproaching those who had citizen status, because he himself, although responsible for all that had been done by the methods I have mentioned, got this treatment.

Here πάντων τῶν πεπραγμένων means "the entire revolutionary reconstruction of Athens"; τοῖς εἰρημένοις τρόποις ὑπ' ἐμοῦ means "by taking orders from Sparta"; and τοιούτων τυγχάνοι means "was put on trial for his life." Mild and vague phrases like this appear in all Greek prose-writers, but in Lysias they are notably common; they are an essential element in his sweetly reasonable style.

This same stylistic trick, in the parodic speech now repeated by Phaedrus, is used for the same purpose at a much lower level. In the first sentence (230e6–231a3)—a sentence which Plato enjoyed, because he made Phaedrus repeat it twice later in the dialogue (262e1–4 and 263e6–264a3)—the scrupulously colorless phrase τῶν ἐμῶν πραγμάτων really means ἡ ἐμὴ ἐπιθυμία σοῦ, and the even flatter phrase γενομένων τούτων means σοῦ ἐμοὶ χαριζομένου: both ideas too bold to be, at least in the habitual style of Lysias, candidly expressed. One of the purposes of the entire speech is to show how skillfully a speaker using the smooth, transparent style of Lysias can express facts which, if named by their true names, would be repulsive. Thus the surrender of a boy to a man is τοιοῦτον πρᾶγμα προέσθαι (231c7), restated as προεμένου δέ σου ἃ περὶ πλείστου ποιῇ (232c1) and as ἐμοὶ πειθομένῳ (233a5); and the success of seducers with boys is called ἔπραξαν ὧν ἐδέοντο (232d5); a seducer's failure is ἀτυχῆσαι ὧν δέομαι (231a1); and so forth.

There are, then, many resemblances in the erotic speech read by Phaedrus to the genuine speeches of Lysias. But we should not conclude immediately that the erotic fragment is a genuine composition of Lysias rather than a parody by Plato. Some features of its style do not resemble anything in the extant corpus of Lysias, and there are some words which are never found in Lysias but do occur in Plato. For instance:

ἐπίστασαι (230e6)

ἀμέλειαν (231b2) [Lysias has ἀμελεῖν]

προφασίζεσθαι (231b3) [Lysias 8.16 has προφασιζόμενοι]

ὑπολογίζεσθαι (231b4)

ἔκλεξις (231d7) [ἐκλέγειν common in Plato, never in Lysias]

συνουσίαν (232b3)

διόπερ (232c4)

βραδέως (233c3)

ἀκουσίων (233c4)

προσαιτοῦντας (233e2) [*Symposium* 203b4 has προσαιτήσουσα]

πλησμονῆς (233e2)

The particular play upon words called the σχῆμα ἐτυμολογικόν is not used by Lysias but occurs twice in this fragment of a speech (ἀτυχῆσαι . . . τυγχάνω 231a1 and ἀκουσίων . . . ἑκούσια 233c4). The scholar who assembles these facts and statistics[4] remarks also that the clausulae of the erotic speech differ somewhat from those of Lysias's epideictic speech at Olympia, which is a fair standard of comparison. Lysias ends 35% of his sentences there with a cretic, 21% with a dactyl, and 13% with a double trochee. The author of the *Erotikos* ends 43% with a cretic, 8% with a dactyl, and 27% with a double trochee. Still, I have not checked these figures, and I should not attach much importance to them except as part of a general pattern.

On a higher level, when we compare the *Erotikos* to the extant works of Lysias, we cannot believe that it is anything more than a hateful travesty.

Its structure is superficially clear and basically weak. It contains nine arguments, but they do not cohere either by being attached to any time-scheme or as parts of a single logical structure. They would convince no one but a foolish listener who was ready to be convinced or who was easily overpowered by a show of intellectual acrobatics. Some of the individual arguments are so flimsy as to be absurd—as when the seducer explains that he, rather than a genuine lover, is likely to be a true friend comparable to the boy's mother or father (233c6–d4). Collectively, they are not a chain of reasoning but a bag of conjuring-tricks. Now in the real work of Lysias, we often find arguments which appear flimsy—particularly in the speeches on trivial subjects, such as the *Olive Stump* (7, e.g., 7.17–22) or the *Cripple* (24, e.g., 19–20). But they have more cohesion than the arguments of the non-lover in the erotic fragment and are far more carefully grouped. Lysias likes a simple structure for his speeches, whereas (as we know) the construction of Plato's dialogues is marvelously complex and richly alive; still, Lysias does not ignore the laws of structure and cohesion altogether, as they are ignored in this pastiche.

---

[4]See H. Weinstock, *De Erotico Lysiaco* (Diss., Münster, 1912) 28–29, 50–51, and 86–97.

There is one single theme which recurs variously throughout the speech and which might possibly be persuasive: the promise, never explicitly made but several times implied, that the seducer will become a true friend of the boy, and that his friendship will last long and benefit him, whereas a lover's passion would harm him and would soon pass away. But this theme too is stated in such cool words and such bleak generalizations and such microscopically measured antitheses that it fails to carry conviction. There is not a single word in the entire speech which shows that the boy, its subject, possessed any spiritual qualities which might make an older man cultivate his friendship for the sake of developing them; and not a single word which makes the hearer feel that the speaker himself has a warm heart and a capacity for loyal and selfless devotion. This again is unlike most of the genuine speeches of Lysias. On the contrary, one of Lysias's finest qualities is his ability to give a lively impression of personal character. In the speeches he writes for others, we can nearly always trace the clear lines of the putative speaker's individuality and even hear the accents of his voice. Although of course they cannot hope to equal the remarkable vivacity of Plato's leading characters, they are much more sharply differentiated than, for example, the speeches of the various actors in Antiphon. And the great speech which Lysias made on his own behalf, accusing Eratosthenes, one of the Thirty Tyrants, of the cold-hearted murder of Lysias's brother—that speech breathes true life and unfeigned passion. Not so the *Erotikos*. It is a speech addressed to a dummy by a machine.

The author of the erotic fragment (we must feel as we read) is a clever but cheep, greedy but controlled materialist. When he wants something, he will muster arguments to get it, and set them out clearly and fluently, without considering whether they are true or relevant or coherent, without even caring. This brings us to a stronger point. The ethos, the moral tone, of the erotic fragment is all wrong. Few modern critics who have written about it have perceived this clearly. Those who have, have preferred to say nothing about the subject. Blass[5] coldly remarks that he does not wish to utter a word about the moral ambiguity of the theme and the way in which the love of boys is expressed; and Helmbold and Holther[6]

---

[5][See F. W. Blass, *Die attische beredsamkeit,* 3 vols. (Leipzig, 1887–98), especially vol. 1, p. 428. Ed.]

[6][See W. C. Helmbold and W. B. Holther, "The Unity of the 'Phaedrus'," in *University of California Publications in Classical Philology* 14 (1952) 387–417, especially 392. Ed.]

think it was "clearly intended as a 'delight', a sort of protracted rhetorical joke." But Plato himself had clear views on the subject. He thought this was a vile proposal. In this very dialogue he makes Socrates say that it is very dangerous, and ultimately undesirable, for two male lovers even if united by genuine passion to have homosexual intercourse. To refrain from satisfying their desire is to gain wings for their flight to heaven after death; it is a noble and a beautiful passion, "the stream which Zeus, when he was in love with Ganymede, named Desire (ἵμερον)"; but to give way even to that passion, even when it is shared, is a drunken prank or a piece of senselessness which is inferior to true nobility (255a1–256e2). To have intercourse without love on either side, this, which we should nowadays call unspeakably vile and vicious, Plato, whose predilections were unlike ours, condemns as mean, vulgar, and earthbound (256e3–257a2). Yet this is the policy recommended by the author of the speech, which Plato makes Phaedrus attribute to Lysias. And to recommend such a course of action, for such reasons as appear in the *Erotikos,* is totally unlike the Lysias whom we know from his genuine speeches.

If, then, the *Erotikos* is a parody of Lysias written by Plato, it is a remorselessly cruel and slanderous caricature. No one of good sense, fine feeling, and mature judgment could read it without despising Lysias, yes, and hating him. At the beginning of the dialogue Phaedrus does indeed admire the speech, to an extent which seems extravagant to us; but that is because he is enthusiastic by nature, deeply interested in love, and easily fascinated by the tricks of rhetoric. As the dialogue proceeds, Socrates skillfully destroys all his admiration for it. First, he delivers a counter-speech on the same subject, which is both wiser (as more closely corresponding to the real emotional facts), more genuinely moving, and better built. This speech (237b7–241d1) explains how dangerous a passionate lover is for a boy; therefore, by implication, it complements the theme of the *Erotikos* that a non-lover is safer; but it is far more deeply tinged with true feeling. Then Socrates delivers a second speech, more skillfully constructed, far more poetically inspired, fuller of psychological wisdom, philosophical depth, and mystical vision than both the previous speeches (244a3–257a2). He ends with a lofty denunciation which, without naming Lysias, utters scorn of the cheap qualities we feel in the *Erotikos* (256e3–257a2).

Socrates now goes on still further to destroy Phaedrus's admiration (or should we say love?) for Lysias. Although Lysias was recently abused as a λογόγραφος ("speechwriter"), Socrates ironi-

cally claims that this ought not to hurt his feelings, since he is on a
par with all politicians. They all write speeches and laws and com-
positions of that sort—although they do not know when they are
writing truth and when lies (257b7–258d6). Next he attacks the
construction of the *Erotikos,* explaining (in terms which have since
his time been justly admired) that it ought not to be a random
group of ideas but should have the unity of a living creature
(262c5–264e7). Here there is one very puzzling criticism, which
does seem to imply that the speech is really part of a speech by
Lysias. Socrates criticizes it for lacking a head (264a4–7). But
surely Plato would not be so unfair as to write a speech which was
incomplete and then make Socrates criticize it for being incomplete. In case Phaedrus should miss this point, Socrates goes on to
praise the structure of his own speech, particularly its careful psychological analysis (265), after which he summarizes the rules for
the construction of speeches given by the manuals of rhetoric,
brushing them aside as obvious and negligible, with heavy irony
(πάντως δ' οὐκ ἀτιμαστέον αὐτὸ σοί τε καὶ ἐμοί 266d2–3). Then,
drawing toward a conclusion, he explains to Phaedrus that all
politicians (including Lysias) are ignorant men talking about important subjects which they do not understand, that they have no
standards, and that they waste their time even in writing down
their thoughts (277d6–e). One exception is admitted: Pericles, "the
most perfect of all artists in speaking," because as well as his natural gifts he got the knowledge of Mind and Intellect (νοῦ τε καὶ
ἀνοίας) from the philosopher Anaxagoras (269e–270a).

Phaedrus is now convinced, and so are most of Plato's readers.
We have watched the systematic destruction of a man's character,
of his career, and of his reputation. Lysias (Phaedrus has been
shown and we are expected to believe) has no sense of morality,
being unable to distinguish lust from love. He has no aesthetic taste,
having a poor monotonous style and being unable to construct a
speech. He does not understand psychology. He has no inkling of
true philosophy, which raises men above temporary whims to a
knowledge of the truth and makes them understand the mind and
will of the gods (273e5–8). And his political ambitions, such as they
are, are far below the wise precedent set by Pericles. In spite of this,
does he not remain an eminent rhetorician? No. As the afternoon
grows cool, as the grasshoppers (benumbed by the eloquence of
Socrates) cease to chirp, and as the dialogue at length draws to an
end, after Socrates has contemptuously touched and with a civil
leer dismissed all the rhetoricians of the period in which the dia-

logue is notionally set—Gorgias, Tisias, and "whoever else it was who discovered the art," and Theodorus, and Protagoras, and Polus, and Hippias of Elis, and Thrasymachus "the mighty Chalcedonian," and others (266c1–273c9)—then, after all this, when Phaedrus has been dominated and is ready to go, Plato remembers one more method of destroying Lysias and applies it. Phaedrus (rather unexpectedly and unconvincingly) here recalls the name of a friend of Socrates, "the handsome Isocrates"; and Socrates gladly forecasts that Isocrates, since he has a nobler character than Lysias and has some philosophy in his mind, will make all previous rhetoricians look like children (279a3–b3, especially 279a4, ἤθει γεννικωτέρῳ κεκρᾶσθαι). Lysias has been slowly but thoroughly killed throughout the dialogue. Like Euripides at the end of the *Frogs,* he is now denied resurrection. He is buried, and a stone is laid on his grave.

Almost every dialogue of Plato serves several different purposes. One purpose, and a pre-eminent purpose, of the *Phaedrus* is to destroy the reputation of Lysias. From the very first page, in which we meet the excited and enraptured Phaedrus, walking straight from Lysias's house into the countryside in order to find quietness and commit his words to memory, through the ambitious trilogy of speeches which makes the core of the dialogue (one speech supposedly by Lysias, one by Socrates refuting him, and a second by Socrates transcending and humiliating him), to the last page, when after being lost to view among a swarm of clever tricksters, he is finally pushed into sunset shadow by the dawning brilliance of Isocrates, Lysias is—although absent in person—a central figure of the dialogue. Plato, speaking through Socrates, annihilates him far more ruthlessly than he diminished Gorgias, far more carefully than (in *Republic* 1) he was to humiliate Thrasymachus, and far more seriously than he criticized Protagoras and Prodicus and the other sophists. Evidently he considered Lysias a figure of major importance, one of the great enemies of truth. Yet—and this is unusual—he would not make Socrates meet Lysias face to face. Socrates destroys him in every possible way but will not talk with him. He must have hated him very much.

Even without the *Erotikos,* this would still be true. But the *Phaedrus* begins with four and one-half pages of erotic prose on which much of Socrates' criticism is based. We have therefore to ask whether these pages were written by Lysias or by Plato. Are they a real work—serious or frivolous, it scarcely matters, since Phaedrus is supposed to admire them seriously—a real work by

Lysias published or known under his name? If so, we can take Plato's critique of the work seriously. Or are they an imitation, a pastiche, a parody, a caricature, a forgery, by Plato? If so, we shall not regard these pages as serious evidence for the truth of Plato's criticisms. In fact, we shall have to ask whether the nature of these four and one-half pages strengthens our admiration for Plato's stylistic agility, or increases our distrust of his intellectual integrity, or both.

Is the *Erotikos* a genuine work of Lysias? The evidence is easy to classify.

External evidence is on the whole opposed to its authenticity. If it did not occur in the text of Plato's *Phaedrus,* it would apparently never have been known at all. It is in none of the manuscripts of Lysias. The only ancient writers who quote it or refer to it are very late. Fronto modeled an erotic letter to Marcus Aurelius on it, referring both to Lysias and to Plato.[7] Diogenes Laertius, whom not all of us are inclined to trust, says of Plato (3.25):

καὶ πρῶτος τῶν φιλοσόφων ἀντεῖπε πρὸς τὸν λόγον τὸν Λυσίου τοῦ Κεφάλου ἐκθέμενος αὐτὸν κατὰ λέξιν ἐν τῷ Φαίδρῳ.

and he was the first of the philosophers to oppose the speechmaking of Lysias, son of Cephalus, picking him out and treating him word for word in the *Phaedrus.*

This is not a very convincing sentence. Dionysius of Halicarnassus *(Letter to Gnaeus Pompeius),* and the rhetorician Hermogenes,[8] and the rhetorician Hermeias[9] also believe this work is genuine. No others do.

On the other hand, fragments from λόγοι ἐρωτικοί written by Lysias have been preserved, although they are very small, and he is known to have written such works (Dionysius of Halicarnassus, *On the Ancient Orators* ['Lysias' 1] and Pseudo-Plutarch, *Lives of the Ten Orators* ['Lysias' 836B]). It is possible, therefore, that this fragment is a genuine work by Lysias, although most of the evidence is against it.

Internal evidence we may divide into evidence from style and evidence from content. The style, as we have seen, looks not like authentic Lysias but like a close and injurious parody of Lysias.

---

[7]See S. A. Naber, ed., *M. Cornelii Frontonis et M. Aurelii imperatoris epistulae* (Leipzig, 1867) 255–59.
[8]See L. Spengel, ed., *Rhetores Graeci,* 3 vols. (Leipzig, 1853–56), especially vol. 2, p. 331.
[9]See L. Spengel, ΣΥΝΑΓѠΓΗ ΤΕΧΝѠΝ (Stuttgart, 1828) p. 126, note 64.

The subject matter is in a different category. The speech is so unlike the extant works of Lysias that—if we did not see his name attached to it by Plato and the stylistic tricks stuck onto it like spangles on a doll—we should scarcely recognize it as his work; we should rather put it down as a jeu d'esprit written by some elegant young homosexual pupil of the sophists with a gift for prose, poor taste, and no morals. It may be only an accident that the two fragments of Lysias's genuine erotic pieces which we possess do convey sincere affection—the very reverse of this cold and cynical utterance—and perhaps Lysias did at one time write this speech or something like this speech.[10] However, virtually all the writings of Lysias which we have deal with larger and more serious subjects: sharp legal disputes, urgent political issues, and (behind some of them) important moral problems. Even at their most trivial, the authentic speeches of Lysias contain a lively personal sense of justice. True, some of them are fakes, ghost-written speeches for others to deliver; but the most ambitious and the most passionate were spoken in Lysias's own voice and came from his own heart—the accusation of Eratosthenes, who killed Lysias's brother and impoverished his entire house, and the noble Olympic speech aimed against Dionysius, the tyrant of Syracuse. Therefore, even if the *Erotikos* were an authentic speech by Lysias, would it be fair of Plato to choose it as a marvelous, an outstanding, and an enchanting example of his rhetorical skill? Conceivably it might be fair if Lysias had posed as an expert on homosexual love affairs—a subject which interested Plato and presumably Socrates very deeply; but there is not a shred of evidence that he did. Therefore, to start from such a peripheral and disagreeable little piece, whether it is authentic or not, and to use it as a clear indication that its author Lysias knew nothing about oratory or psychology or morality—that is surely very dubious argumentation.

One further piece of evidence remains to be discussed: it may be called either external or internal depending on one's point of view. This is the fact that Plato says, or makes one of his characters say, that the *Erotikos* is by Lysias. Many scholars have felt that this clinches the matter and that there is nothing left to discuss. Egger[11] held that Plato in such a matter would not lie—which is

---

[10]See L. Gernet and M. Bizos, edd., *Lysias: Discours,* 2 vols. (Paris, 1924–26), especially vol. 2, p. 282, for the two fragments of Lysias's erotic pieces.

[11][See E. Egger, "Observations sur l'Eroticos inséré, sous le nom de Lysias, dans le Phèdre de Platon," in *L'Annuaire de l'Association pour l'encouragement des études grecques* (Paris, 1871) 17–38. Ed.]

surely begging the question. Jebb[12] went a little deeper. He said that because Socrates analyzes the speech with some care and even has its opening re-read to him twice after he has heard it for the first time, the speech must be the work of Lysias—because Plato would never make Socrates analyze a forged or fictitious work with such a pretense of real concern. However, this is really the same argument as Egger's. Plato himself provides the evidence which permits us to answer it. In the *Menexenus* he makes Socrates repeat word for word a funeral speech for the dead Athenian soldiers, which Socrates says he was taught by Aspasia (he was almost beaten by her when he made a mistake too). The speech does not pretend to be genuine, for it contains a reference to the Peace of Antalcidas (386 B.C.), concluded long after Socrates was certainly and Aspasia presumably dead (*Men.* 245e3–4). In the *Symposium* he makes Aristophanes and other distinguished men utter impromptu speeches which can scarcely have been preserved, even by the miraculous memory of Aristodemus, and which must therefore be fictitious. In the *Protagoras* we read a sophistic display by Protagoras which can scarcely be authentic. Finally, Plato's reports of Socrates' own sayings vary so greatly that they cannot all be true. There is a serious cause for believing that even his account of his own master's speeches at his trial (an event at which Plato himself was present) is largely fiction.

We conclude, therefore, that the *Erotikos* in the *Phaedrus* is not by Lysias. It is a forgery, or a caricature, or to use a faintly Platonic phrase, an ignoble lie (ἀγεννὲς ψεῦδος). If this is true, we have one final question to face. Why did Plato write this parody, and why did he devote so much of one of his most beautiful dialogues to smashing the reputation of Lysias, without even trying to allow Lysias to answer him? The obvious answer is that (as he says in the *Gorgias*) he despised rhetoric as a crowd-pleaser, a cheap trick, an enemy of philosophical truth, and the corrupter of politics; and that therefore he attacked Lysias as typical of Athenian rhetoricians, making his work seem trivial, superficial, materialistic, vulgar, and mechanical.

This is true. But there must be more in it than that. Plato writes with far too much passion to allow us to conclude that that was the main purpose of the *Phaedrus*. Gorgias, whose reputation and whose achievement were far greater than those of Lysias, is much more kindly treated in the dialogue named after him; this dialogue

---

[12][See R. C. Jebb, *The Attic Orators from Antiphon to Isaeos,* 2 vols. (London, 1876), especially vol. 1, pp. 305–9. Ed.]

is more full of Lysias than the *Gorgias* is full of Gorgias, but it is named not for the writer but for one of his readers. Instead of putting a parody of Gorgias's famous style into Gorgias's own mouth and then making Socrates silence him, he scarcely lets us hear Gorgias at all. Socrates enters after Gorgias has finished speaking, never hears one of his real discourses, converses with him in a fairly mild dialogue, and then turns to the pupils of Gorgias, leaving the distinguished old gentleman to listen in tranquillity. Perhaps we might suggest that the *Phaedrus* criticizes positive rhetoric—the instrument of the persuasive, woolly-minded, socially conscious legislator; while the *Gorgias* criticizes negative rhetoric—the rhetoric of the hard, self-seeking, ruthless agitator. Still, there must be some other reason for Plato's unusual concentration on Lysias as a repulsive and dangerous individual. It is a very cruel trick to put such a vile speech as this *Erotikos* into the mouth of a contemporary and then to criticize it as though it were his own genuine work. What should we think if we read a dialogue written by an opponent of Plato (say Polycrates), which showed, with lifelike imitation of phrases and mannerisms, Socrates advising young Plato to refrain from joining his kinsmen in the bloody revolution of 404 B.C., not because killing one's fellow-citizens was wrong, but so that he could survive and rewrite Athenian spiritual history in such a way as to denigrate all the ideals of Athenian democracy? "Some will perhaps call Charmides a traitor; but you will show him as a charming young pupil of Socrates, almost an embodiment—on one level—of the Good. Some will surely call Critias a cold-hearted and insane murderer; but you will remember that he had a massive intellect and display him as a noble idealist, possibly a little bit distorted by the pressure of a corrupt democratic regime. You will dedicate eloquent works to the memory of both of them, won't you?" It would have been possible for an enemy of Plato to write such a dialogue. Had it been written and had it survived, might scholars not be debating whether Socrates ever gave young Plato such advice, whether this explained Plato's motives in writing certain dialogues, whether in fact it was historically true instead of being a slanderous fiction?

I suggest, then, that Plato wrote his *Phaedrus* in order to destroy the character and reputation of Lysias. No doubt he had a number of reasons for doing this. But I suggest that one reason which moved him consciously or unconsciously was that the two men stood on opposite sides of the revolution of 404 B.C.

In that revolution, the Thirty Tyrants, supported by the very Lacedaemonians against whom Athens had been fighting for a whole generation, were dominated by Critias, son of Callaeschrus. The cousin of Critias was Perictione, the mother of Plato. Critias and his men held the city of Athens for some time; one of his ten officers in the Piraeus was his ward Charmides, son of Glaucon. Charmides was the brother of Perictione and was Plato's uncle. It was Socrates who advised Charmides to enter politics, says Xenophon, who actually reports the discussion (*Memorabilia* 3.7). During the regime led by Critias, many citizens and resident aliens of Athens had their property confiscated, or were executed without trial, or both. One of the victims of Critias and Charmides was Polemarchus, the brother of Lysias. He was told to drink the hemlock. He was not even conceded a decent funeral; but his dead body was put in a shed, with a borrowed pillow to prop its head; when his widow visited the body, one of Critias's accomplices took a pair of gold earrings out of her ears and pocketed them (Lysias 12.17–19). Lysias himself just managed to escape from this purge. From exile he supported the democratic resistance under Thrasybulus. After the liberation he returned, but all his property was gone, and his brother was dead. Perhaps his earliest and certainly his best speech is his prosecution of Eratosthenes, a member of the Thirty. Critias and Charmides had been killed fighting against the democrats. This man had survived, and through him Lysias denounced all the brutalities of the Thirty Tyrants.

That was the real beginning of Lysias's public career, at an age when many men are thinking rather of retirement. Doubtless the irrecoverable loss of all his property (which we see dimly reflected in the papyrus fragments of his speech against Hippotherses)[13] impelled him to take up, though nearly sixty years old, the profession of λογόγραφος. But certainly his bitter experiences made him, in any speech where allusions to politics would be appropriate, speak as a strong partisan of the democracy and an unforgiving, unforgetting enemy of the oligarchic revolutionaries. Plato could not, or would not, attempt a direct defense of Critias and the rest of the Thirty. He could not, or would not, attempt a direct attack on Thrasybulus and on those who, like Lysias, supported him in restoring the democracy. But he glorified Critias and Charmides as true philosophers, and in the *Phaedrus* he attacked Lysias with destructive and indeed vindictive energy. Most of Plato's methods

---

[13]For the fragments of this speech, see B. P. Grenfell and A. S. Hunt, edd., *The Oxyrhynchus Papyri* (London, 1919) part 13, pp. 48–74.

in this campaign of annihilation have been examined. Two more remain for analysis.

The first is Plato's view of the philosophical and moral basis of democracy. The second is the connection between homosexual love and political activity.

In Book 8 of the *Republic* we are given a satiric description of "the democratic man" and of the regime in which he lives: entirely devoid of reason and self-control, capricious, unable to discern or to maintain standards of morality (*Rep.* 8.557–61). In the *Phaedrus* Lysias is singled out for particular censure in several strong paragraphs at the climax of the dialogue (277a6–278e2, especially 277b5–c6 and 277c7–278b4). He does not (we are told) understand his subject-matter, politics, and morality; he does not know psychology; and he is mistaken in believing that the written word is superior to oral teaching. The reason for this has already been stated. After contemptuously dismissing Lysias's speech and outdoing it (in his own second speech on Eros), Socrates says: "Let him turn to philosophy, like his brother Polemarchus" (257b3–4). In the heart of that marvelous second speech, Socrates produces a hierarchy of human lives. At the top of this hierarchy stands the man who will be a philosopher or a lover of beauty or someone having a musical and loving nature; at the bottom, eighth on the list, below the artisan and farmer, and just above the tyrant, stands the man who will be a sophist or a demagogue (248a1–e3, especially 248d3 and e3). It is clear, therefore, from the *Phaedrus* that Lysias is one of the worst representatives of an evil political system—evil because foolish, vicious because devoted to pleasure, wrong through ignorance and lack of philosophical preparation. Plato will not, in this dialogue, even consider the idea that a democratic constitution might be proved, by philosophical argument, to be just and good, and productive of just and good men and ideas. His mind is closed.

The second problem in uncommonly difficult and not a little unpleasant to discuss. What is the connection between homosexual love and political activity? Most modern readers of Plato are surprised by the way in which he treats rhetoric in the dialogue called the *Phaedrus*. In practice, rhetoric was a method of gaining political power and sometimes making money: in the *Gorgias* Plato accepts that fact and discusses it; but in the *Phaedrus* he attributes to a man widely known for his political and legal activity a composition dealing exclusively with a disgusting aspect of homosexual love.[14] He then makes Socrates develop the same theme from a more favorable point of view, at great length, and with very fiery eloquence soaring high into quasi-religious mysticism; and finally, as though the connection were perfectly obvious, revert to a criticism of the defects of rhetoric and politics when unexamined by philosophical criteria. Now the connection is far from obvious. Yet Plato felt that there was a connection, and an important one. He hints at it in the very beginning of the dialogue. When Phaedrus tells Socrates the subject of Lysias's composition (ὡς χαριστέον μὴ ἐρῶντι μᾶλλον ἢ ἐρῶντι 227c7–8), Socrates applauds ironically (ὦ γενναῖος 227c9) and says that if Lysias would only write that a handsome boy should favor a poor man rather than a rich, and an older man rather than a younger—"like me and most of us"—his speeches would surely be ἀστεῖοι and δημωφελεῖς (227d1–2). The word δημωφελεῖς is comparatively rare and is therefore meant to be emphatic and to strike a strong ringing note. The note which it strikes is a sneer at democracy: anyone who could get a pretty boy's favors for the many without discrimination rather than for the few who deserve and earn them, would surely be a "benefactor of the demos." Socrates does not believe this, nor are his readers expected to believe it; he simply means that everything democratic is degradation.

Plato goes on to explain the degrees of feeling which exist in homosexual love. There are four different types of homosexual connection. The highest and noblest is that in which two partners truly love each other, but, although one is desirous and the other willing, one beautiful and the other amorous, control themselves, pass their lives in harmony, and (as we should now say) sublimate their passion. The lover here exercises more restraint than the beloved. Plato says that this is all but heaven on earth and the greatest "Olympic" victory (256b3–7). Next to this, and although lower still far from despicable, is the condition of two male friends who love each other and yield to their love but remain true to each other. Such lovers are "wingless but eager to win wings" (256d3–e2). Below that is the relationship which Socrates denounces in his first speech. It is a dangerous relationship: a man loves a boy without being loved in return, treating him merely as a Galatea adored by a Pygmalion, a passive object of passionate love. What we hear of Plato's Athens makes us believe that this was the fashionable

---

[14]See also W. Schmid and O. Stahlin, *Geschichte der griechischen litteratur* (Münich, 1912[6]) vol. 1, p. 694, who regard the connection between the two disparate subjects of eroticism and rhetoric as somewhat forced.

type of homosexual love affair. The numerous youths called καλοί on the vases and in inscriptions were clearly the passive members of such a relationship. Fourth and lowest is the relationship in which the man treats the youth merely as a utensil, in which there is no love on either side, and the entire thing (apart from promises of future "friendship") is reduced to the basest physical contact.

Lysias, in a speech written by Plato to travesty and disfigure his usual style and his central moral tone, is put forward as the advocate of this fourth and lowest relationship. Socrates, in a prose hymn to Eros, warns his hearer against the third relationship, approves the second with reservations, and apotheosizes the first.

It is impossible, therefore, to ignore these two parallel hierarchies, and it is difficult not to equate them. For Socrates, the highest sexual relation is a mutual sexual passion between men, parallel on a lower level to that between Zeus and Ganymede, and yet (since we are only human) controlled and harmonized and raised by philosophy to heavenly happiness. The lowest sexual relation is a loveless association between a man and a boy, purely physical in expression and motivated by pleasure and advantage only. For Socrates, the highest spiritual activity is teaching and communicating philosophical truths orally, writing them in the soul and in the soul alone. The lowest is writing speeches and laws for a democracy—that is, the lowest next to tyranny, which is scarcely human.

The conclusion, although Socrates does not draw it explicitly, is clear. In a democracy, he suggests, men treat one another merely as utensils for pleasure and live without love or true affection, without understanding or true standards. The only valuable and livable community is a small group of men who are united emotionally by devotion and admiration, intellectually by their pursuit of and participation in those higher truths which are concealed from the multitude—in fact, an intellectual aristocracy and an elite of homosexuals.

Intensely as Plato appears to feel the truth of these interlocked propositions, he does not, either in the *Phaedrus* or elsewhere, demonstrate them by methods which can in his own terms be called philosophical. Assertions which are not opposed and are not purged by dialectic examinations, mystical speeches filled with pictorial symbolism, false attributions of doctrines and parodies of works of art—to the detriment of an opponent who, being absent, cannot defend himself or answer—these make up the dialogue called the *Phaedrus,* if indeed it should be called a dialogue and not a romantic drama of love. Much as its author professed to admire philosophy, in this work he preferred to use the methods of its rivals—poetry and rhetoric;[15] but he used them for purposes which were dictated, or at least directed, by personal hatred and political bias. Looking back over the charm of the *Phaedrus* and reflecting on the sunlit grace with which it touches and destroys a good man's character, we can understand the remark of Aristotle, Plato's pupil: "Plato is a friend but truth a greater friend."[16]

[15][Here Highet noted in the margin of his manuscript the words that Cicero had used to describe Plato after reading Plato's *Gorgias: mihi in oratoribus irridendis esse orator summus videtur* (*De Oratore* 1.11.47). Ed.]
[16][A reference to the medieval Latin quotation *amicus Plato sed magis amica veritas*—ultimately derived from Aristotle's *Nicomachean Ethics* 1096a16–17 (ἀμφοῖν γὰρ ὄντοιν φίλοιν ὅσιον προτιμᾶν τὴν ἀλήθειαν). Ed.]

Menander's *Dyskolos**

Chance is a powerful goddess, but she loves to tease. In wartime she takes a curious pleasure in destroying precious things, or like an insane monkey, in hiding them away for protection—only to forget where she put them. In peace she delights to present us with random gifts which are sometimes rare and precious, sometimes lavish and worthless, and sometimes so unexpected as to look like a practical joke. As Menander himself says of her:

καθ' οὓς κρινεῖ τὰ πράγματ' οὐ χρῆται νόμοις.[1]

She has no rules when she is judging men's affairs.

Still, it would be imprudent to show ingratitude to a divinity so potent and so unpredictable; and we are all grateful to Chance for presenting to Martin Bodmer, and through him to us, a hitherto unknown comedy written by Menander called the *Dyskolos* (or the *Curmudgeon*).[2]

If next year Chance were to produce, out of that grab-bag she calls her treasure-house, a very early play written by Shakespeare in the year 1588 (when he was twenty-four) or a farce composed by Molière while he was still an actor touring the provinces, what would it be like? Chance being as irresponsible as she is, we cannot be absolutely sure; but the probabilities are these.

First, such a play would be eminently *actable*. It would contain several of what the modern stage calls 'fat parts': boldly marked characters, strong and simple, almost caricatures; together with one or two clowns, who had speaking parts in the comedy but did not significantly affect the main plot, and whose function was simply to behave absurdly, crack jokes, and put in a dance, a song, or some horseplay at intervals.

---

*Presented in 1959 for the American Philological Association.
[1]See A. Körte, ed., *Menandri quae supersunt: pars altera* (Leipzig, 1959) 110.
[2][See E. W. Handley, ed., *The Dyskolos of Menander* (London, 1965) 40–55, for detailed information about the papyrus containing this play, which was acquired in 1958 by Martin Bodmer. Ed.]

Second, the *plot* of the new Shakespeare or Molière play would be simple. Young writers can seldom manage delicate nuances of character, subtle gradations and intricate complexities of motive. (Terence is an exception, but he was working on material supplied to him by mature playwrights.) The basic naiveté of the plot would, however, be concealed by the author's exuberance. The story might be a wildly improbable situation—two pairs of twins, each pair separated and reared in ignorance of the sibling's existence; or a boyishly simple idea—an elderly judge falling desperately in love with a simple milkmaid; but it would be dressed up with fantastically humorous characters like Shakespeare's Don Adriano de Armado and Holofernes in *Love's Labor's Lost,* with elaborate misunderstandings, disguises, extraneous episodes, eccentric monologues, music, and primitive knockabout. At this level of comedy, everyone enjoys seeing a girl dressed up as a man, or a gentleman disguised as a bumpkin, or a braggart scared and begging for mercy, or a shrew or curmudgeon well-basted; and most people do not feel the play is really complete unless at the end it takes off into the festival gaiety of singing and dancing and merrymaking.

The newly discovered comedy would probably be a curious mixture of *convention and invention.* That is, much of it might perfectly well have been composed by any one of a dozen other dramatists—dramatists of an earlier time, perhaps even of another country, whose plays the new young author had admired and studied. Sometimes, like Molière, he might have spent years acting in comedies composed by other men and then decided he could emulate them. Sometimes, like Pedro Calderón de la Barca, he would have been in the audience many times, would have read the plays of his predecessors, and then determined to outshine them. In either case, he would begin by using much of their plot-structure, some of their standard characters, and some of their fundamental conception of comedy. On the other hand, since he was ambitious, the new playwright would try to outdo them, to enrich their work, to subtilize it, and sometimes even to criticize it. The pupil poet would not be writing at all if he was totally uninterested in the medium which his predecessors used; but even though he might not say so explicitly, he would feel that it could be used to say more about the predicaments of mankind, that its language might be made more expressive, and that its taste could well be improved.

Therefore, if the early play given to us by capricious Chance were by Shakespeare, it might be a borrowed romantic improbability full of conventional characters, but all embroidered with dainty devices of wit, full of eloquent snatches of original poetry, and pranked out with genuinely, inalienably Shakespearean eccentrics and lovers; if it were by Molière, it might be one of the broad farces which amused stolid unsophisticated people in country towns, with a naively simple plot kept going by sheer energy through a dozen unexpected twists of surprise and foolery, with all the characters painted in simple primary colors, but at the same time touching several of the genuine problems of human life and portraying one or two unforgettably real people, or else, in scenes of inspired fooling, outdoing all his predecessors and creating one of those frolics where we see (as Shakespeare says) "fancy outwork nature" (*Antony and Cleopatra* 2.2.203).

Menander is not Shakespeare. Shakespeare soars high above him into certain zones of poetic eloquence and gay invention which were familiar to Aristophanes but (as far as we know) remained, for Menander, unvisited. Menander is not Molière, although the two have a great deal in common. He is himself. He has a character of his own, usually neither energetic nor exuberant as comic dramatists are, and yet as unmistakable and unforgettable as the sensitive features and anxious half-frown of his sculptured portraits. In his newly discovered comedy the *Dyskolos,* we can see that character, although still only half-developed, yet already marked with its own likes and dislikes, already directed by its own προαίρεσις ("purpose"); and at the same time, we can see—like the masks hanging on the wall in the playwright's studio—the conventional characters, the traditional plots, and the accepted conception of drama, within which Menander began the work of creation. The new play is like those other hypothetical early comedies of Shakespeare and Molière. It is eminently actable and contains two first-rate character parts for men together with one good clown. The plot is simple and might even be called flimsy; but it is dressed up with a romantic setting and with many diverse episodes which constantly change pace, and it ends with music and merrymaking. And one of the most interesting things about it is the conflict throughout the play between old and new, convention and creation.

Interesting to us, as students of literary history, that is. The conflict shows us much about Menander which (until this play was discovered) could scarcely even be guessed, helps to illustrate the development of Greek comedy, and changes some of the accepted ideas both of the structure of Greek comedy and of its relation to Plautus and Terence, the adaptors who transferred it to the Roman stage. But partly because Menander did not satisfactorily resolve the conflict, his *Dyskolos* is not a very good play. Once again we see and marvel at the featherheaded cruelty of Chance. She is the ruling power in Menander's comedies, restoring lost children to their parents, separating lovers by a misunderstanding or an accident, creating apparently insoluble puzzles and then solving them arbitrarily with a shriek of idiotic laughter. If Menander had prayed to her to permit a few of his comedies to be preserved in order to educate us semi-barbarians of a later age, which do you suppose he would have chosen? *Glycera,* perhaps named after his sweetheart? The *Girls Taking Hemlock?* The *Double Deceiver?* He had a hundred to choose from, and some of their titles are delightfully intriguing (in both senses); but something tells me he would scarcely have selected the *Dyskolos.* Light it is, but it is thin. Charming it is, but its charm is often irrelevant. No, Menander would not have chosen this little piece as his only play to be transmitted virtually complete through twenty-three centuries; and just for that reason, Lady Chance rescued this foundling from the sands of Egypt, checked its breathing and blood-pressure, made sure that its tokens of recognition were firmly attached, and handed it over to Martin Bodmer, who in 1958 introduced his fosterling to an astonished world. Chance is the true presiding deity of Comedy, even in its preservation.

On the first page of the manuscript fragments containing the *Dyskolos,* there is a summary of the plot, a cast, and a few notes by the illustrious Alexandrian scholar Aristophanes of Byzantium. One of the notes says that the play was performed and won first prize when Demogenes was archon of Athens, which is the year we call 317–16 B.C. (The MS actually reads Didymogenes, but no such name is known among the archons, whereas we can be sure that Demogenes did hold office during Menander's lifetime.) If this is true—and there is no reason to disbelieve it—then when Menander brought out the play, he was only twenty-five years old. He was already a playwright, for his first play, the *Fit of Anger,* had been produced in 321 B.C. (perhaps even earlier, in 324 B.C.);[3] but he was very young still, and his play is a young man's play. Furthermore, although the mature Menander composed many plays of great beauty and charm in the special style which we call

---

[3]See A. Körte, "Menandros (9)," in *RE* 15.1 (1931) 707–61, especially 710–11.

New Comedy, that style did not yet exist at the opening of his career. It was coming into being, and it was Menander who would perfect it; but at this time, he was only working toward it and building upon the work of his predecessors.

His immediate predecessors were the comedians of the middle decades of the fourth century B.C. We do not know enough about this Middle Comedy to describe it fully, since not a single play, not even a single scene, has survived—nothing but twelve baskets of fragments and a few critical comments by Greek and Latin scholars. But we can be sure of certain basic facts about it.

It is tempting to give it exact dates of birth and death: birth in about 400 B.C., with the resurgence of Athens shortly after the Peloponnesian War; and death in 322 B.C., when democracy was abolished and a foreign garrison was installed in the Piraeus. That schematism is too sharp, but the dates are at least helpful to remember. Now most of the Attic comedies produced during those decades had characters who were realistic and engaged in intrigues which were comical but still credible. And there were few or none of those fantastic creations which fill the comedies of Aristophanes with their deliberately impossible adventures: no flying dung-beetles, choruses of wasps, arguments between Right Reason and Wrong Reason, castles in the clouds, journeys to the land of death; no more riotous obscenity in speech, action, and costume; no more grotesque masks for the main characters, and far less of the richly varied lyricism of singing and dancing choruses. Instead, the typical playwright of Middle Comedy often built his plot out of events of daily life, family disputes or social intrigues; or else he parodied well-known myths and famous tragedies, doubtless by bringing them down to earth; and he had these comedies realized by men and women who looked and behaved much like the audience watching them. But he seems to have got more comic effect from character than from plot. He liked to put on his stage certain social and professional types who were easily recognizable and considered to be amusing. Nowadays we see nothing funny about chefs; fishmongers leave us cold; courtesans and gatecrashers appear in the gossip columns and occasionally are interviewed on television but rarely become the subject of comic dramas. But in Athens the playwrights of Middle Comedy loved to put such people on the stage and make them explain (with infinite pomposity and absurd prolixity) the subtlety, the importance, and the rich rewards of their vocations. The diabolically clever slave, the eternally hungry 'extra guest' or parasite, the bold and skillful courtesan, the soldier of fortune returned from Eastern campaigns with his pouch full of gold and his mouth full of strange oaths—these were the people of Middle Comedy. As far as we can tell, they made the audience laugh by displaying their own abnormal qualities at least as much as by the dramatic intrigues in which the playwrights involved them.

Now as Menander grew up and thought of becoming a playwright, he was watching the work of these men. Alexis, one of the best of them, was his uncle and, according to one account, actually trained him (περὶ κωμῳδίας 17).[4] Therefore, when he wrote his early plays, he took over many of their methods and much of their material: some he took with enjoyment; some with a dutiful acceptance, feeling (as Yeats put it) "that no better could be had" (Old Men be Mad 19); and some with a conviction that it was obsolescent. These last features of Middle Comedy he was determined to abolish. In the same way as his predecessors had quietly abolished the lewd gestures and outrageous costumes of Aristophanic lyrical farce, so Menander (and perhaps others of his generation) determined to abolish the crude two-dimensional characters, the detachable monologues, and the episodic plots of Middle Comedy in order to build a more real comic world with real people really involved.

But Menander had another model, a great dramatist who was not a comedian at all. This was the tragic poet Euripides. Like Menander, Euripides came late in the development of his branch of drama; and he altered the nature of tragedy in certain essential ways, which were to appeal strongly to Menander. For example, Euripides virtually abolished the chorus as a part of the action; he strove to keep his men and women from being merely types—remote, mythical, and grand—and instead he made them passionately, disquietingly real, directing the attention of the audience into the subtlest recesses of their characters and their emotions. It was mainly Euripides who altered the relation between gods and men in drama, in such a way that, although the gods still retained their power over mankind, they were often portrayed as acting capriciously in a subhuman and irrational manner very like the rule of arbitrary Chance; and it was supremely Euripides who created, out of standard traditional plots, plays which left the audience's minds full of insoluble questions and a sense of helplessness before the riddle of the universe. The men of Middle Comedy had already

---

[4]See G. Kaibel, ed., Comicorum graecorum fragmenta (Berlin, 1899) vol. 1, pp. 6–10.

both imitated and parodied Euripides. Menander seems to have gone further and to have adopted at least in part his psychology, his melancholy, and his sadly questioning view of human life.

The *Dyskolos* is then a play of later Middle Comedy; but its author, although young, is clearly moving on to a new kind of drama.

Consider first the characters of the comedy. There are twelve speaking parts, plus several mute figures, at least one musician, and a chorus. Of the twelve, two are women—who are, as often in realistic portrayals of Greece, suppressed (they are a terrified and nameless young daughter and a miserable old slave woman); one is a god, who vanishes immediately after starting the comedy (although his presence is felt throughout); three are more or less helpful servants, well-differentiated and well-characterized. Then there are two father-and-son pairs, one rich and one poor. The poor pair are in fact stepson and stepfather only but are drawn together in an adoption toward the end of the play (729–39). The story of the comedy is really built on and around them. The central plot, as Menander conceived it, is that a rich youth falls in love with a poor girl and wants to marry her honorably: he has to overcome first the mistress of her brother, then the stubborn misanthropy of her father, and finally a minor objection raised by his own father.

These four male characters are deftly balanced: a strong, eccentric, poor father and a mild, well-balanced, rich father; a strong, tongue-tied, poor son and a weak, garrulous, rich son. But—here is Menander already exercising one of his own special dramatic gifts—the poor father in spite of his tough surface is not strong enough, is broken, and collapses; while the rich son shows unexpected determination, wins his way through, and proves strong. Again and again Menander does this in his later plays. The hero of the *Periceiromene,* so brutal and militaristic in manner, breaks down completely and even gives up all pretense of being a hard soldier (471–1020); Charisius in the *Arbitrators,* though pretending to be a cold-hearted debauchee, is really sick of disappointed love for his wife (431–35 and 957–58); and in one of Menander's masterpieces, the *Self-Tormentor,* we watch two pairs of fathers and sons, whose characters develop by turning, as it were, through an arc of 180 degrees. There is a famous piece of sculpture in the Lateran showing Menander gazing at a comic mask.[5] No doubt it

---

[5][See M. Bieber, *The History of the Greek and Roman Theater* (Princeton, 1939[1] and 1961[2]) 166 in 1939 edition and 89 in 1961 edition, for this sculpture, located in the Vatican Historical Museum in the Lateran Palace. Ed.]

is merely a traditional scene based on earlier portraits of Euripides and other dramatists. But I like to think that it also represents his way of working: he took a conventional mask and then looked through it to find a character sometimes quite at variance with the outward show.

Fathers and sons, helpful servants, a beloved girl, a kind deity—surely no more characters are required. But Menander inserts two more into the *Dyskolos*. One is a parasite, Chaereas; one is a chef, called Sicon.

In a complex intrigue, a parasite can be an active figure. Witness Phormio in Terence's adaptation of the *Claimant* by Apollodorus of Carystus: he dominates the entire play and makes the other characters pale by contrast with his exuberant boldness. Not so Chaereas in the *Dyskolos*. He is introduced at the beginning of the action, and his function is, specifically, to help his young patron by advising him how to win the girl (55–57). However, he does not give any creative advice whatever; he merely criticizes his patron Sostratus for sending a servant to see the girl's father instead of going himself (74–77); the best plan he can think of to solve the problem is to send Sostratus home and promise to interview the father personally the next day (129–34). His weakness and procrastination infuriate Sostratus, who appears to curse him roundly (135–40). He is terrified into silence and runs off, or at any rate remains dumb for the rest of the scene. He is never seen or referred to again.

Now one of the standard devices of Middle Comedy was that certain eccentric specialists should describe the technique of their vocations in proudly professional terms, boasting of their cleverness and versatility, sometimes actually vaunting their own cool impudence and resolute stubbornness. There is a long anthology of such speeches made by comic parasites in Athenaeus 6.234c–248c, where it is put in the mouth of Plutarch of Alexandria. Apparently this idea was first used by two brilliant writers of Old Comedy—the Sicilian Epicharmus (Ath. 6.235f–236b)[6] and the Athenian Eupolis, who called his parasites κόλακες ("flatterers") and named one of his plays after them (Ath. 6.236e–237a).[7] But it really flourished in Middle Comedy. Speeches of this type appeared in plays by Anaxandrides, Antiphanes the Elder, Alexis, Aristophon, Antidotus,

---

[6]See Kaibel (above, note 4) vol. 1, p. 96.
[7]See J. M. Edmonds, ed., *The Fragments of Attic Comedy*, 3 vols. (Leiden, 1957–61) vol. 1, pp. 375–76.

Axionicus, Timocles, and Antiphanes the Younger.[8] There are some parasites who boast of their skill and daring in New Comedy also: we know them best through their adaptations in the plays of Plautus and Terence.[9]

But in the *Dyskolos,* this very early play by Menander, we see the parasite beginning to fade away and disappear. In the opening dialogue, the parasite Chaereas responds to his patron's request for help by delivering a short speech on his own expertness (57–68). But the speech is immediately dismissed by his patron as being irrelevant and useless (68–69), which in fact it is. (Chaereas says he can either kidnap a courtesan or arrange a regular marriage with a young lady; the daughter of Cnemon is neither one nor the other.) Both the boastful lecture of the parasite and his usual function in comedy are therefore introduced by Menander only to be discarded. Menander knew the convention of the helpful, impudent parasite; he was too young to abandon it altogether; but he knew, and he showed that he knew, it was actually an impediment to the new drama which he was trying to create. The stratagems and swaggerings of a parasite have no place in the world of real people and real love.

Another such conventional character is the cook called Sicon. Audiences of Middle Comedy loved to hear chefs talking proudly of their artistry in the kitchen, their complicated equipment, and their marvelous inventions—as such chefs did in plays by Nicostratus, Eubulus, Epicrates, Alexis, Dionysius, Sotades, and Axionicus.[10] Such a cook belonged, intellectually and aesthetically, to the avant-garde: he was known as μαγειρὸς σοφιστής ("master chef") and sometimes even spoke in esoteric and scholarly language like a literary critic.[11] Just as the parasite of Middle Comedy was a special form of the κόλαξ ("flatterer"), so the cook was very often a special form of the ἀλαζών ("braggart"). Athenaeus, who gives an anthology of their boastful speeches, sometimes very funny (7.290b–293e), begins by observing: ἀλαζονικὸν δ' ἐστὶ πᾶν τὸ τῶν μαγείρων φῦλον (7.290b). There are several cooks in the

---

8[See Edmonds (above, note 7) vol. 2, pp. 48, 52, 230, 252–54, 262, 426, 460–62, 468, 484, 500–502, 522, 544–46, 560, 564, 606–10, 616, 622, and 626. Ed.]

9See G. E. Duckworth, *The Nature of Roman Comedy* (Princeton, 1952) 265–67.

10See Edmonds (above, note 7) vol. 2, pp. 30, 108, 352, 386, 406, 430, 432–36, 446, 456, 458–60, 464, 534–38, 552–54, and 566.

11See Edmonds (above, note 7) vol. 2, pp. 582–84, for the fragment from Straton's comedy.

plays of New Comedy, including a wonderful boaster in a fragment of Hegesippus (Ath. 7.290b–e). Menander himself did not disdain to use them in his mature plays: there are cooks in the *Samian Woman* and in the *Arbitrators;* and we have two interesting speeches among the fragments from both the *Trophonios* and the *Pseudheracles.*[12]

In the *Dyskolos,* the chef Sicon has much of the energy and self-confidence of Middle Comedy cooks: he plays a rich part, from his first entrance dragging in a recalcitrant sheep (393) to his final exit garlanded, singing and dancing (964). However, he stands outside the plot of the play. What does he actually do? He prepares and carries out the cooking and serving of the sacrificial meal and banquet (all off-stage). He tries to borrow a cooking-pot from the Curmudgeon and fails (498–521). He watches with amused disgust and comments on off-stage action, while the Curmudgeon is falling into the well and being fished out again (620–65). And finally, with the help of a young slave, he makes fun of the helpless old Curmudgeon in a riotously farcical ending. He does nothing whatever to help or hinder the actual intrigue of the comedy. His real function is something different, something quite unusual. In a comedy where the chorus has dwindled into a group of extraneous singing and dancing revelers who come onto an empty stage usually unannounced and then disappear again, Sicon the chef performs some of the same functions that were—in the plays of Aristophanes—performed by the leader of the integrated chorus and his men. The final scene of the *Dyskolos,* which we shall discuss shortly, shows this very clearly and delightfully.

Like the parasite Chaereas, the cook makes a speech vaunting his skill. He does not praise his cuisine, but—in a typical Middle Comedy monologue—his experience and his diplomatic address (487–99). (Menander has therefore assimilated the cook Sicon to the Middle and Old Comedy type called the κόλαξ—the word itself is used in 492. There is some praise of his skill as a maître d'hôtel in 942–45, but it is brief and, coming at the end of the play, incidental.) But just like the speech by the parasite, this monologue turns out to be quite pointless. Sicon's boasted diplomacy fails ignominiously (500–513), and then, just as Sostratus dismisses the pretensions of the parasite (68–69), so Sicon dismisses his own boasts as false and useless (514–21). The riotous door-banging and shouting of the last scene (911–30) are fun in themselves, but they are also a

---

[12]See Körte (above, note 1) 141 and 158.

parody of the intensely tactful κολακεία ("flattering") which Sicon earlier boasted of being able to command.

In the parasite and the cook, therefore, Menander was using two characters who were traditional in Middle Comedy but who were irrelevant to his plot. He made each of them speak his piece and vaunt his skill; then he rejected and nullified their boasts. The parasite he banished from the play. The cook he kept alive, not as an active personage in the intrigue but as a surrogate for the chorus of Old Comedy. To bring traditional characters on stage, to make them say their pieces, and then to dismiss them, is to criticize the traditions from which they were taken. What Terence did explicitly with painfully blunt phrases in his prologues, Menander did with more tact but no less firmness in the body of his plays.

Turn now to the plot itself. The story clearly has two threads: (1) Cnemon the Curmudgeon has quarreled with his wife and stepson and cannot believe in human kindness until his stepson risks death to save his life; (2) Sostratus, a rich and pampered youth, falls in love with a country girl and cannot win her unless her father believes he is not a gentleman but a real working farmer.

These two threads are interwoven through the complex character of Cnemon the Curmudgeon, but they do not have much real affinity. The first shows a perverse man crushed and corrected, while the second shows a simple man deceived. Menander forces the two threads to meet three times: first in Cnemon's acceptance of his new son-in-law (751–60), which is very perfunctory and scarcely justifies Sostratus's masquerade with a sheepskin coat and a mattock (in fact, Cnemon, who has so many of the traits of both the surly man and the distrustful man in the *Characters* of Theophrastus [αὐθάδες 15 and ἄπιστος 18] would surely have seen through Sostratus's disguise if he had not been in a state of shock); second, in the rapid arrangement of a second alliance between the two families, in which the young peasant Gorgias is wed to an invisible sister of the rich Sostratus (784–849); and third, in the scene of farcical horseplay at the end where two servants force Cnemon, now the only holdout, to attend the betrothal party with the rest of the two families (935–58). Of these three links between the two threads of plot, the first is very brief, and the third very flimsy. The second, although it appears to be more serious, is notably artificial; and Menander feels this. First of all, Sostratus has to persuade his father to accept the new marriage between the young farmer and Sostratus's own sister. The father resists for a minute or so, and then, after a crudely sententious lecture by his son, gives in, crying:

"It's only money; hand it out freely!" (784–820). Then the impe-
cunious Gorgias first refuses the match, but after a short and unconvincing conversational exchange, gives way with unexpected
rapidity (821–40).

These two threads, and the way in which they are interlaced,
show Menander still trying his prentice hand and using materials
from several different kinds of drama. One thread is essentially a
juvenile love romance, in which the problem is solved by disguise
and cheating—rich boy pretends to be poor and wins poor girl. This
dramatic pattern may well have originated in Middle Comedy,
where love intrigues of daily life were first put on the stage;[13] certainly it was to be one of the mainstays of New Comedy. But the
other, the trial and breaking of the Curmudgeon—is that not
something far more serious? Admittedly, his adventures are petty
because they depend on his own stinginess, and comical because
they are induced by a series of trivial chances; yet they nearly end
in his death, and they do cause his complete physical and emotional collapse. The tough working farmer, whom we first hear of
running over the hills with shouts and curses (117–21), whom we
see growing more savagely energetic continuously up to the climax (584–601), is suddenly converted into a pathetic victim who
cannot stand up alone (700–701, 740, and 928–29), who is close to
death (730), who speaks as though his active life were over (739
and 747), and who is last seen as a bedridden, helpless, and paralyzed old man (905–10). The speech in which he gives up his hard
independence and accepts a dependent old age (713–47) is profoundly serious and contains some sad moralizing which reminds
us of Hesiod's *Works and Days*. What shall we say of this change?
Is it not a περιπέτεια ("reversal") modeled on those that afflict the
heroes of tragedy? It is a long way from the Persian capital Susa or
the palace of Thebes to the little farm at Phyle; yet both Xerxes and
Oedipus and Creon and Cnemon here are witnesses to the tragic
truth πάθει μάθος (Aeschylus, *Agamemnon* 177)—learn through
suffering, suffering even to death.

One thread of plot in the *Dyskolos* is therefore a love problem
solved through cheating, which is a comic and romantic theme.
The other is a strong lonely character broken by suffering self-
induced, which is a tragic theme. The former motive came to
Menander from Middle Comedy. The latter he took from tragedy,
and he was to use it again and again—although always bounding

---

[13]See A. Körte, "Komödie," in *RE* 11.1 (1921) 1207–75, especially 1264–65.

it by the limits of ordinary emotion and quiet middle-class social life—in the comedies of his maturity. However, in this early play, so that the tragic περιπέτεια should not be too painful, he disguised and lightened it by rounding it off with a κῶμος, a farcical revel, which he took from Old Comedy.

The entire fifth act of the *Dyskolos* is best understood as being a survival from Old Comedy. We can find parallels for it, not in any of the surviving plays of Menander but in certain plays of Plautus. The *Persian* has an entire final act devoted to singing and dancing and drinking and jesting; Wilamowitz believed that it was based on a play of Middle Comedy.[14] The *Stichus* similarly ends in drinking and dancing and buffoonery, and we know that it came from one of the two plays called the *Brothers* by Menander himself. It has been suggested that these scenes in Plautus are derived from "pre-literary Italian farce";[15] but we can now see that they are Greek, and perfectly literary in nature and in origin. Menander in the *Dyskolos* (and doubtless elsewhere) and other Attic Middle and New Comedians chose sometimes to maintain the festal conclusion of a comedy which Aristophanes and the other Old Comedians preferred. Thus, at the conclusion of Aristophanes' *Acharnians,* Dicaeopolis is the center of a great revel, on which the chorus comments with delight; the revel ends with Lamachus being carried out helpless while Dicaeopolis dances off to the chorus's cries of victory. The *Wasps* ends with a dance by Philocleon and a song by the chorus; the *Lysistrata* with singing and dancing by a Laconian and cries of victory from the Athenian chorus; the *Frogs* with a triumphal procession escorting Aeschylus up to Athens; the *Ecclesiazusae* with Blepyros going off to the banquet with girls and wine and dancing; the *Peace* with a marriage festival led by the hero Trygaeus; and the *Birds* with a marriage festival led by the hero Pithetaerus and culminating in cries of victory. Now we have the *Dyskolos.* Its last scene begins with music (880) and is accompanied by the noise of a revel off-stage, which is in fact a double marriage festival (901–2) full of drinking and dancing (946–53). On-stage the principal character, the Curmudgeon, is not glorified like the heroes of Aristophanic comedies; he is mocked and buffeted and scared. The persons who surround him are not two

---

[14][For Wilamowitz's views on Plautus's *Persian,* see U. von Wilamowitz-Moellendorff, *De tribus carminibus latinis commentatio*—a paper prepared in Göttingen during the 1893–94 academic year and reprinted in his *Kleine Schriften,* 6 vols. (Berlin, 1971–72) vol. 2, pp. 249–74, especially 260–74. Ed.]

[15]See Duckworth (above, note 9) 381.

semi-choruses, as so often in Aristophanes, but they are agile and energetic, and their horseplay almost becomes a dance at the end (954–57). Just as in an Aristophanic play, the final scene of all is a triumphal procession bearing the main character off—with song, garlands, and music—to take part in a revel. Here then quite unexpectedly, we can see a strong and generous survival of the comic technique of Aristophanes in the sophisticated work of a New Comedian.

In meter also, the *Dyskolos* is a transitional play. Old Comedy was wonderfully various, using a multitude of meters. Most of the surviving work of Menander is a continuous series of iambic trimeters, loose and graceful, but monotonous. However, among the fragments of Middle Comedy there are traces of other spoken meters—passages of that great old standby of popular writing, the trochaic tetrameter, and some passages of a less usual meter, the iambic tetrameter—which appeared in plays by Anaxandrides, Antiphanes the Elder, and Anaxilas.[16] In an early play, the *Samian Woman,* Menander uses trochaic tetrameters for a scene of excitement and tension. In the *Dyskolos,* at two important crises, he changes from the standard iambic trimeters: first, after the rescue of Cnemon from the well, into a long passage of trochaic tetrameters (ca. 705–83, ending Act 4); and finally, at the end of Act 5, into iambic tetrameters which continue until the exit passage (880–958). Thus, about one-sixth of the entire play is written in gay dancing meters, which are more lively and varied than the regular iambics of mature New Comedy and its dramatic model Euripidean tragedy.

Finally, let us look at the spiritual side of the play. The *Dyskolos* begins with an explanatory prologue, spoken by a god. The god is Pan. He loves romantic mountain scenery like that of Phyle, and he is close to the Nymphs, who naturally sympathize with the wild, shy, primitive girl who is Cnemon's daughter. His presence in the comedy is justified. There are gods in Old Comedy who take part in the action. But Pan here utters a prologue (1–49) which is as carefully regular as the prologue of many a Euripidean tragedy. Is this the first appearance of a Euripidean expository prologue on the comic stage?

After his speech ends, Pan points out the hero and vanishes. Nevertheless, the presence of both Pan and the Nymphs is felt throughout the play. They are responsible for the love intrigue. It is unusual, even unnatural, for a rich youth to fall in love with a poor

---

[16]See Edmonds (above, note 7) vol. 2, pp. 58–60, 170, and 346.

girl and wish to marry her: only a miracle could bring that about, and Pan and the Nymphs were responsible for the miracle. The entire play takes place outside the sanctuary which the Nymphs share with Pan. The chorus, although extraneous, is a group of worshipers of Pan (230). At the end of the second act, preparations for a sacrifice to Pan are beginning; the sacrifice, the feast, and the ensuing revel accompany the action throughout the remaining three acts. The sufferings and fall of Cnemon occur without the agency of Pan; but the love story is a direct intervention of a divinity in human affairs, met with a pious and happy response by the men and women affected. The god made Sostratus fall miraculously in love (39–44) and then sent an ominous vision to his mother (409–18), which his mother undertook to avert. The sacrificial animal and banquet equipment are sent out from her house to the shrine at Phyle (393–426). Servants and guests arrive (430–41). The sacrifice is completed inside the shrine; the cooking, baking, and serving begins (546–51); and other guests are invited in to share the meal (607–19). The father of Sostratus arrives—late, to be sure, but there is still something left for him (773–83). Gorgias with his mother and sister join the party (866); and with the new betrothal in prospect, Callippides and Sostratus plan an all-night revel before the wedding (850–60). The music spills out from the shrine onto the stage (880), and at last, not merely from wanton cruelty but from a wish for that complete affection and communion which should be part of a religious celebration, Cnemon is taken out of his lonely sleep and carried in to join the banquet (911–58). In other plays by Menander there is little interest in traditional religion. Sometimes it is criticized, and sometimes its extravagances are satirized. Here it is only the Curmudgeon himself who speaks against religious ritual (444–53). All the other characters accept religion and engage in its rites: Sostratus is quite serious about it (309–13), and so is Cnemon's daughter (36–39 and 197–99), while his mother is a devotee, whose prayers, nevertheless, are rewarded. In this, therefore, the *Dyskolos* goes back to the origins of comedy. Although light and gay, the play is concerned with the relations of god and man: it begins with a divine miracle and omen; it continues with prayer and sacrifice; and it ends with a festival held in a sanctuary, which, although it was accompanied by drinking and dancing, was nevertheless, for those happier Greeks of an earlier day than ours, a holy communion.

Suppose we sum up. What has the discovery of the *Dyskolos* taught us about Greek drama and in particular about Menander?

About Menander it has confirmed one suspicion which had already lodged in our minds. He wrote too much and too quickly. The acute psychological observation for which the later Greeks and Romans admired him, and which is observable in the *Dyskolos,* was not always balanced by skillful plot construction. He was not working for eternity but for the theater of his own day. He turned out about one hundred plays; among them there were, we now know, some trifles and some careless, hasty dramatic sketches.

On the other hand, this play demonstrates clearly what we could only guess before, that Menander did possess a store of genuine high spirits and enjoyed simple gay knockabout farce. In a famous critical epigram found in Suetonius (*De Poetis* ['Terence' 5]), Julius Caesar characterized the Roman Terence as *dimidiate Menander* ("Menander cut in half") and also complained that he lacked *vis* ("energy"). The *vis* of Menander is scarcely ever seen in Terence. Before this discovery we could see hints of it in his *Periceiromene,* where there is a mock siege; in the *Samian Woman,* where there is a fight between two old men on the stage; in the *Perinthia,* where a master threatens to burn his slave to drive him away from an altar of refuge; and perhaps elsewhere. But it also appears frequently in the *Dyskolos:* the breathless description by Pyrrhias of the Curmudgeon's attack on him (81–121); the mounting excitement of the objects falling into the well one by one followed by their master (574–625); and finally the mad attack on Cnemon's house by two partly drunk clowns, shouting at the top of their voices, knocking and kicking the door to the terror of its helpless owner (911–58). All these incidents give vigor and zest to the play, and make it perhaps cruder but certainly more dynamic than the plays of Terence. If Terence was Menander cut in half, then the other half went to make up T. Maccius Plautus.

The student of Greek drama will learn from the *Dyskolos* what he had been implicitly told by a great German scholar[17]—that it is wrong to draw sharp lines between the various phases of developing Attic comedy and to try to classify each phase by pointing to characteristic qualities which cannot be found elsewhere. Thus, in this single play, which is either a late Middle Comedy or a very early example of New Comedy, we can see:

a prologizing god modeled on Euripidean tragedy;

a romantic love story derived from Middle Comedy;

---

[17]See Körte (above, note 13) 1226–75.

the downfall of a strong man learning through suffering, modeled ultimately on tragedy;

a psychological type-study derived from Middle Comedy, but (I should strongly suggest) deepened by Menander's study of the *Characters* of Theophrastus, which were written within a year or so of the *Dyskolos;*

two extraneous comic figures, cook and parasite, taken from Middle Comedy but criticized by Menander as obsolescent;

two linked father-and-son pairs, possibly Menander's own invention as they were certainly one of his favorite devices, but possibly coming from Middle Comedy also;

two scenes in long trochaic and iambic meters, expressing extra energy and emotion, handed down from Aristophanes through Middle Comedy;

a final scene of knockabout farce ending in song, dance, drinking, and revelry, which derives from Aristophanes and was to be taken over by Plautus in his Roman adaptations;

and an overall religious pattern of miracle and omen, prayer and sacrifice, banquet and Dionysiac revel, which goes back to the very origins of Greek comedy.

Menander wrote too much and too rapidly, but he was a deeply sensitive man and a poet of versatile imagination. In the mind of such a man, many powerful currents meet to make even such an airy bagatelle as the play of the *Dyskolos*.[18]

---

[18][See G. Highet, "The *Dyskolos* of Menander," *Horizon* 1.6 (July 1959) 78–89—Highet's translation of this play into English in the meters of the original Greek—reprinted in R. J. Ball, ed., *The Classical Papers of Gilbert Highet* (New York, 1983) 22–57. Ed.]

Dio Chrysostom[*]

He is an engaging and ambitious writer, who strives to attain two of the finest ideals of classical Greek prose—the suave persuasiveness of Lysias and the bold mythopoeic imagination of Plato. He lived a difficult and adventurous life: now a friend of monarchs, now a penniless wanderer; now a comfortable bourgeois devoted to the home of his fathers, now a lonely mystic striving for the revelation of arcane truths; now delivering a nobly eloquent speech on the nature of the highest godhead to the Panhellenic audience at Olympia, now addressing the population of a Greek city-state in terms combining humorous criticism with serious reproof, and now using his oratory to quell a mutinous Roman army. He left a large body of work: nearly eighty pieces have survived, and we know of many others which are lost (including a history of the Getae, a Thracian tribe on the lower Danube). A restless man with an eager mind and a remarkable capacity to enjoy strange situations and even sometimes to bring dangers on himself—small, tireless, garrulous, versatile—a true son of Odysseus.

We see four distinct stages in his career. Born in one of the most beautiful cities in the world, Prusa (now Bursa) on the slopes of Mount Olympus in Bithynia about 40 A.D., he came from a distinguished family of the local aristocracy, and was independently wealthy and well-educated. His first vocation was as a public lecturer traveling about the Greek-speaking world of the eastern Mediterranean. Such a man was called a σοφιστής ("sophist") and was thought of as being in opposition to philosophy. Putting it crudely, he was an heir of Gorgias and Protagoras and the professional intellectuals of the fifth century B.C., rather than of their critic, the ugly barefooted stonemason Socrates, who could not bear to give lectures or listen to them.

However, like many an intelligent young man, he was—after an initial resistance to the attractive power of philosophy—converted. His conversion, and what it meant to the growth of his thought and character, have sometimes been slightly misunderstood. Synesius of Cyrene, who greatly admired his writings, implied that his ca-

---

[*]Presented in 1975 at Harvard University (= Loeb Classical Lecture).

reer should be divided into two neat parts—first a shallow sophistic period, and then exile and transformation into a serious philosopher.[1] But in fact he was converted to philosophy while he was quite young, by the Italian Stoic C. Musonius Rufus. This man was deeply involved with the opposition to Nero and was banished after the disaster of the Pisonian conspiracy. Dio himself refers so often to the vanity and folly of Nero that I suggest he was turned away from the self-advertising life of the sophists by the spectacle of Nero's self-degradation, which in a later speech he called a disease (32.60). If so, he came to philosophy when he was in his twenties.

But in middle life, Dio underwent a much more serious and fundamental spiritual change. He himself says that only after this change was he called φιλόσοφος ("philosopher") and felt able to accept the title (13.11). It was precipitated by a disaster which destroyed his whole life and might easily have blotted him out of existence. Suddenly, after dining with satraps and kings (7.66), he became a homeless beggar. He was involved in the fate of the cousin of the cruel and suspicious emperor Domitian, T. Flavius Sabinus, who was executed early in Domitian's reign. Dio was, in effect if not by explicit decree, banished from Rome and Italy, and also from his homeland Bithynia. He wandered about for years in complete loneliness and utter destitution—sometimes in mainland Greece and the islands, and sometimes on the remote northeastern frontiers of the Greco-Roman world. Philostratus (*Lives of the Sophists* 1.7) says that he carried only two books with him—Demosthenes' nineteenth speech (the *False Embassy*) and Plato's *Phaedo*. This information may be based on something stated by Dio himself; certainly it reflects his chief interests—honest government, ethics exalted by metaphysics, and a pure vigorous Attic style. This exile lasted for more than ten years, until the assassination of Domitian. Thus it covered the central part of Dio's mature life, the time when most men are busy making their careers, from the early forties to the late fifties. At the end of it, he says that his health was much impaired, but he was still full of spiritual energy.

This was Dio's second conversion. It moved him from Stoicism to a modified form of Cynicism. He was never, mark you, a complete Cynic. He never did deliberately disgusting things in public like Diogenes and some of Diogenes' followers. He never held or showed the complete contempt for all culture, all social life, and all

---

[1][See H. von Arnim, ed., *Dionis Prusaensis quem vocant Chrysostomum quae exstant omnia,* 2 vols. (Berlin, 1893 and 1896) vol. 2, pp. 313–19, for the text of Synesius. Ed.]

organized civilization, which marked the most thorough and out-rageous of the Cynics. No, rather he became a blend of Diogenes and Socrates. Like Socrates, he gained knowledge of his mission from the Delphic oracle, which told him to continue living and acting as he was doing, until he reached the ends of the earth (13.9)—that is, not to be a recluse, or a city-bound philosopher like Socrates, but to be a philosophical pilgrim. Like Diogenes, he had no home, wore one poor thin ragged garment, had a long beard and hair, and carried a wallet for scraps like a beggar. This was a deeper conversion than the first. It was close to being a religious conversion. Certainly it makes us think of those later converts to Christianity who tormented their bodies with fasting and macera-tion in order to gain spiritual strength, and who shunned the great cities in order to exist in rude cabins or caves on the edge of the desert.

But at this time Dio says that people started to consult him and ask for his help in the problems of life; and he implies that he had now grown wise enough, perhaps by detachment from his own affairs, to help them. Certainly he developed a stronger personal authority. There is a story (which again must come from Dio him-self) that when Domitian was murdered in 96 A.D., the Roman troops in a frontier post were about to mutiny and resist the elec-tion of the new emperor Nerva, when Dio calmed them by jump-ing up on an altar, denouncing the crimes of the dead tyrant, and persuading them to follow the will of the Senate and the Roman people (Philostratus, *Lives of the Sophists* 1.7). Now he thought of himself as φιλόσοφος πολιτείας ἀψάμενος, a "philosopher engaged in politics" (48.14).

The fourth stage of his career now began. Like so many other of Domitian's victims (for instance, Juvenal exiled in Egypt) Dio started back toward his home. He established friendly relation-ships with the new emperor Nerva and after an interval with Nerva's successor, the formidable Trajan. This was the climax of his long adventurous life. He addressed hortatory and complimen-tary speeches to the emperor. He represented the emperor as a semi-official envoy to great Greek cities. He referred often to his friendship with the emperor. At the same time, or shortly after his foreign missions were ended, he spent many months and a huge quotient of spiritual effort in his own province of Bithynia, attempting to confer aesthetic and social benefits on his city of Prusa by pulling down old buildings and erecting new ones; and endeavoring to appease the rivalries between the various city-states of Bithynia, each of which, with true Greek πλεονεξία ("greediness") and φιλαυτία ("selfishness"), was struggling to out-do the others in competing for honors and financial concessions from the central government at Rome. The last we hear of Dio is that he is involved in a particularly spiteful and nasty lawsuit before Trajan's especially delegated trouble-shooter, Pliny the Younger (*Epist.* 10.81–82). He would then be over seventy, ap-proaching the end of a complex and hazardous career.

The letters written by Pliny from Bithynia to Trajan give a squalid picture of the bickering and inefficiency and dishonesty of these irresponsible Greek provincials. Any satirically minded ob-server, reading them, will think of the grandiose schemes of to-day's emergent nation-states, with their expensive missions to the United Nations and their financially absurd five-year plans at home. When he thinks of our own foreign aid programs, the ob-server will sympathize with the emperor Trajan, being informed that the aqueduct at Nicomedia has already absorbed millions of dollars, is still unfinished, and is now being pulled down. To this Trajan replies: "See that water is brought into the city. But *medius fidius* take enough time to find out who is responsible for this waste of money. Perhaps the people in charge have been doing favors for one another, by starting the aqueduct and then abandoning it. When you find out, report to me." (*Epist.* 10.37–38). That is the de-grading and silly little world in which we last hear the voice of Dio, defending himself against the charge of misappropriation brought before Pliny by an escaped convict, calling himself a philosopher. The charge of treason—high treason—was added, because Dio had buried his wife and son in a garden near a library which con-tained a statue of the emperor. That particular charge Trajan dismissed; but he told Pliny to order Dio to produce the accounts of the enterprise for which he had been in part responsible.

And so it ends, not with a bang but a whimper. Neither in his be-havior as reported by Pliny, nor in his own self-justificatory politi-cal speeches, is there anything of the arrogant nihilism of the Cynic, or the proud independence, mingled with passionless phi-lanthropy, of the Stoic. He had ceased to be the pilgrim of eternity, the interpreter of the divine order, the adviser of monarchs. He be-came a μικροπολίτης, a "citizen of a small city," a major notable in a minor community which was only a tiny part of the vast empire of Rome.

Dio was a fairly close contemporary of Quintilian. The two men both owed their advancement to the two sons of Vespasian's brother Flavius Sabinus, the cousins of Domitian. But Quintilian never mentions Dio, and Dio never speaks of Quintilian, and they live in mutually exclusive worlds. His Greek contemporaries Plutarch and Epictetus never say a word about Dio (although they had friends in common, and although Plutarch wrote two pieces called *To Dio* or *Against Dio*), nor does he vouchsafe them a single sentence. However, Dio lived through his books. Not long after his death, they made him a classic. The name Chrysostomos first appears in the third-century A.D. rhetorical writer Menander as though it was already established.[2] (It may even have been given to him to distinguish him from the historian, who, named Cassius Dio Cocceianus, was surely a kinsman.)

His surviving books are only part of his work, perhaps not even half of it. There are just under eighty pieces extant. They vary widely in size, scope, style, and character. Dio is anything but a monotonous or conventional writer. Although he often belabors a single point too long, it is impossible to tell what he is going to say next; and although his reading is narrow, his range of subjects is wide.

Most of the pieces are informal talks or lectures (διατριβαί or διαλέξεις) on ethical, political, aesthetic, and educational themes. There are eleven dialogues and one letter. There are also some formal speeches, some of them very long indeed. I have timed one at two hours. Some of these works are not worth reading twice, and some not even once. Others will repay prolonged and careful study.

The most remarkable is the *Borystheniticus* (36). This describes Dio's visit to the Greek city of Olbia, in what is now southern Russia near the site of Odessa. Besides Dio we know of only one other Greek writer who visited this remote spot, and that was Herodotus over five centuries earlier (Herodotus 4.18 and 4.53). Remembering that Dio wrote a history of the neighboring tribe of Getae, we might compare him to Herodotus, as a traveling ethnologist. Yet when we look more closely at the speech, we see that his chief interest was not the surrounding barbarians but the Greek or half-Greek citizens of this outpost of civilization.

Besides this, Dio left a famous and much admired tale of his visit to an almost equally lonely part of the Greek world, his *Euboicus* (7). Here he tells how he was shipwrecked on the rough coast of Euboea, met a huntsman who took him home, and was simply but kindly entertained. Dio's host describes his rough poor existence,

---

[2][See L. Spengel, ed., *Rhetores Graeci*, 3 vols. (Leipzig, 1853–56), especially vol. 3, p. 390, lines 1–2. Ed.]

free from both the corruptions and the comforts of the city; and we see that Euboea, once a prosperous region of central Greece, has slipped back many centuries into depopulation and into semi-barbarism. (This is denied by John Day in a 1951 article, but his arguments are curiously weak and inadequate.)[3]

The two speeches make a marvelous pair: one on the little Greek city struggling to maintain its identity far away in the wilds; the other on the small Greek family group surviving, virtuous and happy, in an area fast reverting to near savagery—the men of Olbia clinging to their knowledge of Homer and their cult of Achilles (although surrounded by wild Scythian nomads); and the family of Euboea living out its life with only an occasional visit to the neighboring city, whose size and complexity (though it is half-deserted) completely astound the poor huntsman. Each is more than a mere description. In the *Borystheniticus,* Dio talks with Greeks, scarcely seeing them as Greeks because of their barbarian costume—long swords, and trousers like the Scythians; but they are still Greek and hunger for Greek speech and elevated thought, so that the piece ends with a superb cosmological myth, based on Zoroastrian doctrine and told by Dio in a manner not wholly unworthy of his master Plato. As for the *Euboicus,* it too begins with a travel tale: a storm-stayed wanderer finds a hunted stag where it has leapt over a cliff to the seashore; he hears, above the boom of the breakers, the baying of hounds; he climbs up, meets the hunter, helps him to skin the stag and cut it up, and goes home with him to dinner. And then the huntsman tells Dio of his life, with a complex story of how he was once haled to town and prosecuted for failure to pay land-taxes, but delivered in the nick of time by a stranger who rose dramatically in the assembly and certified his honesty, saying that he himself when shipwrecked had been rescued and sheltered by the huntsman's family; the huntsman is rewarded as a patriot by being given his farm free of taxes; and the idyll closes with a marriage between the huntsman's daughter and her cousin. It is like a romantic play from New Comedy;[4] and from that painting of simple happiness Dio takes off into a convincing and

---

[3][See J. Day, "The Value of Dio Chrysostom's Euboean Discourse for the Economic Historian," in P. R. Coleman-Norton's festschrift, *Studies in Roman Economic and Social History in Honor of Allan Chester Johnson* (Princeton, 1951) 209–35. Ed.]

[4][See G. Highet, "The Huntsman and the Castaway," *GRBS* 14 (1973) 35–40—an article in which Highet first proposed the connection between the *Euboicus* and New Comedy. Ed.]

sometimes moving description of the beauties and virtues of country life uncorrupted by urban complexities and vices.

The big book on Dio published in 1898 by Hans von Arnim (and composed with Wilamowitz looking over his shoulder) has a reassuring air of authority and completeness.[5] Von Arnim writes lucidly, sometimes even gracefully. As you read, he makes you feel that all, or almost all, the problems of Dio's life and works have been solved. But when you turn back to Dio's text, you find this impression is exaggerated, even false. I hope it is not ungrateful to put it in this way, but sometimes I feel that the book by von Arnim resembles some of the statues which Dio says decorated the agora in Rhodes (31, passim): it is a fine piece of sculpture in a handsome pose; it is clearly inscribed DIO VON PRUSA (ULRICH VON WILAMOWITZ-MOELLENDORFF ZUGEEIGNET);[6] only it is not Dio but somebody else.

On reading and rereading Dio, one finds many different problems emerging, which neither von Arnim nor—so far—anyone else has discussed as intensely as they deserve. Let me mention some of them, although I shall not claim to have solved them or even to have defined them adequately.

First, the external structure of the discourses. The patriarch Photius, who read all that we now possess of Dio's work, and the future bishop Synesius, who read far more, speak of their subject-matter without even mentioning their form.[7] Yet it is apparent to a careful reader that many of them are truncated. The *Euboean* speech (as von Arnim showed)[8] lacks both its beginning and its ending, but it is a fine spacious piece, in which it is not difficult to detect such mutilations. But again and again in other pieces Dio will start a train of thought which, allowing for his habit of digression (πλανᾶσθαι ἐν τοῖς λόγοις), develops promisingly and carries forward our interest, and then, without warning or explanation, stops—so abruptly that neither Dio himself nor any intelligent editor who had a fuller version at his disposal can possibly have published the work as it now stands. Occasionally a brevity of this kind is only an introduction to a longer work, which may or may not have survived. (For instance, in 57, Dio writes a pro-

---

[5]See H. von Arnim, *Leben und Werke des Dio von Prusa* (Berlin, 1898).

[6][See von Arnim (above, note 5) for this inscription, found between the title page and preface. Ed.]

[7][See von Arnim (above, note 1) vol. 2, pp. 313–25, for the text of Synesius and Photius. Ed.]

[8][See von Arnim (above, note 5) 492 and 502–3. Ed.]

oemium to one of his discourses addressed to the emperor, which he is now going to read to a different audience—doubtless the citizens of Prusa; and as he loves to do, he assumes the mask of a distinguished figure from myth or history: he becomes not Dio Cocceianus but Nestor giving sage counsel to Agamemnon.) If so, it has a right to stand by itself, like the fifty-six prooemia of Demosthenes. But many other pieces throughout Dio's work are nothing but fragmentary beginnings, like the sixteenth satire of Juvenal, which—after announcing a highly important theme, the privileges of professional soldiers, surely worth developing for two or three hundred lines—breaks off at line 60 in the middle of a sentence. There is a serious gap in the tradition of Dio, somewhere—the sort of gap which (as far as I know) does not exist in the tradition of his contemporary Plutarch or of his successor Lucian. At some time before the present corpus was formed, many of his discourses were mutilated.[9]

Then, the frequent internal incoherence of the text. This problem is better known and goes back even further, as far as Dio himself. His admirers named him Χρυσόστομος ("Goldenmouth"), but he might better have been called Ποικιλόστομος ("Fancymouth") or Υγρόστομος ("Rivermouth"), for his thought wanders and retreats and advances and swirls as bewilderingly as the ripples of the tide between ebb and flow on the sandy seashore. His works are full of digressions and inconsistencies; and also, it seems clear, of alternative versions of the same passages, both written by (or spoken by) Dio; and furthermore, of interpolations made by later readers who wished to make Dio's work clearer or more elegant; and naturally, of scribal errors and confusions, some of them perhaps dating back to the shorthand copies of Dio's speeches, which (according to von Arnim's conjecture)[10] were taken down while he improvised.

To produce a satisfactory text of Dio Chrysostom would be a major undertaking. Beyond its inherent difficulties, which are mainly philological, it would be a worrisome and often irritating task. To edit an author is rather like writing a biography. One is forced into close contact with the man, listening to his favorite cadences, hearing him repeat his jokes and restate his ideas and rehandle his imagery again and again; and even if he is a very dis-

---

[9][For Highet's study of this subject, explored in an article published after his death, see his "Mutilations in the Text of Dio Chrysostom," in R. J. Ball, ed., *The Classical Papers of Gilbert Highet* (New York, 1983) 74–99. Ed.]

[10]See von Arnim (above, note 5) 175–81.

tinguished writer, this can be irksome. With Dio I confess it is sometimes very wearing.

For example, one of his favorite personae was Socrates. He loved to adopt Socrates' pose of ignorance or ironic self-depreciation. For instance, he begins his thirty-fifth speech in Celaenae: "Not to give an exhibition of my art as an orator, nor asking for money, nor hoping for applause, do I appear before you. I know that my talents are not enough to satisfy you . . . It is my nature to speak simply and poorly and just like any ordinary man, while you cannot endure any speaker unless he is terribly clever." Or again, to his own fellow-citizens in Prusa (42.2): "I have never at any time claimed to be able to speak or reason or know any more than the ordinary man." He does this so often, and it sits so badly with his remarks elsewhere about his wide wanderings over the world and his almost herculean sufferings and his influence with great Roman potentates, that it comes to remind us of Uriah Heep, a notorious character in Charles Dickens, who says (*David Copperfield,* chap. 16):

> I am well aware that I am the umblest person going . . . let the other be where he may. My mother is likewise a very umble person. We live in an umble abode, Master Copperfield, but have much to be thankful for.

This pose of humility is called προσποίησις ἰδιωτισμοῦ by von Arnim.[11]

Speaking of Dickens, I cannot resist the temptation to add that there are other passages in which Dio Chrysostom reminds me of someone far less "umble" and far more unctuous than Uriah Heep—an overwhelmingly eloquent orator who, like Dio, cultivates anaphora, polyptoton, rhetorical questions, and similar devices with remorseless repetition. He improvises a speech about the wretched dirty barefooted street-urchin Jo, and he asks his audience (*Bleak House,* chap. 25) why Jo is poor,

> devoid of parents, devoid of relations, devoid of flocks and herds, devoid of gold and silver, and of precious stones.

It is

> because he is devoid of the light that shines in upon some of us. What is that light? What is it? I ask you what is that light? . . . It is . . . the ray of rays, the sun of suns, the moon of moons, the star of stars. It is the light of Terewth . . . of Terewth . . . Say not to me it

---

[11]See von Arnim (above, note 5) 444.

is *not* the lamp of lamps. I say to you, it is. I say to you, a million times over, it is. It is!

These are the words of Mr. Chadband, "a large yellow man, with a fat smile, and a general appearance of having a good deal of train oil in his system" (*Bleak House,* chap. 19); but they occasionally remind me of Dio Chrysostom fervently praising παιδεία ("education") and λόγος ("speech, oratory, eloquence"), and claiming that only the wise man (such as himself) is truly free, all the rest of mankind being madmen and slaves.

A further problem has not yet been sufficiently studied but will yield to analysis—Dio's relation to Rome and to the Romans. Sometimes it recalls to my mind the attitude of the Hindus and Moslems of India to the British during the existence of the British Indian Raj. In some ways Dio admires the Romans. In other ways he despises and detests them, as though he were one of a few articulate human beings in a planet governed by powerful and intelligent apes. Usually he conceals this dislike. We must look carefully to enucleate it. Take for instance the twenty-ninth discourse. This is a speech delivered in Naples during the funeral of a handsome and brilliant athlete called Melancomas, who died young. Melancomas was a boxer. There is one report that he was loved by Titus (Themistius, *Oration* 10).[12] If that is true, the speech would be a gesture of courtesy, even sympathy, to the Flavian prince. Yet it contains two points which are implicitly anti-Roman. Dio says that the athlete's life and training were more difficult and more dangerous than those of a soldier (29.9–13). Now anyone who has read Josephus's account of the Roman siege and capture of Jerusalem—a great contemporary feat of arms—will see that this is nonsense (*Jewish War,* Books 5–6). Furthermore, Dio has special praise for Melancomas because he won all his matches without actually striking a single blow, partly by feinting and partly by wearing down his opponent's endurance, thus (says Dio) demonstrating his supreme self-control (29.11–12). But (although Dio does not say so) it also shows that this Greek athlete and his ideals were superior to the Roman gladiators and *venatores,* who faced armed men and wild beasts in the arena and had to conquer them with steel and bloodshed. (On the introduction of gladiatorial contests into Greece, notice the bitterness of Dio in 31.121: "The

---

[12]See J. Hardouin, ed., ΘΕΜΙΣΤΙΟΥ ΛΟΓΟΙ ΛΓ: THEMISTII ORATIONES XXXIII (Paris, 1684) 139 and 454. See also von Arnim (above, note 5) 143, who comments on Themistius's reference to Titus and Melancomas.

Corinthians watch the duelists outside their city in a ravine which is big enough to hold a crowd and so filthy that no one would bury a free man's corpse in it. But the Athenians witness this noble spectacle in the theater right beneath the Acropolis . . . so that often a man is slaughtered in the front rows, where the chief priest of the Mysteries and the other priests must sit.") Dio hates to think of the military prowess of the Romans. Again and again he speaks of the Homeric heroes, and of the courage of the Athenians and Spartans who defended Greece against the Persians, and of Alexander the Macedonian conqueror. But there he stops. You would never guess from reading his work that Rome had brought the art of warfare to entirely new heights of courage and skill and organization. As far as I recall, he mentions Hannibal only once; and then it is to declare that Hannibal almost captured Rome, but did not wish to do so because of his political opponents at home in Carthage (25.7).

Not only does Dio dislike the Romans. He does not really understand them. His collected works begin with four speeches about monarchy. One of them certainly (the third) and another possibly (the first) were delivered to the emperor Trajan. So they are parallel to the *Panegyric*—the *gratiarum actio* ("expression of thanks") which Pliny the Younger addressed to the emperor in 100 A.D. But they say very little, very little indeed, beyond the obvious truism (worthy of Mr. Chadband) that a good monarch ought to be a good man, filled with prudence, courage, self-control, and wisdom, and discerning in his selection of friends. (Pliny, with his truly brilliant evocation of Domitian's lonely suspicious perverse behavior as the instructive contrast to the frank open character of Trajan, tells us far more in a few pages.) Dio does not really discuss, probably he could not really understand, the social and political and administrative problems of the Roman empire. As Arnaldo Momigliano has said, Dio "leaves the real structure of the Roman empire out of account and does not connect his theory of monarchy with his views on Greek city life."[13] Really, Dio reminds me of the philosopher Phormio, who delivered a lecture on military strategy and the duties of a commanding general, with Hannibal in the audience (Cicero, *De Oratore*, 2.75–76). One of the most dubious pieces of rubbish in that intellectual "pawnbroker's shop"[14]—the *Lives of*

---

[13]See A. Momigliano, "Dio Chrysostomus," in *Quarto contributo alla storia degli studi classici e del mondo antico* (Rome, 1969) 257–69, especially 265.
[14]See C. P. Jones, "The Reliability of Philostratus," in G. W. Bowersock, ed., *Approaches to the Second Sophistic* (University Park, 1974) 11–16, especially 16.

the Sophists by Philostratus—is the statement in his account of Dio that Trajan put Dio by his side in his triumphal chariot and that he used to say: "I don't understand what you are talking about, but I love you as I do myself" (1.7). If you will believe that (as the Duke of Wellington said when a man greeted him as Mr. Smith), you will believe anything.

Dio and Trajan. One more of many problems in their relationship is this. Some of Dio's largest, most carefully composed, and most ambitious works are speeches which he made to the citizens or governing bodies of various Greek city-states, enjoining them to amend their behavior and in particular to improve their attitude to the Roman officials who were set over them. These speeches cannot have been easy to deliver. Indeed, I sometimes have the impression that Dio's Socrates persona here fits him better than usual and that he is in actual danger of being shouted down, even physically assaulted. Some of these Dio gave as an unofficial ambassador of Trajan. How well they succeeded, what was their effect, we cannot tell. At least they cost him much time and effort. How is it then that a few years later Trajan refers to Dio as though he had scarcely even heard of him, and writes to Pliny (his representative in Dio's province of Bithynia) in terms of cold objectivity—as though Dio had never served him on diplomatic missions of some importance, but were merely one of the innumerable squabbling Greek pettifoggers who made the lives of one another, and of their Roman παιδαγωγοί ("baby sitters"), a misery? Momigliano conjectures that some of his speeches may have offended Trajan.[15] How, he does not explain; and it is hard to divine. I might rather suggest that Trajan was disappointed, even disgusted, by the change which overtook Dio as soon as he moved back out of the great world into his own native province and once more became a μικροπολίτης, absorbed in the small claims and petty rivalries and shortsighted assertions of φιλότιμοι ("ambitious men")—which have always, since the first book of the *Iliad,* been such a dominating feature of the Greek character.

The *style* of Dio is a distinguished achievement. All the later writers of Greek prose face the same dilemma. If they write the ordinary language spoken by the people in the street—the koine—they will be thought vulgarians incapable of aesthetic feeling and separated from the great masterpieces of classical literature. If they try to write in the elevated literary language of Thucydides or

---

[15]See Momigliano (above, note 13) 265–66.

Plato, they will scarcely be understood. Each later Greek writer must therefore form his own blend of contemporary language, literary reminiscence and adaptation, and purely personal phrasing. Perhaps it is not too fanciful to compare this with the work of the 'oral poets' many centuries earlier, who mingled the formulae created and handed down to them by bards several centuries in the past, with phrases newly coined by themselves and with snatches of the spoken language of their contemporaries—the result being that each made his own individual style. In this task Dio was successful. His contemporaries found his speech attractive; his successors soon promoted him to the rank of classic. And today those who read Dio with care will soon realize that they are not being exposed to an artificial product but to a living voice, which responds sensitively to many different situations and expresses many diverse types and nuances of thought.

I find the most striking thing about his style is his ability to coin *new words,* or at least to introduce new words to the language. There are so many, and they are so well suited to the genius of the Greek tongue, that in Dio's time it was still nothing near dying or even fossilizing (e.g., κακοδουλία ["servant trouble"] 38.15).[16] (In relatively unimportant points of accidence and syntax he often follows the practice of the koine. So the second person of οἶδα is not οἶσθα but οἶδας, and -μι verbs are disappearing, with ὀμνύω replacing ὄμνυμι. The negative μή gains ground over οὐ, partly because this was a refinement of later Greek, and partly because it helps Dio to avoid that shibboleth of post-Isocratean style, the hiatus.[17] The perfect tense too is sometimes confused with the aorist [ἀγήοχα, not ἦχα, as the perfect of ἄγω].) On the other hand, because Dio is a well-read man, he uses some pure Attic forms which had long dropped out of circulation: the dual of nouns and verbs, and the optative, and ποῖ and ὅποι, which he sometimes overcorrectly employs to mean "where," with verbs of rest. And he has a large stock of words and phrases remembered from the best prose writers, especially Plato and Xenophon, Demosthenes and Thucydides and Herodotus; some, but not so many, come from classical poetry.

16[See also G. Highet, "Lexical Notes on Dio Chrysostom," *GRBS* 15 (1974) 247–53, and "Lexical and Critical Notes on Dio Chrysostom," *GRBS* 17 (1976) 153–56. Ed.]

17See also B. L. Gildersleeve, "Encroachments of μή on οὐ in Later Greek," *AJPh* 1 (1880) 45–57.

On a higher level than words and phrases, Dio's style bears a good deal of analysis. Its *texture* is extremely varied. Some of the discourses jog along with little change in sentence-structure, few syntactical oddities, little to tax the intellect, or indeed to engage the close attention of the reader or hearer. But quite often a carefully wrought passage will contain sentences so long, so complex, and so loaded with unusual words and stylistic devices, that it must be painstakingly dissected. In these cases we wonder whether Dio may not be trying to obfuscate his audience. In those later centuries almost any eminent writer was a bit of a spellbinder, a spellbinder who—like Apuleius in his *Florida*—may be listened to with admiration but without complete understanding. And furthermore, some of Dio's themes are so lofty—for instance, the relation of the Demiurge to its creation (36.55–60)—that he deliberately chooses to clothe them in esoteric language and obscure syntax.

But most of the time Dio's sentences are, when most complicated, ingeniously naive. A modern Greek automobile driver hired to take the foreign visitor from Sparta to Olympia via Arcadia will set off at a quiet pace and apparently try to maintain it steadily for a few miles, but only apparently, for often as he coasts down a hill, he will take advantage of his naturally increased speed and start up the opposite slope without losing a single kilometer per hour, and he will many times round a curve or evade an obstacle—and how provokingly multitudinous the obstacles are, especially in the backward parts of the Peloponnese, where the forces of progress have not yet exercised their full transforming authority!—doing so, when it is necessary and even sometimes when it is not imperative, with an élan, a chivalrous impetus that eventually helps him to attain the maximum speed, which he feels has been throughout the desire of his foreign passengers, accustomed as they are to fine broad six-lane concrete highways unimpeded by poor little narrow village streets through which one must force one's way with blasting horn and scraping fenders, and not delayed by bleating groups of uncooperative goats, scrambling everywhere and degrading the landscape with dialectal cries and pastoral effluvium, so that by the time he is zooming down the curving road which clings to the mountainside without a guardrail between the car and the precipice, glancing back over his shoulder from time to time to reassure his guests, or taking one hand off the wheel to wave it in a gesture of nonchalance, and maintaining a steady eighty kilometers an hour as though he were on a flat plain without any risk worse than a blowout, then he is truly fulfilling his nature, being reckless, aristocratic, confident, irresistible, a re-incarnation of Achilles plunging forward with a war shout behind his furious horses.

In the same way as a modern Greek driver, Dio Chrysostom will start out quietly enough but keep going steadily faster and faster round numerous detours and past many near collisions until he reaches an almost unforeseeable destination three-quarters of a page later. To watch him performing one of these feats reminds the onlooker of the infant Hercules, who in his cradle caught and strangled two snakes dispatched by his stepmother Hera. In one hand Dio grasps sense, in the other syntax; and he squeezes them until the very particles scream for mercy.

One of his masterpieces in this line comes in the thirteenth speech.[18] It is important for him, this passage. It describes his chief mission. After he returned from exile, he says, he preached to the Romans as Socrates had once preached to the Athenians; and in this speech he reports what he said to the audience in Rome:

> In this way I tried to talk to the Romans—when they invited me and asked me to speak, not taking them aside by twos and threes in wrestling-schools and walks, for it was impossible to meet them like that in the city of Rome, but to large groups gathered together—explaining that they needed better and more careful education if they wanted to be happy, genuinely and truly happy and not by the opinion of the mass as now. Suppose, I said, someone were to take them over and convert them, explaining that there is nothing good among the things they aim at and struggle eagerly to acquire, and believe the more they acquire the better and happier they will live, but that, for the practice of self-control and courage and justice, if they could forget everything else and get hold of teachers, whether Greeks or Romans or perhaps among the Scythians or Indians a teacher of these subjects might be found, just like a teacher of shooting or riding, or a doctor qualified to cure the illnesses of the body, someone capable of healing the mind's diseases and qualified to expel lust and greed and other such maladies from their victims, then, recruiting this teacher to join them (through persuasion or friendship, for money and other rewards will never influence such a man), and installing him in the city hall, they should make it mandatory by law for all the young people to go to him and be with him, yes, and their elders too, until they all got wisdom and fell in love with justice, and—despising gold, silver, ivory, fine food, rich perfume, and sexual pleasure—lived happy lives, governing first and foremost themselves, and then the rest of mankind. For then, I said,

---

[18] 13.31–34. The text printed by von Arnim (with constant interference by Wilamowitz) must be emended by the restoration of an arbitrary cut or two, and the insertion of a few connectives.

your city will be great and strong and truly a ruler, while as
things are, its greatness is doubtful and quite unsafe.

This may be a platitude, an extended platitude. Yet it is a truth. And
put in that strange persistently persuasive style which, although
copious enough, still does not risk putting its hearers to sleep with
the monotonous to-and-fro balanced rhythm of Isocrates, it is a
noble and moving truth. At moments like this, Dio achieves real
distinction. His prose becomes something like poetry. It recalls the
music of Orpheus, whose hearers

> hung on his voice, motionless, listening,
> and listened still when he had ceased to sing.[19]

---

[19][Highet's translation of the last two lines of André Chénier's evocation of
Orpheus (*Hermès* 2.4.11):

> Aux accents de sa voix demeuraient suspendus,
> Et l'écoutaient encor quand il ne chantait plus.

Highet applied these words to Chénier himself in *The Classical Tradition*
(New York, 1949) 403. Ed.]

LATIN LITERATURE

Julius Caesar*

Julius Caesar has been dead for more than two thousand years, twenty centuries; but people are still arguing about him. Everyone agrees that he was brilliantly clever and dashingly brave, and that he changed the history of the Western world. He was, in that sense, a great man. Yet people cannot agree on one simple question: was he a good man or a scoundrel? Was he the savior of Rome, or a vile traitor who richly deserved to die? We have all made up our minds about George Washington and Adolf Hitler. April 30, 1945, when Hitler killed himself among the flaming ruins of his capital, is a day to remember in all the history-books, and every February 22 we are proud to celebrate the birth of the father of this country. But Julius Caesar still divides intelligent people in a sort of intellectual civil war. I had a schoolteacher who always wore black for mourning every year on the Ides of March, the day Caesar was killed. She idolized him. I know one or two historians who cannot discuss him without losing their tempers—they hate him so much—and several more who won't hear a word spoken against him. I myself—well, let us wait a little. Before we talk about the man, let us look at his books. Through them we ought to be able to find out more about his character and his motives—not 'what made him tick' but what drove him through life like a blazing comet through the sky.

Caesar wrote several books, for he was a highly intelligent man with lots of original ideas. The others were lost during the Dark Ages of later European history; but two have survived and have always been read in schools and colleges wherever Latin is studied. These are the *Gallic War* and the *Civil War*. Not many active and successful generals write books about their campaigns. I can think of Eisenhower's *Crusade in Europe* and Grant's *Memoirs* and Frederick the Great's *Principles of War,* but scarcely any more. Why did Caesar take the trouble to write them? He was tremendously active and always busy (they say he used to dictate four different letters to four different secretaries at once); he was fully occupied with politicking and fighting and revising the calendar and

*A 1968 lecture in typescript (printed here) and on cassette (= *AFSS* 23087).

reforming the senate, not to mention making love to Cleopatra. You can understand a retired general like Grant and Eisenhower writing a book on his war service, but Caesar had no thought of retirement. When he was struck down by Brutus and Cassius and the others, he was only fifty-five, younger than Abraham Lincoln was at the time of his murder; and he was full of mighty plans for the future.

People usually start with Caesar's *Gallic War*. I prefer the other one myself because the Civil War is a more important subject, but the *Gallic War* is more carefully written and richer in incident. Whichever you start with, you are bound to be surprised, probably disappointed, perhaps disgusted by the style. Both books are dry, factual, and on the whole unexciting. They are full of stereotyped phrases like *quibus rebus cognitis,* "after learning this" (*BGall.* 1.19, 4.30, 7.56, 7.72). There are some stirring incidents, but you have to look carefully for them. Usually, when Caesar or someone else makes a speech, we are not allowed to hear his voice and his actual words. Instead, the gist of it is reported, paraphrased, in 'indirect speech.' There are one or two exceptions to this. For instance, in *BGall.* 7.77–78, Caesar has been besieging a town in Gaul. The garrison runs out of food. The chiefs hold a council of war. Some are for giving up and surrendering. Some propose to make a desperate sally and try to break through Caesar's lines. One chief stands out. He says the first plan is cowardly and the second silly. He declares that the fighting braves should eat the women and the children and the old and unfit men, and so continue their resistance. Now Caesar gives this speech in the chief's own words—or at least, what he pretends to be the chief's own words—full of fire and energy and bitter hatred for the Romans. But he does so for a special purpose. Normally, Caesar avoids the emotional impact of a direct speech; and in the whole of his two books, although he is often reported as speaking himself, we only once, at a big crisis (*BCiv.* 3.85) hear his own voice; and then he utters only twenty-three words.

Yes, the style is extremely dry and curt and businesslike. It does not give us anything like the impression of Caesar's character which we get from reading about his life in other historians, and in biographers like Plutarch and Suetonius. He was a romantic, dashing, impetuous man with a pretty wit and an astonishing gift for doing the unexpected and getting away with it. When he was a young man of twenty-five, sailing to study in Greece, his ship was captured by pirates and he was held for ransom; while he waited for the ransom to arrive, he used to make jaunty speeches to the pirates, telling them to look out, because when he got away he intended to capture them and crucify them; in time the ransom arrived; Caesar was set free; he collected some ships, sailed after the pirates, caught them, and crucified them every one (Plutarch, *Caesar* 1–2). He had many other adventures like that, he took hundreds of outrageous risks, and in general he led a life which was brilliant and colorful—the very opposite of the colorless style in which he describes his two campaigns. There has to be a good reason for this.

If we analyze Caesar's style in detail, we find out that it is even more sparse and dry than it looks. The Latin language has a fairly rich vocabulary. Julius Caesar cuts it down to the barest essentials. There are lots of ordinary Latin words, which every other writer uses but which he will not touch. For instance, he never writes the word *quamquam,* which means "although," or *ideo,* which means "therefore." Never. Yet these are quite regular words, and nobody else writing Latin tries to avoid them. Can you imagine a modern general writing two books about his experiences in war and deliberately never saying "although" or "therefore"?

If we go on analyzing, we find more peculiarities along the same line. If several words can be used to mean the same thing, Caesar will choose one of them and stick with it all the way through. For instance, there are three synonyms all meaning "river"—*flumen, fluvius,* and *amnis.* Now there are plenty of rivers in the *Gallic War:* Caesar makes a big thing of the bridge he built across the river Rhine (*BGall.* 4.17); but always and everywhere he uses only the word *flumen,* never *fluvius,* and never *amnis*—not even for change. That means that he has to use it seven times in the one chapter about the Rhine bridge, which is pretty monotonous. Now when you and I repeat a word like that, it is because we are bored, or tired, or just stupid. Caesar was seldom bored, and never tired, and he was one of the brightest men who ever lived. Why does he do it?

There is something else that strikes everyone the moment he or she starts reading Caesar. This is that, although he is writing about himself and describing his own plans, his own successes and occasional failures, and even his own motives for action, he does not say "I sent out cavalry" or "I crossed the bridge." Instead he writes "Caesar sent out cavalry" (*BGall.* 7.45) and "Caesar crossed the bridge" (*BGall.* 4.17). This of course makes the whole thing colder and more formal. It is difficult for us to identify with a man who talks of himself in the third person, as though he were somebody else.[1]

For this curious trick, there are several reasons. One is that, outside his books, he often talked of himself in the third person. In real life, instead of saying "I" he said "Caesar." Certainly it was a special habit of Caesar. When he divorced his wife for being connected with a scandal, he said: "Caesar's wife must be above suspicion" (Plutarch, *Caesar* 10.6). Once he was crossing the dangerous Adriatic Sea in a small boat on an urgent mission; a storm came up and the boatman panicked; Julius said to him: "Take courage: your passenger is Caesar" (Plutarch, *Caesar* 38.3). Now William Shakespeare, who was a marvelous psychologist, noticed this when he was reading about Caesar and put it into his play. There is a fine speech in Act 2, where Julius is told that there have been many omens of disaster to bring in the Ides of March. Finally, the priests who have offered up sacrifices tell him he should not leave his home to go to the senate-house (2.2.39–40):

> Plucking the entrails of an offering forth,
> They could not find a heart within the beast.

But Julius replies (2.2.41–48):

> The gods do this in shame of cowardice:
> Caesar should be a beast without a heart
> If he should stay at home today for fear.
> No, Caesar shall not. Danger knows full well
> That Caesar is more dangerous than he.
> We are two lions littered in one day,
> And I the elder and more terrible,
> And Caesar shall go forth.

Trust Shakespeare to notice these little details which reveal the mysteries of the human heart.

Well then, Caesar often spoke of himself in the third person, so it was perhaps natural that he should write of himself in the same way. But there is another and more potent reason. This stems from the character of his books.

What are they, these books, the *Gallic War* and the *Civil War?* Histories, you might think. No, they are not. Caesar called them *commentarii,* which is not the same as *historiae* ("histories"). For

---

[1][In the rest of this paragraph—which Highet excised from the lecture—he stated that the translators John Warrington (1953) and Rex Warner (1960) made Caesar write "I crossed the bridge" in order to make him sound more natural, thus distorting the impression that he intended to convey. Ed.]

the Romans as for most of the Greeks, history was not the same as a plain narrative of facts. It was artistic; it was emotional; it had strong descriptions, battles and riots, and fires and storms; it had eloquent dramatic scenes, debates and court-trials, with passionate speeches on both sides. Without the romantic love interest, history for the Romans was meant to have something like the emotional impact of Tolstoy's *War and Peace* and Dickens's *A Tale of Two Cities*. Therefore, it could not be 100% true and factual. Of course, historians often *say* they are writing without prejudice and giving only the essential data; but in fact they always color their story by the way they select and arrange some facts and omit others. Julius Caesar did not want to write like that. The name of his books is *Commentarii*. The word does not mean "histories" and does not mean "commentaries" either. In English a commentary is a book which explains and discusses an important and famous work, and clears up difficulties in understanding it. So you can have a commentary on the Book of Job in the Bible, or a commentary on a play of Shakespeare, or a commentary on the opinions of the Supreme Court. But in Latin *commentarii* means "notes" or "memoranda." For example, a student's notes taken at a lecture are *commentarii;* a doctor's records of his cases are *commentarii;* after Cicero died, his secretary published his work-sheets, his *commentarii* for some of the speeches which he had delivered just from bare outlines. Therefore, by calling his books *commentarii,* Julius Caesar means his readers to believe that they are something plainer, and simpler, and more factual than artistically written history. The title *Commentarii* means something like Data, or Log-Books, or Work-Sheets, or Source-Materials, or Factual Records. Though we have no exact word for *commentarii* in English, the meaning is clear—a book simpler, plainer, drier than history, and more truthful. The facts.

Now Cicero had excellent taste in literature. He understood Caesar very well. In a book published two years before Caesar's assassination, he says that Caesar's *commentarii* are meant to provide the material for others to use when writing history (*Brutus* 75/262). And there we have the main explanation for the name *Commentarii,* for the cold, dry, monotonous style, and for the curious trick of writing "Caesar crossed the bridge" instead of "I crossed the bridge." When he wrote these books, Caesar intended to present them to his world as the facts, the bare facts, pure reporting, nothing more and nothing less, straightforward, unbiased, not distorted by any emotion and not disguised by the graces of fine writing. He wanted them to be like a candid-camera photograph unretouched, and not like a big elaborate oil painting filled with tricks of design and color and light and shade.

When he was writing the *Gallic War,* he knew that there were many Romans who thought he was a pretentious upstart, and as a soldier, merely an amateur. In particular, he envied the tremendous reputation of his rival, who was to become his victim— Pompey the Great. Two grandiose histories of Pompey's victorious career as a general were already circulating, and written in very flowery language. Julius Caesar, on the other hand, had done no serious campaigning until he was in his forties, while Pompey had commanded an army at the age of twenty-three and had beaten far more important and dangerous enemies than Caesar had to face in Gaul. When Julius wrote the *Gallic War,* he meant it to convey one message—many others, but this one message certainly—Caesar is as brave and skillful a general as Pompey.

Then later, when he wrote the *Civil War,* Caesar had another job to do and was trying to persuade his readers of another—well, shall we call it a propaganda point? It was that, when he marched an army into his own country and put the legal government to flight, he was not really a public enemy and was not guilty of high treason, but was simply sticking up for his rights. Can you imagine an American general sending a fleet of bombers under his own orders over the city of Washington in order to enforce his demands on the President and the Congress? That was what Julius Caesar did when he crossed the frontier at the Rubicon and entered the territory of Roman Italy.

Therefore, Caesar's two books are part of the political and military strategy which he used to become the sole ruler of Rome and the Western world. To put it bluntly, they are not works of art; they are not history in the normal sense. They are propaganda, of the type which we get from politicians all the time, every day, now, and here—although more skillfully written. They are what he wished his contemporaries and posterity (meaning us) to believe. The simple unpretentious form, the bare terse style, and all the rest of his devices are meant to make his readers believe that the books contain the truth, the whole truth, and nothing but the truth.

Well, do they? Are they truth? Or are they something else? Are they propaganda?

Experts differ about this. Some admire Caesar so much that they will swallow nearly every word he wrote. Some believe his books are a very cunning confidence-trick. The French historian

Rambaud has written a persuasive book about Caesar and "the art of distorting history."[2] Then there are some who try to have it both ways: they *say* Caesar's books are "naturally not unbiased"; but they *imply* that on the whole they are reliable. I myself think that in spite of—no, because of—their apparent simplicity and frankness, they are brilliantly skillful propaganda. When you read them, you will be making a serious mistake if you do as Caesar wants you to do and plow through chapter after chapter taking it all in, just as he presents it. Instead, you should constantly ask yourself *why*. "Why is he describing this? What does he want us to believe here? This is an exciting incident, but what is behind it?" For instance, you remember the speech of the Gallic chief who proposed killing and eating the noncombatants. Why does Caesar put that into straight direct speech? He never mentions the man before that particular council and never brings him in again, so it is not to build up the man's character as a future hero or villain. Surely it is because he wants to show us that some of the Gauls were cruel and bloodthirsty savages; that by conquering Gaul, Caesar was delivering Rome from a clear and present danger; and that Caesar's army, which could challenge and beat such desperate fighters, was a gallant force, the finest soldiers of Rome, magnificently trained and commanded by General Julius Caesar. And why the big description of building a bridge across the Rhine, only to pull it down again? To show that he understood military engineering and to show that he was upholding the prestige of Rome, establishing her influence on the further side of an important frontier, beyond which lay dangerous hostile tribes.

What is the conclusion then? What was Caesar? There is a joke about a timid young priest who was invited to lunch by his bishop. To make conversation, the bishop said: "I have just been reading a new biography of Napoleon." The poor young priest could not think what to reply. He gulped, and took a deep breath, and then said: "Ah, Napoleon! Able fellow, wasn't he?" He could not guess whether the bishop would think Napoleon was a good man or a bad man; but there was no doubt of one thing, Napoleon's ability. This is correct. Napoleon was a marvelous organizer. He reformed French law, the French administrative system, the French schools and universities, and built a new France. Caesar too was such a man. When he came to power, the Roman Republic was almost five hundred years old. It had lived more than twice as long as the

---

[2][For the arguments employed, see M. Rambaud, *L'Art de la déformation historique dans les "Commentaires" de César* (Paris, 1952[1] and 1966[2]). Ed.]

Republic of the United States of America at this moment. It had become the ruler of the whole rich Mediterranean world, without greatly changing its ancient constitution. There were lots of things in it that needed reform right away, and quite a number that ought to be abolished for good. Many of these Julius Caesar, after attaining power as a dictator, abolished or reformed, and when he was killed, he was planning to do much more along the same lines. In this he was a real benefactor.

And another thing. He was not a cruel man. In battle he fought hard and pursued the enemy relentlessly; but once the fighting was over, he was merciful and kind—at least to his fellow Romans. He was no Stalin with secret police and labor-camps. But like Napoleon, he was incurably self-centered. He had to be the greatest man in Rome, far superior to all others, almost a god. In the last year of his life he was wearing the magnificent crimson robe of a triumphant general, sitting on a golden throne, and allowing his statue to be put beside the statues of the gods. He even named one of the months of the year after his own family name, which is why we call the seventh month July, from Julius. And still worse, he was getting ready for a new war, which would certainly be a tremendous strain and might (like some wars) turn into a disaster. At the age of fifty-five, he intended to march east into Asia Minor with a huge army, invade and conquer the countries which are now Iraq and Iran, then strike north through the Caucasus to the Ukraine, and come back into Europe through Germany, conquering all the time, or so he hoped. Now that he had beaten Pompey the Great, he had only one rival left—Alexander the Great, who was dead, but who was famous as the greatest soldier who ever lived; and Caesar intended to outdo Alexander's conquests.

This would have been terribly dangerous. But what was most dangerous of all, what was fatal, was the fact that Caesar conquered not only the Gauls but the Roman Republic. He wrecked it. Of course he was able. Of course he carried out reforms which were sorely needed. But he was a dictator; and by his grandeur and his power he prepared the way for the other dictators who gradually became emperors and who crushed half the life out of Rome. As Winston Churchill once said, democracy is the worst system of government ever invented except all the others.[3] Once a republic

---

[3][This famous statement comes from a speech that Churchill delivered on November 11, 1947, before the House of Commons, in which he remarked that (his exact words follow) "democracy is the worst form of government except all those other forms that have been tried from time to time." Ed.]

has been taken over by one-man rule, it is almost impossible for it ever to recover its freedom, to make a new declaration of independence; and it is very very difficult for men of talent and energy to make a career in it without toadying to the dictator *whether he is good or bad*—a genius like Caesar, or atrociously cruel like Stalin, or insane like one of Caesar's successors, the emperor Caligula. Caesar was a great man. But it would have been better for Rome and for the world if he had been killed in the year 54 B.C. when he was invading Britain, rather than in 44 B.C. after he had become dictator. Remember, Caesar had no sons, but by adopting his nephew Octavian, he set up what is worse than a dictatorship—a hereditary monarchy, with power increasing each generation. Only a few generations later the last of that particular family dynasty—with the treasury bankrupted by his crazy extravagance, with the army mutinying—was declared a public enemy by the senate, and with a little assistance from one of his servants, killed himself. This was the emperor Nero.

Vergil's *Aeneid*[*]

I am the best possible man to talk to you about Vergil, because I am a teacher of Latin, and yet I hated Vergil for many years. Then I learned—quite slowly—to understand him; and now I admire him and love him greatly. I really hated him when I was young. I thought he was gloomy and dull. I believed his language was affected and artificial. I saw him as a poor, thin, carbon copy of Homer's *Iliad* and Homer's *Odyssey*.[1] For a few years, while I was teaching in the Humanities (or Great Books) course at Columbia University, I struggled to keep Vergil out of the reading lists. I never read him for pleasure. I never taught him. And then—gradually—I got converted. I started reading him again (I forget why) and thinking about him. Then I began to teach him and found that my classes were keen and enthusiastic. I got caught up and began to do research on his poetry. The more I did, the more rewarding it was. I found out more and more beautiful and powerful things in his work, things which I had simply been blind to for many years. Now I teach him every year and enjoy it; I think my pupils enjoy it—at least they talk very well about him; and I am writing a long and laborious book about him, which is a pleasure.[2]

I am not the only one by any means. Vergil has often been misunderstood and often been cordially disliked. There are only two reasonably good appreciations of his poetry by American scholars (Brooks Otis and George Duckworth);[3] little or nothing in French and Italian; and until recent years, only two or three sympathetic books in German. Now things have changed, and good books on

[*]A 1968 lecture in typescript (printed here) and on cassette (= *AFSS* 23117).

[1][See G. Highet, "The *Aeneid:* Penetrating a Book," in *The Powers of Poetry* (New York, 1960) 244–50—another lecture in which Highet recalled his negative view of Vergil. Ed.]

[2][See G. Highet, *The Speeches in Vergil's Aeneid* (Princeton, 1972)—the book that Highet eventually published on Vergil—and his "Speech and Narrative in the *Aeneid,*" *HSPh* 78 (1974) 189–229, in which he examined a subject not fully considered in his book. Ed.]

[3][For the two appreciations of Vergil's poetry to which Highet may well be alluding, see B. Otis, *Virgil: A Study in Civilized Poetry* (Oxford, 1963), as well as G. E. Duckworth, *Structural Patterns and Proportions in Vergil's Aeneid* (Ann Arbor, 1962). Ed.]

Vergil are coming out in many different countries; but still, it is clear that for many generations he was too difficult for most readers to understand. However, I now know—I do not think—I know that he is a great poet, up there on the same level as Homer and Dante and Shakespeare. Ah! Perhaps that is what turned me on to reading Vergil. I had been reading Dante. Dante is a great poet, and Dante calls Vergil his father, the supreme poet. Yes, that must be it. Anyhow, I have had a very pleasant time finding out what makes Vergil great.

To begin with, he is a fine musician. Poetry is made out of words. Words are not marks on a page. They are sounds—and we all know this now that we hear so much poetry sung to music. So if you try to read Vergil only by spelling out the words printed on the page, you are missing many of the effects at which Vergil himself worked so hard. You are like someone trying to enjoy a Beethoven symphony simply by reading the score, without hearing the orchestra. Today we are all rediscovering the fact that all poetry should be read aloud or recited aloud or sung aloud, and that a musical accompaniment often helps it to penetrate our minds. Vergil's poetry is its own musical accompaniment, but it must be read aloud. He himself had a marvelous reading voice and gave recitals of his poetry which deeply moved those of his friends who heard them. This is why it is almost useless to read translations of Vergil's poetry into prose—all the music and rhythm are destroyed. And this is why we read Vergil's poetry in Latin—because it contains special beauties which cannot be reproduced in any other language. Every page of everything he ever wrote is full of the most remarkable effects of rhythm and sound, echoing and enhancing the emotion, or explaining the action which he is describing. For instance, here is a man striking a spark from flint, and feeding it into dry leaves, and starting a fire. You can hear the scratch of the flint, and the flame catching, and the fuff of the fire spreading (*Aen.* 1.174–76):

> ac primum silici scintillam excudit Achates,
> suscepitque ignem foliis, atque arida circum
> nutrimenta dedit, rapuitque in fomite flammam.

And here is an angry goddess, denouncing her rival, hissing and spitting like a serpent (*Aen.* 10.94–95):

> tum decuit metuisse tuis: nunc sera querelis
> haud iustis adsurgis, et inrita iurgia iactas.

And here is my favorite, from one of the poems about life in the country, which he wrote while he was very young. First you hear the bees buzzing in the hedgerow—a sleepy sound in a hot afternoon (*Buc.* 1.53–55):

            saepes
Hyblaeis apibus florem depasta salicti
saepe levi somnum suadebit inire susurro

and then the call of the wood-doves and pigeons high in the elm-tree. They say "coo-coo . . . coo" (*Buc.* 1.57–58):

nec tamen interea raucae, tua cura, palumbes,
nec gemere aëria cessabit turtur ab ulmo.

Very few major poets have been able to make such music as that. Homer scarcely even tried, for he was working in a different style. Dante did it now and then. Shakespeare did it often, although he was better at rhythm than at melody-effects. Browning and Tennyson both tried to rival Vergil in this and almost succeeded— one comic, the other romantic. Making music with words is a great art.

However, it is only a part of making poetry. Poetry is also made of emotion and of meaning, of many different kinds of meaning. And here we have one reason why I hated Vergil for so long, and why many young readers dislike him, although perhaps they faintly realize that he is a fine artist. The emotion is downbeat. He is a sad, pessimistic poet. His world is gray and blood-red and black, not gold and blue. No one has a good time in the *Aeneid.* Yes, there are the early poems called the *Bucolics,* which have some cowboys and shepherds singing and playing music, and cutting up touches, with a few jokes and some gaiety. But the *Aeneid* is a black poem. It is the gloomiest of all the great epic poems. The *Iliad* of Homer ends with the death of a hero, but it is more balanced and calm as it comes to a close; the *Odyssey* of Homer ends with a triumphal victory against heavy odds; Dante's *Comedy* leads to a marvelous transcendence of humanity in the vision of God; even Milton's *Paradise Lost* has a slightly hopeful ending, because although Adam and Eve have been expelled from Paradise, they have each other, and they have been told that mankind will eventually be redeemed. But the *Aeneid* is one long recital of effort and frustration and pain and killing; this comes out in almost every page you read. For instance, there is a passionate love story in Book 4 between Dido and Aeneas. She is beautiful, he is brave and handsome, they are both lonely, they desire each other, they are united—and then he is told by God Almighty that he must leave her and go on to lead his people to the Promised Land. The agony which the two lovers go through when they have to part, that is wonderfully described. He grows cold and says less and less, because he has been commanded by God to give her up, and cannot even argue about it. She pleads with him, tries to persuade him to stay, finally curses him and sends him away with a terrible death-wish. She kills herself. This is very powerful, very true. But were the two lovers happy in their love for a time? We must suppose so; but their happiness is never described. Now love scenes are not taboo in epic poetry. In Homer's *Iliad* you have the love of Paris and the beautiful Helen, the love of Hector for his wife Andromache, and even the love of Zeus for his consort Hera; there is much lovemaking in Homer's *Odyssey;* even in Milton's *Paradise Lost* there are two exquisite love scenes between Adam and Eve (Book 4 and Book 9).[4] But in the *Aeneid* the delight which Aeneas and Dido take in exchanging their love is only alluded to, in something like twelve lines. The misery and hatred into which it turns are described for four hundred lines. That is Vergil's view of human life—that on the whole it contains much more pain than happiness. If he had been a playwright, he would not have written romances or comedies, but grim tragedies.

The entire plot of the poem is predominantly sad. Aeneas is an exile, searching for a home—which is always a gloomy situation. He fought for ten years against the Greeks who besieged his home, Troy; the Greeks won and burned the city to the ground. He managed to escape with his little son and his old father, although he lost his wife. At the head of a group of exiles he builds ships and sets out to find a new place to live. They try one country after another, and every time their settlement fails. Finally they learn that their home is to be in Italy, and they set sail westward; but before they reach it, the goddess Juno, who hates all the people of Troy and helped to destroy the city, causes a hurricane which wrecks some of the ships and drives the rest ashore on North Africa. Then comes the love affair between Aeneas and the beautiful queen Dido. God tells Aeneas to leave; he does; and she kills herself. At last the Trojans land in Italy. They are about to settle down and Aeneas to

---

[4][Here Highet is very likely referring to 4.492–502, where after counting their blessings, Adam and Eve kiss in a loving embrace; and 9.1011–45, where after eating the forbidden fruit, Adam and Eve burn with lust and use each other purely for sexual pleasure. Ed.]

marry the daughter of a local king, when Juno contrives to get a war started. A war! Aeneas has already fought for ten long years and wandered the world for seven. He is exhausted. There is nothing he wants less than a war, nothing more than peace. However, to save his people, he must fight. And here a terrible thing happens. He grows bitter and furious, and he begins to fight savagely like a berserker. It would happen, you know. When a good fighter with plenty of experience is forced into combat against his will, he will use his full strength without holding back. Aeneas hoped to find peace. Instead he got war. Right, he says to himself, if they want war, I'll give them war. He crushes the enemy. He attacks the city of the old king who had promised him his daughter. At last he meets his chief opponent, the young prince Turnus, in a duel. Aeneas disables him with a spear-blow in the thigh. Then, in one of the most painful scenes in epic poetry, he stands in front of Turnus wondering whether or not to spare his life, while the wounded man begs for mercy. But Turnus is wearing a piece of armor, a sword-belt, which he took from the dead body of one of Aeneas's friends; and when Aeneas sees this, he plunges his sword in the man's chest. This is a terribly grim ending for the poem.

Toward the end of Homer's *Iliad,* Achilles kills Hector and mistreats his corpse; but afterward he is reconciled with Hector's old father and gives him the body to take home for burial. Toward the end of Homer's *Odyssey,* all the suitors who had invaded the home of Odysseus are killed; but they are killed fighting, and the odds are greatly in their favor. Thereafter there is a reconciliation scene. Both the Homeric epics end calmly, therefore. It is only the *Aeneid* which ends with the hero raging with dark fury and killing a helpless man. The truth is that the people of Homer's day thought that war was a regular and necessary part of human life; it meant suffering for those who were beaten, but glory and loot for those who won; and although Homer sometimes calls it "dreadful war," he clearly likes writing about it, and his audiences liked hearing about it. But for Vergil, who had seen the terrible civil wars of Rome—he was twenty-two when Julius Caesar beat Pompey at the Battle of Pharsalus—war was something like crime and something like raging madness; it infected even a soldier like his Aeneas who was fighting in a just cause, and made him cruel and ruthless. I have studied the *Aeneid* in detail for years now, and I keep finding new evidence to prove this. For example, you know how Homer likes to compare his heroes to brave animals like lions. Vergil does that now and then; but once, in a battle where Aeneas is fighting furiously and successfully, he compares him to a hideous mythological monster with a hundred arms who once dared to fight against the gods, that is, not to a brave beast like a lion but to a devil (10.565–70). Only Vergil would risk such a comparison, because he felt the full hideousness of war. (Statius of course copies this passage [*Thebaid* 2.595–601], but he keeps copying Vergil—repeatedly.)

But there is something darker still about the end of the *Aeneid*. All through the poem the goddess Juno, wife of the supreme deity Jupiter, has been persecuting the Trojans. Although destiny cannot be altered, and destiny says they will settle in Italy, still she thinks she can delay it, and out of pure spite, makes things as miserable for them as she possibly can. Hence the war which she stirs up. As the war draws to its climax, Jupiter tells her she has done enough, she can do no more, she must stop. Pretending to be humble and submissive, she bows her head and consents; but in exchange she makes a small request. Now that the Trojans have landed in Italy, she says, and are going to be established there as the ancestors of the Romans far in the future, will Jupiter grant one little thing? Let the Italians keep their own language and their own customs, and let the Trojans merge with them. Jupiter agrees. You see what this means. It means that Juno has won. She has managed, after seventeen years of effort, to destroy not only the city of Troy but all the Trojans. Within a few years they will all have disappeared—all but a legend. True, something else will take their place. According to the tradition which Vergil is using, the mixed breed of Trojans and Italians will produce the Romans—Julius Caesar claimed to be a direct descendant of Aeneas—and that is a greater destiny than the mere survival of the people of Troy. But the fact remains that what Aeneas and his subjects have been trying to accomplish—to find a home where they can settle and continue their lives—will not now be achieved. You know from the Bible how long the Jews struggled under Moses to reach the Promised Land, and how hard they fought under Joshua to make their way into it and to beat down the resistance of its peoples, who were endeavoring to keep them out; but at last they succeeded. But imagine if God had said that they must pay a price for their entry into the Promised Land—that they could come in, and settle down, but mingle with the nations already there, and lose their identity as Jews, as the children of Abraham. Even though some other, some greater destiny had been offered in return, it would have been felt as a dreadful, an unendurable loss.

Yes, it is fundamentally a very sad book, the *Aeneid*. There are other kinds of sadness in it too. When you read it first, you are only vaguely aware of them, but as you study it, they come out more distinctly. For instance, there is the sorrow of loneliness. Aeneas has no friends. His young wife disappeared in the sack of the city. His lover Dido killed herself. He has a faithful squire, Achates, but he hardly ever talks to him, and Achates only once says anything to Aeneas (1.582–85). His son, young Iulus, is with Aeneas quite a lot, but Aeneas never says a single word to him until the very last book—when he makes a short and inspiring speech of farewell to him before going out for the duel with Turnus (12.435–40). This is very unlike the *Iliad* of Homer, where the heroes are always chatting away, and Achilles has long talks with his good friend Patroclus. Perhaps Vergil thought the Greeks talked too much. Many Romans thought so. But the loneliness of Aeneas is un-Roman too. Almost all the great Romans we know of had lots of friends and talked freely to them. Vergil's patron the emperor Augustus had Maecenas, and Agrippa, and many more. One of the best books in Latin is a collection of delightfully easy and witty letters from Cicero to his old friend Atticus. But Aeneas has no one like that in his life. I think this may be a reflection of Vergil's own character. Although he had good friends, such as the poet Horace, he was painfully shy, and restless, and unhappy most of the time. To him loneliness was another part of the long torture of living.

In spite of all this pathos and suffering, the *Aeneid* is a very beautiful poem. There are twelve books, each a unit in itself with its own rhythm, and all blending into an overall pattern which is bound together by dozens, perhaps hundreds, of tiny links—meaningful phrases, recurrent images, and so forth. Here is one of these links, just one. The poem begins with Aeneas quite helpless, facing shipwreck and death by drowning in a storm at sea; the poem ends with Aeneas standing over a beaten enemy and killing him. Now when the hurricane strikes, Vergil says that Aeneas's limbs grew slack and cold with shock and terror—the words in Latin are *solvuntur frigore membra* (1.92). They never occur anywhere else in the poem until the last page; as the wounded Turnus is stabbed to death, *solvuntur frigore membra*—his limbs grow slack and cold in death (12.951). Vergil uses the phrase in these two places, the beginning and the end, to show how the wheel of fortune comes round full circle and how character changes under stress. At first it was Aeneas who almost died in the storm called up by his enemy Juno; at the end it is his enemy Turnus who dies under Aeneas's cruel sword. This kind of thing makes it worth studying a difficult poem in Latin and studying it carefully. Vergil took eleven years to write the poem, and he meant to spend three more years on it before publishing—which would have averaged out at two lines a day. Yet he was not a slow worker: he could compose quickly and freely, and even improvise verses when he was hot. But like James Joyce, he spent a long time on polishing and improving, and tightening up the structure by putting in these small unobtrusive links, and on varying the verse-rhythm so that the reader hardly ever finds the same pattern in any two successive lines, and the tempo is always subtly changing. He wrote only three major poems or groups of poems, and he worked over them with the greatest care. I said he was a musician; and he wrote rather like Beethoven, who wrote fast and with great excitement, but would spend years, many years, on an important piece of music before he allowed it to be performed or published. If you enjoy music, it is a constant delight to play the sonatas of Beethoven over and over again—I have been doing so for forty years—and each time to find out some new subtlety or strength in them which you had missed before. So with Vergil (and with Homer and with Dante), you do not appreciate all his deep thought and all his rich music at the first reading, nor at the twentieth. If it could all be gulped down and digested in one evening, it would be perfectly ridiculous for anyone to study the *Aeneid* carefully in Latin for a year, or for several years, or for a lifetime. Buy a paperback; read it; throw it away: that is good enough for many books, I think for most books. But some books are meant to be like Beethoven's symphonies, or the Parthenon, or St. Peter's in Rome—to last for centuries, and to give something to everyone who does not merely visit them for a few minutes, but studies them, and thinks about them, and allows them to enlarge his mind and his soul.

Is it all sorrow and misery and cruelty and endurance, the *Aeneid?* Is there no happiness in it anywhere, no serenity? Yes, there is. Three times Aeneas is happy. Once in Book 8, when after landing in Italy, he goes up the river Tiber to get allies for the impending war and sees the tiny colony which has settled on what will be the site of Rome in the future; a little later, when he looks at the shield made for him by the god Vulcan, which shows some of the wonderful scenes from the history of Rome, in which his descendants will play a part; and before that, in the greatest book of the whole poem, Book 6. There he visits the world of the dead to talk with his dead father. From him he learns that most of the dead do not simply lie in the ground as corpses; they have immortal souls; and their souls are made clean after death, in purgatory (except for a few hopeless cases who are tormented in hell); and then, after a thousand-year interval, they are born again in new bodies. With that his father shows him the souls of the great men who are to be the citizens and rulers of Rome in the future: Romulus the founder; Augustus the first emperor and second founder; Cato and Scipio and the great republican heroes; and two armored figures whom he begs not to make war, civil war, and not to turn their swords against their own country—they are Julius Caesar and Pompey. This long and magnificent vision shows Aeneas that his efforts and sufferings have not been useless, and that they will produce a noble civilization in the future. It is more encouraging than the words of God to Moses in the Bible; for Moses was told that although he had led the children of Abraham to the frontiers of the Promised Land, he was not permitted to enter it himself (Deut. 32.52). And yet, this happens in the other world, not in this world. It is a vision, far removed from Aeneas's own life and time, so far that he can hardly understand it. All he knows is that if he performs his duty, this marvelous future will be created. All he knows is that if he does his work on this earth—even if it means fighting a dirty little war and killing a helpless opponent—a national and a world plan will be fulfilled. He does not enjoy it. No one does. Vergil does not. You and I do not as we read it. But there are two motives in human life which it is very hard to reconcile: one is happiness; the other is duty. Vergil was unhappy himself, and he made his hero and his hero's people unhappy; but like Moses and the children of Israel, they performed their duty, and they lived and produced a great nation and a great ideal.

Tibullus the Rebel[*]

In his rapid survey of Latin literature, Quintilian comes to elegy and deals first with Tibullus. *Tersus atque elegans,* "polished and elegant," he calls him (10.1.93). Superficial as many of Quintilian's capsule criticisms are, this is so thin as to convince us that he really cares nothing about elegiac poetry—that is, nothing about its content. He is interested only in style. Ovid, in a similar survey written for a different purpose, gives Tibullus quite a lot of space, and quotes or paraphrases passages from his poetry (*Trist.* 2.447–64). Instruction in adultery and sexual cheating—that, says Ovid, is the main subject of Tibullus's poetry. This is special pleading, since poor foolish Ovid is trying to defend his own *Art of Love;* but it contains a certain amount of the truth, though not by any means all. What does Tibullus say?

I want to discuss the themes of Tibullus's elegies.[1] It is not often easy to do this with personal lyric and elegiac poems. For instance, what are Ezra Pound's *Cantos* really about? For that matter, what is the most famous poem of this century, T. S. Eliot's *The Waste Land,* really about? Charles Baudelaire's *The Flowers of Evil,* A. E. Housman's *A Shropshire Lad*—can we say what is their subject, or what are their principal topics and how interconnected? Yet when we read an impressive book of poems such as these, we always feel that we are in contact with a man who is showing us various sides of his personality. They may be in conflict one with another, yet they combine to make up a single character. That character may change through time, as it does in Pound's *Cantos;* it may also be changing in the course of the poems, even through the actual composition of the poems, as in *The Waste Land.* But it is still one character, unlike all others in this myriad-minded world; and an essential function of criticism is, from the poems, to evoke that character and understand it.

You will see that I do not accept the 'persona' hypothesis as applied to personal poetry such as certain types of lyric and elegy—

---

[*]Presented in 1976 for the American Philological Association.
[1][For Highet's earlier views on Tibullus, see his *Poets in a Landscape* (New York, 1957) 156–72. Ed.]

except in the most trivial sense.[2] Each of us wears at least one persona, which he exhibits to the world almost all day long. Unless he
is a criminal or a hardened hypocrite, his persona is not something
detached and alien, but part of himself—the aspect which he
wishes to display to others. Every man and woman wears a mask;
but the mask in some degree resembles him or her. No one except
a confidence man, or a corrupt beggar, or a transvestite, walks
with a crutch he does not really need, or puts on a wholly deceptive
disguise. Therefore, if the real Tibullus thought certain topics were
important enough, moving enough, for him to spend many hours
turning them into poetry, then I believe that the "I" who speaks
through the poems and calls himself "Tibullus" (1.3.55 and 1.9.83)
has the voice of the real man, uttering some (though by no means
all) of the real man's essential feelings and thoughts.[3] Epic, drama,
didactic poetry, formal lyric, and fictional narrative are on a different plane—obviously. But we are talking of personal lyric and
elegy; and frankly, I cannot emulate the White Queen, who told
Alice that the way to believe impossible things was to "draw a long
breath, and shut your eyes."[4] I cannot believe, for example, that
when Keats wrote that on first looking into Chapman's Homer he
felt like an astronomer discovering a new planet, this was the false
or affected utterance of a fake persona, and that the real John
Keats, after Cowden Clarke showed him Chapman, shoved the
book aside and started playing bumblepuppy whist.[5]

Tibullus's work as we have it amounts to sixteen poems. Eleven
are mainly devoted to love. But seldom does he touch on those types
of love which are rich and satisfying and durable. He is rarely
happy. He speaks of two girls, whom he calls Delia and Nemesis,
and describes as corrupt and deceitful, heartless and mercenary. If

---

[2]I have made this point at greater length in "Masks and Faces in Satire,"
Hermes 102 (1974) 321–37.
[3]I cannot understand G. Williams's comment on Tibullus's poems of unhappy love in *Tradition and Originality in Roman Poetry* (Oxford, 1968) 505:
"These relationships are not so much the material of poetry as of a situation, only vaguely apprehended, within which Tibullus can express his own
private reflections on the human condition."
[4][A reference to Lewis Carroll, *Through the Looking Glass and What Alice
Found There* (London, 1872) chap. 5. Ed.]
[5][For the anecdote about Keats and Clarke, see C. C. Clarke, "Recollections
of John Keats," in C. C. Clarke and M. C. Clarke, *Recollections of Writers*
(London, 1878) 120–57, especially 128–31. For the rules of whist and other
card games, see D. Pool, *What Jane Austen Ate and Charles Dickens
Knew: From Fox Hunting to Whist—The Facts of Daily Life in Nineteenth-
Century England* (New York, 1993) 62–66. Ed.]

love were logical, we should ask what on earth he sees in either of them. He does not describe them as particularly beautiful or affectionate or seductive or—like Propertius's Cynthia—talented. Ovid has several delightful poems about pretty women—what Milton calls "their shape, their colour, and attractive grace" (*Paradise Regained* 2.176)—through which it is possible to imagine the charms of his mistresses. Both Ovid and Propertius write in passionate delight of an afternoon or a night spent in bed with their beloved (Ovid, *Amor.* 1.5 and Prop. 2.15). But Tibullus talks of his girls mainly as cruel cheats, unloving and for most men unlovable. There are several fine poems by Propertius in which Cynthia reproaches him (clearly with some justification) for wronging her (Prop. 1.3, 2.29, 4.7, and 4.8); their tone is that of deep though troubled passion, almost devotion. Nothing like this appears in Tibullus.

What does he expect from these girls, and what does he get? Companionship, of a kind. He sounds like a very lonely man: at least he writes much and feelingly about the pains of separation; he never mentions the idea of raising a family of children; he seems to have few friends, and to relax and enjoy himself only seldom, on festivals. Companionship is important for a sickly man. In his very first poem (1.1) Tibullus has a premonition of death—like Keats in his sonnet "When I have fears that I may cease to be"—and expects Delia to be at his deathbed. In elegy 1.3 he is seriously ill, writes his own epitaph, and imagines himself as entering the Elysian Fields. He (or his persona) was possessed by the thought of illness and premature death; and in fact he died young.

But it is not the companionship of his women that chiefly concerns Tibullus. He spends much effort complaining about their infidelities and their cruelties. And in this he differs from Propertius and from Ovid. When a woman breaks a promise to them, or is unfaithful for a caprice, or is seduced by a rich rival, they grow indignant. They complain volubly. They sometimes slap the girls or pull them around by the hair. They go off with other girls. But on the whole, Tibullus is not strong enough to indulge in any of these emotional counterattacks. He weeps. He calls for drink to drown his sufferings (1.2.1–4 and 1.5.37–38). Significantly, when he does try making love to another woman as a substitute, he grows impotent (1.5.39–42); he curses his rival and the go-between who destroyed his happiness (1.5.47–58); and then gives up, beaten—*heu canimus frustra* (1.5.67). Again and again he reverts to this theme: his own weakness, the triumph of his rivals, the uselessness of struggle and effort, and the deceitfulness of hope. (His second girl is called Nemesis, and Nemesis is often shown as the antithesis of Hope [*Anth. Pal.* 9.146 and sculptures of Nemesis].)[6] He admits this weakness; he exhibits it freely; almost we might say he glories in it.

The final poem in the collection (2.6) begins with a half-comic military march, like *non più andrai, farfallone amoroso* ("no more you'll wander, my amorous butterfly") in Mozart's *The Marriage of Figaro* (Act I, No. 9). Aemilius Macer is off to the wars (1–2).[7] If the god Love is kind to soldiers, I shall go soldiering too and—only Tibullus would have summed up a soldier's life in this way—"carry water in my shiny helmet" (7–8). But no, it is useless (11–12):

> magna loquor, sed magnifice mihi magna locuto
> excutiunt clausae fortia verba fores.

And he relapses once more into half-hysterical self-pity: he is insane (18); he would have killed himself but for Hope (19–20); he will sit weeping at the grave of his girl's sister and pray for the ghost's help (29–40); no, he will not, for that will upset his girl Nemesis; and the poem ends in desperation, as he pictures her in the arms of a rival, trying different sexual positions, and curses the bawd who arranges her assignations with others (41–54). After its bright and gay opening, the poem runs downhill—through threats of suicide and madness, through the violent death of a young woman (an event which is irrelevant but serves to darken the atmosphere further), to end with a rather feeble imprecation, *satis anxia vivas* (53)—always downhill.

That is only one example of Tibullus's principal theme—his subordination to the girls he loved. "As long as I am with you, Delia, let me be called a lazy good-for-nothing" (1.1.57–58). "I shall submit to harsh rules: if I praise another girl, let Delia scratch my eyes; if she thinks I wronged her, let me be dragged through the streets by my hair" (1.6.69–72). "Only to be with Nemesis in the country, I would dig the soil and follow the plow in spite of sunburn and blisters" (2.3.5–10); "make me a slave in fetters, and flog me" (2.3.79–80). "She demands money and jewels and fine clothes—so I must take to robbery and murder, or to stealing temple treasures" (2.4.21–24); "to please her I would sell my ancestral home or drink deadly drugs" (2.4.51–60).

---

[6]See F. Marx, "Albius Tibullus," in *RE* 1 (1894) 1319–29, especially 1322–23.
[7][See Marx (above, note 6) 1323—a key source for identifying Macer as Aemilius Macer. But see E. O'Neil, "Tibullus 2.6: A New Interpretation," *CPh* 62 (1967) 163–68—an article that presents compelling arguments for identifying Macer as Pompeius Macer. Ed.]

No other Latin love poet known to me degrades himself (or his persona) in this way. Catullus struggles against the domination of Lesbia but combines his love with hatred, which is a manifestation of his independence (Cat. 72, 75, and 85); and finally, after a painful effort of will (Cat. 8), he converts it into bitter contempt and detestation (Cat. 11 and 58). Propertius and Cynthia present themselves as two strong characters who could live neither together nor apart; and in that marvelous ghost-poem, unequalled for me in all Latin poetry, he is still wronging her after her death and yet is still held by her love (Prop. 4.7.93–96). As for Ovid, a man whose sexual drive he himself said was *in has omnes ambitiosus amor* (*Amor.* 2.4.48), he (or his persona) never suffered much or long from the torments of passion. But Tibullus is, in the colloquial phrase, a loser.

Now it is tempting to propose that he was a masochist, like Algernon Charles Swinburne, who could not derive any satisfaction from a woman unless she made him suffer, who worshiped what he called "splendid and sterile Dolores, Our Lady of Pain" (*Dolores* 11–12). But this would be an over-simplification. Tibullus brooded on his unhappy loves, but from them and from his own failures he does not say he obtained any pleasure.

I suggest that this attitude is one aspect of a larger feature in Tibullus's character. We might call it *defeatism* or *escapism*. It appears not only in his loves but in his attitude to two other things more important to the Romans—wealth and war. The first lines of his first poem (1.1) bring them together in a curious way. "Let others heap up yellow gold and possess huge tracts of farmland," he begins (1–2). And you expect him to go on, like Horace, "by sailing through dangerous seas to trade in costly merchandise" (*Carm.* 1.1)—but no. Instead of that, he says "by enduring constant danger in the face of the enemy and being awakened early by the bugles of war" (3–4). And then he proceeds: "Not me. Let me be poor and inactive, provided I have a fire burning constantly on my hearth" (5–6). By this he means a working-class sufficiency, but not *la misère* ("destitution"). (So in 1.5.31–34, he looks forward to entertaining Messalla, with Delia serving at table unassisted by any domestic slave—*epulas ipsa ministra gerat.*) Surely this is strange: not the contrast of wealth and poverty, common enough, nor the contrast of the soldier's life with that of the peaceful farmer; but the implication that the chief reason for joining the army is to become a millionaire, with a safe full of yellow gold. This is, of course, a theme known from Greek New Comedy (and its Roman adaptations), where the mercenary soldier, enriched by his campaigns

in the wars of Alexander's successors, is a comic and slightly repulsive figure. But how is it relevant to the epoch in which Tibullus
was living and writing?

In two ways. First, it refers to Octavian and his henchmen. With
the Battle of Actium, fought about five years before Tibullus published his first book, Octavian became *de facto* the ruler of the
Western world and came into control of enormous wealth. His
supporters, even men from unknown families such as Agrippa, got
their shares of it and acquired more for themselves as commanding generals. Agrippa owned vast estates—*culti iugera multa soli*
(Tib. 1.1.2)—in Egypt and Sicily, and the whole of the Thracian
Chersonese. As after most successful revolutionary wars, there
was a vast redistribution of wealth, and much of it went to commanders who had fought on Octavian's side.[8] Furthermore, the
years following Actium saw many more wars fought on different
fronts—in Gaul, Spain, Africa, and Thrace; many wars, followed
by triumphs, and the display of the spoils taken by the Roman victors from the vanquished.[9] The Romans never forgot the hard epigram once addressed to them by a Gaul—*vae victis,* "woe to the
conquered" (Livy 5.48.9). Thence too came broad lands and heaps
of gold. Even on a lower level, a legionary officer—once a slave—
could acquire a big property in the wine-growing country of
Falernum and show off his wealth in the knights' seats in the theater, says Horace, *Epod.* 4 (cf. Tib. 2.3.59–60). Second, it glances,
although guardedly, at the legionary soldiers of Octavian. After
Actium he disbanded a number of legions, and—just as after
Philippi—he had to find land for them to settle on. Even if he paid
the townships for it—as he claims he did (*Res Gestae* 16)—the
evicted landowners, without the steady income brought in year
after year, would feel impoverished.

Poverty as a new experience—that is one of Tibullus's recurrent
themes: *felicis quondam, nunc pauperis agri,* he calls his estate
(1.1.19), and adds that his household gods once (*tunc,* not further
defined) received "countless bullocks" in sacrifice but now get only
one ewe-lamb (1.1.21–22; cf. 1.1.33–34, 37–38, 41–44, and 2.1.15–
16). It is never made clear whether Tibullus's estate was cut down
after he was a grown man (that is in 30 B.C.) or earlier, at the
same time as the confiscations around Mantua which afflicted

---

[8]See R. Syme, *The Roman Revolution* (Oxford, 1939) 369–86, especially 381.
[9]See M. P. Charlesworth, "Wars in the West and the Balkans," in S. A.
Cook, F. E. Adcock, and M. P. Charlesworth, edd., *The Cambridge Ancient
History* (New York, 1934) vol. 10, chap. 4, sect. 2, pp. 116–18.

Vergil. At one point he speaks of the wealth of his ancestors
(1.1.41–42); and we might argue that in the rest of the poem he is
consoling himself for their losses and exhorting himself to accept
his own status as a young heir whose inheritance has all but vanished. He never says that he himself was once rich. Constantly he
ranks himself among the poor (1.5.61–66) and contrasts his own
indigence with his rich rivals. That sensitive critic Georg Luck
says: "The poet's references to his *paupertas* . . . are little more than
literary convention; the erotic poet had to be penniless by definition."[10] Yet I do not remember Ovid complaining of poverty; and
Propertius, although richer rivals came on the scene sometimes,
had a household which was far from indigent: see Prop. 4.7, with
an expensive mistress beautifully dressed, a gold statuette of
Cynthia, and a number of slaves.

Throughout his work, Tibullus never once mentions Octavian
(later styled Augustus), or the Battle of Actium, or the restitution of
the Republic, or the divine ancestor Julius Caesar, or Agrippa, or
any one of Augustus's achievements, or any one of Octavian's supporters—except his own patron M. Valerius Messalla Corvinus.
He never mentions Horace, or Vergil, or their patron Maecenas.
Studied silences in such sensitive, expressive poets as Tibullus
mean a great deal. At the very least, they convey lack of interest,
failure of commitment; they can also mean cautious rejection, positive disapproval, or downright hatred.

Nevertheless, Tibullus speaks of himself now and then as though
he had thought about becoming a soldier. It never comes to anything. In his first elegy (1.1) he says emphatically: "Let others go
soldiering! Not me!" In his last (2.6) he says exactly the same. In elegy 1.10 he laments that he is being dragged off to war (*trahor,*
with an unnatural and emphatic lengthening of the final vowel)
and that death is waiting to strike him down (11–14); and the
poem ends with a prayer to peace (67–68). In elegy 1.3 he has broken down at the beginning of his tour of duty as an officer with
Messalla. He is ill in Corfu; he explains that he did not want to join
the expedition in the first place and kept trying to find evil omens
which would show that heaven wanted him to stay at home (15–
22). Nowadays it would be a Section Eight discharge. We can be
sure that he (or his persona) never heard a bugle blow the charge
or faced the swords of an enemy. He wishes he were living in another world, an earlier epoch, a primitive golden age of peace, un-

---

[10]See G. Luck, *The Latin Love Elegy* (London, 1959[1] and 1969[2]) 63 in 1959 edition and 71 in 1969 edition.

der Saturn (37–48). Now, under Jove, *caedes et vulnera semper* (49–50).

But is there not a direct claim by Tibullus, made in one of his most finished poems, that he served as a member of Messalla's military staff? In elegy 1.7 he celebrates Messalla's birthday (1–2), recalls his recent triumph over the Aquitanians in 27 B.C. (3–8), and then evokes his patron's missions in the West and the East (9–22). After an odd and irrelevant digression on Egypt as the cradle of Neolithic civilization (29–48), he returns to Messalla (55–56), his present activity in reconstructing Italy as a highway-builder (57–62), and his birthday festival (63–64). In this poem Tibullus appears only as a poet: *canam* (13), *referam* (17), *possim dicere* (23); and as a celebrant (*dem . . . honores* and *liba . . . feram* 53–54). Except for one word. Just after the evocation of Messalla's triumph, he says: *non sine me est tibi partus honos* (9), and to this will bear witness . . . and then a list of place-names. Now this remark seems very wrong. First, it is wrong in tone. Messalla was a very great man, one of the chief men in the Roman world—*consul, augur, triumphator*. It is utterly inappropriate for Tibullus to write: "It was not without me that you earned your triumph." Second, it conflicts with all the rest of Tibullus's poetry, in which he keeps saying how he detests war, and danger, and foreign travel, and effort, and suffering—not because he has tried it and found it repulsive (he has no veteran's reminiscences about wounds and bloodshed) but because it is against his whole nature. This was seen by A. E. Housman, who cleared up the problem by a tiny emendation: he changed *non sine me* to *non sine re*, "not without substance"[11]—that is, Messalla's triumph was earned by genuine achievement, and to this will bear witness the lands through which he traveled as a conqueror and pacifier.

War, then, and wealth Tibullus finds equally repulsive. He makes them more repellent by combining them, rather artificially. The Rome of his time was deeply involved in wars, both civil and foreign; and many of its citizens were occupied in getting and spending. Tibullus repeats again and again that these ways of life are not for him. He withdraws, partly into the world of love adventures and furtive assignations, partly into a small quiet country home.

---

[11][See J. P. Postgate, *Corpus Poetarum Latinorum* (London, 1894) vol. 1, pp. xv and 274, for this emendation, which Housman apparently did not publish on his own but forwarded instead to Postgate for inclusion in the above volume. Ed.]

Yet a poem by Horace seems to make nonsense of these statements. It is a short poetic letter (*Epist.* 1.4) addressed to someone
called Albius. In this piece Albius is described as doing (or likely to
be doing) several things of which no trace whatever appears in the
poetry of Tibullus: writing something to outdo the works of Cassius
Parmensis (whatever that may mean); meditating on philosophical problems, apparently moral; and reading Horace's *sermones*
with a critical eye. Furthermore, Horace says Albius is rich, famous, popular, and robust in health. He has everything—except
(Horace delicately implies) that he suffers from a tendency to
melancholy brooding. I confess I cannot solve this discrepancy except in one of three ways: either Tibullus's poems are largely sham
and lies, the emotional antics of a fictional persona, in which case
the jarring inconsistencies within them are simply bad and careless writing;[12] or else Horace is addressing another man altogether
called Albius (this was the proposal of Baehrens);[13] or else Horace
did not really know Tibullus but wrote to him with pretended fa-
miliarity (I have sometimes thought I glimpsed this fake familiar-
ity in other letters of his). (There is also a little lyric of Horace
[*Carm.* 1.33] consoling Albius for the loss of a girl called Glycera,
not to a *richer* man—which is how Tibullus in his poems always
lost his girls—but to a *younger* man. Here there is one feature
which does look like the Tibullus we know, that he composes
miserabiles . . . elegos. But the name Glycera never appears in his

---

[12]So H. C. Gotoff, "Tibullus: *Nunc levis est tractanda Venus*," *HSPh* 78
(1974) 231–51, especially 231, who speaks about Tibullus's "endlessly and
shamelessly posturing characters." Mr. Gotoff begins by saying: "At the
time he was writing, he was young and handsome, rich and talented, and
living in an age when young poets of his background and interests had access to the highest court circles and the most desirable beds in the capital of
the world." No evidence is offered for this bold general statement. If it is
true, what was he doing with women like Delia and Nemesis?

[13][See E. Baehrens, *Tibullische Blätter* (Jena, 1876) 7–11, for this early challenge to the traditional view of identifying the Albius addressed by Horace
with Tibullus the elegist. The Albius = Tibullus question became the subject
of a scholarly debate at the beginning of the twentieth century between two
classicists who interpreted Horace's verses differently: for arguments
against identifying Albius with Tibullus, see J. P. Postgate, *Selections from
Tibullus* (London, 1903) 179–84, and "Albius and Tibullus," *AJPh* 33 (1912)
450–55; for arguments in favor of identifying Albius with Tibullus, see B. L.
Ullman, "Horace and Tibullus," *AJPh* 33 (1912) 149–67, and "Rejoinder to
Mr. Postgate," *AJPh* 33 (1912) 456–60. See also R. J. Ball, "*Albi, ne doleas*:
Horace and Tibullus," *CW* 87 (1994) 409–14, for a review of this spirited de-
bate and for further arguments in favor of the identification. Ed.]

work. I suppose it could have been that of an earlier love; or it might be a substitute for Nemesis.)

Ovid has a pretty rococo elegy on the death of Tibullus (*Amor.* 3.9), although he never knew him personally (*Trist.* 4.10.51–52). He is evidently working with Tibullus's poetry and quotes it repeatedly. Tibullus 1.3, written in loneliness and fear of death at Corfu, he cites as though it were factual (*Amor.* 3.9.47–52). Delia and Nemesis, says Ovid, both kissed the dead poet and challenged each other about his love (*Amor.* 3.9.53–58). This point is just the kind of thing that Ovid, who knew women so well, would invent. In elegy 1.1 Tibullus says to Delia: *te teneam moriens deficiente manu* (Tib. 1.1.60). But Ovid makes Nemesis (who dominates Tibullus, Book 2) quote this to outdo her rival Delia and say: *me tenuit moriens deficiente manu* (*Amor.* 3.9.58). It is not much of a poem, but at least it shows that Ovid considered Tibullus's poetry to be largely autobiographical. Ovid, although he lived in the same social world as Tibullus and was a skilled psychologist, was not so clever and sophisticated as modern critics who can distinguish "the poetic personality as opposed to the personality of the poet" and speak of the personage who utters the memorable words *vivamus, mea Lesbia, atque amemus* (Cat. 5.1) as "Catullus' Lothario."[14]

Besides war and wealth, the Romans of Tibullus's time had two other great concerns. These were politics and religion.

What would we not give for another collection of letters such as Cicero's to illuminate the period of the Roman Revolution, or for the autobiographies which we know were written by Agrippa and by Augustus himself? Political life has rarely been as exciting and produced so many powerful and capable men as in that momentous half-century. For politics, however, Tibullus appears from his poetry to care not the paring of a finger-nail. The senate, the consuls, the Roman people, the provinces and their governors, mean nothing to him whatever.

Religion, on the other hand, he treats with great gravity. His poem on the country festival of the *lustratio agri* (2.1) is a little masterpiece. It is made particularly attractive by the fact that Tibullus himself speaks as the director of the festival. He utters the prayer to the ancestral gods while the sacrifice is being made (17–24); he interprets the omens as good (25–26); he toasts the absent Messalla as patron of the feast (35–36); and being a poet, instead of making a speech to the feasters, he gives them a poem skillfully moving from the deities of agriculture to the deity of love (37–80),

---

[14]See Gotoff (above, note 12) 232 and 241.

and summoning Cupid to the festival (81–82). Yet there is something out of harmony in the poem—as usual in Tibullus. Its setting is rustic. The revelers are country people, farm workers and their wives and children (*rusticus* 21 and *coloni* 23). The beginnings of civilized life, yes, and of music and the dance and the minor arts are placed firmly in the countryside. But as soon as Tibullus starts to talk of love, the scene (and the tone of his poetry) shifts away from the country to the city. If the god of love was indeed born in the countryside among the cattle and the mares (as Tibullus says in 67–68), then we should expect the poet to sing of young lovers in the country, as Shakespeare does (*As You Like It* 5.3.21–24):

> Between the acres of the rye,
>   With a hey, and a ho, and a hey nonino,
> These pretty country folks would lie
>   In springtime, the only pretty ringtime.

Instead, he takes us into the city, where a girl escaping from her bedroom in a dark house is stepping over the *custodes*—sentinels placed by her husband or the man she lives with—to slip out and meet a lover (75–78). Just so Propertius's Cynthia says she used to climb out of a window and make love to him lying on the cold pavement (4.7.15–20). That was in the Subura, at the heart of Rome. But I find it hard to imagine a farmer's wife or daughter out in the Italian countryside deceiving her *custodes* to meet a lover. But this is part of a basic conflict in Tibullus's nature. He cannot decide whether love means the deep affection of husband and wife—as it does when he speaks of sleeping peacefully with Delia in his farmhouse *solito . . . toro* while the storm rages outside (1.1.43–48), and of growing old and gray together with her (1.6.85–86)[15]—or furtive adventures, which usually involve cheating on a husband or a rival (1.2.15–42).

One more of Tibullus's poems centers on religion: an invocation to Phoebus Apollo to welcome Messalla's son Messalinus as a member of the Sacred College, *quindecimviri sacris faciundis* (2.5). This is, on the whole, serious. It glides very skillfully from a description of the site of Rome as it was in prehistoric times (23–38) to the Sibyl's prophecy to Aeneas (39–64), and thence—after a dark reference to the ill-omened year 44 B.C., although without a mention of Julius Caesar (71–78)—to an evocation of the pastoral rite of the Palilia (79–104). For a moment Nemesis rears her

---

[15]See Gotoff (above, note 12) 242 on 1.6.85–86. On this Mr. Gotoff comments: "He is sentimentalizing, for pathetic effect."

pretty head. With another of those jarring inconsistencies which mar his work so often, Tibullus forgets that he is addressing Apollo the god of poetry and declares he could not write a line without his darling little disease, Nemesis (105–12). But after that he recovers himself admirably, to end the poem with a prophecy, forecasting that in time young Messalinus himself will celebrate, like his father, a triumph (113–22).

We should therefore see Tibullus as a rebel, fighting against the main movements of his time, swimming against the stream; or at the very least, as an outsider. He turns away from the great spectacle which is unfolding around him and from all the powerful men who were helping to shape it. With one exception: that is Messalla. Messalla played a big part in the civil wars: fighting at Philippi; combating Sextus Pompey; and commanding the center for Octavian at Actium. Nothing of all that interests Tibullus; at least he never mentions it. Messalla was emphatically aloof from the circle of Octavian's close friends and quickly resigned the post of *praefectus urbi,* which made him governor of Rome as though it were a conquered province. That aloofness reappears in Tibullus's silence about nearly all his important contemporaries.

Although the τόπος ("formula") is familiar from other poets, it is nevertheless used with what appears to be emphatic conviction by Tibullus—retirement, retreat from the world, rejection of responsibility and of danger—let others do this, not me. He does not even take his role as a poet seriously. Ovid fills his elegy on Tibullus's death (*Amor.* 3.9) with grand and pious declarations asserting that the poet ought to be sacred, that his works at least are immortal, and that Tibullus is now in heaven with Calvus and Catullus (and perhaps Cornelius Gallus). Horace builds his first ode out of a traditional comparison of men's interests and pursuits, concluding with the ideal of his own life—to be a lyric poet (*Carm.* 1.1). Not so Tibullus. He does not talk gravely of his art. He never mentions other poets, or imitates them obviously and explicitly—unlike Horace and Propertius and Ovid. (He does occasionally use a theme or a phrase from Catullus.) All the poets of his time retired from the world to some extent: they wrote *recusationes* ("excuses"), hated the profane mob, and lived in seclusion when they could escape from Rome with its duties and its attractions. But they had a wide circle of friends and a large gamut of interests. Tibullus was a self-sentenced exile.

About homosexual activity, Catullus wrote a little, nothing whatever to compare with his poems about the love of the two sexes. Horace has a few light allusions to it, while Propertius and Ovid ignore it. Vergil, himself homosexual, has one famous poem on homoerotic love (*Bucolics* 2) and a few veiled allusions in the *Aeneid*. Tibullus, however, makes it important. He writes a short *Ars Amatoria* on pederasty, making Priapus the speaker (1.4). He makes this bolder, and for most tastes more offensive, by saying that he wanted his friend Titius to have all this valuable advice but that Mrs. Titius forbade it (73–74). And he ends with another vacillation, by appointing himself professor of homosexuality, and immediately canceling the appointment by saying he is dominated—again this note of self-distrust and surrender—by the boy Marathus; his claim to expertise is a fraud, *vana magisteria* (75–84). Later in the same book there is another poem on pederasty (1.9). Tibullus's beloved boy has been seduced by a rich and dirty old man (53–76). After vehement reproaches, Tibullus exultantly says: "You will be sorry too late, when another boy rules my heart" (77–84). This emphatic bisexuality is not mentioned by Ovid in his memorial poem and is usually neglected by modern critics. It is another aspect of Tibullus's rebellion against Roman ways and conventions.

Let me finish with a curious and tentative suggestion, on which I should be grateful for your opinions. Most elegiac poetry is notably personal, as contrasted with didactic and epic and ceremonial lyric. The elegists appear to talk freely, intimately, about themselves and their loves and hates. They do not explain much. They begin and end their poems abruptly; and they dart from one theme to another with unexpected or truncated transitions. Sometimes they enjoy juxtaposing poems which conflict with each other. (There is a famous example of this in Ovid's *Amores,* Book 2. In an impassioned monologue Ovid defends himself against Corinna's charge that he has been having an affair with her maid Cypassis, and swears to heaven that the accusation is utterly false [2.7]. In the next poem he addresses Cypassis herself, saying: "How on earth did she find out? Anyhow, let's have another bout now—or else I'll admit everything" [2.8].) Of all the Roman elegists whom we have, Ovid is the smoothest, in that he preserves within nearly every poem something like continuity. Catullus has some difficult transitions, and Propertius even more—although once we grow accustomed to his peculiar oblique manner, we understand them better. But I confess that I find the transitions in Tibullus's elegies often very slipshod, or obscure, or willful; and aesthetically disappointing. Some nineteenth-century critics felt this too and decided that the manuscript was full of holes. Professor Robert Ball has shown that this is a mistake and that many of Tibullus's transitions can be explained, not logically but imaginatively, like daring modulations in music.[16]

True. And yet I cannot keep myself from feeling that Tibullus is often *deliberately* eccentric, capricious, arbitrary, careless; and that he cultivates this erratic manner to make a contrast, both with the careful formality of Vergil's and Horace's poetry, and with the traditional character of Roman life and thought. The Romans were slow thinkers; but they had built up a huge body of laws and military strategy and religious ritual and administrative skills, which aimed at perfect regularity and efficiency. Their private and public morality varied; but they always admired *gravitas* and *constantia*—seriousness, dependability, consistency, steadiness. Of course anyone who reads Cicero's letters knows that Cicero and many other intelligent Romans vacillated and changed their views and held personal opinions which sometimes contradicted their public conduct. But they did not publish such things in beautifully arranged *libelli*. Tibullus did. He combined incompatible themes in the same poem. One, particularly absurd, sticks in my throat. In a poem devoted to praising his patron Messalla (1.7) he spends a long time talking about Egypt. Mysterious country, nourished by the Nile, one of nature's marvels. Mankind was taught agriculture and civilization, not by Triptolemus or Athena or Dionysus, but by Osiris. Osiris is summoned to attend the celebration of Messalla's birthday. This, although Messalla had helped to win the Battle of Actium, in which the queen of Egypt and her consort Mark Antony were defeated. Osiris was one of the chief gods of Egypt. Surely the appearance of Osiris at Messalla's festival would be as discouraging as that of the Stone Guest at Don Juan's banquet.[17] But Tibullus does not notice the inconsistency; or perhaps he does not care.[18]

---

[16][See R. J. Ball, *Tibullus the Elegist: A Critical Survey* (Göttingen, 1983) for detailed analyses of Tibullus's sixteen elegies—the book that grew out of the doctoral dissertation completed under Highet's direction. Ed.]

[17][Here Highet may well have been thinking of Mozart's *Don Giovanni*—the most famous adaptation of the Don Juan story—where the Stone Guest attends Don Juan's banquet before dragging him off to hell. Ed.]

[18][But see Ball (above, note 16) 112–17, especially 115–16, for a review of how the scholars of the 1970s related Tibullus's 'hymn to Osiris' to the context of the elegy in which it appears, by establishing archetypal and antitypal connections between the Egyptian god and the Roman general. Ed.]

Petronius's Dinner Speakers*

Recently one of the boldest experimental novelists now writing in English published a long comic novel entirely without narrative. There *was* a story line, highly original and filled with satiric exaggeration, but the plot was developed and the characters were portrayed solely through their voices. The novel was *JR*, by William Gaddis (New York, 1975). It became a flop *d'estime*.

This technique is peculiarly modern—modern as opposed to classical, Greek and Roman. Shakespeare is full of turns of phrase and of speech-rhythms which are special to one character alone; so is Robert Browning, and Charles Dickens, and James Joyce. There are some Greek writers who do this—Plato, Aristophanes, Theocritus—but not many. In Latin it is done on a large scale by only one surviving author—Petronius, in his *Satyrica*.[1] That is one of several qualities which make him unique.

I propose to examine his methods of characterization through speech in the banquet scene, where people talk most freely and interestingly. This has been done before, several times, but I hope I can contribute a few new observations.

Let me remind you about the speakers at Trimalchio's party. Besides the host himself, who is inexhaustibly garrulous (and that although he gave another banquet the evening before [34.7]), there are seven chief speakers, not counting several who surface to say only a few words and then disappear again.[2] These are—in order

---

*Presented in 1976 for the American Philological Association.

[1][For Highet's defense of the spelling *Satyrica,* see his two earlier articles on Petronius—his "Petronius the Moralist," *TAPhA* 72 (1941) 176–94, especially 176, and his "Whose *Satyricon*—Petronius's or Fellini's?" *Horizon* 12.4 (Autumn 1970) 42–47, especially 42. Ed.]

[2]Such are Dama (though the name is a conjecture by Heinsius to replace H's *clamat*) in 41.10–12 and Plocamus in 64.3–4. In even small details Petronius is a subtle satirist. When Trimalchio leaves the room, his guests sigh with relief and begin general conversation *sine tyranno* (41.9). The first to sound off is Dama. He asks for a good big drink, informs the company that he is already drunk, and is never heard from again. Not even a hiccup. [For Heinsius's conjecture, see P. Burman's edition of Petronius (1709[1] and 1743[2]) 185–86 in 1709 edition / vol. 1, p. 252, in 1743 edition. Ed.]

of their appearance—Hermeros,[3] Seleucus, Phileros, Ganymede, Echion, Niceros, and the late-entering Habinnas.

The first thing that we observe about their speeches is that Petronius's methods of characterization are far more delicate than those of most modern writers. They depend far less on the repetition of easily recognizable verbal habits. Shakespeare makes Falstaff's attendant Pistol habitually utter Marlovian blank verse when others are speaking prose (*Henry V* 2.1.62–63):

> O braggard vile, and damned furious wight!
> The grave doth gape, and doting death is near . . .

Corporal Nym keeps saying "that's the humor of it"; and Captain Fluellen talks Welsh-English (*Henry V* 3.2.59–63):

> For look you, the mines is not according to the disciplines of the war . . . for look you, th' athversary, you may discuss unto the duke, look you, is digt himself . . . under the countermines.

So Dickens's Mr. Jingle always talks in telegraphese abbreviations (*Pickwick Papers,* chap. 2):

> Tall lady, eating sandwiches—forgot the arch—crash—knock—children look round—mother's head off—sandwich in her hand—no mouth to put it in . . .

Sam Weller mixes up "v" and "w", and inserts "as the man said" after every little epigram. This is tolerable over a long novel but would be unendurable in a single chapter. Petronius skillfully confines himself to much smaller and neater effects.

Certain guests—like colloquial talkers all over the world—have small pet phrases. Others may use the same phrase, but one man will bring it in, sometimes for emphatic repetition, sometimes unconsciously echoing himself, two or three times only a few sentences apart. For example, *ad summam* ("in short," "in a word") turns up quite frequently: first in the mouth of a slave (31.2), then in Echion's monologue (45.12), and thrice in Trimalchio's final tirades (71.1, 75.10, and 77.5). But Hermeros, the most truculent

---

[3]Introduced first without a name as *is qui supra me accumbebat* (36.7) and named in 59.1. Eduard Fraenkel can scarcely be right in excising *is ipse qui supra me discumbebat* in 57.1: for this would mean that the man making the important speeches found in 37.2–38.16 is left unidentified, contrary to Petronius's practice elsewhere. [For the excision proposed by Fraenkel, see K. Müller's edition of Petronius (1961) xl–xli and 57—an edition containing a number of other suggestions made by Fraenkel, which Müller incorporated in this volume with Fraenkel looking over his shoulder. Ed.]

and voluble of the guests, uses it three times in a few lines (37.5, 37.10, and 38.2) and thrice again in a later speech (57.3, 57.9, and 58.8). Threatening cheeky young Giton, he also uses *curabo* three times in one breath (58.2, 58.5, and 58.7) and *bella res* twice (58.12 and 58.13). (Trimalchio also has *curabo* thrice, although at larger intervals [74.14, 74.17, and 75.9].) He twice uses the odd phrase *in rutae folium conicere* (37.10 and 58.5: "to make someone look like small potatoes"). Niceros, and only he, has *homo meus* (62.4) and *miles meus* (62.13). Then Echion has *etiam si* twice in a few lines (46.4 and 46.5), while Seleucus repeats *quid si non* (42.5 and 42.7). Seleucus also specializes in one type of phrase which we know from Plautus to be true native Italian. Fraenkel calls it "identification," and he gives as a model example *muscast meus pater: nil potest clam illum haberi* (*Mercator* 361).[4] So Seleucus declares *baliscus . . . fullo est* (42.1)—meaning that the bathman wears out your body just as a fuller wears out clothes by rough treatment; *medicus enim nihil aliud est quam animi consolatio* (42.5); *antiquus amor cancer est* (42.7); and his *aqua dentes habet* (42.1) and *utres inflati ambulamus* (42.4) are not far removed from this pattern.

All the speakers make mistakes in Latin. But here a caveat. Although they use some foreign words, they do not appear to be thinking in some other tongue and translating their thoughts into Latin. Indeed, we know from their own mouths that at least three of them came to Italy as young boys, so that they learned Latin when they were young enough to adopt it as their own tongue (Ganymede, 44.4 and 44.6; Hermeros, 57.9 and 58.13; Trimalchio, 75.10). Hermeros even recalls his Latin-speaking schoolmaster's words as he sent the boys home from school (58.13). The errors they make are generally quite simple things, almost on a level with those we hear every day in the United States—e.g., "Febuary," which will soon be joined by "libary," and "we played pretty good," and "af*flu*ent society," and "cohort" meaning an assistant. Some forms which look wrong to our eyes may well be archaisms that survived on the lips of the people. The nominative *Iovis* for *Iuppiter* (47.4 and 58.2) is justified by Ennius (*Annales* 63/241), while *bovis* for *bos* (62.13) comes into Varro (*Menippeae* 1, *Aborigines* 3). We

---

[4]E. Fraenkel, *Plautinisches im Plautus* (Berlin, 1922) 23–58. Jokes of this pattern occur in Aristophanes and a few other Greek writers, but not in Menander or Terence. Fraenkel points out that most of the Plautine examples have a purely Roman context and appear in the speeches of funny slaves.

should not even assume that *argutare* used in the active voice (46.1 and 57.8) is a solecism, for there it stands in a polished elegy of Propertius (1.6.7). Some of the speakers make more and worse blunders than others, like the drunk, who is the only man to say *vinus* for *vinum* (41.12); Trimalchio and one of his slaves get it right (31.2, 34.7, and 39.2). This is one of Petronius's methods of differentiating and characterizing these men.[5] Nevertheless, they nearly all have a pretty good command of Latin syntax and accidence. An ignorant fellow like Echion can say, quite neatly and correctly, a sentence expressing an unreal condition by two subjunctives—*si non didicisset, hodie famem a labris non abigeret* (46.8). Many more illiterate things are scrawled on the walls of Pompeii; and indeed one scholar points out emphatically that Petronius does not endeavor to reproduce all the eccentricities and blunders of the popular language of his time.[6] These men talk Latin which is unintellectual but energetic, simple but vivid, faulty—yes—but not barbarous.

One further general comment. A reader accustomed to contemporary American and European novels and magazines is really surprised to see how little real *dirt* gets into their talk. True, they make jokes about illicit love affairs between free people and slaves (43.7–8, 45.7–9, 69.3, and 75.11), yet they sometimes protest that their love is not merely a physical sex urge but is based on virtue (61.6–8 and 75.3–5). There are some crude expressions, but far fewer of the real *praefanda* than we find, for instance, in Martial. When Hermeros is denouncing Ascyltos and Giton in a speech blazing with anger (57–58), there are only two little obscenities in his long outburst; his tone is violent but not brutally cruel. There is relatively much more filth and savagery in Catullus; and we can hear worse things today in many a film and many a stage-play.

All the men have non-Roman names, and very grand ones indeed. There is one Ganymede, named for the favorite of Zeus; there are three men with erotic appellations—Hermeros, Phileros, and Niceros. One man has a name from the Greek myth—Echion.

---

[5]Yet W. Arrowsmith in his translation—*The Satyricon of Petronius* (Ann Arbor, 1959) 76—neglects the anomalous forms, making no attempt to reproduce them in English. No one who reads "as you hope to make a fortune" could guess that it was meant to render *sic peculium tuum fruniscaris* (75.3).

[6]G. Suess, *De eo quem dicunt inesse Trimalchionis cenae sermone vulgari* (Dorpat, 1926) 3 and 77–82. If we had more of the Atellan farce, which had such forms as *dicebo* and *vivebo,* we should then have a higher opinion of Trimalchio's guests and their language.

Echion was one of the warriors sprung from the dragon's teeth sown by Cadmus. After nearly all had killed one another, he with four others survived (Ovid, *Met.* 3.118–28). Therefore this Echion, and he alone, talks about bloodletting: he loves to see swordsmen killed—*ferrum optimum . . . sine fuga* (45.6). Another guest is named after Alexander's general, who ruled a great empire in Asia, Seleucus. (Trimalchio's pet pageboy with the dirty teeth also has the name of an Asian monarch, Croesus [64.5].) The significance of the name Trimalchio is well-known. It combines the intensifier *tri-* with the Semitic root for "king" *(mlkh);* but it has the vulgar termination in *-io,* like his household gods Felicio and Lucrio (60.8, cf. Martial 3.82.32). As for Habinnas, his name is clearly foreign. It is not in the *Corpus Inscriptionum Latinarum,* but a cognate *Abinnerici* (genitive) is; Αβεννήριγος appears in Josephus *(Jewish Antiquities* 20.22); Αβίνας is found in P. Jouguet, ed., *Papyrus de Théadelphie* (Paris, 1911) 65–66 for #5, lines 1, 9, and 17; and there is a city called Αβίννα in Susiana.[7]

These men are neither Roman nor Greek. They are Asians; they stem from the hybrid culture which grew out of the empires of Alexander the Great and his successors. (You will recall that Petronius was governor of the Asian province of Bithynia [Tacitus, *Annales* 16.18].) Ganymede says *cum primum ex Asia veni* (44.4). Hermeros declares he accepted slavery although he was of royal birth, in order to become a Roman citizen rather than a *tributarius* (57.4); and his claim is not unprecedented, since Claudius's freedman Pallas claimed descent from the kings of Arcadia (Tacitus, *Annales* 12.53), and Nero tried to have his sweetheart Acte connected with the royal house of the Attalids (Suetonius, *Nero* 28, and Dio Cassius, *Epitome* 61.7.1). Hermeros therefore was born in one of the half-barbarous frontier states. Trimalchio calls his friend Habinnas a Cappadocian (69.2) and does so as though he himself came from a neighboring region—that is how the Swedes talk of the Danes, and the Scots of the English. Once he tells his guests that he continued investing and taking profits until his wealth was as great as that of his *patria* (76.9). Either he is exaggerating his humble origins and his acquired wealth, or he comes from a small client kingdom. This is all part of the wave of Levantine immigration which Juvenal later was to denounce, declaring that most of

---

[7]M. Hadas, "Oriental Elements in Petronius," *AJPh* 50 (1929) 378–85, especially 383; A. H. Salonius, *Die Griechen und das griechische in Petrons Cena Trimalchionis* (Helsingfors, 1927) 6–7.

these scum were not true Greeks and that the Asian river Orontes had flowed into the Tiber (Juv. 3.61–66).[8]

Some of them, perhaps most, are *old men* approaching the terminus of their lives. Hermeros was a slave for forty years, starting as a boy of school age (57.9, 58.7, and 58.13), and then bought his freedom—so he is at least sixty. Ganymede too came to Italy when he was a boy (44.4 and 44.6), and he speaks as though that were long ago, a couple of generations back, when things were very different. Plocamus, whom the host calls up to sing, is old and gouty; his engine has run down (64.3). Trimalchio himself has made his will and is prepared for death; but a soothsayer has given him thirty-odd more years to live (77.2)—from which Gilbert Bagnani ingeniously conjectured that at the time of the banquet he was sixty-nine.[9]

Now it has often been suggested that the *Cena Trimalchionis* is modeled on Plato's *Symposium,* particularly since the irruption of the drunken Habinnas is parallel to the arrival of the drunken Alcibiades.[10] One resemblance which I have not seen pointed out is that there is no give-and-take of conversation as there is in Horace's symposium (*Serm.* 2.8). With rare exceptions, each guest makes one speech and then falls silent. But the *Cena* is not a party of young men like the *Symposium;* it is far more like a fiftieth class reunion. The *Symposium* of Plato has a central theme, appropriate for young fellows—Love. The *Banquet of Trimalchio* has a central theme, right for old men—Death.

Death runs all through it in a remarkable way. One of the guests is an undertaker (38.14–15 and 78.6), and another makes grave-monuments (65.5); he has indeed been commissioned to build the sepulcher of Trimalchio himself (71.5–12 and 74.17). Right at the start of the dinner a silver skeleton is thrown on the table, and the host, to encourage his guests to enjoy themselves, recites a short macabre poem on death (34.8–10). As soon as the conversation be-

---

[8][See G. Highet, *Juvenal the Satirist* (New York, 1954) 65–75, especially 71–72, for Highet's earlier comments on Juvenal's xenophobia, as he observed it in the context of *Satire* 3. Ed.]

[9][Bagnani's *Arbiter of Elegance: A Study of the Life & Works of C. Petronius* (Toronto, 1954)—the only work of this scholar cited by Highet—does not consider this question, as far as I have been able to determine. For the conjecture about Trimalchio's age, see Bagnani's two articles on Trimalchio—his "Trimalchio," *Phoenix* 8 (1954) 77–91, especially 84–91, and his "The House of Trimalchio," *AJPh* 75 (1954) 16–39, especially 35–36. Ed.]

[10]See A. Cameron, "Petronius and Plato," *CQ* 63 (1969) 367–70, who refers to earlier literature on this subject.

comes general, Seleucus announces that he has just come from a funeral and describes the last days of the dying Chrysanthus (42). This is followed by an obituary of Chrysanthus (43), and shortly afterward by a description of two gladiatorial shows with much emphasis on killing (45). A little later Trimalchio recalls having seen the Sibyl at Cumae; she said ἀποθανεῖν θέλω (48.8: "I wish to die"). Thereafter an acrobat falls on him; the guests regret the accident because they might be compelled *alienum mortuum plorare* (54.1: "to mourn for a stranger"). When two tales of the supernatural are told, the first begins with a death, that of Terentius the innkeeper (61.9), and the second is about witches stealing a corpse during a wake and killing the man who resisted them (63.4–10). Then Habinnas enters. He has come from a banquet given to honor a dead slave and resented having to pour half his wine over the bones of the dead (65.10–11). As the evening draws on, Trimalchio launches a bizarre series of speeches and displays centering on his own death and funeral. First he reads his will (71.1–4). Then he goes through the design of the elaborate monument on his grave and recites the inscription on it verbatim (71.5–12). Everybody mourns aloud as though he were already dead (72.1). After an interval Trimalchio hears a cock crowing and says it is a sign of someone's death (74.2). Then, inspired by a quarrel with his wife, he makes a long speech covering his entire career (75.8–77.6). Since this is not merely factual but is interlarded with sentences of praise—*virtute mea ad hoc perveni* (75.8) and *ad hanc me fortunam frugalitas mea perduxit* (75.10)—it reminds us of the *laudatio funebris* ("funeral eulogy") pronounced over an important person by a close relative. Last of all he has his own graveclothes brought out and exhibited along with the perfume to anoint his corpse, and then lies down as though already dead, and calls the trumpeters to play a funeral march (77.7–78.7).

I should have thought that such a superstitious man would consider all this to be an evil omen and would avoid such talk and such display. But Petronius was a fine psychologist and has shown us why Trimalchio does all this—because he believes the soothsayer who told him he had still more than thirty years to live. Look at his energy—playing handball, eating, drinking, kissing a pretty slave-boy, and talking incessantly on scores of different subjects. In his heart he believes death is far, far away. Nevertheless, during the evening he has to evacuate several times (27.5–6, 41.9, and 47.1–7), and a physician might well give him a dark prognosis. Like the old men in Juvenal who have hot baths after dinner, he will die soon and unexpectedly (Juv. 1.144).

Two more characteristics shared by all the speakers at this feast. They have total recall; and their horizon is limited to their community, to the *colonia* in which they live. Old men and women (especially if they are uneducated) can talk for hours about incidents that occurred forty or fifty years ago (Nestor is the first of a long line); and they do not care whether every detail in their story is relevant or not. So here. Habinnas, after protesting that his memory is treacherous, spends twenty-two lines on describing every single course at the banquet he has just attended (66). Others recall trifles from the past. Ganymede remembers Safinius, who "used to live by the old arch" (44.6). Niceros says that when he was still a slave, his people lived in a narrow lane, "where Gavilla's mansion is now" (61.6). Hermeros boasts that he arrived off the boat when he was a longhaired boy—"the town hall wasn't built yet" (57.9). All are long-time residents of the colony. And they expect all their listeners to understand all their local allusions. Echion sets out to praise the magistrates, who have been criticized by Ganymede, and talks like a small-town newspaper: Titus is going to put on a good show (45.5–6); Glyco has sent his accountant to fight wild beasts, but Glyco's wife is no good anyhow (45.7–9); Mammaea plans a public banquet, and if he gives it, he will beat Norbanus in the election (45.10–13). These people have never been mentioned before and will never be mentioned again, but apparently they are well-known local personalities. No one ever mentions any great event happening outside the confines of this little town—except the tale of the emperor who executed the inventor of unbreakable glass (51) and a few notes about prices in Rome and elsewhere. This is a small puddle, full of frogs who think themselves big batrachians.

Of the individual guests, the most voluble talker is Hermeros, Encolpius's informative neighbor. He has 133 lines (1,108 words) according to Mr. Dell'Era and his IBM machine.[11] To him we owe character sketches of two other freedmen (38.6–16) and of the hostess Fortunata, whom he dislikes (37.2–7); also a description of Trimalchio's luxurious habits (37.8–38.6); and—concealed inside his invectives against Ascyltos and Giton—his own autobiography (57–58). He is both the most ostentatiously humble and the touchiest of the guests, twice speaking to his neighbor as servant to mas-

---

[11][See A. Dell'Era, *Problemi di lingua e stile in Petronio* (Rome, 1970) 41–44. Ed.]

ter: *ignoscet mihi genius tuus* (37.3); and *servus tuus* (41.3), which often appears in the Bible and sounds Semitic.[12] But he bursts out in a rage when Encolpius's companions laugh at Trimalchio (57–58). His main interest is wealth acquired by men of humble origins and spent on conspicuous waste, especially on eating and drinking and house-furnishings. For such things as fine horses, beautiful slaves, and works of art, he shows no sympathy whatever. He does not conceal, but rather chooses to emphasize, the lower-class background of the hostess Fortunata and the other guests. Juvenal's friend Umbricius left Rome because he loathed such vulgar ways of making money as the profession of undertaker (Juv. 3.32), but Hermeros declares it a *honestam negotiationem* (Pet. 38.14).

He uses relatively more Greek words than the others: *topanta* (37.4), *saplutus* (37.6), *babae babae* closely followed by *babaecalis* (another of these unconscious repetitions [37.9 and 10]), *phantasia* (38.15), *thesauros* (57.9), *athla* (57.11), *Athana* (with a South Italian vowel [58.7]), *deurode* (58.7), *geometrias* (58.7), *alogias* (58.7), and *rhetoricam* (58.8).

Furthermore, he speaks more abruptly, in shorthand phrases like Dickens's Mr. Jingle, than any of the others: *nec quid nec quare* (37.4); *familia vero babae babae* (37.9); *amici de medio* (38.13); *phantasia, non homo* (38.15); *bellum pomum, qui rideatur alios* (57.3); *ego et tu sponsiunculam* (58.8); *Occuponem propitium* (58.11); *at nunc mera mapalia* (58.14).

One little oddity. The freedmen avoid using the ablative absolute. Although there are nearly 200 in Petronius's book, only four appear in the freedmen's speeches. Three are given to Trimalchio; and one introduces the dignified and elaborate final sentence of Hermeros's description of the proud bankrupt (38.16).[13]

Like several of the others, he is painfully conscious that he has never had a higher education, with such rubbish as *geometrias* and *critica* (58.7). He tries to compensate for this in two ways: by

---

[12]So Hadas (above, note 7) 380. But this is flatly denied by Suess (above, note 6) 8, who cites a religious designation of Janus as *divum deus* (Varro, *De Lingua Latina* 7.27) and *mearum cura curarum* from *Catalepton* 5.6, in the *Appendix Vergiliana*. A. Stefenelli, *Die Volkssprache im Werk des Petron im Hinblick auf die romanischen Sprachen* (Diss., Vienna, 1962) 66, says that the Italians of today say *il suo servo* for "I". And M. L. Wagner, "Über die Unterlagen der romanischen Phraseologie," *Volkstum und Kultur der Romanen* 6 (1933) 1–26, especially 13, says once he asked a Spanish guide who discovered certain grottoes, and got the reply *un servidor,* meaning the guide himself.
[13]This is noted by J. H. Howard, *Case Usage in Petronius' Satires* (Diss., Bloomington, 1899) 11.

proposing riddles as a test of intellectual agility (58.8–9) and by challenging his opponent to see which has better credit at the banker's (58.11).

By the way, several scholars have written studies connecting the language and some of the incidents of the *Satyrica* with modern Neapolitan and South Italian speech and folklore.[14] One of them recalls how, when he was staying at Anacapri with a Neapolitan friend, every morning as he left the house to have a swim, his friend would call out *col piede destro*—exactly like Trimalchio's slave, with his *dextro pede* (30.5). He had to start with the right foot; otherwise the whole day would be ruined.[15] Again, we are told that well through the dinner party, the cook brought in snails in a silver basket and sang in a hideous tremolo (70.7). Now in modern Naples, most of the street-cries are brisk and jolly; but the snail-sellers, who come out in the evening, advertise their *maruzze* with a long mournful chant. The cook is imitating them.[16] So it is not hard to see typical Neapolitan abuse in Hermeros's *lacticulosus* (57.8) = *puzza ancora di latte* ("still smelling of [mother's] milk") and *terrae tuber* (58.4) = *tartufo* ("truffle").

The drunk, conjecturally called Dama (41.10–12), speaks only 5 lines (43 words)[17] but manages to make an undue number of mistakes: *balneus* and *vinus* masculine; *versas,* a frequentative, for the simple *vertis;* two syncopations, *calfecit* and *calda.* But like many hard drinkers, he talks very fancily and imaginatively about booze: a drink puts warm clothes on you (another example of "identification"); *staminatas* ("good hairy ones"?) and *matus* ("spiflicated" or *kaputt*—only here and *Anth. Pal.* 487a20); probably *pataracina* is quoted from him too.

Seleucus (42), who speaks next, has 19 lines (155 words).[18] He is the most tactless of all. He begins by saying that he does not take a bath every day and that today he could not bathe because he was "to a funeral" (42.1–2). These are not topics to be introduced in social conversation, but neither he nor his friends show the slightest awareness of this. One of the most obscene Greek words in the whole *Cena* appears right at the beginning of his speech—the word *laecasin.*

---

[14]Stefenelli (above, note 12) and Wagner (above, note 12).

[15]Wagner (above, note 12) 6.

[16]Wagner (above, note 12) 6–7.

[17][See Dell'Era (above, note 11) 44. Ed.]

[18][See Dell'Era (above, note 11) 44. Ed.]

He is followed by Phileros (43), whose description of the deceased Chrysanthus covers 28 lines (218 words).[19] He is an advocate (46.8), and so he takes an adversary relationship to Seleucus, making out the dead man to have been a vile monster, admirable for nothing but his wealth—*solida centum* (43.2). Even his talent for making money is described in the disgusting statement "he would pick a cent out of a dunghill with his teeth" (43.1). Phileros used to be a peddler (46.8), and he still cannot speak very clearly; one of his specialties is the misuse of *ille,* which makes his account of Chrysanthus's quarrel with his brother very unclear and inelegant.

Now the subject is changed by Ganymede (44). He has 42 lines (340 words).[20] He is a poor man compared with the other guests. (Everyone is poor compared with Trimalchio.) He starts by complaining bitterly of the price of bread (44.1–2). This is very notable, following directly after the description of Chrysanthus, who died a very rich man (42–43) and in the midst of a banquet where so much elaborate food is wasted. Ganymede speaks for the *populus minutus,* mistreated by corrupt officials (44.3), and expresses admiration of old Safinius, who greeted everyone by name, *tamquam unus de nobis* (44.10). Toward the end he admits—with how much truth we cannot say—to being on the edge of bankruptcy (44.15). Although, like the others, he is an immigrant from Asia (44.4), he is deeply devoted to the old traditional Italian religious rites (44.17–18)—surely a sign of genuine Romanization. About his speech, which is quite vivid and convincing, there is only one noteworthy detail—he loves participial adjectives: *minutus* (44.3), *stolatae* (44.18), and *lanatos* (44.18).

Of all the guests, next to the voluble Hermeros, the rag picker Echion (45–46) makes the longest speech—76 lines (599 words).[21] This is a masterpiece of brutality and vulgarity. First he refutes Ganymede's criticism of the municipal officials by declaring that there will shortly be fine gladiatorial shows, with plenty of men killed, including some freed slaves (45.4) and a man fighting against wild animals (45.7–9). With obvious gusto he says no wounded fighter will be allowed to escape; there will be *carnarium in medio ut amphitheater videat* (45.6). Elsewhere *carnarium* means a place to hang up meat or generally a pantry. Here the context, as well as Echion's bloody-minded sadism, show that it

---

[19][See Dell'Era (above, note 11) 45. Ed.]
[20][See Dell'Era (above, note 11) 45–46. Ed.]
[21][See Dell'Era (above, note 11) 46–47. Ed.]

means "the butchery," that is, the *spoliarium*—where disabled gladiators had their throats cut (Seneca the Younger, *Epist.* 93.12). Usually this was done off-stage, but this time—as a special treat— it will be done *in medio* for all to enjoy. Let me remind you that some people in Rome would drink the warm blood of a dying gladiator, instead of Geritol.

Echion is not rich, for he says he is looking forward to a public banquet at which the host, a candidate for public office, will hand out two *denarii* to each diner (45.10). His host Trimalchio had done just that some time earlier (71.9–10).

Thereafter Echion turns to Agamemnon, the professor of rhetoric, and attempts to flatter him by saying that he has two boys who are devoted to learning; one of them can already multiply by four (46.3–8). This is an elegant combination—the voluble rag picker praising bloody butchery and patronizing intellectuals.

His language contains many blunders and vulgarisms. He cannot even get *loqui* right but makes it active instead of deponent— two times, in a direct address to the teacher of literature (46.1). (Seleucus has it correctly in 42.3, and oddly enough Echion gets the imperative correct in 45.1.) Only he uses *quia* as a conjunction with words of saying and thinking (45.10 and 46.4): this was to become common in later Latin, but Echion is the first to say it in extant texts. He alone commits such a gross debasement of accidence as *pauperorum* (46.1). He also has one magnificent hapax legomenon—*burdubasta* (45.11), which Hadas says is Aramaic for "pit of shamefulness." (The second element looks like the Hebrew *bosheth,* meaning "shame," which pious Hebrews used instead of Baal—e.g., in the name of Saul's son Ishbosheth, altered from Ishbaal.) And he finishes his eulogy of literature addressed to Professor Agamemnon with an exquisite malapropism—*litterae thesaurum est* (46.8). (Hermeros gets *thesaurus* right in 57.9.) Like several of the other guests, he sometimes tries to be extra elegant, hyperurbane: so *artificii docere* (46.7) is a polite attempt to avoid saying *de* with the ablative;[22] and only Echion produces fancy periphrastic futures such as *habituri sumus* (45.4) and *daturus est* (45.10).

Niceros (61–62), who talks for 55 lines (398 words),[23] telling the story of the werewolf, does least to conceal his origins as a slave. When we recall that Augustus would never admit any freedman

---

[22]Suess (above, note 6) 70–71. Contrast *de iure* (46.7), *de scriblita* (66.3), and *de melle* (66.3).
[23][See Dell'Era (above, note 11) 47–49. Ed.]

to his table—except Menas and one special agent (Suetonius, *Augustus* 74)—we can imagine the effect made on Petronius's audience by a story which begins "when I was still a slave" and goes on to tell how the narrator saved up his *peculium* (61.6–8). He guarantees the truth of his tale by the oath *genios vestros iratos habeam* (62.14), which implies that the other guests are masters and he still a servant. He is quite uneducated and is afraid the *scholastici* may laugh at him (61.4). Well they might, for he specializes in getting cases wrong: *persuadeo* with the accusative (62.2); *adiuto* with the dative (62.11); *exire* with the dative of motion (62.1); and a beautiful anacoluthon about the wolf which *omnia pecora . . . sanguinem illis misit* (62.11).

Habinnas the Cappadocian is drunk when he arrives and combines affectations of elegance with brutal bad taste. In all he speaks 49 lines (380 words).[24] First he takes the best seat in the house (65.7) and then refuses to stay unless the hostess Fortunata sits down (67.1–3). Very gallant, but a few minutes later he plays an embarrassing practical joke on her (67.12–13). He refers to his wife Scintilla as *domina mea* (66.5, cf. 67.9), but then tells with apparent gusto how she vomited at a dinner party (66.5), inveighs against her extravagance with an extreme epigram—*caldum meiere et frigidum potare* (67.10), and later launches into a eulogy of a slaveboy, obviously his catamite—*recutitus est et stertit* (68.8), informing the company what he paid for the little wretch—*illum emi trecentis denariis* (69.1). His wife protests (69.1), but he publicly caresses the slaveboy (69.5). She swallows this in silence. These women know who is boss. Throughout the entire banquet Fortunata is heard speaking only half a dozen words, and Scintilla, only nineteen.

These seven men are the chief speakers at Trimalchio's banquet—similar in language and in level of culture, but very different in emotional tone and subject-matter. Altogether they speak 402 lines. You will scarcely be surprised to hear that their host Trimalchio speaks nearly as much as all put together—400 lines (3,021 words).[25] He is an inexhaustible talker. His subjects, like his interests, are few in number, but he goes back and forward over them like a cross-town bus.

His chief interest is *himself*—his physical health, his wealth, his past, his future, his wife, his will, and his funeral. To this all-important topic he devotes ten passages, some of them very

---

[24][See Dell'Era (above, note 11) 49–50. Ed.]
[25][See Dell'Era (above, note 11) 36–41. Ed.]

lengthy, from which we can easily extract an outline of his biography.

Next in importance, judging by the number of references and words devoted to it, is the subject of food and wine and utensils for eating and drinking, and the techniques of table service. He mentions these eleven times.

His guests are given orders and permissions and encouragements seven times.

His slaves occupy his conversation ten times at least. His attitude to them is very awkward. Having himself been a slave, he does not know how to behave to his own slaves. Therefore he wavers between extreme severity and excessive friendliness. He calls them *putidissimi servi* in 34.5. At the entrance his guests see a warning notice proclaiming that any slave who goes out without permission will get 100 lashes (28.7). A slaveboy who picks up a dropped dish is punished with slaps (34.2). A cook is warned to be careful; otherwise he will be transferred to the *viatores,* the dispatch-runners (47.13). Later, when he forgets to gut the pig, he is stripped for flogging and stands gloomily between two torturers (49.6). It is a joke, but a cruel joke. (Martial [8.23] speaks of flogging a cook quite as a matter of course.) During the reading of the daily *acta* of his estates, we are told casually that a slave was crucified for cursing Trimalchio's *genius* (53.3). After an accident, a slave who made the mistake of using white rather than purple wool for his master's bandage is flogged (54.4). Toward the end of the banquet, when he is quite drunk, he calls for a servant to display his funeral clothes, and in the most genial way says: "Keep mice and moths out of them, or else I'll burn you alive" (78.2).

At the same time, he is far too familiar with his domestics. He sets individual slaves free quite casually—a *puer speciosus* (41.6–8) and a *puer* (54.1–5). As the banquet proceeds, he kisses two boys (64.11 and 74.8) and makes a party out of a slave's beard-cutting festival (73.6). Finally he invites all the staff to join his guests at table (70.10–12), which tells his guests what he thinks of them.

One trait very marked in Trimalchio's character is capriciousness. He simply does not notice his glaring inconsistencies. Just before having his will read, he declares that according to its provisions all his slaves are to be set free—*me salvo cito aquam liberam gustabunt* (71.1). This is the very opposite of what he means, which is *me mortuo.*[26] At another moment he directs that a statue of Fortunata be placed on his tomb, holding a dove as a symbol of true

---

[26]Noted by Suess (above, note 6) 75.

affection (71.11); shortly afterward he has thrown a wine-cup in her face and rescinded the order (74.10 and 17). Then, in a laudatory account of his career, he emphasizes that his own merits brought him to his present eminence (75.8 and 10), but then proceeds to explain that his owner and patron left him a huge sum of money (76.2), and that Fortunata once sold all her clothes and jewelry to help him through a financial difficulty—*hoc fuit peculii mei fermentum* (76.7). A moment later he is calling her "this viper" (77.4).

The best educated man at the party, Agamemnon the rhetorician, is never invited to speak—except once, when his words are not reported and when Trimalchio cuts him down (48.5–6). But Trimalchio loves to display his own learning and to recite poetry, some of it his own. Five large passages are devoted to his cultural monologues, all full of mistakes in history and mythology far more monstrous than his errors in grammar and accidence. There are also recitations from Vergil, with the text corrupted by insertions of comic verse (68.4–5), and a battle scene from Homer represented by Greek-speaking actors, which Trimalchio explains with ludicrous inaccuracy (59.3–5). Virtually all his display of learning is wrong—as wrong as his taste and his behavior. (In 55.5–6 he repeats a fine poem which he attributes to Publius [so the MS]. I cannot understand this. Judging by his gross blunders in mythology and history, and comparing the dismally poor poems which he quotes or improvises elsewhere, I cannot see how he could have recited *from memory* sixteen lines of highly elaborate poetry [*pietaticultrix gracilipes crotalistria*] without apparently a single boo-boo and without explicating it later. The joke may be that the poem was written by someone well known to Petronius's audience and that Trimalchio got its authorship wrong; but that is much more subtle than the rest of his foolish blunders and not so funny.)

In spite of his Semitic name and his Asian origin, Trimalchio is eager to become a genuine Roman. While the *Homeristae* are performing in Greek, he ostentatiously reads a libretto in Latin (59.3). He has a library of Greek books and a library of Latin books (48.4); but he never quotes anything from Greek literature, and he gets Greek myths wrong. He can make bilingual puns though (56.7–9). He prefers Atellan farce to Greek comedy, and he has instructed his clarinet-player to play in Latin (53.13). I suppose this means simple Italian folk songs and no foreign music. So Henry Fielding's Squire Western objected to hearing his daughter play Handel on the harpsichord (*Tom Jones,* Book 4, chap. 5):

His most favourite tunes were *Old Sir Simon the King, St. George he was for England, Bobbing Joan,* and some others.

All Trimalchio's estates are in Italy (71.12 and 38.1–3). He prefers to be called by his praenomen Gaius, the mark of a free man (30.3, 50.1, 53.3, 67.1, 74.7, and 75.2). He is one of the *seviri Augustales* and would dearly love to be a Roman knight. In his epitaph he makes no mention of his Asian origin, but like an antique Roman, styles himself *pius, fortis, fidelis* (71.12).

Trimalchio's language has one special quality which expresses his character: it is self-assertive, emphatic, even over-emphatic. Take his story of visiting the Sibyl. How does he say that he actually saw the old prodigy? *Sibyllam . . . ego ipse oculis meis vidi* (48.8). (This is pointed out by Dell'Era.)[27] Although there are plenty of superlatives in the general narrative of the *Satyrica,* only twelve appear in the conversation of the freedmen; of these six are used by Trimalchio.[28] His former master and mistress he styles *ipsimus* and *ipsima* (69.3, 75.11, and 76.1); odd that he never once names them. Double negatives are used once by Seleucus (42.7) and once by Habinnas (75.1); twice at close range by Trimalchio (76.3 and 76.5). The one thing about which he is evasive, euphemistic, even shy, is his sexual life with his owners when he was a young slave. Yet he cannot keep his mouth shut about it, as anyone with decent feelings would do; he keeps coming back to it. Once, coining an intensive compound to avoid the regular *futuo,* he says *ego sic solebam ipsimam meam debattuere* (69.3); then later he says *ad delicias ipsimi annos quattuordecim fui . . . ego tamen et ipsimae satisfaciebam* (75.11); later still he says the soothsayer told him about his past, including the secret *tu dominam tuam de rebus illis fecisti* (77.1).

Looking at their names (one Ganymede and three Erotes), and reading their reminiscences, and watching their behavior with slave boys, we are tempted to conjecture that all these men, when they were young, were used as 'chickens' by their slave owners, really enslaved until they said and believed *nec turpe est quod dominus iubet* (75.11)—the ultimate human degradation.[29]

---

[27][See Dell'Era (above, note 11) 68. Ed.]

[28]Howard (above, note 13) 11.

[29][For a recent study of characterization in Petronius's banquet episode, see the revised doctoral dissertation of B. Boyce, *The Language of the Freedmen in Petronius' Cena Trimalchionis* (Leiden, 1991). Ed.]

Apuleius's *Golden Ass*[*]

Let me tell you a story. It is one of the most peculiar stories in the whole world.

Once upon a time there was a young man called Lucius. Like most young men, he was inquisitive, energetic, irresponsible, and optimistic. He liked wild adventures. He loved pretty girls. He was a bit of a donkey. His father died and left him some money, and he set out on his travels. In time he came to a part of the world which was famous for something not to be found everywhere, something rare and almost unbelievable—not its scenery, nor its climate, nor its food, nor its wealth and luxury, nor the beauty of its women—none of these. This country was famous because it was a home of magic. It was not Haiti, but it had the same kind of reputation as Haiti: voodoo festivals, sinister drums beating in the darkness, love spells and death enchantments, men possessed by powerful spirits, sorcerers who could raise the dead and control them as the Haitian wizards control the zombies. Even the rocks beside the road might be human beings, petrified by some malevolent witch.

Young Lucius found all this very exciting, particularly after he heard some firsthand accounts of the power of these magicians. He had a letter of introduction to a businessman in the capital of the country. He presented it. He was asked to stay; he accepted. The house was not very comfortable (because the owner was a moneylender, who watched every cent), but there was a very pretty housemaid, with a fine figure and a beautiful head of hair, long wavy hair. Lucius liked good figures, and he loved long wavy hair, and quite soon he had become very good friends with the girl. Her name was Fotis. I do not know how long he might have lingered in that house, but he learned that his hostess, the moneylender's wife, was an experienced witch, and naturally he was anxious to see her at work. He wanted to find out whether or not there was anything in this stuff about magic. So he persuaded Fotis (the maid) to tell him when a spell was being cast. He had means of persuading her.

One day she told him that that very evening her mistress was going to change herself into a bird and fly out to visit a young man

---

[*]Presented in 1955 on Highet's radio program (= *BMCT* 21–22).

she loved. After sunset, stealthily, walking on tiptoe, the young couple approached the witch's bedroom, peered through a chink, and watched her; they saw the whole process. First she undressed completely. Then she opened a cupboard containing several jars of ointment. She chose one, took off the lid, and smeared herself from head to foot with the magical salve. Then she muttered a spell or a prayer. Gradually her skin grew into feathers, her arms changed into wings and her toenails into talons, her nose grew crooked and sharp, her face changed into a furry mask, and her eyes became large and staring. She was an owl; and with the hoot of an owl, she stretched her wings and flew off into the darkness.

Lucius was terribly excited by this. He had always wanted to fly through the air. Now he told his sweetheart that he must try the same prescription and become a bird—if only he could find some way of changing back into a man. She reassured him. She said that she knew all the antidotes, for she always had to rub her mistress down on her return, to restore her to the shape of a woman. So she went into the witch's room, fetched out a jar of ointment, and gave it to Lucius. He rubbed it all over himself and said a short prayer for a successful flight; and then he watched his arms, to see the feathers appearing. They did not. No feathers grew. No wings were fledged. Instead the skin on Lucius's arms became coarser and coarser and heavier and heavier. His fingers bunched together into hard lumps; so did his toes. His body thickened into something strong and gross. His spine tingled, and he felt a long tail growing out of it. Worst of all, his face swelled up and became long and hairy, with two tremendous ears sticking out of it. He had not become a bird. He had changed into a jackass.

Poor Lucius! He tried to say something to his sweetheart, but he couldn't speak. He could only look sadly at her out of his big watery eyes and shake his long ears. As for her, she had the good grace not to laugh. She cried and said it was all her fault for picking out the wrong box of ointment. However, she knew the antidote for this transformation too. To change back into human shape, all Lucius had to do was to eat some fresh roses. First thing in the morning, she said, she would go out and get some for him, but meanwhile, being a jackass, perhaps Lucius would be more comfortable in the stable?

With a heavy heart Lucius trotted down to the stable, where he was welcomed by his own thoroughbred horse with a kick in the face. He had only six or seven hours to wait until the morning, when he would eat the fresh roses and change back into a man—

but there's many a slip between the rose and the lip. That same night the moneylender's house was broken into by armed gangsters, who carried out all his valuables, loaded them on the horse and the jackass, and drove away into the trackless hills.

And now Lucius's adventures really began. No one knew where he was, not even his sweetheart. He couldn't speak. Once, when he was passing a village, he tried to shout for *help,* but nothing came out except *haw.* Worst of all, he was kept tied up so tightly that he could never get near a rose garden, and presently the season for roses passed, so that he saw himself condemned to many months of suffering worse than slavery. Whenever you see a donkey looking sadly at the ground, or lifting its head and baring its teeth and pumping its lungs in that comical yet despairing *heehaw,* reflect whether it may not be a young man bewitched and longing for some fresh roses.

Lucius's first adventure was that the gangsters who had stolen him went out on another expedition. They returned with a beautiful young woman, disheveled and weeping. She was the daughter of a rich man; they had kidnapped her and were holding her for ransom. After she had spent some time there, Lucius broke his rope in an unguarded moment, stopped to take her on his back, and bolted off for freedom, but—alas!—the bandits caught them, took them back to their headquarters, and set about planning a hideous death for them both. Just before the torture and murder started, another gangster with a famous reputation joined the group, contributed $10,000 in gold to the treasury of the gang, and proposed a party to celebrate. The gangsters accepted; they drank freely; the drinks were all drugged, and they fell fast asleep. The new bandit was the kidnapped girl's fiancé, who had risked his life to save her. The gangsters were overpowered, the girl was taken back home, the marriage took place, and the donkey Lucius was smothered with thanks and stuffed with barley—but no roses.

He waited. Yet he was still plagued by disaster. Just after the honeymoon ended, the young couple was killed by a jealous lover, and Lucius was sold to the first bidders, who happened to be a fantastic group of traveling fakirs, combining religious fanaticism, vice, and petty swindling. It was not long before they were arrested, and Lucius was sold again. This time he was bought by the owner of a mill, who used him as a machine—harnessing him to a heavy mill wheel, blinkering him and whipping him round and round to turn the millstone. Surely he had touched bottom by now, thought Lucius, the poor bewitched outcast, who could see nothing ahead but death. Fortunately, the miller was driven to suicide by his wicked wife, and Lucius was sold once again.

This time he was bought by the servants of a rich and distinguished government official. They were in charge of the old gentleman's kitchen, so that for the first time Lucius had a chance to eat something better than barley and hay. You see, he had retained all his human tastes as well as his intelligence. After every big dinner party, while the servants were relaxing, Lucius used to eat up most of the leftovers—a little leg of chicken here, some cheese straws there, a touch of marzipan, a few fruit tarts; it was a delightful change after all that vegetarian diet, and he soon grew fat and sleek. The servants began to notice it. They kept watch and caught Lucius at his banquet. But this time he was not flogged. They thought it was so wonderful to see a donkey eating like a civilized human being that they laughed heartily. Their master overheard; he joined them, laughed even more heartily, and invited the jackass to supper. Lucius was delighted. He did himself well, choosing all the tastiest things, even when they were least like a donkey's usual diet. The old gentleman watched with amusement and finally offered him a large goblet of honeyed wine. Sure enough, the donkey licked his lips and drank off the wine with leisurely appreciation.

Anyone who can eat and drink like a gentleman is at least half-human, thought the rich old official, and he had the jackass trained—how to recline politely at table, how to dance, and how to communicate in sign language. Lucius had been careful not to be *too* intelligent right away. If a donkey shows signs of excessive intelligence, people are apt to distrust it, particularly in government circles; any politician knows that. So he learned slowly but steadily, and he was better and better treated, until the awful purpose of all this training was disclosed. His master was a Roman government official, who was expected to give a huge gladiatorial show; the climax of it was to be a display both obscene and cruel, given in the circus by the donkey and a condemned murderess—after which they were both to be eaten alive by wild beasts.

On the day of the performance—the day scheduled for his disgrace and death—Lucius thought of committing suicide, but he could not find any way of killing himself. So he behaved as gently and mildly as possible, cropping the new grass of spring, until his attendants left him alone to watch the opening of the circus show. Seizing an exciting moment in the ring, he strolled gently away, turned a corner, and ran six miles at full gallop until he reached the sea, and there, in a lonely corner of the beach, he lay down and fell asleep.

When he woke, the moon was rising. He gazed at her—it's a bizarre and haunting scene, isn't it?—the hunted and condemned donkey, with his great moony eyes, gazing at the rising moon; he thought of her as a divinity. He plunged his big head seven times in the sea to purify himself, and then he prayed to her as the Queen of Heaven to have pity on him and rescue him from his bestial state. In answer to his prayer a goddess appeared—the divinity of nature—but known, she told him, as Isis. Next day, she warned him, there would be a procession in her honor, in which the high priest would carry a wreath of roses. Lucius was to eat the roses and be transformed back into a man; thenceforth he would be dedicated to her service. With delight Lucius accepted this condition.

Next morning he went to meet the procession. The crowd parted before him. The priest stood still and held out the garland of roses, which seemed for the moment like a crown of victory. With trembling lips and pounding heart Lucius ate them. And gradually his beastly face changed back into human shape, his rough hair fell away, his great hard teeth shrank into their proper size, his ears diminished, his tail vanished, and his hooves changed into soft hands and feet. He was a man. Within an instant he was covered with a pure white linen robe and became a part of the procession of worshipers.

Of course his friends and relatives had thought he was dead. Now when they heard of his miraculous reappearance, they hurried to send him money and clothes. He was restored to humanity. But he could not resume his old way of life. He became a devotee of the goddess, and went through more and more intimate and difficult initiation ceremonies, which marked him as a dedicated man. Also he embarked on a steady career as a lawyer and had much success. His practice grew and prospered. Neither he nor his clients ever realized that he had qualified to be a lawyer by spending a long, long time as a miserable jackass—flogged, underfed, speechless, and hopeless.

*   *   *

Now I must tell you the name of the story and who wrote it. It is called the *Metamorphoses* or *Transformations*. And it was written about the year 150 A.D. by a mysterious and attractive character called Apuleius. A new English translation of it has recently come out, done by that intelligent eccentric Robert Graves and called

The Golden Ass of Apuleius.[1] Much as I dislike the book, or some aspects of it, I must admit that it is one of the great stories of the world. It is more than a mere story.

The fantastically decorative style of the book (which makes it so hard to read in Latin) does not appear at all in Graves's translation. He makes it seem straightforward, no nonsense, clear, brisk and energetic. The original Latin is richly musical, and exquisitely complex in structure, and full of very strange words, and overgrown with a tropical exuberance of phrasing; it sounds like Marcel Proust without his occasional simplicity, like James Joyce without his frequent vulgarity. There is no modern writer who has woven such a rich fabric of style throughout an entire book, and so there is no translator who can render the *Golden Ass* in any style intelligible to us without making it appear so exotic as to be ridiculous. How can I convey the feeling of the Latin to you? Can you imagine the subject matter of Henry Miller and Franz Kafka, couched in a style like that of John Ruskin and J.-K. Huysmans, with a strong flavor of Richard Burton's translation of the *Arabian Nights?* That would approach Apuleius.

Quite apart from the style, I have simplified the structure of the book so that you could follow and appreciate the story. There is not one story but many—fifteen or twenty stories interwoven with the main fabric, after the pattern we know from the *Arabian Nights.* Some are funny, some are shocking, some are weirdly fanciful. One at least is of immortal beauty. This is the tale of a beautiful girl who (because of an offense against a god) was condemned to marry a monster. She did not see the monster and yet came to love him. One night, when he had fallen asleep, she ventured to bring in a lamp and found that he was not a monster; he was handsome, divinely handsome; but by discovering him, she lost him and had to go through endless trials before she was reunited with him. And his name was Cupid (or Love); and her name was Psyche (or the Soul). The entire story is an allegory of the power of love over the human soul—how unconsciously it comes upon us, how difficult it is to appreciate, how much suffering it inflicts upon us, and how (after all is endured) love becomes the true meaning of our lives.

But how about the main story—this long piece of fantasy about a man turned into a donkey and turned back again by eating roses and being dedicated to the moon? Do you suppose this thing has

---

[1][See R. Graves, *The Golden Ass of Apuleius* (New York, 1954)—published by Pocket Library in 1954, but originally published by Farrar, Straus, and Giroux in 1951. Ed.]

any real meaning? Frankly, the first time I read it, I thought it had none. And then I remembered the tale of Cupid and Psyche. There it was, inset into the *Golden Ass*—this story of the loving girl and the invisible bridegroom, who was thought to be a monster and who proved to be love itself; a story told by a drunken old hag in a gangsters' hideout to a terrified girl and overheard by a tormented donkey. No, this was not merely a silly piece of fantasy-fiction; it must have a deep symbolic meaning, and it must have been written by an intelligent and imaginative man. Therefore the main story must also have some meaning. Frankly, the casual reader, if he were exceptionally clean-minded or dirty-minded, might conclude that the tale had been written merely to titillate; the pure would turn from it in disgust; the others would gloat over it. Only the gross-minded, if they had any intelligence, would also begin to learn from it; they might begin to find out that they too were jackasses, and they might start to discern something of their character and their destiny.

Lucius was a young man. He had a sensual love affair with a pretty girl who meant nothing more to him than a handsome body and a lovely head of hair. He tried to fly like a bird but turned into a donkey. He was humiliated and threatened with death; he was scorned and maltreated; finally he was flattered by being treated like a human being, but only so that he could be still more grossly humiliated and then killed in torment. He appealed to God. He was miraculously saved. He became a fully mature man, with a career and a sense of morality and a religion which would not desert him thereafter.

What kind of story is this? Surely it is a variation of one of the most interesting types of story in the world—the tale of a young man's growing up. The ladies will not understand this entirely, nor wholly sympathize with it, but it is true. Every youth has to pass through a period when he is a bit of a beast. He may look more or less human, but he is gross and hairy; he kicks everything with heavy hooves; he cannot speak rationally, but he brays loudly, and even if he complains, it does not sound like a rational complaint but rather like *heehaw, heehaw.* He eats prodigiously; he is excessively, even repulsively, ungraceful; he upsets everything by merely turning around; and yet somehow we know that inside that hairy hide and behind those crude features there lurks a human being. And he himself, poor Lucius (or whatever we call him)—when he gazes in the looking glass, sees a donkey, and yet he feels like a poet, a lover, a hero—if he could only find the roses which will bloom next spring. This is a novel about growing up—what the Germans call a *Bildungsroman*—like James Joyce's *Ulysses,* and Thomas Wolfe's novels, and Henry Fielding's *Tom Jones,* and Charles Dickens's *David Copperfield,* and Thomas Mann's *Joseph* series, and many more. Growing up—it is one of the great themes of fiction. What tragedies it involves, and what comedies, and what farces! The adolescent is a hero and at the same time a clown; he is a donkey trying to become a saint or at least a reasonable human being.

But the story is something else as well. It is told in the first person; the young man speaks of himself as "I" (= "I, Lucius"). Now and then he drops hints about his origin and his career. They are not prominent, but they are there, and a careful reading discloses them. He says that he came from a place in North Africa called Madaura; he explains that he studied philosophy and religion; and he tells us that he became an experienced speaker. Now we have several other books by the same author, Apuleius, and we know some external facts about him. From these we learn that the author himself came from Madaura in North Africa, studied philosophy and religion, and became an experienced speaker.[2] (And in fact the individual and skillful style of his book is enough to show that he was a brilliantly gifted writer.) Therefore his work is in some sense an autobiography. The author can scarcely mean that he was magically transformed into a jackass and driven off by gangsters, but by putting in so many hints which identify him with his hero, he means that he went through the same *kind* of adventure. The book is also a symbolic confession. In Apuleius's time the jackass was a symbol of coarseness, cruelty, and sensuality. The story, which looks like a magical romance about a man changed into a beast, is an indirect description of the author's own youth— telling how through irresponsibility and grossness he became more like an animal than a man, and how he at last emerged from this state through a religious conversion which seemed like a miracle. With this in mind, it is astonishing to reread the *Confessions* of St. Augustine, who was also born in North Africa (some two hundred years later), who followed the same career as a student of philosophy and an orator, who fell into the same pit of sensuality, and who—after similar agonies—was rescued from it by a miraculous conversion.

---

[2][See St. Augustine, *City of God* 8.12, on Apuleius's homeland; Apuleius's *Florida* 18 and 20 for the subjects that he studied; and his *Apologia* for his experience as a speaker. Ed.]

There is one important difference between the two books. St. Augustine became a devout Christian. Apuleius became a devotee of Isis and Osiris, and of other mystical divinities. He was not a Christian at all, and in one passage he even seems to take a nasty crack at Christianity. Still, at the time he wrote, Christianity had not spread widely and had not developed the kind of philosophical system which would appeal to such a man. Instead, the whole Western world had a large and superficial state religion, to which almost anyone could subscribe as a matter of duty, with his eyes half-shut; it also had several highly developed and mutually conflicting systems of philosophy; but it had very few religions which really responded to fundamental human needs, to the sense of awe, to our feeling of inadequacy, to our longing for the symbolic and the mystical, to our wish to quit ourselves of our own impurity. Several such religions were coming out of the Middle East. They all filled a deep need in the hearts of men of that age. One of them was the worship of the Queen of Heaven; whether she was called Isis (as she is here), or the Corn Queen, or Mother Nature, or Diana of the Ephesians, she had many devotees; she made them happy and (at least some of them) good.

As we look back, it seems as though the whole pagan world had been groping to find a satisfying religion and had made many false experiments before at last discovering it in Christianity. If you accept that, then this peculiar book about the youth who became a donkey and emerged to become a religious votary is also a symbolic description of the religious conversion of the Greek and Roman world—a world which, beginning as naive and sensual, became beastly, and then, almost through a miracle outside logic, became aware of loftier spiritual values. It found, arising from the sea of doubt, a deity which was the divinity of nature and of purity and of universal law. And so the book about the miraculous donkey is (whether its author knew it or not) an anticipation of one of the greatest events in history—the conversion of Greece and Rome to the Christian religion.

So then, silly and even repulsive as it appears, this book—the *Metamorphoses* or *Transformations*—is a symbolic masterpiece which conceals many important truths. (By the way, the man and the donkey—do they not remind you of those two faithful comrades, Don Quixote and his squire Sancho Panza—the adventurous, idealistic spirit and the coarse, humorous body mysteriously attached to it?) The ambitious youth who wants, without much work but rather by magic, to become an owl, the symbol of intellec-

tual wisdom, and who only manages to become a donkey—is he
not a familiar type? Some scholars have failed to see the symbolism; they have even thought that the book must be two different
works—the early part, with its coarse sensuality and its wild adventures, forming one volume; and the end, with its lofty religious
vision, a sequel written by someone quite different.[3] See the effect of
'scientific method' as applied to literature. Apuleius wanted to explain the process of conversion, in which a human being is regen-
erated, so that he becomes a different being almost unrecognizable
even by himself. So scholars have suggested that the book must be
by two different people.

But we must not blame them too much. The book has not yet
been completely understood. Realistic books are easily assimilated;
symbolic books last for centuries. Read this strange story yourselves and see what you think of it. It is a picaresque vision of a
world not too unlike our own, with just as much sex, with much
less cruelty, with rather more vulgarity, with much better aesthetic perception, with the same kind of religious groping, and with
the same irreducible residue of that element which remains even
in the prisoner and in the tortured half-animal, man, the essential
vitamin of the spirit, Hope.[4]

---

[3][For a survey of these scholars' opinions, see C. C. Schlam, *The Structure
of the Metamorphoses of Apuleius* (New York, 1968) 4–31—a doctoral dissertation for which Highet served as an adviser. Ed.]
[4][See C. C. Schlam, *The Metamorphoses of Apuleius: On Making an Ass of
Oneself* (Chapel Hill, 1992)—the culmination of this scholar's research on
this challenging and entertaining Latin classic. Ed.]

Apuleius's Cupid and Psyche*

Here is a marvelous story. It was told many hundreds of years ago by a skillful storyteller. It has often been interpreted in art and music and poetry and later fiction and even psychology, but it has never been fully understood. It was first told (so far as we know) in a very odd place for a very strange purpose.

A girl was kidnapped by gangsters and held for ransom. She was overcome with terror and grief—grief because she had been engaged to be married and was actually stolen upon her wedding morning; terror because the bandits might torture her if her ransom were not paid at once. The gangsters hid her in a lonely cave in the hills and set a horrible old woman to look after her. The girl had hysterics and threatened to kill herself. In order to divert her and perhaps to encourage her, the old woman told her the story of Cupid and Psyche.

Psyche was the name of a young and beautiful princess. She was so beautiful (this was long ago in the pagan days) that people began to say she was beauty incarnate; she was the divine embodiment of beauty; she was the goddess Venus—alive, visible, tangible, in a breathing and beautiful body. They worshiped her. And she? She felt lonely and unhappy.

She had good reason. The real goddess Venus was infuriated. She called in her son Cupid to help—Cupid, not a pretty little child with toy wings and a toy bow, but a grave and handsome youth, the living expression of passionate desire. She told him to make the girl Psyche fall in love with some hideous monster, some being beneath the lowest levels of degradation; and he set about obeying her.

Now although Psyche was so beautiful—or perhaps because she was so beautiful—she could not find a husband. Her father asked a divine oracle where to find a bridegroom for her. Instead of receiving an encouraging response, he was told that he must take his daughter to the top of a lonely mountain and leave her there, to become the mate of a demon, a cruel and irresistible devil. Her parents mourned for her as though she had died in a disastrous accident; they were sure they would never see her again, and they

---

*Presented in 1957 on Highet's radio program (= BMCT 90–91).

were in agony about her ghastly future. But they had to obey the commands of heaven. They took her to the mountaintop, and left her, and went home, and closed the doors and windows of their house, and pulled the curtains tight and dark, and wept for their lost child.

The girl stood on the top of the mountain—alone, trembling and crying, waiting for the monster which was to approach her. At first nothing happened, nothing whatever. Then a gentle wind began to blow, the warm west wind. It surrounded her and played with her dress; it lifted her off the ground, carried her lightly down into a green valley, and laid her to rest on a bed of grass and flowers. There she slept for a time. When she awoke, it was still daylight. She saw a quiet wood nearby, through which there flowed a clear stream. She followed the stream through the wood—the water glowing dull silver in the dusk and glimmering among the dark trees like a bright path—and soon she came to a great palace, beautifully built and sumptuously furnished, but quite empty, standing alone as though waiting for its lady and its lord.

She went in. She was welcomed, not by servants but by disembodied voices and invisible hands, which made her comfortable, helped her to bathe and dress in a wedding dress, and served her a bridal dinner to the accompaniment of music from unseen musicians. The night grew late. Terrified and lonely, and yet unexpectedly happy, she went to bed. The house was silent until about midnight a whispering began, and grew closer and closer. It was her bridegroom. In the darkness she could not see him; but he did not behave like a monster; he behaved like a lover, and soon she was his wife and he her husband. Before daybreak he left her. He returned again the following night and the night after that, always in darkness. In time, although she had never yet seen him, she grew to look forward to his visits, to fear him no longer, and in fact to love him as he loved her.

She had almost forgotten her parents, and they had given her up for lost. But she had two sisters older than she—one married to an invalid and one married to a cripple. They had always envied her her youth and beauty. Now they searched for her until they found her living in the lonely palace. Psyche welcomed them sweetly. Although she could not introduce them to her husband and could not even describe who he was, she said he was terribly kind; she made up a rather unconvincing story about him; he had a short beard, and was away a good deal because he liked hunting. The two sisters saw through this at once. They explained to her tactfully but firmly that she had been destined to marry a horrible and lethal monster; she had now done so and was simply trying to conceal her own ignorance and terror. She ought, they said, to take action, dominate the situation, and defend herself before being destroyed. They advised her the very next night to prepare a concealed lamp and a knife. After her husband had visited her and fallen asleep, they said she should quietly bring out the lamp, and when she saw the monster sleeping beside her, then cut its throat or plunge the knife deep in its heart. She was pregnant too, they added, and this was the only way of protecting her child as well as herself.

Poor Psyche was torn with a horrible conflict. She did not love her sisters, but they were older than she, they were experienced married women, blood was thicker than water, and somehow she had to trust them. She did love her mysterious husband, but she had never looked into his eyes; she was all alone in the world, and perhaps he really was a cruel monster which was merely softening up its prey. And she had an irresistible curiosity, so that she had to know more, even if it meant killing the thing she loved.

Next night, when the sisters were gone, she took into the bedroom a burning lamp carefully muffled and covered, and beside it she laid a razor-sharp knife. When her husband had come in and gone to sleep, she waited for a while until his breathing grew slow and deep. Then, on tiptoe and trembling, she took out the knife and uncovered the lamp and brought them both toward the bed. It was not a bestial monster that lay there. It was a god—the god of love, naked and handsome and eternally young, the tips of his wings flickering as though in the invisible flame of his ardor. His bow and arrows lay at the foot of the bed; eagerly she snatched them up and tried the tip of an arrow with her thumb. It was sharper than she had thought; it pierced her skin, and now she fell even more in love with love; she kissed her husband so passionately that her hand trembled, and the lamp which she was holding spurted out a drop of hot oil upon his smooth white shoulder. He awoke, looked at her with grief and horror, and flew away into the darkness.

Now Psyche was truly deserted. Her home was home no longer. She left it empty as it had been when she came, and wandered out through the world searching for her lost husband. She did not find him; he was lying ill, partly with the pain of the burn, partly with the pang at his heart. Instead she was arrested by the servants of the goddess Venus, and dragged away and flogged. Venus berated her furiously, with particular fury because poor Psyche was pregnant and it enraged Venus to think that she in her divine loveliness might have to become a grandmother. Then she set her a number of impossible ordeals to undergo: first, to sort out thousands and thousands of mixed seeds—wheat, barley, poppy, and so forth; second, to bring back the golden wool of the dangerous rams of the Sun; third, to fetch a jar full of the water of the deadly river Styx; and last, to visit the world of death and procure a box containing some of the beauty of the queen of the dead.

All these ordeals were impossible for a human being to perform; but Psyche, although human, was the wife of a god and was carrying a baby at least half divine. The ants took pity on her and sorted out all the mixed seeds. The reeds of the river advised her how to get the golden wool of the rams, by waiting until sundown and gathering it from the bushes. An eagle soared up to the mountain where the river Styx burst out and brought her back a jar of its water. To reach the world of death, she thought of jumping off a high tower and killing herself; but the tower spoke to her and advised her what perils she would face and how she could evade them. After she had passed them all successfully, once on the way down to death and then on the way back, she made her final, almost fatal mistake. She opened the box containing the beauty of the queen of the dead and fainted away in a deathlike swoon.

Only a final miracle saved her. Her husband Cupid recovered from his heartbreak and pang, searched until he found her lying helpless, touched her with his arrow to rouse her from her trance, and then appealed to the highest of all the gods, Jupiter himself. Jupiter had often suffered from Cupid's caprices and his wanton arrows; now he was amused and merciful, and glad to see Cupid settling down. He took Psyche up into heaven, made her immortal, and married her to the young god of love. In due time she had a child, a little daughter, whose name was Pleasure.

There it is, one of the strangest and most famous stories in the Western world, the story of Cupid and Psyche. Cupid means passionate love; and Psyche means the soul. The story is told in a gangsters' hideout by a drunken old hag to a terrified girl, and is overheard by a tormented donkey—who is really a young man transformed to animal shape by magic mismanaged, and who remembers the story and writes it out later, after he has been restored to human shape. (His adventures, with the tale of Cupid and Psyche and other weird fantasies among them, are told in a book called the *Metamorphoses* or *Transformations,* by the Roman-African writer Apuleius. He lived in the second century A.D., and we have talked about him before in these lectures. There is a very graceful translation of the story of Cupid and Psyche by Walter Pater in his *Marius the Epicurean*.)[1]

One of the oddest things about the story of Cupid and Psyche is that it does not look like a piece of random invention by a capricious author. It sounds like a folk tale, a product of the imagination of that great poet—the naive, ingenious, irrational, miracle-loving mind of the ordinary people. Of course, as soon as Apuleius wrote it down in book form, it was enthusiastically taken up; and when it was rediscovered in the Renaissance, it became the material for dozens, scores of works of conscious art—operas, pictures, groups of sculpture, novels, and poems. (Many of its most beautiful restatements are described by Professor Elizabeth Haight of Vassar, in a charming little book called *Apuleius and His Influence*.)[2] Yet no one has been able to trace it before Apuleius, anywhere in Greek or Roman literature. It seems as though he had heard it somewhere, one evening in a caravansary, on the lips of a storyteller in an Eastern bazaar, or perhaps sung by a rude poet in some barbarian language, and had himself transformed it into permanent literature, adding its religious and philosophical overtones, and so made it immortal.

*   *   *

The story of Cupid and Psyche, told by the sophisticated writer Apuleius in the second century A.D., has fascinated both artists and authors ever since it was put into writing. Beautiful and sensual sculptures, paintings, and pieces of music have been modeled on it. Wordsworth stood and gazed at one sculptured group of Cupid and Psyche in a Roman gallery for some time, and then, turning away, said bitterly: "The devils!"[3] And more recently it has been translated into novels, even into books of psychological interpretation.

---

[1][See Apuleius, *Metamorphoses* 4.28–6.24, for the story of Cupid and Psyche in the original Latin, and W. Pater, *Marius the Epicurean* (New York, 1885) chap. 5, for the translation that Highet admired. Ed.]

[2][See E. H. Haight, *Apuleius and His Influence* (New York, 1927). Ed.]

[3][Although I have not been able to verify this anecdote, I have come across Wordsworth's account of his seeing a *painting* of Cupid and Psyche done by Washington Allston—a painting that Wordsworth observed while meeting with Allston in London and admired for the rendering of the naked figures. For Wordsworth's description of Allston's painting, see A. G. Hill, ed., *The Letters of William and Dorothy Wordsworth* (Oxford, 1993) vol. 8 (= a supplement to the seven volumes of letters published by Oxford between 1967 and 1988), specifically pp. 57–61, for Wordsworth's letter of May 7–9, 1812. Ed.]

In 1957 two eminent British novelists published novels which were based on the above myth, and in 1956 the psychologist Erich Neumann, who is spoken of as the successor of C. G. Jung, produced an elaborate psychical analysis of the story. The three books are so different from one another and from the original story that you might well ask yourself whether you were approaching one single theme or several; but the basis of the Greek myths is that they fertilize the imagination, so that a playwright can take a simple story and turn it into a tragedy, an artist paint it, and a lyric poet transform it into a series of sonnets or a broken meditation.

The first of these books on the legend is a novel by C. S. Lewis, called *Till We Have Faces*.[4] This is not a straight novel, no; Mr. Lewis could not write a straight reportorial 'she said, and he said, and then she stubbed out her cigarette before turning away' novel even if he tried. This book is something between an allegory (like one of his favorite books, *The Pilgrim's Progress*) and an imaginative reconstruction of a distant age, such as the romances of Mika Waltari and Sholem Asch. Instead of retelling the story of Cupid and Psyche in the rather artificially 'classical' setting which its first writer used, C. S. Lewis has pushed it into the remote frontier lands outside of Greece, into the Crimea or the Ukraine or the Caucasus—the country where Stravinsky set *The Rite of Spring* and Naomi Mitchison her best romance, *The Corn King and the Spring Queen*. He makes it not simple Greek, but primitive.

C. S. Lewis tells the whole story from the point of view of one of the evil forces in it, one of the bad sisters who wrecked Psyche's life and broke up her marriage and condemned her to suicide or worse. And with a strong effort of the moral imagination, he makes us understand and sympathize with this bad sister. Orual she is called (the name sounds like "horrible," and many other names in Lewis's retelling are significant in the same way). Orual is the eldest of three princesses; her father has no sons; she realizes slowly but agonizingly that she herself will never be a pretty girl or a beautiful woman or a happy and much-desired wife; so she decides to be something more like a man—fighting in battles, sharing in political meetings of minds, and justifying her spirit, since her body is unworthy of her. Meanwhile one pretty and foolish sister grows up beside her, doing nothing very much with her life except for having fun; and then (from her father's second marriage) a

---

4[See C. S. Lewis, *Till We Have Faces* (New York, 1957). For Highet's review of three other novels by C. S. Lewis, see his "From World to World," in *People, Places, and Books* (New York, 1953) 130–37. Ed.]

younger and more beautiful sister is born. She is Psyche. Orual hangs over the new baby as though it were her own baby, and she helps it to grow up. And so their lives proceed, with a tough father growing weaker, a soft and rather degenerate simple sister, a beautiful new young child-sister, and Orual herself, trying to keep the family together, trying too hard. It could be made into a play about a small family with similar problems today. Still, the central problem in Lewis's tale is essentially a religious one. When the elder sister tries to break up her young sister's marriage, she is not only an unmarried woman who misunderstands a happy bride, not only a sex-starved woman trying to wound a sister fulfilled, but a cold rationalist trying to argue with a soul which has undergone a religious transformation.

The main thread of the story we know, until the final catastrophe when the young wife Psyche takes in the dagger and the lamp to confront and perhaps to kill her husband; the palace of love is destroyed; and the heartbroken girl wanders off into exile weeping, forever weeping.

The rest of the story, as C. S. Lewis tells it, is the story of Orual, the evil sister. As we see her life through her eyes, we realize that she is not bad, simply well-meaning. Because she is so efficient and means so well, she rearranges the lives of everyone near her and manages to wreck or at least to distort them all. And then, still seeing through her eyes as she grows old (this part is very moving and sad), we go on to understand that she realizes how much she has destroyed those whom she loves: one sister gone, a suffering wraith; another sister blighted into sensual silliness; herself more of a man than a woman, and yet yearning for womanhood; and all her intimates eaten up with her energy and her lust for domination. Just at the end of the book, when very old, she begins to look through the screen of reality: she dreams dreams and sees visions; she suffers, as old and sensitive people sometimes suffer, in the torment of the spirit; and she goes through the ordeals which (according to the legend) Psyche herself had to undergo; and in the end she finds that she herself has in her own way fulfilled the destiny of Psyche and has somehow become Psyche, or the twin of Psyche. I have read this part several times; I do not think I can explain it or fully understand it; but it haunts me as others of Mr. Lewis's allegories have also haunted me. *Till We Have Faces* is a highly interesting and moving book.

Another distinguished English novelist, Charles Morgan, has produced another meditation on the myth of Cupid and Psyche.

This is so widely different from C. S. Lewis's strange romance that we are bewildered to think how many meanings a single myth can have. It is called *Challenge to Venus*.[5] This is an entirely modern novel, the tale of a love affair between a tall, strong, quite naive and undeveloped Englishman passing through Italy, and an Italian lady—young, widowed, beautiful, and aloof. Mr. Morgan is a fine and rather elaborate stylist; his story is told with more conscious attention to the graces than that of Mr. Lewis; it is more sensual and perhaps a little shallower, but more easily understandable.

The principal link between this novel and the myth is the character of the lovely young Italian woman. She is very beautiful, almost fabulously beautiful. She belongs to a family which has always prided itself on remaining above human entanglements, remote from complicated human emotions; and when she yields for a single night to her attraction for the Englishman, she means it to be nothing more than a casual gesture. When she finds that its effects overwhelm her as well as him, she is astounded, horrified. He has never seen anything so beautiful; he likens her to the exquisite goddess in Botticelli's picture of the birth of Venus; and in one charming scene, alone in her bedroom, she assumes the same pose to compare herself point by point with the goddess. But she herself is terrified by the new powers and demands which arise in her; and at last, rather than continue to challenge the goddess and become fully beautiful and filled with love, she gives up her new lover and (like Psyche) goes off into hopeless and homeless exile.

Recently the same myth has been analyzed by a skilled psychologist, the follower and the principal successor of C. G. Jung—Dr. Erich Neumann. His book is called *Amor and Psyche: The Psychic Development of the Feminine*.[6] Although rather opaque in style, this book is highly revealing, and seems to me to show how scholars in the future must treat those old stories—the myths which are apparently so childish and yet are so haunting, stimulate so many artistic imaginations, and outlast many philosophical doctrines, many statements of so-called scientific fact.

The girl is called Psyche, which means the soul. Her lover is called Cupid. Dr. Neumann turns his name back into Amor, which must have corresponded to its Greek original, Eros—love, love indistinguishable from passion. This being so, surely the myth has

---

[5][See C. Morgan, *Challenge to Venus* (New York, 1957). Ed.]
[6][See E. Neumann, *Amor and Psyche: The Psychic Development of the Feminine,* trans. R. Manheim (New York, 1956)—originally published in German (Munich, 1952). Ed.]

something to do with the growth of the soul. Dr. Neumann says that it is an allegory of the progress of the soul of woman from youth, through fear and revolt and ordeal, to maturity and happiness.

In the first stage Psyche is doomed, by the ordinance of heaven and the consent of her parents, to be married to a hideous monster. Her wedding is more like a funeral, and when she is left alone to await her bridegroom, she is terrified, hoping only for a quick death without pain. This (according to Neumann) represents the passage from girlhood into womanhood—which is sometimes called the plucking of the flower (as though the flower were killed by him who plucked it) and which is always accompanied by the fear of the unknown.

Then, after Psyche's husband comes to her in the darkness, she grows to love him without ever seeing him. She lives in a fairy palace surrounded by invisible servants, waiting only for the approach of night. This is the stage which some women inhabit throughout their lives, the stage from which the immature never emerge—the stage of primitive sensuality. They are in love with sex alone. They are bodies without minds.

But Psyche's sisters find her and scold her for her stupidity. They tell her that her husband must be a monster and that she ought to discover him and then kill him. At this point Neumann's interpretation becomes more difficult and more fanciful, but it is not impossible. He says that the sisters are part of Psyche herself. They represent the wish of women to be left alone, or to be dominant in every love relationship, to have the man merely as an appendage, to resist all his attempts to dominate, and to threaten him with death or mutilation if he does not submit.

The insistence of the matriarchal element breaks up the marriage for a time. But Psyche herself does not wish to break it up. In order to maintain it and renew it, she willingly undergoes several ordeals, which she can pass only by supernatural help—which means through calling on powers she possessed without knowing them. Neumann's interpretation of the ordeals is still more fascinating. For instance, when Psyche is confronted with a huge pile of mixed seeds which she must sort out, these (he says) are the disordered welter of fruitful predispositions which are part of the nature of woman and which she must bring into order so that they will become more consciously useful. So her final ordeal, bringing back the beauty of the goddess of death, is completed successfully, until Psyche has returned to the upper world, and then—only then—she opens the box containing the mystery, and dies. For the second time she has risked death for her husband, this time willingly and consciously; he flies to her side, and with a significant prick of the arrow of love, restores her to full life. And she becomes immortal and bears an immortal child whose name is Pleasure. A woman can love a man truly only if she suffers for his love and becomes aware of all the ordeals which it demands of her and faces them bravely. Then the two make each other immortal through their love and produce a child which is the image and the final fulfillment of them both.

These are only three of the most recent interpretations of the myth of Cupid and Psyche. These myths are part of our permanent inheritance from the world of Greece and Rome, and as long as they continue to interest our thinkers and fascinate our artists, that world is still alive within us.

CLASSICAL TRADITION

Dante's *Comedy**

When my son was about sixteen, my wife and I took a house in Bermuda for the summer. We soon realized that this was not in all respects a good idea. The place was beautiful, but there was a slightly heady atmosphere of luxury; and for a strong and handsome boy there were too many temptations. We even wished that we had gone to a ranch out West instead. However, the boy got through it and turned out well—partly because of a curious stratagem which I invented.

I was preparing my lectures for next year at Columbia, and I asked him to help me work on Dante's *Comedy*. He was flattered, and anyhow it was too hot to do anything for a couple of hours after lunch. So every day he and I read one short section of the *Comedy* and discussed it. He used a good translation into English verse; I had a lucid translation in prose. He also had the marvelous illustrations by Gustave Doré, while I was helped by Grandgent's notes to penetrate some of the difficulties of the poem.[1] I knew a little Italian too, enough to read the finest passages aloud. There are one hundred cantos in the *Comedy;* the house was rented for three months, and so with a little skipping he and I finished the poem by the end of the summer. It was a fine intellectual exercise for both of us (it is easy to stagnate in a land of bright sun and blue sea). More than that, it was excellent training in moral principles. Many young people nowadays do not know the difference between right and wrong. My son learned them. He has never forgotten the whole experience. Nor shall I.

---

*Prepared in 1972 for Winthrop Laboratories (a pharmaceutical company that no longer exists) for the series *What Makes It Great?*—a series of booklets on the humanities designed for members of the medical profession.

[1][For the translation used by Highet, see J. A. Carlyle, T. Okey, and P. H. Wicksteed, trans., *The Divine Comedy of Dante Alighieri* (New York, 1932), containing an introduction by C. H. Grandgent. For the translation used by Highet's son, see L. G. White, trans., *Dante Alighieri: The Divine Comedy* (New York, 1948), which also contains the lively and fantastic illustrations of Gustave Doré. See C. H. Grandgent, ed., *La Divina Commedia di Dante Alighieri* (Boston, 1933)[2], for the Italian text and English commentary that Highet also used for preparing his lectures on Dante's masterpiece. Ed.]

I had always been prejudiced against Dante. Brought up in a Scottish Presbyterian household, I had thought of him as a Papist bigot. Proud of being a rational modern youth, I had despised him as a medieval mystic. And when, aged sixteen or so myself, I found a translation of the *Inferno* in my father's bookcase and read it, I was repelled by what looked like his sadistic delight in describing ingenious tortures. I was wrong of course, wrong all the way. After joining the Columbia faculty, I was invited to teach the famous Humanities course in which the great books of the past were read and analyzed. Homer, Vergil, Shakespeare, Goethe—these I could do easily, but my prejudice made me shrink from Dante. The first time around I taught him poorly, sticking to hard facts. Next year, however, I was surprised to find myself almost looking forward to teaching Dante. I remembered more about the *Comedy* than I had expected. It had its hooks into me. And I began to realize that it was a magnificent poem and a stupendous achievement of rigorous consistent thought. Then came the summer in Bermuda, when I spent three months with the *Comedy,* always somewhere inside my mind. A year or two later I had learned Italian in order to read all the original, and found it more strange and beautiful than I could have guessed even from the best translations.

Fortunately there are English versions which do give us a pretty good idea of the poem. The meaning, though not the poetry, comes across in the prose version by Carlyle, Okey, and Wicksteed, with Grandgent's explanatory notes. In verse it is always a good idea to read several different translations, each of which will have some merits the others do not; I can recommend those by Dorothy Leigh Sayers, Melville Best Anderson, and Lawrence Grant White. But always remember, every translation of a great poem is inadequate. I can read Latin almost as easily as English; the best English version of Vergil's *Aeneid* makes me wince. I love Shakespeare devotedly; the best translations of his plays into French and German give me acute nausea. That after all is why we learn languages (including 'dead' languages)—to enjoy the originals. In the same way, if you have never seen the Cathedral of Notre-Dame except in photographs, you will be dumbfounded when you actually stand inside it, gazing at the huge pillars, the vast and noble perspectives, the soaring arches and flying galleries, and the unearthly glory of the great rose window. And you will feel that years would not be too much to give to learning and understanding its purpose and its design.

The *Comedy* is like a cathedral built by one man.[2] It is the first long highly-organized poem written in any modern language. Dante himself said that his master in poetry was not any French, Italian, or Provençal author—although he indeed admired some of them—but the Roman poet Vergil (*Inferno* 1.85). Vergil's masterpiece, the *Aeneid,* is an epic poem about ten thousand lines long; its component parts are so skillfully and delicately interconnected that, even though it has been intensively studied for centuries, scholars are still discovering new subtleties in its structure. The *Comedy*—by the way, he did not call it the *Divine Comedy* (*divina* is simply an epithet of praise conferred on it by admiring Italians, as they call a famous soprano a *diva*)—the *Comedy* does not in the least resemble the *Aeneid* in appearance; its architectural plan is totally different. But like the *Aeneid,* it is a massive unity in which a myriad diverse parts build up a superbly integrated whole. No one can read it quickly. Nobody can read it all through in one continuous effort, any more than he could look at all the paintings in the Louvre. When my son and I finished three months of reading it continuously, only one canto each day, we had just begun to appreciate and understand it. It is meant to be lived with. Anyone who really lives with it will find that it changes his life.

It is the story of a journey—a spiritual pilgrimage made in a dream or vision. The pilgrim is Dante Alighieri himself. When he began to write the story, he was plunged deep in misery. Because of a feud within his city, Florence, he had been put on trial in his absence, found guilty of financial misdoing while in public office, and sentenced to perpetual banishment. Once honored and powerful, he was now a poor outcast with no home and apparently no future.

Three things sustained him. One was poetry. He was himself a brilliant poet in the modern style, but he loved the Latin masterpieces and knew himself to be capable of far greater things than any contemporary. One was love. Still a boy, he had fallen in love with Beatrice Portinari; and although she was dead and he had married someone else, his soul was still nourished by his love for Beatrice. (Her name means "She Who Blesses.") One and foremost was religion. Although he opposed the temporal dominion of the Pope and indeed held the reigning Pope Boniface VIII to be a

---

[2][In an earlier version of this lecture, presented on his radio program in 1954 (= *BMCT* 8), Highet remarked that he came to know Dante's *Comedy* only after rereading it many times—in the same way that J.-K. Huysmans, in his novel *The Cathedral* (Paris, 1898), came to know the cathedral of Chartres by living near it and by almost inhabiting it for many weeks. Ed.]

damnably wicked man, he was a devout Christian and lived in God's eternity more than in the changeable, imperfect world of time.

His journey begins in despair. It takes him through hell and purgatory and heaven to the vision of God. He describes it stage by stage, sometimes almost step by step, so vividly that we experience it along with him. The earth Dante conceives as a gigantic disc. On this side of it is the world we inhabit. Within its depths is the vast gulf of hell, piercing almost clear through to the other side. At its center is Satan himself. He was hurled down from heaven after his rebellion against God and is now pinned deep within the earth—although powerless to move, infecting it with his evil presence, eternally hating, eternally suffering, the impotent monarch of the hopelessly damned. On the other side of the earth disc, inaccessible except through a miracle, is the Garden of Eden, where Adam and Eve once had dwelled; and the mountain of purgatory, rising into heaven.

At the beginning of the poem Dante goes downward into hell. He is guided further and further down in the lowest depths. Lowest of all he confronts the mighty and horrifying figure of Satan; and to reach the other side of earth, he is forced to touch Satan's titanic body, to be carried by his supernatural companion through its forest of hair, until he emerges on the other side to see the stars. Now he descends no more but mounts steadily though still effortlessly up the purgatorial mountain and into the earthly paradise. Thereafter he ascends into the sky, no longer climbing but moving as rapidly and easily as the flight of thought—first into the nearer zones dominated by the moon, the sun, and the planets; and then outward from our world, into the universe inhabited solely by stars and by the souls of the blessed shining like stars; until at last he sees, surrounded by an infinite multitude of angels and glowing with an indescribable radiance, the three Persons in one Substance which is God.

No man could make this journey without divine sanction and without superhuman guidance. Dante has three guides. Through hell and purgatory he is led by Vergil—whom he revered above all other poets, and who in his *Aeneid* had written a powerful description of a similar pilgrimage through the world of eternity. Because he had the misfortune to live and die before the birth of Christ, Vergil is condemned—not to endless torment like the damned but to eternal exclusion from the vision of God; therefore he leaves Dante after taking him through purgatory and returns to the realm at the edge of hell where dwell all the virtuous pagans. Then Dante meets the beautiful and saintly Beatrice, now an immortal spirit; and with her as his guide and teacher he reaches the outermost. Finally, after she returns to her throne among the blessed, Dante is guided by the saintly Bernard of Clairvaux to the ultimate, ineffable vision of incarnate Power, Wisdom, and Love. There the poem ends.

Most visions are illogical, fantastic, and dreamlike—just think of the Book of Ezekiel and the Book of Revelation in the Bible. But Dante's vision of the other world is a triumph of logic. In fact, if I were asked to tell the significance of his poem in one sentence, I should say: "The universe is rational." Everything God does has a perfectly sufficient reason. Man does not always understand this. Dante himself, at the beginning of his pilgrimage, does not; but his guides instruct him and reply to his questions, and he talks with many immortal souls, in hell and purgatory and heaven, who explain their destinies, and every stage of the journey deepens his insight. Accompanying him, we learn as we go.

Thus, hell is not simply a burning fiery furnace. It was created by Wisdom, and so it has a plan. It consists of three main sections for the three main types of wickedness as classified by Aristotle, whom Dante refers to as "the master of those who know" (*Inferno* 4.131). These are incontinence—gluttony and sexual lust, for instance; violence—including violence against nature, such as sodomy; and worst of all because it makes the very soul a lie, deceit. Lowest in hell are the traitors, lapped in the eternal ice which formed in their cold hearts during life; and Satan, the arch-traitor to God, forever chews and mangles the three arch-traitors of mankind—Brutus and Cassius and Judas Iscariot. Within each of the three large sections—which do not intercommunicate, so that Dante and Vergil have to be miraculously transported from one to another—there are subsections, each for a special type of sin punished in a special way. Political grafters, for instance, are plunged into a lake of boiling pitch—because politicians are often tempted to take graft but cannot touch pitch without being defiled. Dante converses with many of the damned. He is deeply sorry for some of the incontinent and faints with grief when he hears the dreadful story of the lovers Paolo and Francesca, for he himself has been a slave of love. For the violent he has mainly scorn, seldom compassion. The traitors, who deliberately perverted their souls, fill him with loathing, and the most terrible moment of the poem comes when he must make physical contact with the incarnation of treason and escape from hell by being carried along the body of Satan.

Purgatory also is the work of Reason. It is a mountain with seven circular ridges: on each sinners are purged of one of the seven deadly sins. They suffer and weep, but they have hope in their suffering, since they know their punishment is just and is preparing them to enter paradise. What is inflicted on them is reasonable. Gluttons are starved into spiritual health; sluggards never rest but run perpetually; the proud are bent earthward, carrying huge stones; and they cheer and encourage one another. Here Dante can walk, although with great difficulty; and we feel his effort as he toils up to the summit.

There, in the Garden of Eden, he is met by Beatrice. But this is not a meeting of lovers long parted. She is a blessed and immortal soul; he is a sinful man. She is gracious to him but severe; her first words to him are a rebuke. Humbly he accepts it; and as is right, he remains humble while she conducts him upward and outward through the radiant heavens, teaching him as they go. There too he meets many great men and women of the past, who speak to him of their lives and resolve many problems that have perplexed him. Heaven also is not a simple, undifferentiated abode of bliss. Saints and blessed souls roam through infinite space like stars; but like the stars they group themselves into constellations by spiritual sympathy. In one magnificent scene Dante and Beatrice see a gigantic eagle shining in the sky. It is a complex of bright spirits. These are the great princes who were famed on earth for their justice—Joshua, Charlemagne, Godfrey the leader of the First Crusade, and many more. They are kindred spirits; collectively they assume the shape which best typifies their power and nobility.

But why did Dante call this awesome apocalypse a *Comedy?* The title is for me the only serious weakness in the work. Men of the Middle Ages had forgotten the true nature of drama—because the professional theater, a creation of Greek and Roman paganism, had been abolished. Misunderstanding a definition formulated by Aristotle, they thought 'tragedy' meant a story that began nobly and ended sadly, and 'comedy' meant a story that began gloomily and (like Dante's pilgrimage) ended happily. Also, 'comedy' was written in plain, simple words, and 'tragedy' in lofty language; so Vergil's *Aeneid* with its complex Latin was a 'tragedy,' and Dante's poem in the modern dialect of Tuscany (which even women and the uneducated could understand) was a 'comedy.'

If you have ever studied a Gothic cathedral, walking around and through it, climbing its towers, examining it from many angles, you will have been astonished at the intricate interplay of arch and column and buttress, all solid stone but interwoven like silk. So the entire *Comedy* is built on many symbols which all support one another and bind the entire structure tightly together. For instance, Three. God for Dante was Three in One. So the entire poem is in three parts and in ninety-nine cantos with one introductory canto; and in each canto the lines are interwoven in rhyming triplets. Just as God's presence pervades the universe, so trinity and unity pervade the poem. One single word, repeated at three key points (*Inferno* 34.139, *Purgatory* 33.145, and *Paradise* 33.145), asserts unity in trinity—a beautiful word, a beautiful symbol. Each of the three parts ends with "stars"; but the three repetitions communicate growing nobility and majesty. After the hideous journey through hell, reaching the other side of earth,

> we issued forth again to see the stars.

Having climbed Mount Purgatory and passed through the earthly paradise, Dante is

> pure and prepared to mount up to the stars.

And finally the vision of God is a vision of

> Love, which moves the sun and the other stars.

I have said enough and yet not enough. Many books, larger than the poem itself, have been written about the *Comedy*. Some of them are helpful, a few necessary. But it is as with all great things in life: no description, no analysis equals the actual experience. The *Comedy* is difficult, often forbiddingly difficult. But so is life itself; and to know the *Comedy* is to enlarge one's own comprehension of the highest values in life.

Shakespeare's *Julius Caesar**

It is not very easy, nor very common, to watch a poet actually working and to see how he makes a poem. There is one pretty good book on the subject, *Poems in Process,* written by Phyllis Bartlett; and one great book on a single poet, *The Road to Xanadu,* written by John Livingston Lowes.[1] But there are not many studies of this sensitive subject, and there is room for many more.

William Shakespeare was an expert magician, but it is sometimes possible to catch him at work and see how he develops his marvelous tricks. Although he made up his characters (from his own vast imagination and his own subtle observation), he did not make up his plots but took them from history books and collections of short stories. Although he himself composed most of his poetic declamations and descriptions and dialogues and narratives, yet he sometimes built them upon pieces of plain prose written by someone else. We can see, without too much trouble, how he does this.

Shakespeare knew some Latin, which he got at high school in Stratford, and a few words of Greek. He was always interested in the life, the history, the myths, the poetry, and the philosophy of the Greeks and Romans. Long after he had left school and while he was building his career as a playwright, he was still reading the Greek and Roman classics, sometimes in the original and sometimes in translation. How many of his plays and long poems do you think deal with themes drawn from ancient Greece and ancient Rome? No less than twelve altogether—twelve out of forty major works. He may not have learned much Latin at the Stratford school, but it was taught to him so well that it stuck in his mind and generated a continuous, even an increasing interest, a passion that lasted throughout his creative life.

One of the classical books which he studied with most care was that indispensable old standby, the *Parallel Lives of the Greeks and Romans* by Plutarch. This book had been turned into beautiful

---

*Presented in 1959 on Highet's radio program (= *BMCT* 172).
[1][See P. Bartlett, *Poems in Process* (New York, 1951); see also J. L. Lowes, *The Road to Xanadu* (Boston, 1927), on Samuel Taylor Coleridge. Ed.]

French (about the year of Shakespeare's birth) by Jacques Amyot, and largely from that version it was put into sound if uninspired English in 1579 by the Elizabethan master of prose, Sir Thomas North, in a book which at once became a best seller and is still in print. A second and enlarged edition appeared in 1595, when William Shakespeare was thirty-one years old. It hit him hard. He thought it was a superb book. A few years later he produced the first of his great plays on Roman subjects, the tragedy of *Julius Caesar.* He had written some dazzling comedies and some stirring historical plays before *Julius Caesar;* but in this drama he explored the human soul more deeply and thought more intensely about the problems and agonies of political life. We cannot say that he solved the problems on which he meditated. His mind, like the minds of nearly all his contemporaries, was too firmly set in the mold of feudal nobilities and hereditary monarchies to understand what a true democracy is and how it can be overthrown by an ambitious and unscrupulous egoist; but he visualized the actual murder of Julius Caesar and the turmoil of the Civil War so clearly that it is now difficult to think of them without hearing his words and seeing the scenes which he put on the little stage of his "wooden O."[2]

If you read North's translation of Plutarch's life of Julius Caesar and then go through Shakespeare's tragedy of Julius Caesar, you will be astonished to see how closely and carefully Shakespeare has followed not only the incidents but sometimes the very words of the biography. But he does not do this mechanically. He is selective. Apparently what he did was to read and reread the life of Caesar, then block out his play, and then introduce into it episodes and utterances which he took out of the text of North's translation. We can see how he worked by looking at one section. After Julius had attained supreme power in the Roman Republic and was king in everything but name, the opposition to him grew very strong. The descendant of the man who overthrew the last king of Rome, Brutus, was picked out to lead the opposition; the bitter Cassius was its chief driving force. As the time of Caesar's murder drew near, omens were observed; a wise man even warned Caesar about the very day, the Ides (that is, the fifteenth) of March. Now see how Plutarch tells the story and then how Shakespeare uses his narrative. Plutarch says (*Caesar* 62.4–63.3):

---

[2][See *Henry V,* prol. 13, for this phrase—probably a reference to the Globe Theater, an authentic replica of which now stands on the south bank of the Thames on the site of the original structure. Ed.]

Now they that desired change and wished Brutus only their prince and governor above all other, they durst not come to him themselves to tell him what they would have him to do, but in the night did cast sundry papers into the praetor's seat where he gave audience, and the most of them to this effect: "Thou sleepest, Brutus, and art not Brutus indeed." . . . Caesar also had Cassius in great jealousy and suspected him much; whereupon he said on a time to his friends: "What will Cassius do, think ye? I like not his pale looks." Another time when Caesar's friends complained unto him of Antonius and Dolabella, that they pretended some mischief towards him, he answered them again: "As for those fat men and smooth-combed heads, I never reckon of them; but these pale-visaged and carrion-lean people, I fear them most"—meaning Brutus and Cassius. Certainly destiny may easier be foreseen than avoided—considering the strange and wonderful signs that were said to be seen before Caesar's death. For touching the fires in the element, and spirits running up and down in the night, and also the solitary birds to be seen at noonday sitting in the great marketplace—are not all these signs perhaps worth the noting? . . . Divers men were seen going up and down in fire; and . . . there was a slave . . . that did cast a marvelous burning flame out of his hand, insomuch as they that saw it thought he had been burnt, but when the fire was out, it was found he had no hurt. Caesar self also doing sacrifice . . . found that one of the beasts which was sacrificed had no heart; and that was a strange thing in nature, how a beast could live without a heart. Furthermore, there was a certain soothsayer, that had given Caesar warning long time before, to take heed of the . . . Ides of March . . . for on that day he should be in great danger. That day being come, Caesar going into the Senate-house and speaking merrily to the soothsayer, told him: "The Ides of March be come." "So be they," softly answered the soothsayer, "but yet are they not past."

There we have quite a short section of a biography, with a number of solid facts in it: propaganda to get Brutus to lead the opposition; Caesar's suspicion of Brutus and Cassius; the omens and prodigies—fire, strange birds, the sacrificial animal without a heart, and the warning of the soothsayer. All these are told by Plutarch in rapid, continuous narrative. Shakespeare was struck by them and determined to introduce them into his tragedy. To do so, he had to make them emotional; he had to relate them to the lives of his leading characters; and he had to dramatize them, to make them actually happen on the stage, or if not, to have them vividly described. Furthermore, for the sake of his drama, he had to arrange them at intervals in such a way as to increase the tension which starts with the rising of the curtain and continues to rise thereafter. All this he did with consummate skill.

In Shakespeare's play (1.2.12–24), Julius and his magnificent retinue have scarcely entered before a voice calls: "Caesar!" Julius says: "Ha! Who calls?" and the music sinks into silence. "Who is it in the press that calls on me? I hear a tongue, shriller than all the music, cry 'Caesar!' Speak; Caesar is turned to hear." The voice says: "Beware the Ides of March." The soothsayer is brought forward after a pause and repeats his warning: "Beware the Ides of March." Caesar—not cruelly but grandly, neither cynically nor superstitiously—says: "He is a dreamer. Let us leave him. Pass." The procession continues. Caesar's grandeur grows to its climax. On the day of the murder (3.1.1–2), Caesar enters again, sees the soothsayer again, and with his characteristic loftiness says to him: "The Ides of March are come." "Aye, Caesar," replies the mystic, "but not gone."

Caesar's suspicion of Brutus and Cassius is described rather briefly by Plutarch, as though it were almost a comic weakness in the dictator. Listen to what Shakespeare makes of it (1.2.190–201):

CAESAR
  Antonius!
ANTONY
  Caesar?
CAESAR
  Let me have men about me that are fat,
  Sleek-headed men, and such as sleep a-nights.
  Yond Cassius has a lean and hungry look;
  He thinks too much; such men are dangerous.
ANTONY
  Fear him not, Caesar, he's not dangerous;
  He is a noble Roman, and well given.
CAESAR
  Would he were fatter! But I fear him not.
  Yet if my name were liable to fear,
  I do not know the man I should avoid
  So soon as that spare Cassius . . .

You see how Shakespeare has taken the idea from Plutarch but altered the clumsy words of Plutarch or of his translator. Plutarch said "fat men and smooth-combed heads" and "pale-visaged and carrion-lean people." Shakespeare wrote "men . . . that are fat, sleek-headed men, and such as sleep a-nights." He abolished Plutarch's "pale-visaged," which sounds too weak and worried and neurotic. He changed "carrion-lean" to "lean and hungry," which is far more graphic and more active; and then he added the penetrating, the immortal phrases: "He thinks too much; such men are dangerous."

It was not too difficult for Shakespeare to alter Plutarch's words. But how was he to deal with the supernatural prodigies? He could not put them on the stage—this was not a magical play like *Macbeth*. If he made a wizard or an astrologer describe them, they might be thought to be mere hocus-pocus. If he made a crowd rush in shouting about them, it might be considered mass hysteria. So he had to have them described by someone reliable, someone credible. In *Julius Caesar* he produced a storm of thunder and lightning. Through the storm, terrified and staggering, he brought the toughest and most cynical of all his characters, Casca, the man whom only a few hours earlier he had seen watching with bitter cynicism the attempted coronation of Caesar. Such a man, so seldom deceived, cannot be lying, cannot be suffering a hallucination, when he describes the astounding prodigies of that miraculous night, so that we believe him when he describes them (1.3.5–10 and 15–28):

> I have seen tempests, when the scolding winds
> Have rived the knotty oaks, and I have seen
> Th' ambitious ocean swell and rage and foam,
> To be exalted with the threat'ning clouds;
> But never till tonight, never till now,
> Did I go through a tempest dropping fire . . .
> A common slave—you know him well by sight—
> Held up his left hand, which did flame and burn
> Like twenty torches joined; and yet his hand,
> Not sensible of fire, remained unscorched.
> Besides—I ha' not since put up my sword—
> Against the Capitol I met a lion,
> Who glazed upon me and went surly by
> Without annoying me. And there were drawn
> Upon a heap a hundred ghastly women,
> Transformed with their fear, who swore they saw
> Men all in fire walk up and down the streets.
> And yesterday the bird of night did sit
> Even at noonday upon the marketplace,
> Hooting and shrieking . . .

There was one more significant incident which also forecast Caesar's death, an omen which could not be brought into this fine dramatic narrative. Plutarch described it in the same context, but rather dully:

> Caesar self also doing sacrifice . . . found that one of the beasts
> which was sacrificed had no heart; and that was a strange thing
> in nature, how a beast could live without a heart.

Now it is impossible to have an animal killed and sacrificed upon the stage. Shakespeare therefore had the incident happen off stage, so that it could be reported to Caesar; and instead of Plutarch's naive little comment, he invented a magnificent riposte, which prepares for the first climax of the tragedy and manifests the grand courage of his Caesar (2.2.37–43). On the morning of his murder, Julius sends a servant to tell the augurs to do sacrifice and to report back to him. The servant returns.

CAESAR
                What say the augurers?
SERVANT
    They would not have you to stir forth today.
    Plucking the entrails of an offering forth,
    They could not find a heart within the beast.

Plutarch commented that this was a very unusual physiological phenomenon. Shakespeare makes Julius reply:

    The gods do this in shame of cowardice:
    Caesar should be a beast without a heart
    If he should stay at home today for fear.

Even in these splendid dramatic speeches, Shakespeare has caught one tiny but significant psychical oddity. He makes Julius talk of himself in the third person: "Caesar should be a beast without a heart"; "Speak; Caesar is turned to hear." This is correct. When Julius was divorcing his wife, he said: "Caesar's wife must be above suspicion" (Plutarch, *Caesar* 10.6). At school Shakespeare had read some of Caesar's report on his war in Gaul, in which he never says "I decided" but always "Caesar decided"—as though he were writing the history of someone quite different and stating the impersonal truth. Shakespeare remembered this, and he saw it again in Plutarch, and he put it into his play. For the true dramatist, everything is material: a memory from a schoolbook; a note in a newspaper; a tiny affectation noted in a man whom he does not even know but reads about in some old book written in a so-called 'dead' language. From his Latin lessons in high school, from his later reading of Plutarch, and from his own psychical insight, Shakespeare created the character of a brave and ambitious and domineering man, with his flatterers, his dependents, and his enemies, so vividly that, once we have seen them speak and move, or even read the words Shakespeare put into their mouths, we can never forget these actions and words, and we find that history has been replaced by poetry.

America's Classical Heritage[*]

The United States of America was not born out of a vacuum. It was created by ideals which already existed, which had existed for many centuries. Yet the founders of the Republic believed that these ideals had long been forgotten. They thought it was a daring and incredibly difficult task to convert these ideals once more into fact and to work out their application and their consequences. Sometimes they almost despaired and felt that the enterprise was doomed. In the beginning they failed, and they had to revise their plans and reshape them more accurately and realistically before the present structure of the United States could be put on a working basis.

In the end, however, they succeeded—those intelligent idealists, those practical dreamers. The United States works. It works so well that our neighbors abroad occasionally fail to give us credit for carrying out a plan far bolder than any other in modern history; and now and then they call us crude materialists, forgetting that the very pattern of our life is made of ideals which are still working their way into reality.

The principles on which our Republic is founded are many and powerful. It would take months to discuss them all and show how they are ingrained in our laws, in our attitudes to religion, in the shape of our society, in habits so familiar that we seldom think of them, and in institutions so important that we scarcely question them. But one group of them deserves special attention because it is least known and among the most important. This is the group of ideals drawn from ancient Greece and ancient Rome.

Take out a dollar bill and look at it. On one side you will see the face of George Washington, the father of our country. On the other side there are two circles: these are reproductions of the Great Seal of the United States. They carry three short phrases in Latin. All three are adapted from the poetry of Vergil (or from poems attributed to him). This is because the Founding Fathers believed that Vergil was not only one of the greatest poets who ever lived but

---

[*]Presented in 1954 on Highet's radio program (= *BMCT* 46).

something like a seer, who understood the hidden forces which build or destroy civilization.

On the left-hand side of the dollar bill, the circle shows a pyramid, which I imagine is Masonic in origin. Above are the words ANNUIT COEPTIS ("he has favored our enterprise")—adapted from the prayer in Vergil, *Georgics* 1.40–42.[1] They are set around an eye within a halo, which is surely a symbol of God; therefore they mean that God himself has approved of the foundation of the Republic. The pyramid bears in Roman numerals the date 1776.

Below the pyramid is the phrase NOVUS ORDO SECLORUM ("a new order of the ages")—a new beginning of history. This is adapted from Vergil, *Bucolics* 4, the wonderful poem which foretells the opening of a new age of the world, with the birth of a miraculous child who shall bring in the reign of peace and reestablish the virtue which our first forefathers knew; a poem which—although it was written forty years before the birth of Jesus—seemed to the early Christians like a clear prophecy of the coming of the Messiah.[2] This motto also shows how the founders of the United States felt that they were doing a work which was qualitatively unlike anything then in existence and was partly divine in origin.

On the right-hand side of the dollar bill, the Great Seal shows the well-known figure of the eagle, with the thunderbolts of war grasped in its left claw and the olives of peace in its right. Both olive branch and thunderbolts are Greco-Roman symbols; and so originally is the eagle itself. (Benjamin Franklin did not like it and proposed that the national bird of America should be the turkey; but he was overruled, and perhaps he was not wholly serious.) In its beak the eagle bears a scroll with the phrase E PLURIBUS UNUM ("one out of many")—a quotation adapted from the *Moretum* (at that time believed to be Vergil's)—which is a succinct description of the several states joined in a single union.[3]

You may think that these are trifles, and rather old-fashioned trifles at that. If you do, you will be mistaken. They are meaningful

---

[1][In its original context Vergil's phrase *adnue coeptis* (*Georgics* 1.40) is directed to Augustus, whom the poet asks to favor his undertaking to write about the subject of farming. Ed.]

[2][In its original context Vergil's phrase *magnus saeclorum ordo* (*Bucolics* 4.5) identifies this glorious new age of peace as one that will commence during the consulship of Pollio. Ed.]

[3][In its original context the Latin phrase *e pluribus unus* (*Moretum* 104) refers to the single color demonstrated by the individual ingredients contained in the farmer's salad. Ed.]

symbols, and symbols which are preserved for many centuries show a deep underlying resolution and bear witness to a set of enduring ideals. Not all but some of the ideals which inspired the Founding Fathers were the ideals of Greece and Rome. When they set up the new Republic, they modeled it partly on the free Greek and Roman states. That is, for instance, why the upper chamber of Congress is called the Senate; the word means "the assembly of elders" and is borrowed directly from the Roman legislative body. That is why the Congress building is set upon a hill called the Capitol—after the hill in the city of Rome where the records of the Republic were stored. Great ideas such as these do not age and are not rendered obsolete by any material progress; they may be forgotten from time to time in the temporary insanities which beset mankind, but they re-emerge after long intervals to create mighty states and beneficial institutions.

Recently I have been reading a book on this entire subject. It is a selection from the most important books which the Founding Fathers themselves read with particular attention; therefore it is a partial mirror of the ideas which went through their minds during one of the most vital, formative periods in history. It is called *Our Long Heritage* and is edited by Wilson Ober Clough.[4] (I am sorry to say that it contains far too many misprints.) Only one section of this anthology is filled with selections from the Greek and Roman books which the American statesmen knew; and yet it is indeed possible to read the entire work, and all through it—in the utterances of Edmund Burke and Jean Jacques Rousseau and the wise Montesquieu—to trace the classical tradition of logic, and the sense of history, and the respect for man simply as man.

Now the Founding Fathers did not think that all the Greek and Roman writers were equally valuable or equally important. Plato, for example, they scarcely read. Both John Adams and Thomas Jefferson spoke slightingly of him, because Plato distrusted and despised democracy, hoping for that delectable impossibility—a government of philosophers or an educated aristocracy. They thought much more of the historian Thucydides, that calm realist who had seen the disintegration of his own country through war and revolution. John Adams, who was to become the second President of the United States, quoted Thucydides' description of the ravages of class war in his *A Defence of the Constitutions of Government of*

---

[4][See W. O. Clough, ed., *Our Long Heritage* (Minneapolis, 1955)—a book previewed by Highet in 1954 and reprinted with revisions in 1961 under the title *Intellectual Origins of American National Thought.* Ed.]

the United States of America,[5] as a warning to all those who might
believe that perjury and treachery could solve the problems of
their country. Here is a selection from that splendid analysis of a
constantly recurring disease; even through the thick velvet curtain of baroque prose, it gives a vivid picture of the cruelties and
treacheries involved in class war.

> Oaths, if ever made for present reconciliation, had a temporary
> force, so long as neither knew how to break them; but never when
> either party had power to abet their violation. He who at inviting
> opportunity durst incur the perjury, if the adversary was off his
> guard, executed his rancor with higher spirit than from enmity
> open and avowed. Such a step was thought most secure; and be-
> cause he had thus surpassed in guile, it was certainly extolled as
> a masterpiece of cunning. Large is the number of villains, and
> such obtain more easily the reputation of dexterity than their
> dupes can of goodness. The latter are apt to blush; the former
> most impudently triumph. The source of all these evils is a thirst
> for power, in consequence either of rapacious or ambitious pas-
> sions . . . Seditions in this manner introduced every species of out-
> rageous wickedness into the Grecian manners. Sincerity, which
> is most frequently to be found in generous tempers, was laughed
> out of countenance and forever vanished.

This horrible account, the best which has ever been written in so
small a space, was quite clearly in the minds of several of the men
who created our Republic; they took instruction from it; and they
did what they could to warn their contemporaries and successors
against the dangers it describes.

But also they were deeply interested in a more stable state than
those of Greece—the Roman Republic. They studied it to find out
how it had lasted for so many long and difficult centuries, in order
that they also might build a country which would last; and they
found a guide in the Greek philosopher Polybius. This man, instead
of despising Rome as many Greeks used to do, came to admire its
strength and its wisdom and its stability. He concluded that these
virtues were based not on any concentration of power but on a
mixture of powers, in which any excess was checked and any defect was counterbalanced. The Founding Fathers determined to
take over this principle of checks and balances; and so, what the
Romans did almost instinctively and a Greek philosopher diagnosed and explained, the first Americans put into practice in con-

---

[5][See J. Adams, *A Defence of the Constitutions of Government of the United
States of America,* 3 vols. (London, 1787–88), especially vol. 1, preface, for
Adams's citation and analysis of Thucydides 3.81–84. Ed.]

structing the three bodies—legislative, executive, and judiciary—through which the American people governs itself.

Mr. Clough's book is full of problems, some of which go very deep into American life and thought. One of these is the famous phrase in the Declaration of Independence, that among the rights given to men by God are "life, liberty, and the pursuit of happiness." That is a strange phrase, is it not? Life, yes, certainly. Liberty, most surely. But can the pursuit of happiness be called a right? And is it the only right except life and liberty which ought to be mentioned in such a document? Who coined the phrase, and what did he mean? The phrase was written by Thomas Jefferson. It was not an empty phrase either. It seems clear that he coined it as an alternative to two or three other possibilities. Men who were more orthodox in their religious views would surely have said something like "the pursuit of virtue" or "the service of God" rather than "the pursuit of happiness." Jefferson rejected those ideas because he wished to preserve complete religious freedom for his new country. On the other hand, he also rejected the formula of the English political philosopher John Locke, who had named—among the most important of man's rights—property. Jefferson wanted something less material than property and more free than any single religion. Toward the end of his life he described himself as an Epicurean; and he inserted in one of the most fundamental documents of our country a phrase which can be traced back to Greek philosophy. The fundamental theme of the political system of Epicurus is not virtue, certainly not religion, not duty (all these Epicurus thought artificial), and not pleasure (that is the mistake which primitive minds have often made); but the pursuit of happiness.

The Republic was founded in 1776. Yes, but its spiritual ancestry goes back for many centuries beyond that date. No great institution was ever built without long and penetrating thought, without the slow forging and the repeated testing of certain central principles. One of the reasons why the United States has survived and grown stronger in a world full of danger and turmoil is that it was in part based upon the clear, penetrating thought of the Greeks and upon the shrewd and realistic statesmanship of the Romans. They are among the wisest of our spiritual ancestors.[6]

---

[6][For a comprehensive examination of the American classical heritage, see M. Reinhold, *Classica Americana: The Greek and Roman Heritage in the United States* (Detroit, 1984). Ed.]

In Search of Classical Oratory*

We make so many inventions, so many wonderful and terrible inventions, that we are apt to think that human knowledge is constantly increasing. Well, it may be—but not steadily and not without loss. Our technology is improving rapidly; but we are forgetting many things, both useful and beautiful, which our ancestors knew.

In particular, there is one art which was once widely known and has now been almost forgotten. This is the art of making a speech. It was thoroughly understood by our forefathers in the eighteenth and in the nineteenth centuries; long ago the Greeks and Romans brought it to a marvelous height of development; but nowadays it has virtually vanished—so much so that most people do not even know it ever existed.

Of course people go on making speeches, some of them very good too. That is because speaking is a faculty natural to mankind, like singing and dancing. But there is all the difference in the world between a room full of ordinary dancers, practically untrained, shuffling round the floor to the simple 1-2-3-4 music of a dance band, and the complex and sensitive movements of a ballet troupe. There is all the difference in the world between two or three men bawling out *Home on the Range* in the locker room after a golf game, and a trained chorus and soloists singing Richard Wagner's *Mastersingers*. And in the same way, there is all the difference in the world between the average modern politician, laboriously reading out a dull, solid, shapeless speech which he and his associates have hammered into shape during the preceding week, and an orator like Daniel Webster, or Edmund Burke, or the Roman Cicero, standing before an audience with no prepared text in his hand, and both captivating and dominating all those who listen to him. It is the difference between the amateur and the professional. It is the difference between improvisation and art. But at least the Saturday night dancer knows that there is an elaborate technique of professional dancing; the man singing in the locker room does not think he can equal a Wagnerian tenor; and yet the average modern public speaker does not even know that there was once an

---

*Presented in 1956 on Highet's radio program (= *BMCT* 64–65).

art of speechmaking, with tried and tested principles, and with many magnificent models to imitate. He thinks it is enough to write out a statement and then get up and read it—or even worse, to stand up and talk off the cuff, telling a few funny stories, stringing his thoughts together just as they happen to occur to him, and punctuating the whole thing with "er . . . er . . . er . . ." In the same way, most audiences nowadays do not realize that oratory used to be an art; most of them have never heard a really good speech in their lives; they are content if a speaker says something forcible about the Cold War or the farm problem, and they do not understand that oratory depends not only on *what* is said but on *how* it is said.

The Greeks and Romans developed the art of making speeches, and they improved it constantly over a period of something like five hundred years. The two finest orators who ever lived were a Greek, Demosthenes, and a Roman, Cicero. It was through careful study of their speeches and of the Greek and Roman books about oratory (at first or second hand) that the most distinguished orators of the eighteenth and nineteenth centuries formed their own styles and produced their own masterpieces. Now that tradition has all but died away; the concept of oratory as an art has practically vanished. And yet we are living in a time when oratory has become more and more influential, when speakers can be heard by far wider audiences than ever before in history, and when a politician who cannot at least speak well enough to carry some conviction has virtually no chance to be anything more than a dim figure in a back room.

Unfortunately there is no single good modern book in existence which explains all that an orator needs to know. I wish there were. Dozens of people have asked me where they could find one; but there is none in any language known to me. And the Greek and Latin books on oratory, valuable though they are, are nearly all too highly specialized. They assume that the reader already knows the basic principles of speaking, and they go on from there—rather like a book on singing which starts by expecting its readers to have five years of voice training and to be ready to study operatic roles. The best of them are by three very distinguished men: Aristotle's *Rhetoric,* Cicero's *On the Orator,* and Quintilian's *Training of the Orator.* These are full of meat; one could spend a year studying Aristotle alone; but they are not for beginners—and what we need most is a book for beginners. I wish that I had time and experience enough to enable me to write such a book; but I fear I have not. I can, however, outline the principles of Greek and Roman oratory, in the hope that it may stimulate someone else to do so, or at least help some speaker who is anxious to learn the fundamentals of his craft.

To begin with, the ancients laid down that there were three different types of speech—three and only three, each with its own functions, each separate from and unlike the others. They called them—first, the legal speech; second, the deliberative speech; and third, the display speech. The aim of the first, the legal speech, is to persuade a court of the guilt or innocence of an accused man, or of the justice or injustice of a legal claim. The aim of the second, the deliberative speech, is to persuade a group of people to adopt some policy. A candidate's address to the voters, a director's speech at a board meeting, a sermon, a general's message to his troops before battle—all these and many more are deliberative speeches; they are aimed at getting the hearers to make some political or moral decision. The purpose of the third type, the display speech, is to please the audience, and usually to extol some individual or institution, but not primarily to elicit any decision. For instance, a speech proposing the health of the newlyweds at a wedding luncheon, a commencement address in a school or university, a Fourth of July oration, a funeral sermon—all these are display speeches. Outside these three types—the legal speech, the deliberative speech, and the display speech—the Greeks and Romans held that there were no speeches, properly so called; of course there were many subdivisions within each type, but only these types were considered to be real oratory; and the first aim of every speaker was to determine exactly what kind of speech he was going to make so that he could have the clearest possible idea of its purpose.

Now if this is true, and I think that it is, it will solve one of the problems which confront many people today who speak in public—the problem of definition. For instance, is a treasurer's report a speech? Is the President's State of the Union Message a speech? Is a lecture to a college class a speech? Is a talk on a new cure for diabetes a speech?

The answer apparently is that so long as a man speaking in public is doing nothing except giving facts, he is not making a speech. He is simply conveying by word of mouth information which could also be conveyed by print and paper. A treasurer's report consists of bare facts and figures; the only reason why he reads it aloud is so that he may be questioned about facts in it. The State of the Union Message might just as well be printed and circulated; it is usually

sent to Congress, not read by its author;[1] no immediate policy decision is taken after it is communicated—so it is scarcely a speech. A
medical talk is almost wholly factual. If the speaker wishes to persuade his audience that they ought to adopt one type of treatment
rather than another, then his remarks become a speech and are
subject to the rules of oratory; but if he is merely making an objective report without recommendations, then he is not engaged in
speechmaking. A lecture to a college class—that is a more difficult
problem. We have all heard lecturers who, even if they were dealing with moving and important subjects, persisted in reading out
their lectures in the driest and most impersonal, unimpressive
tones; and we have all wondered why they did not simply mimeo-
graph their material and circulate it to the students, as indeed
many lecturers in European universities do. Students themselves
often do not know why they go to lectures and complain that they
would rather read the subject matter for themselves. Both these
students and these lecturers have misconceived the nature of a
lecture. Some lectures must be at least partly speeches because
they are aimed not only at giving facts but at persuading the audience; and other lectures give not only the facts but the processes of
thought which produced and tested the facts, so that the students
themselves will learn to recapitulate and imitate them. Thus it
would be absurd to lecture on meteorology merely by reading out
statistics about the origin and growth of cyclones; the good lecturer
will examine various theories, analyze various explanations, and
teach his hearers both by the workings of his thought and by its results. And it would be ridiculous to lecture on Shakespeare's plays
and treat them merely as laboratory specimens to be examined
impersonally and coldly; the aim of the lecturer is both to explain
the subtleties of Shakespeare's art and to persuade his hearers of
its importance. Insofar as he persuades them, he is more than a
mere lecturer; he is an orator.

So then, there are three types of speech—legal, deliberative, and
display. For each of these the Greeks and Romans worked out an
appropriate pattern—clear, economical, and logical. Their aim

---

[1][For an examination of this interesting subject, see A. M. Schlesinger, Jr.,
"Annual Messages of the Presidents: Major Themes of American History,"
in F. L. Israel, ed., *The State of the Union Messages of the Presidents
(1790–1966)*, 3 vols. (New York, 1966) vol. 1, pp. xiii–xli, especially xiii–xvii.
Although Presidents have clearly differed in their method of presenting
Congress with the State of the Union Message, since the administration of
Franklin Roosevelt they have chosen to deliver the Annual Message in per-
son, in what has obviously become a nationally televised media event. Ed.]

was simply to make speaking more effective; and they worked over and over these patterns in the same way as modern scientists work over and over the structural problems of airplanes, trying to reduce drag, to diminish the waste of power, to increase the pilot's ability to maneuver, and so forth. It is in this field, the field of rhetorical structure, that the ignorance of the average modern speaker is shown most painfully. He usually does not know how to start his speech or how to finish it; he jots down eight or ten important points which he wishes to make, juggles them about until he gets some sort of continuity, and then tries to think of a good opening and closing sentence. He is like a ten-year-old boy building an airplane out of wood and wire, without understanding the principles of aerodynamics.

For instance, the basic pattern for a deliberative speech (that is the type to which political oratory belongs) is a scheme of five parts, each with its own function to fulfill. If you are making such a speech, the Greeks and Romans said it was a mistake to rise and plunge straight into the subject. If you do, the audience will take some time to warm up and will miss much of what you are telling them. Instead you begin by establishing contact with your hearers. In a short passage called the exordium, you set out to arouse their interest, explain briefly why you happen to be addressing them, and give them time to get accustomed to the tone and rhythm of your voice. After this, while their attention is still fresh, comes the second and most important part of your speech—the statement of the policy which you want them to adopt. It must not be too brief, but it must be absolutely clear. Next come the arguments which prove the validity of your proposal, and then the counterarguments designed to destroy the proposals of your opponents. (Do you know that there are only three major arguments to recommend to any proposition? You can say that it is profitable; you can say that it is necessary; or you can say that it is just and honorable. There is scarcely any forceful argument which cannot be subsumed under one of these heads; as soon as you know them, you have a scheme which will help you in arranging your own arguments in the most effective way possible.) Last of all comes the peroration. In it you may summarize what you have said, but you should not put in any further facts. The Greeks and Romans thought it was not usually effective to end with a great outburst of emotion. They defined the purposes of the peroration as—first, to move the audience (so as to mold them to your will), and then, to calm them down (so that the mold will set and remain fixed thereafter).

*   *   *

So much for the framework of the speech. It is basic. Its purpose is to put the reasoning of the orator in the clearest and most effective order. But speechmaking is more than merely intellectual; it is also moral and emotional; and therefore the classical writers on oratory believed that every speaker who aspired to excellence should control three different types of persuasion.

One of these was naturally argument—proof by logic. Many, though not all, of the ancients believed that this could best be learned through training in philosophy; and nearly all of them maintained that every orator ought to have at his disposal a large number of general themes which he had carefully thought over and which he could draw upon to illustrate any particular argument. Today, for example, anyone entering politics would be well advised to have thought out all the pros and cons in the essential conflict between the liberties of the individual citizen and the claims of the state, and to introduce topics drawn from that theme whenever they were relevant. But the greatest of all logicians, Aristotle, filled many pages with arguments even simpler and more central than that—the argument from analogy, the argument from analysis, and so on.

But logic alone will neither win a case nor convince a meeting. Two other kinds of persuasion are needed. The Greeks called one of them pathos and the other ethos.

Pathos means emotion of any kind; and no one will deny that the emotion of a crowd listening to a speaker is a most powerful and unforgettable force. You remember the fierce shouts of the audiences that listened to the recent European dictators: it was hard for us to tell which was more terrifying—the harsh voices of Hitler and Mussolini, or the eager yells that replied to them. The greatest of modern dramatists has shown this effect in one tremendous scene of the tragedy of *Julius Caesar,* where Mark Antony, standing over the body of his murdered master, begins with the gentlest and simplest exordium (3.2.74–75):

> Friends, Romans, countrymen, lend me your ears:
> I come to bury Caesar, not to praise him . . .

And yet, within a short speech in which he uses almost every trick of rhetoric, he manages to convert the calm citizens into a raging mob shouting (3.2.204):

Revenge! About! Seek! Burn! Fire! Kill! Slay!

This is one of Shakespeare's most brilliant feats, to have reconstructed a supremely effective speech made by a Roman orator of remote antiquity. In a democracy most speakers do not wish to rouse such savage passions; or if they do, they refrain from carrying them to such a dangerous and destructive pitch. But *some* emotion should be stirred in the audience by every speech, whether it be hope, or solid confidence, grief, fury, or shame, or the spirit of self-sacrifice, or the spirit of just indignation. And how can the speaker arouse emotion in his hearers? The Greeks worked out many rules, drawn from experience, to help him in doing so—too many to go into here; but they agreed on one important fact, that he must not permit himself to become more excited than his audience. He must feel emotion, yes, and he must communicate it, but (like an actor in a tragic drama) he must remain in control of himself, his thoughts, and his listeners.

The third type of persuasion is one which we all know well, because we have all seen it in the speeches of President Franklin Roosevelt and Sir Winston Churchill. The ancients called it ethos; and they meant by it the type of conviction which is produced by a speaker who sounds and looks like a good and wise man. Because you trust such a speaker, you are inclined to believe what he says and to allow yourself to be persuaded by him. This quality is rare. Sometimes it exists in men who are otherwise fairly poor orators: President Eisenhower is a good example of its force, and so was President Washington. (Whether, on the other hand, it is possible for a complete scoundrel to deceive many audiences by creating in them a false idea of his own worth and wisdom, I do not know; but I think it must be, for the career of Adolf Hitler is there as a proof. However, such deception is extraordinarily rare and extraordinarily difficult.) To persuade an audience by means of ethos, two things are usually needed: first, a deep and a noble character strengthened through many trials; and second, a manner and a style which convey the value of that character to the audience. However noble and virtuous a speaker may be—if he talks foolishly, if he argues incoherently or flippantly, and if his voice and manner are unimpressive, he will fail to convince us. Some of President Lincoln's speeches which read as masterpieces of prose were unsuccessful when he delivered them, because of his awkward appearance and his provincial voice and accent. I have heard addresses by eminent men of religion, which sounded as though they were being delivered by a particularly fatuous Sunday

School teacher to a particularly doltish class; and although I could not doubt the virtue of their speakers, I could only regret that they had been quite unable to convey ethos, the conviction of their worth.

This takes us to another quality which every orator needs but which few now study—it is style, the art of using words. After the speech has been planned, after the arguments have been arranged, the whole framework must still be clothed in words. If the words are poorly chosen and clumsily placed, they will obscure the values of even the most powerful thought and sterling character. If they are brilliant and memorable, they will stay in the memory even when the ideas which they embodied have ceased to move our minds. Nobody nowadays cares very much about the doctrine of bimetallism (except perhaps a few senators from the 'Silver States'), but many people remember the superb climax of William Jennings Bryan's speech on the subject: "You shall not press down upon the brow of labor this crown of thorns; you shall not crucify mankind upon a cross of gold."[2]

Now style is not a gift; it is a faculty which can be developed by thought and practice. Lincoln's *Gettysburg Address* was the result of many years of study and was worked over very carefully several times before being delivered.[3] There are two indispensable ways to practice rhetorical style—both used by the Greeks and Romans. One is to read the best models, the most famous speeches of all times, to study their effects and to try to rival their imagery and their phrasing. (There is a good treasury of the world's great speeches edited by Houston Peterson.)[4] The other is to work with a friend or tutor who is sensitive to style and who, after hearing you speak, will go over the speech with you word by word and sentence by sentence, pointing out deficiencies and advising you how to remove them. One of the finest English speakers, William Pitt the Younger, was trained at home by his father. Still in his early teens, he was made to translate entire speeches from the Greek and Roman orators—not word for word, but rather as though he were paraphrasing them in English—while his father listened and then criticized his choice and arrangement of words. The result was

---

[2][Delivered on July 8, 1896, at the Democratic National Convention. Ed.]
[3][Delivered on November 19, 1863, at the dedication of the national cemetery on the Civil War battlefield of Gettysburg, Pennsylvania. Ed.]
[4][See H. Peterson, ed., *A Treasury of the World's Great Speeches* (New York, 1954[1] and 1965[2]), in which each speech is "prefaced with its dramatic and biographical setting and placed in its full historical perspective." Ed.]

that by the time he entered Parliament (at the age of twenty-one)
he was so fluent, commanded so many powerful images, and could
speak with such sustained energy, that he dominated the House
and could move even his bitter opponents to applause. But practice
is essential. Any speaker who is in doubt about the effectiveness of a
speech he has written should deliver it several times—either alone,
or to a small and sympathetic audience such as an intelligent wife,
or even to a tape recorder. Thin patches and ugly repetitions will
become far more apparent at the third recitation and can then be
removed with confidence.

Of course the Greeks and Romans went far further into delicacies of style than we nowadays even think possible. They studied
the harmonious arrangement of separate syllables—not so as to
make their speeches regularly rhythmical, like poetry, but in order to produce the indefinable effect of nobility which a loose but
pervasive prose rhythm always conveys, and to stamp their words
more deeply on the memory of their hearers. Modern research
has revealed the presence of underlying rhythmical patterns in
many of the most powerful sentences of Cicero and Demosthenes.
One famous speech by Demosthenes *(On the Crown)* begins: "I
pray to all the gods and goddesses that . . . " The thought in English
is impressive; but the words are not. However, in Greek they form
a rhythmical pattern which is inimitably solemn and impressive:
τοῖς θεοῖς εὔχομαι πᾶσι καὶ πάσαις . . . Sir Winston Churchill has
often brought off similar effects with great success. Lincoln's
Gettysburg Address is filled with them, right down to the very last
words—"that government of the people, by the people, for the people, shall not perish from the earth." Notice how the pace of the final clause, after the powerful triplet on the people, gradually slack-
ens. Lincoln would not say "shall not die out in the world" or "shall
not perish among mankind"; instead he used a strong four-syllable
phrase, and then a slower, stronger, three-syllable phrase—"shall
not perish / from the earth."[5]

One further virtue of the Greek and Roman orators is now
largely neglected by politicians, although it is still practiced to some

---

[5][For Highet's own analysis of the *Gettysburg Address* as a skillfully constructed oration, see his essay "The *Gettysburg Address*," in *A Clerk of
Oxenford* (New York, 1954) 84–91—an essay belonging to a long tradition of
publications dealing with Lincoln's most famous and most quoted speech.
Interest in Gettysburg culminated in the publication of G. Wills's *Lincoln
at Gettysburg* (New York, 1992), which received the Pulitzer Prize for its il-
luminating treatment of the subject and examined the influence of classical
oratory on the construction of Lincoln's memorable little masterpiece. Ed.]

extent by legal orators and preachers. This is memory. The ancients seldom read their speeches. They seldom used notes. Usually they prepared their speeches with great care, then learned them by heart, rehearsed them again and again until they sounded entirely spontaneous, and delivered them apparently off the cuff—even to the mock hesitations and the apparently improvised jokes. In the schools of rhetoric, young speakers were given elaborate training in the art of memory. We hear of astonishing feats performed by their virtuosos. Cicero's rival Hortensius could remember not only his own speech but the entire outline of his opponent's speech and its most important paragraphs—which he would quote in order to refute them in detail. When he was preparing a two-hour speech on an important case, Cicero studied and memorized his speech in the same way as a modern pianist studies and memorizes a concerto, or a singer the leading role in an opera. You would think it ridiculous to see Walther in the *Mastersingers* carrying about a score of the opera and reading his words and music off it as he sang. The ancients thought it was just as ridiculous to see an orator standing on the platform reading off his speech and hesitating when he turned the page.

Last of the five virtues of the orator is that which Demosthenes considered the most important of all: delivery—the power of the voice, the play of the features, the mocking, passionate, or exciting gesture. This art again is almost wholly neglected today. Probably this is because most speakers are tied to the microphone and the manuscript. If you are afraid of moving about on the platform because you may become inaudible and will certainly lose your place in your prepared script, all you can do is to hang onto the reading desk like a pigeon roosting, and look up and down, up and down, at the audience like a pigeon feeding. But that is not the most effective oratory. One of these days we shall see a speaker who has courage enough, talent enough, and training enough to ignore the microphone (or even to wear a small portable mike), to memorize his speech, and to deliver it with energy and conviction. Whoever he is, he will be a powerful man; and he will be the true successor of the Greek and Roman orators.

Schliemann's Excavations[*]

The earth is full of buried treasures—treasures made by man, hidden, forgotten, and lost, lost sometimes forever. Not all the earth. There are few such treasures in the new continents—North and South America outside the regions of the great pre-Columbian empires, southern and central Africa, and Australia. But elsewhere, in those lands which men have inhabited and fought over for many thousands of years, lie enormous, undreamed-of, exquisitely beautiful, and unthinkably strange treasures. Many are the buried treasures in the earth and (we now begin to realize) in the sea; few are those who know how to find them. The men who do not simply break into a hillock on their grandfather's field or accidentally run a bulldozer into a queen's dowry, the men who search for the site unknown even to those who live above it, the men who look through history and pierce through geology to the wealth and magnificence of the past—these are the true searchers; these are archaeologists, the explorers of oblivion.

One of the most famous among these men, if not the greatest, one of the most widely publicized, if not the most deeply respected, and one of the most sensationally, even scandalously successful— whom some would call the P. T. Barnum or the Mike Todd of archaeology, while others would pinpoint his mistakes and do everything in the diametrically opposite manner—was the gloomy, self-absorbed, nervous, half-educated but brilliantly self-trained hypochondriac millionaire named Heinrich Schliemann. It was he who discovered Troy and excavated the fortress of Mycenae.

Many millionaires are a little mad. Some of them have inherited their money and come to think (half-consciously of course) that they must be specifically favored by providence; some of them have made their money by a combination of skill and luck, and they tend to think that—when they can do something with one of the essentials of human social life which almost nobody else can do— they must be partly superhuman. Heinrich Schliemann belonged to the second type. He was born in the most frightful and discouraging poverty. Before he was thirty he was quite often faced with

---

*Presented in 1958 on Highet's radio program (= *BMCT* 156).

death by starvation or by cold and fatigue. He survived. He made not one single large fortune but three at least. And then he turned away from money to capture something else even more difficult which had eluded the eager grasp of all his predecessors—the wealth and glory and vivid life of the Greek heroic age.

The tale of Schliemann's life is told in a number of books—although, as far as I know, there is none which deals fully both with his strange character and career and with the meaning and impact of his archaeological discoveries. The latest is *The Gold of Troy* by Robert Payne[1]—interesting, bright, and easily read, though rather superficial. If I had a son of about fifteen who wanted to be a scholar, I think I should give him this book; adults should read it with reservations; still, it tells some of the story well.

What did Schliemann do? In a single sentence: he was one of the first men to give myths and legends a firm root in history. When he was born, no one was really sure whether ancient Troy was just a piece of pure fiction, like the Never-Never Land of James M. Barrie, or the Utopia of Sir Thomas More, or a positive fact of past history; and those who thought it was a positive fact could not really imagine what the city had been like when it still stood. Troy was a thing of fable. Those who wanted to imagine it went to one or two small hills in the lonely plain of northwestern Turkey near the Dardanelles, surrounded by swampy rivers, licorice fields, and wretched villages. One hill was called by the Turkish name of Bunarbashi, and the other by the Turkish name of Hissarlik. Most people thought that Troy might be under Bunarbashi, a few that it was hidden under Hissarlik. No one had seriously tried to find out. (There had, of course, been spectacularly successful excavations further east, where the Englishman Henry Austen Layard had dug up ancient Nineveh; but no one had yet made a real attempt to reveal Troy.)

Probably because Hissarlik was unpopular, Schliemann went to it, hired some laborers, and told them to start digging there. On the very first day he discovered the foundations of a large building, forty feet by sixty feet. And thereafter, against countless difficulties—an atrocious climate, the passive resistance of the Turkish government, the objections of the local landlords who owned part of the site, the finagling of the workmen, and the proliferation of the local fauna (including vipers)—he discovered much of a very ancient city. He dug up traces of a primitive religion, including

---

[1][See R. Payne, *The Gold of Troy* (New York, 1959)—previewed by Highet in 1958. Ed.]

some very explicit sexual symbols; many examples of plastic art so naive that it surprised and rather disgusted him; enormous jars, which in remote antiquity were signs of wealth, for they meant that the owner had much food and drink to store away; huge primitive fortifications; weapons made not of steel or iron or even bronze, but of copper and obsidian; and many other strange, at that time all but inexplicable treasures. Finally, he himself found and (with infinite circumspection) smuggled away—from Turkey to Greece and from Greece to Germany—a huge hoard of silver and of gold: three silver vases, six silver daggers, two enormous crowns made of multiple gold rings, and over eight thousand golden rings and golden buttons. This, said Schliemann, was the treasure of King Priam. It was not, but it was certainly the treasure of some king of Troy, buried in some infinitely remote era of the past.

The Turks, naturally enough, were furious with rage when they learned how Schliemann had conveyed this priceless discovery out of the country; they sued him, and he had to pay compensation; but he retained the treasure. Eventually, after much soul-searching, he presented it to the German nation. It sat in a special wing of the Ethnological Museum in Berlin from 1881 until 1939. Then it was once again buried deep in the earth. In 1945 Russian troops discovered it and sent it back through their lines; and now it appears to be lost once more.[2]

There is another treasure discovered by Schliemann which is not lost—or not yet. After his great find in Troy, he left and went to the enemy of Troy—to the ruined palace of Mycenae in southeastern Greece, once (according to legend) inhabited by the kings of Argos who led the Greek expedition against Troy and its allies, twelve hundred years or so before the birth of Jesus. Here there was no doubt, as there had been at Troy. The site was known and identified. There were the ruins of palace and fortress, clear to see, crouched upon a hill like a wolf watching a herd of cattle in the plain. But here it was believed that there was nothing left to discover. One magnificent and terrible royal tomb had been opened and robbed long, long before Schliemann got there. No one could see anything else of any value. Shepherds used the ruins for shelter, and sometimes bandits hid in them. But Schliemann, like a modern oil man, knew that the real values are buried; and he had

---

[2][But see C. Moorehead, *Lost and Found: The 9,000 Treasures of Troy* (New York, 1996) 5–11 and 266–93, on the 'rediscovery' of the treasure, which the Russians admitted to having after almost fifty years of silence and decided to put on display in 1996 at the Pushkin Museum. Ed.]

a remarkable power of divination, which came from his delighted absorption in the distant past. Near the entrance to the fortress of Mycenae there was a circle of vertical stone slabs like a very small Stonehenge. Obviously it was ceremonial and important. And so Schliemann started his men digging there. They dug for weeks in the summer heat with little success; and for weeks in the autumn rains; they began to find primitive symbols, primitive weapons, fragments of pottery; and then, as they got deeper, they found skeletons, royal skeletons wearing their golden crowns, deep below the detritus of ages. Grave after grave was revealed. Schliemann had struck one of the royal cemeteries of Mycenae, where those wicked and powerful monarchs lay buried with their golden necklaces, golden wine jars, golden crowns, and sword pommels of rock crystal. At last, toward the end of his magnificent bonanza, he made the most spectacular discovery of all—the death masks of the kings.

When you enter the National Museum in Athens and turn into the big room which contains Schliemann's finds, you see all round you a dazzling display of ornaments and utensils, many of them gold; some are childishly primitive; others are worked with such delicacy that their artists must have been the fourth or fifth generation of specialists. All is splendid; all is strange. But the strangest thing is that, as you walk in, you are confronted by the faces of the men who owned these things. Apparently, just after a prince of Mycenae died, the court goldsmith was ordered to mold out of thin gold plate a face which, during and after the interment, would cover and somehow immortalize the perishable face of bone and flesh. Such a face was a real portrait; and so the death masks seem not to be the symbols of conventional monarchs, like so many mummy cases and statues of the Pharaohs, but rather to be real men, with the same peculiar life as a modern portrait by a Titian or a Rembrandt—a point that Mr. Payne makes very convincingly.[3] It is indescribably impressive to look at these countenances, dead and yet alive. One shows an elderly man with a heavy ridge of brow overhanging two large, tired eyes, closed at last in sleep; beneath them rises a powerful ridge of nose; and below that is a mouth closed tightly in a permanent grimace of combative resolution. Like Shelley's Ozymandias of Egypt, he has the "sneer of cold command." But the one which I recall best still retains in death a hideous tight-lipped smile beneath a curling mustache and below

---

[3][See Payne (above, note 1) 179–210, especially 196–201, regarding the golden masks. Ed.]

two large, round eyes—which in their day saw everything and watched everything. Such eyes and such a smile had the tyrant Atreus at the climax of his long diplomatic intrigue with his brother Thyestes, when, after welcoming his rival back to his disputed palace, he killed Thyestes' children, and cooked their flesh, and served it to Thyestes at the welcome banquet.

I need scarcely add that Schliemann's discoveries were doubted and even denied. People said that he had forged them all to make a reputation;[4] others suggested that they were not Greek or Trojan, but Oriental, brought in by Arab or Phoenician traders; and some thought they might be quite modern—loot stored up by Frankish conquerors in the Middle Ages. However, they were all real, although difficult to interpret. Schliemann never doubted that they were real. How could he, when he himself had first seen them come to light, when his own beautiful Greek wife had crouched for hours in the excavations, delicately picking off the encrusted clay and earth, as though she were picking off the years, one by one through the first thousand, and then the second, and then the third?

What kind of man was Schliemann himself, who discovered all this mystery and majesty? The story of his character and career is well told in Mr. Payne's book. Heinrich Schliemann was born in 1822, the son of a poor parson in a poor parish in a poor German province, East Prussia. He was denied a proper schooling and took a job in a general store at the age of fourteen. Between fourteen and twenty he formed his tough, angular character and his strong, wiry body. After many grave disappointments—social, financial, and marital—he determined that in order to live a decent life he had to make money. So between the ages of twenty and twenty-four, he learned seven languages—French, Spanish, Portuguese, English, Italian, Dutch, and finally Russian. That—together with his indomitable will and the hard experience in commercial methods which he had already acquired—made him his first fortune, as a general importer of all kinds of merchandise into rich, backward Russia. He made his second in California, where he arrived just after the great San Francisco fire and worked for some time as one of the first reliable bankers who had international connections. His third he made importing even more desperately needed mer-

---

4[See (most recently) D. A. Traill, *Schliemann of Troy: Treasure and Deceit* (New York, 1995) 1–13 and 298–306, in which the author uses Schliemann's diaries and correspondence to argue that Schliemann repeatedly distorted facts pertaining to his life and to his excavations. Ed.]

chandise into Russia during the Crimean War. Before he was forty years old, he was worth over a million dollars, which would be equivalent to at least twenty million today.

He did not start out as a classical scholar, but he became a famous classical discoverer. He had all the talents required by the explorer. First, he had absolute confidence. When he had made a decision, he stuck to it, even if it meant weeks of apparently fruitless digging, many speculations which turned out to be hopeless, public frustrations, and the contempt of the experts. Second, he had enormous energy, far more than the average professor had. In his youth he had fought his way across the Isthmus of Panama, among savage primitives and even savager white men, and he could not be daunted by a few striking workmen or a few slothful officials trying to save their own gold-brick department. The world is my enemy, he told himself in bad times; and at other times he thought the world was his instrument. And finally, he had an ideal. He did not like the society in which he had had to live and make money. He thought the ancient Greeks were simpler and nobler; he spoke and wrote classical Greek by preference; he read Homer every day for hours; and his chief aim for many years was to reconstruct the spiritual values of a world he thought superior to the bitter, snarling, greedy, scratching, petty world which he had inhabited and then dominated.

It is ironic that one of his greatest discoveries should have been the grim, wily face of a monarch of three thousand years ago who viewed the world as an instrument, a den of slaves, a piece of plunder. But an artist transformed that old king's face into a work of art; and an ideal transmuted Schliemann's life, which might have been part of a vulgar comedy by Honoré de Balzac, into something like a romance and something like an epic.

Housman's Critical Prose[*]

Loveliest of trees, the cherry now
Is hung with bloom along the bough,
And stands about the woodland ride
Wearing white for Eastertide.

Most of us know these beautiful lines, the name of the book from which they come, and the name of the author. They appear in *A Shropshire Lad* (2.1–4) by A. E. Housman, who published the book in 1896 and died forty years later, in 1936. But not so many of us know the prose writings of the same man. Not so many of us even realize that, besides being a poet, he had another career, quite differently oriented and calculated to earn him a very dissimilar type of fame. Housman was a classical scholar, and he was one of the bitterest, most venomous, and most ruthless critics who ever put pen to paper. Most professors are pretty mild people. The French occasionally needle one another, and the Germans used to bowff sharply at their rivals; but Housman earned a worldwide reputation for relentless savagery.

The type of work on which he spent his life is a little hard to understand without special training. He was devoted to one central purpose—to establish, to justify, and (where strictly necessary) to explain the exact text of the Greek and Roman classics. This is much more difficult to do than it sounds. We have virtually nothing that corresponds to a first edition of any of these books—nothing contemporary with the men who wrote them and with their first readers. What we have is copies of copies of copies of the originals. Now in every one of these copies there are some things which do not make any sense as they stand, either because the man who wrote the manuscript copy did not reproduce accurately what he had in front of him (through fatigue, or ignorance, or the difficulty of reading a strange script), or else because he was copying from a book which had some imperfection in it (damp stains which had blurred the writing, torn or missing leaves, pages or sections mixed up, and so on). If you take any two of these manuscript copies, you will find that they scarcely ever correspond to each other in the

---

[*]Presented in 1956 on Highet's radio program (= *BMCT* 51).

same way as two copies of a modern machine-made book will correspond. Names appear in one form here and in another form there. One copy puts the poems in a different order from another. One copy will have a line, or even a whole page, which is not to be found in other copies. Which is right?

Suppose there are three hundred copies of a Greek poem. Which shall we take to be closest to what the poet himself wrote? Which shall we print? The most elaborately and beautifully written? The oldest? The one which has a huge mass of medieval notes explaining it? Or should we follow the majority? Or perhaps should we trust none of them implicitly, but try to work back through them all to the original, in the hope of coming out with something like the poet's actual words? And what happens when we find a line or a passage which is totally unintelligible, although it is in every one of the three hundred copies? The scribes themselves, it is obvious, did not understand it. What shall we do? Leave it out? Or try to reconstruct what the poet had in mind? If so, how can we possibly penetrate through two thousand years of darkness to the original light? And can we ever be certain that we are anywhere near the truth?

These then, put very simply, are the problems which occupy classical scholars. Similar problems, and others even more ferociously difficult, beset everyone who attempts to study the origin and the transmission of the Christian and Jewish scriptures; and at any moment a new discovery, like that of the Dead Sea Scrolls, may make their job even more complicated. People who are not specialists usually think that the chief problem is *reading* the manuscripts, actually making out what they say; but this is not so. Good manuscripts are almost as easy to read as print. A few of the letters are a little different in shape from our own, but one can learn them in a day. The ink is still strong and the letters are well formed; the only difficulty comes when some later scribe has erased a word and written in some change, which he thinks is an 'improvement.' No, the real difficulty is, having read the manuscripts, to judge how closely they represent the original, the actual words of the poet or the philosopher or the historian whom we are studying. On that task A. E. Housman spent much of his life.

He reconstructed the text of three Roman poets: a satirist, Juvenal; an epic writer, Lucan; and an astronomer and astrologer, Manilius. In addition, he edited several smaller poems and wrote many articles suggesting changes in the accepted text of authors, both Greek and Latin.[1] His work was always valuable and occasionally brilliant; but by its very nature it can interest only specialists. What we can all appreciate is one of its by-products—the extraordinarily pungent prose in which he discussed his textual criticism and the work of other scholars living and dead. In this he sounds more like Dean Swift[2] than anyone else in the English language; and indeed they were both moved by the same fundamental impulse—indignation. Some of the best prose in the world has been produced by the Power of Negative Thinking.

You remember that one of the chief problems confronting a critic is to decide, when he has many different copies of a Greek or Latin poem (all in manuscript), which of them he should follow and indeed whether any of them could be followed absolutely. Now here is A. E. Housman discussing the same problem. (And remember, this was written within ten years of the appearance of *A Shropshire Lad.*) He has explained that one of the manuscript copies of Juvenal's poems is undoubtedly better than the others, but he adds that this does not mean we ought to believe it always, absolutely, and merely to print what it says, ignoring all the other copies. I know it is a very special and technical subject, but hear with what energy and what venom Housman handles it:[3]

> In thus committing ourselves to the guidance of the best MS we cherish no hope that it will always lead us right: we know that it will often lead us wrong; but we know that any other MS would lead us wrong still oftener. By following any other MS we shall only be right in the minority of cases; by following [manuscript] P we shall be right in the majority: that is all we look for. A critic therefore, when he employs this method of trusting the best MS, employs it in the same spirit of gloomy resignation with which a man lies down on a stretcher when he has broken both his legs. But far other is the spirit in which it is hailed by the reciter of formulas. He is not dejected by its inadequacy, but captivated by its ease. "Here" says he "is a method, sanctioned by critics, employed in scientific enquiry, and yet involving not the slightest expenditure of intellectual effort: this is the method for me"; and he espouses it for ever. In places where critics rise up and walk, where judgment has scope and authority is superseded, he remains supine and marvels at the vagaries of pedestrians: presumptuous

---

[1][For these articles—all published between 1882 and 1936—see J. Diggle and F. R. D. Goodyear, edd., *The Classical Papers of A. E. Housman,* 3 vols. (London, 1972). Ed.]

[2][Jonathan Swift was appointed Dean of St. Patrick's Cathedral in Dublin in 1713. Ed.]

[3]See A. E. Housman, ed., *D. Iunii Iuvenalis Saturae* (Cambridge, 1905[1] and 1931[2]) pref. xv–xvi.

beings who expect to reach their goal by the capricious and arbitrary method of putting forward first one foot, and then, with strange inconsistency, the other.

That is good prose, I think you will agree, but it is not calculated to make friends and conciliate people. The German critics, at whom most of those barbed shafts were aimed, may not have been wits or epigrammatists of the same order, but they were shrewd enough to see that Housman was calling them mental cripples. They replied with bitter reviews of all his work, and for many years he was the most unpopular of all classical scholars. He retorted even more violently. Here is another statement of the same position, from the preface to his edition of Manilius:[4]

> An editor of no judgment, perpetually confronted with a couple of MSS to choose from, cannot but feel in every fibre of his being that he is a donkey between two bundles of hay. What shall he do now? Leave criticism to critics, you may say, and betake himself to any honest trade for which he is less unfit. But he prefers a more flattering solution: he confusedly imagines that if one bundle of hay is removed he will cease to be a donkey. So he removes it. Are the two MSS equal, and do they bewilder him with their rival merit and exact from him at every other moment the novel and distressing effort of using his brains? Then he pretends that they are not equal: he calls one of them "the best MS," and to this he resigns the editorial functions which he is himself unable to discharge.

Bitter as it is, this still does not name names. A little later in the same preface, we see Housman denouncing his predecessors and his competitors by name. The poet Manilius on whom he was engaged had been edited by two Germans, who committed the fatal error of believing that one particular manuscript held the whole truth, or nearly the whole truth. (Each of them chose a different manuscript to worship, which made it funnier.) Here is Housman, commenting on them:[5]

> To elude what Byron calls "the blight of life—the demon Thought," Messrs. Jacob and Bechert have committed themselves respectively to the Vossianus [manuscript] and the Gemblacensis [manuscript], the devil and the deep sea. Having small literary culture they are not revolted by illiteracy, having slight knowledge of grammar they are not revolted by solecism, having no sequence of ideas they are not revolted by incoherency, having nebulous thoughts they are not revolted by nonsense.

---

[4]See A. E. Housman, ed., *M. Manilii Astronomicon,* 5 vols. (London, 1903–1930[1] and 1937[2]) vol. 1, pref. xxxi.
[5]See Housman (above, note 4) vol. 1, pref. xxxix.

This is only the beginning of an enormous tirade which ends in an epigram, famous among classical scholars; the epigram denounces such critics as[6]

> gentlemen who use MSS as drunkards use lampposts—not to light them on their way but to dissimulate their instability.

In case you may be repelled by Housman's acrimony, let me remind you that he had a great deal of neglect and misrepresentation to endure. He spent about thirty years in editing and publishing the Roman poet Manilius. When he reached the end of his task, he looked back (that was in 1930), and this is what he wrote:[7]

> All [the volumes of this edition] were produced at my own expense and offered to the public at much less than cost price; but this unscrupulous artifice did not overcome the natural disrelish of mankind for the combination of a tedious author with an odious editor. Of each volume there were printed 400 copies: only the first is yet sold out, and that took 23 years; and the reason why it took no longer is that it found purchasers among the unlearned, who had heard that it contained a scurrilous preface and hoped to extract from it a low enjoyment.

But there were other reasons for his asperity. These were: first, that he himself deeply loved poetry—all poetry, in whatever language—so that when he saw it mishandled by lazy or incompetent critics, he was disgusted; and second, that he admired accurate reasoning as one of the activities which distinguish men from animals, and therefore, when he saw sloppy argument and herd-thinking among his fellow scholars, he felt as revolted as you or I should do if we saw a man eating out of a trough like a pig.

One of the most painful events in the recent history of classical scholarship occurred in 1930, when Housman, in the preface to the last volume of his edition of Manilius, spent over two hundred lines of small type in pillorying a miserable Dutch scholar who had published an edition of the same poet, in showing up his mistakes one by one, and (worst of all) in pointing out with bitter satisfaction the passages in which the Dutchman—instead of making his own mistakes—had copied the mistakes of other men without observing them.[8]

---

[6]See Housman (above, note 4) vol. 1, pref. liii.

[7]See Housman (above, note 4) vol. 5, pref. v.

[8][See Housman (above, note 4) vol. 5, pref. xxvi–xxxii, for this tirade—an attack on J. van Wageningen's *Commentarius in M. Manilii Astronomica* (Amsterdam, 1921). Ed.]

It is witty, Housman's critical prose, and it is splendidly crisp; but it is often disagreeable to read—simply because it makes us believe that he enjoyed giving pain. Insofar as that is true, his prose work deserves to be relegated to the dustier shelves of the library. But it has one incontestable merit which makes it worth reading—once at least—by all students of literature and history and art. That is that he takes his subject seriously. He loathes amateurs; he will not endure inadequate and slipshod discussion of any subject; and thus, by the very acidity of his comments on scholars now dead and gone and forgotten, he reminds us again and again that great poetry and great prose ought to be handled with the most profound reverence, and that of all the powers man possesses, the power of clear thinking is the most vitally important and yet the most easily abused.[9]

---

[9][For Highet's further views on Housman, see his "Professor Paradox," in *A Clerk of Oxenford* (New York, 1954) 173–81—reprinted in *The Powers of Poetry* (New York, 1960) 114–21. Ed.]

Cavafy's *Waiting for the Barbarians**

What are we waiting for, assembled in the city square?

 It is the barbarians who are coming today.

Why is there such idleness in the Senate?
Why are the Senators sitting there without making laws?

 Because the barbarians are coming today.
 Why should the Senators make any more laws?
 The barbarians, when they arrive, will make the laws.

Why did our Emperor wake up so early in the morning,
and why is he sitting at the biggest gate of the city
on his throne, in state, wearing his crown?

 Because the barbarians are coming today.
 And the emperor is waiting to welcome
 their leader. In fact he has prepared
 to give him a piece of parchment. There
 he has written many titles for him and names.

Why have our two consuls and the praetors gone out
today with their crimson, their embroidered togas?
Why are they wearing bracelets with so many amethysts
and rings with bright glittering emeralds?
Why are they carrying their expensive walking-sticks
with choice carvings in silver and gold?

 Because the barbarians will arrive today,
 and such things impress the barbarians.

Why have our worthy orators not gone out as usual
to sound off their speeches and say their say?

---

*A 1966 translation of a poem originally published by Constantine Cavafy in
1904.

Because the barbarians are coming today;
and they are bored by eloquence and oratory.

Why has this uneasiness suddenly started,
this confusion? The faces, how serious they have grown.
Why are the streets and squares emptying so quickly,
and everyone going home so deep in thought?

Because it has grown dark and the barbarians have not arrived.
And some people have come from the frontier
and said there are no barbarians any more.

And now what will become of us without barbarians?
These people were a sort of solution.[1]

---

[1][At the end of this piece Highet wrote: "Is this the world of Byzantium or of 1966?" Ed.]

Joyce's *Ulysses*[*]

Most of us have heard, however vaguely, of *Ulysses,* the vast and complicated novel by the Anglo-Irish writer James Joyce. For ten or fifteen years after it was first published (in 1922) it was notorious; then it became famous; now it is in its special way a classic. And it has fully earned both its notoriety and its fame. It is so outrageously obscene and blasphemous that it could not at first be published in the United States or Canada or Britain. Joyce had to have it set up by French printers and issued in Paris. When copies were sent over for importation into the United States and Britain, they were seized by customs authorities and burned. (I remember that, after buying my copy in Paris, I had to smuggle it past the customs officer in a handful of innocent magazines; this was made easier by the fact that it had a limp paper cover, but I still turned a little pale and breathed a little heavily.)

Ulysses was the subject of a famous trial (in 1933), at which the United States endeavored to have it declared obscene under the Tariff Act and therefore subject to seizure and confiscation if imported. (Presumably it would follow that, if any American publisher tried to print it, all his copies would be seized and destroyed.) Judge John M. Woolsey, in a clear and well-written opinion, determined that the book was not obscene within the legal definition of obscenity—that is (roughly), that it was not pornographic: it did not attempt to stimulate lustful thoughts.[1] He was of course absolutely right. *Ulysses* is full of filthy words and disgusting scenes, and there is a great deal of sex in it, but it is emphatically not pornographic. Indeed, one of the recurrent themes in it is a pornographic French romance called *Sweets of Sin,* with a hero called Raoul who happens to like perfumed underwear; but whenever this romance is evoked, it produces merely contempt mingled with amusement and disgust mingled with boredom. In the closing sen-

---

[*]Presented in 1958 on Highet's radio program (= *BMCT* 137).
[1][See J. Joyce, *Ulysses* (New York, 1934[1])—this or any later edition published by Random House—for the transcript of Judge Woolsey's decision to lift the ban on Joyce's novel. Ed.]

tences of his opinion, Judge Woolsey said that *Ulysses* was not aphrodisiac but emetic. That pretty well sums it up.

It is famous also for its obscurity. Joyce deliberately made it as difficult to understand as possible, heaping up double and quadruple and decuple meanings, constantly interrupting the movement of the narrative with apparently irrelevant parodies and reminiscences, stepping into them out of the minds of his characters, from objective to subjective, half a dozen times in the same page, and varying the style and pace of his story so widely that it is hard to believe two neighboring chapters were written by the same author in the same book. This is perfectly legitimate; in fact it is marvelous artistry, for when people are experiencing different states of consciousness, surely they ought to be described in different styles and rhythms; but it is difficult to understand as it was surely difficult to write. For instance, the next-to-last chapter deals with two men who are just sobering up after a drunken brawl; so it is all set out in carefully—rather too carefully—logical questions and answers. In the last chapter of all, the subject is a woman, who is lying in bed in the darkness half asleep, dozing and remembering and letting her mind wander. Since one's thoughts at such a time flow on and on in a continuous meandering stream with no abrupt interruptions or long pauses, the whole chapter is one continuous paragraph of eight sentences, forty-five pages long. This is astoundingly skillful writing, but it does not make *Ulysses* easy to read.

Most books fall into groups and follow patterns. *Ulysses* in many ways is unique. It is the only book in modern times to be written successfully in fifty or sixty different styles. It is the only book which spends over seven hundred pages on describing the events of a single day in a single place. (The place is Dublin, Ireland; the day is June 16, 1904—which Joyce enthusiasts, after the name of one of his heroes, call Bloomsday.) It is perhaps the only modern novel which is modeled, both as a whole and in each of its separate parts, on a classical epic poem. The poem is Homer's *Odyssey*. The overall correspondence is that in the poem the hero Odysseus spends many years in dangerous wandering and at last returns home to be reunited with his son and his wife, and his son, who has been waiting and searching for him, grows through his trials into a man; while in *Ulysses* Leopold Bloom, a wandering Jew, spends many hours—and faces various dangers and trials—roaming through Dublin until he at last reaches home and his wife, and Stephen Dedalus, a penniless, parentless student, finds a substitute father in Bloom and through his trials becomes more mature. But

I wonder whether many readers would have noticed the correspondence of the two stories, and the still more elaborate correspondence of the various episodes, if Joyce had not told a friend about it and pointed out many detailed parallels, which the friend (Stuart Gilbert) then explained in a book.[2] For instance, Odysseus putting out the eye of the giant in his cave with a burning log corresponds to Bloom waving his burning cigar in the face of a tough Irish nationalist in a pub. However, that is probably the most amusing thing about *Ulysses:* it is a long parody told in many varieties of parodic language. It would be fair to call it one of the most ingenious books ever written.

The result is that it is in its way a classic. It is studied in some colleges and in all universities which have good graduate schools of literature. Shelfloads of articles and books have been written to interpret it, and more come out every year.

Ulysses is respected but not enjoyed. It is seldom quoted with appreciation as other novels of its time are quoted. It is seldom imitated by young writers, in the same way that William Faulkner and Ernest Hemingway, Marcel Proust and Franz Kafka are imitated. Its own successor from Joyce's hand—*Finnegans Wake*—though much less comprehensible, seems to be quoted more often and recalled with more pleasure. You know how frequently we recall the best whimsicalities of Laurence Sterne's *Tristram Shandy,* the frail delicacies of Virginia Woolf's *Mrs. Dalloway,* the subtleties of Thomas Mann's *Death in Venice,* and the bold melodrama of Charles Dickens's *Great Expectations.* Do you ever hear or read about anyone evoking *Ulysses* with the same spontaneous affection? When a book, however remarkable, becomes remote in that way, it may still be a classic; nevertheless, it is not a living classic but a mummy.

In fact *Ulysses* is too full of repulsive elements. To begin with, the language is often simply revolting, and the scenes described (although certainly true to real life) are often positively nauseating. The people and the talk are natural, but they are nasty. Practically no women and not many men can read certain passages without the most profound disgust—a disgust which passes quite easily into scorn and even hatred for the author who spent time and energy and loving care on describing such things. Samuel Johnson's epitaph for Oliver Goldsmith was: "He touched nothing that he did

---

[2][See S. Gilbert, *James Joyce's Ulysses* (London, 1930[1] and 1952[2]). See also G. Highet, *The Classical Tradition* (New York, 1949) 504-7, for a summary of the central parallels. Ed.]

not adorn."[3] The epitaph for James Joyce in *Ulysses* might be: "He touched nothing that he did not defile." One example. In a climax of the book, the young student Stephen is in a disorderly house, drunk. The ghost of his mother appears to him, tells him that she loves him still, and pleads with him to return to the Church and abandon his proud atheism. At the high pitch of his excitement he replies with one syllable, which is the most vulgar and sordid obscenity in the language.

Another repellent, less emotional, is the sheer difficulty of the book, which often masks the commonplace in intricacy. Now that readers must not only plow back and forth through the novel but digest bushels of commentary upon it, many find the effort unrewarding. You remember in Dickens's novel Sam Weller's remark to his son (*Pickwick Papers,* chap. 27):

> Vether it's worth while goin' through so much to learn so little, as the charity-boy said ven he got to the end of the alphabet, is a matter o' taste.

Joyce himself, with his appalling, his infinite vanity, said: "I demand that my reader should give up his entire life to reading my works."[4] But few will feel inclined to do so.

Still less is the average reader likely to spend a lifetime reading and rereading a book about one day in the life of the city of Dublin at a not very important period of its history. Dublin has its charms; and it has produced some good poetry, some fine drama, and some amazingly bright conversation. Yet who would willingly read seven hundred pages about its lower middle-class characters during one single day? Perhaps an Irish nationalist might, you will say. Yet there is an additional difficulty. Of the two chief characters, one is not Irish at all but a Jew born in Hungary; while the other is Anglo-Irish, a man who despises the Celtic twilight and the nationalist movement, and talks with vital excitement only about

---

[3][A reference to the statement *nullum quod tetigit non ornavit*—from one of two epitaphs in Greek and Latin composed by Johnson for Goldsmith, both found in James Boswell's *Life of Samuel Johnson* (London, 1791). See G. B. Hill and L. F. Powell, edd., *Boswell's Life of Johnson,* 6 vols. (Oxford, 1934–50)—the standard scholarly edition of this work—especially vol. 2, p. 282, for the Greek epitaph, and vol. 3, pp. 82–83, for the Latin epitaph. Ed.]

[4][I have not been able to verify this statement, to which Highet also alludes in *The Classical Tradition* (above, note 2) 696, in a portion of a footnote on Stuart Gilbert that seems worthy of quoting here: "Joyce is reported to have said that what he demanded of his reader was to give up a lifetime to reading Joyce's books. Apparently he imagined himself as a modern Aquinas, and Gilbert as the first commentator on his *Summa Dublinensis.*" Ed.]

Shakespeare and other non-Irish figures. And as for the Catholic Church, which means so much to Ireland, its rites are blasphemed on the first few pages and often later; and its priests and rituals are bitterly mocked again and again. It is an ambitious book, *Ulysses;* but it contrives to be parochial without being patriotic.

And how about the story? A novel which goes on for over seven hundred pages ought to have a plot in which interesting things happen, important decisions are taken. But a cold critic, not disposed to hagiolatry, would say that *Ulysses* is merely a series of trivial episodes, brief incidents of city life with little continuity, little development, and much repetition. At the climax what happens? Stephen swears vulgarly at his mother's ghost, is knocked unconscious by a casual ruffian (who happens to be a British soldier), and is rescued by Bloom, who takes him to Bloom's own house, sobers him up, and sends him off home. Bloom goes to sleep after a short love passage; and his wife thinks over her past and her present. That is all. For a moment Stephen represents the little son whom Bloom lost years ago; and Bloom replaces the weak, useless father whom Stephen despises. That is a touching but a flimsy link, for the two men have nothing really in common; their temporary association dissolves that night. Meanwhile the entire last chapter is taken up with a huge soliloquy by Mrs. Bloom, who has never met Stephen Dedalus for more than a moment and who has remained in the background throughout the day. Unless—are we meant to conjecture that young Stephen will have an encouraging love affair with the aging Molly Bloom, and thus outdo Hamlet, and become Oedipus as well as Telemachus? It is possible, but it is scarcely hinted at; if the idea is important, it should be developed.

This flaccid and disjointed story is designed as a counterpart of one of the tightest and best-constructed stories in all literature— Homer's *Odyssey.* Why? As a piece of cleverness? That, yes; but much more because of one of Joyce's fundamental beliefs, perhaps his fundamental creed. The *Odyssey,* although it stoops to squalor, is heroic; Joyce's *Ulysses,* although it rises to intellectual distinction and moral energy, is sordid. The *Odyssey* had a plan; the adventures of Stephen and Bloom are ineffective and planless. Bloom is pitiful and weak; Odysseus is energetic and noble. The wife of Odysseus has many suitors and resists them all; Mrs. Bloom has many suitors, accepts them all, and wishes for more. The life of ancient times was good and great; modern life is one long squalid failure. That is the meaning of *Ulysses.*

Joyce hated the city in which he was born and brought up; he despised his father; he resisted his mother; he scorned the Church; he sneered at the Irish; he envied and secretly admired and hated the English; he coldly rejected the few fellow intellectuals whom he knew; and finally, he loathed himself—all of himself except for his nimble and tenacious mind with its remarkable gift for languages, and his sensitive if shallow taste for music. The central purpose of *Ulysses* was to permit Joyce to express in permanent form all this scorn, all this elaborate hatred. Read through it two or three times, and you will find that somewhere, somehow, Joyce manages to distort and befoul an enormous range of human activities: natural physical acts which most of us seldom think of, important expressions of physical passion, religious doctrines, literary masterpieces, philosophical systems, wealth and poverty, food and drink, dirt and cleanliness, passion and modesty. Everything becomes—when he touches it—mean, nasty, and false. This purpose sprang from his own bitter youth and his own warped character—warped who knows how early? But it was intensified by two of his chief literary models. One was the harshly cynical Gustave Flaubert, who dedicated his life to pouring scorn on his contemporaries and fellow men—the vile bourgeois, whom he called the *mufles* (the "boobs"). (H. L. Mencken took it up much later as the "booboisie.") The other was, like Joyce himself, an Anglo-Irishman with overweening ambition and little love in his heart, whose greatest work shows a single lonely man, wandering through a world which is inhabited by contemptible pygmies, then by terrible and revolting giants, then by crazy pseudo-intellectuals, and finally by stinking, lustful, treacherous humanoid beings, the Yahoos. I wonder if Jonathan Swift himself might not have been appalled, if he had read *Ulysses* and seen his own Dublin inhabited by Yahoos described by an intelligent Yahoo, with his pen dipped in acid mingled with filth.[5]

---

[5][See G. Highet, "The Personality of Joyce," in *Explorations* (New York, 1971) 135–46, for his analysis of Joyce's character, with its fascinating conflicts and contradictions. Ed.]

Kazantzakis's *Odyssey**

Just about twenty years ago, before the beginning of World War II, I heard from various friends about a colossal new poem which they said I ought to read. It was a work of huge dimensions and overweening ambition, running to more than 30,000 lines. It was written in modern Greek and was labeled a sequel to the famous epic in ancient Greek, the *Odyssey* of Homer; but (they also said) it ranged far more widely than Homer's epic poem and had a deeper spiritual significance. It was also more difficult to read: Homer's language was picturesque but regular, while this new sequel to his *Odyssey* was filled with bold phrases unique in their conception and with obscure words taken from remote dialects of modern Greek. Its name was simply the *Odyssey;* its author was an eccentric and brilliant Cretan called Nikos Kazantzakis. At that time I did not know much about Kazantzakis; none of my friends had read the whole of his *Odyssey,* and nobody was able to give me a coherent account of the poem. In the world of literature you often hear of proud enterprises like this: you are told that so-and-so has been working for thirty years on a rocket to take him to Saturn; you register the fact and then you wait to hear whether his mission was ever achieved. Usually it does not even get off the ground. But the rocket of Kazantzakis was launched and is in orbit. It is well worth watching and admiring.

The original poem in modern Greek I have never read, partly through lack of time and partly because I do not yet know modern Greek well enough for such an enormous undertaking. But now we have a translation of it into modern English, made with tender loving care, in collaboration with the author himself and with the assistance of advice from many good contemporary critics and poets. It is by Kimon Friar, an American of Greek descent. The book is called *The Odyssey: A Modern Sequel.* The publishers have done a praiseworthy job.[1] Mystics, poets, revolutionaries, Greek-

---

*Presented in 1959 on Highet's radio program (= *BMCT* 170).

[1][See N. Kazantzakis, *The Odyssey: A Modern Sequel,* trans. K. Friar (New York, 1958), and the critical companion volume by P. Prevelakis, *Nikos Kazantzakis and His Odyssey,* trans. P. Sherrard (New York, 1961)—both of them published by Simon and Schuster. Ed.]

Americans, pantheists, philhellenes, classicists, eroticists, and other-worldists should buy this book and begin to read it slowly and with relish. It will take them plenty of time. There are 776 pages, together with notes, a synopsis, and a copious introduction. In the *Odyssey* of Homer the hero had no guide, except for the occasional visits from his kindly guardian Athena; and in the sequel by Kazantzakis he has neither guide nor plan. In reading this sequel we have an excellent guide, Mr. Kimon Friar, who communicates to us with self-forgetting devotion both the words and the thoughts of his author, the obscure and intense Cretan bard.

And we need guidance. Homer's *Odyssey* is easy to read—provided that you can read a translation of a poem dealing with a distant epoch and describing the manners and beliefs of its people. The *Odyssey* of Kazantzakis is furiously difficult to read—more difficult in thought, although perhaps not quite so difficult in expression, as that other modern *Odyssey* published a few years earlier, Joyce's *Ulysses*. One reason for its difficulty is that it is not a straight narrative aimed at a single target, like the *Odyssey* of Homer.

Homer tells the story of a single hero returning from a foreign expedition, through many difficulties and traps, to his home. The milieux are sometimes fantastic, but the social framework, theology, and historical background are always the same; and the tale, although cunningly arranged and diversified, is always told on the same level; apart from a few treacheries and disguises, things are what they seem. Not so with the *Odyssey* of Kazantzakis.

The modern *Odyssey* begins even before Homer's *Odyssey* (in its traditional version) ends—at the moment of supreme triumph, when Odysseus has just returned, smuggled himself in disguise into his own house, killed all the men who were importuning his wife and trying to take over his property, and hanged all the servants who had collaborated with them. On its first page we see Odysseus laughing grimly and washing off the blood of his enemies.

After that we know what Homer intended. A prince of the Bronze Age, who had been far away on a difficult enterprise and had survived all the perils of his return, had no higher ambition than to remain in his own house, enjoying his glory, his spoils, and his well-earned tranquillity. That is how we see Menelaus, the husband of Helen, and Nestor, the oldest veteran of the expedition, when we meet them in Homer's *Odyssey*. They are peaceful, safe, and rich. And so, says Homer, Odysseus himself would settle down.

But there was something in the character of Odysseus which made it difficult for later readers and for later poets to accept that. He was too experienced a traveler to enjoy farming and rent collecting; to put it more kindly, he had enjoyed fantasy, both in deed and in word, too intensely to make him accept reality without revolt; or to put it more coarsely, his homeland was too poor and boring to keep him in it. This was seen by Dante, who met him in hell and heard from his own spirit how he had died—far, far from home, outside the pillars of Hercules—that is, out in the Atlantic Ocean, where he was voyaging on a route no other sailor had ever attempted; and because he was passing the frontiers placed for man by almighty God, he was swallowed up by a whirlpool and sent to everlasting damnation (*Inferno* 26.90–142). Tennyson, in a noble dramatic monologue called *Ulysses,* took up the same theme and made Ulysses say that he could not possibly endure to sit idly at home while the sea called and the future challenged; so he sailed off into the unknown.

This non-Homeric theme is the theme which Kazantzakis has adopted. He sees Odysseus as the eternal searcher, the Wandering Jew, the Flying Dutchman, the explorer of the world, the displaced person who does not want a home. His hero cannot settle down. He has no interest in Penelope, he despises the piggish peasants who are his tenants and subjects, and he is too tough for his stay-at-home son Telemachus. As soon as he gets his son married off to the charming little princess Nausicaa who once gave him shelter, he builds a ship and he leaves Ithaca forever, with a few loud-voiced, hard-fisted, highly sexed, greedy, and optimistic comrades, called by names such as Rocky, Granite, Orpheus, and Captain Clam.

He sails first to Sparta, where he carries off the beautiful Helen (always so tempting and so willing to be carried off). Then to Crete, where he takes part in a series of wildly decadent rites of sexual play and bullfighting, and at last massacres the court and destroys the palace of Knossos. (If you have read Mary Renault's fine historical novel *The King Must Die,* you will be delighted by some of the coincidences between these two poetic reconstructions of a distant era.) Then to Egypt, where he helps to lead a social revolution, which is utterly crushed. From Egypt he leads an exodus of the oppressed southward into the land of the Negroes, and through it, past the dangers of savagery, to the lake which is the source of the Nile. And there, after much meditation and many visions, he founds what is to be an ideal city, rather on the lines of Plato's Republic; but it is soon annihilated by a tremendous earthquake.

From now on, the last journey of Odysseus becomes less and less a factual story, and more and more a spiritual journey through the labyrinth of thought and vision. He is alone, both a hermit and an ascetic, visited by strange and apocalyptic visions. Moving ever southward through Africa, he meets (among other curious people) a prince and a prostitute who are both struggling to escape from the pettiness and the torture of individual life. The prince is a sort of Buddha, and the prostitute a sort of Maya; yet all the people Odysseus talks to are scarcely more authentic than those he sees in his dreams. He builds a boat and sets sail toward the frozen sea. His last contact with humanity comes when he meets a few primitive people living on the ice, passes a long Antarctic winter night with them, and then watches in horror as they are all swallowed up by a gigantic collapse of the floe on which they make their home. He himself sails ever south, until he meets an impenetrable wall of ice, which crushes him—or rather crushes his body (23.1305–8):

> As a low lantern's flame flicks in its final blaze
> then leaps above its shriveled wick and mounts aloft,
> brimming with light, and soars toward Death with dazzling joy,
> so did his fierce soul leap before it vanished in air.

That is only a short outline of this splendid work. The poem itself is an enormous creation—33,333 lines of poetry—three times at least as long as Homer's *Odyssey*. And the poetry (as far as I can judge from a translation) is remarkably original and stirring. It is written in big, swinging lines of eight beats (in Greek) rendered by loose iambic lines of six beats (in English)—like Robert S. Bridges' *Testament of Beauty,* although much freer and more athletic, and Richmond Lattimore's translation of the *Iliad,* although rather more compact and regular. From the first page to the last it is packed with imagery. The images are often mixed and incongruous; the poet does not care, for he hates logic and loves the hyperbolical and the impossible. But they are nearly always boldly original. Here is a description of one of the commonest of all happenings, the passage of time from summer to winter (7.734–41):

> Yesterday and Tomorrow, like two rampant lions,
> stood back to back in the sun's flame-eyed disk and rolled
> it gently down to earth to frisk and play with it.
> The sun rolled on, and all earth's creatures changed their dress,
> their emerald shirts grew faded, tore, and fell away,
> the gaunt trees shed their leaves, the heavy rains came down,
> cranes carried the young birds and then flew off like carters
> of fierce swift-footed time, and soared on toward the sun.

The emotions are as intense and improbable as the images. If you have read Kazantzakis's recent novels *Zorba the Greek* and *The Greek Passion,* you will recall how his heroes are fabulously strong, prodigious drinkers and desperate fighters, supermen careless of convention and immune to fatigue, Herculean lovers (one of them breaks three beds on his wedding night). The same is true of the chief characters in his *Odyssey:* they lust and fight and travel and starve and laugh more like Titans than like men; their battles are equal to the fiercest Homeric combats or the great adventures of modern Greek παληκάρι ("brave men"); and their sexual passions outdo anything in the tamer life of classical Greece. Furthermore, the entire poem is studded by dreams and fables and symbols and visions—some of them inspired by wild Greek folklore—which takes us even further out of the frontiers of reality. To read the poem is go on a voyage of exploration into the unknown and unimagined.

But you will ask, what does it all lead to? We see Odysseus leave his home, and kidnap and plot and destroy and plan and brood and dream and journey, and at last die. For Homer his aim is clear. He is trying to get home, if possible with the loot he got from Troy, if not, alive. In this poem what is his aim? As we thread our way through the dense maze of symbolism which fills the central and later books, we see that Odysseus is an exceptional human soul in search of truth. He passes through all these experiences and savors them, to find out whether through them he can understand life. He rejects first one solution and then another, but he goes on experimenting until his death. During the revolutions which he leads in Crete and Egypt, he sounds remarkably like a communist, leading the oppressed workers against the feudal exploiters with the help of blond barbarians from the north. But he soon drops that altogether. After the failure of his ideal state in central Africa, he loses interest in society altogether and grapples all alone with the central problem of human existence. From time to time, at earlier stages, he and his friends are attracted by the boldest way of solving the problem, which is to deny that there is a problem and to say that life is its own justification. The young in one another's arms, birds in the trees, the mother with a baby, the strong man in his pride, simply live life and do not try to dissect it.

But this *Odyssey* is essentially a poem about growing old and facing death. The modern Greeks (according to Kimon Friar, the translator) believe that when a man is born, the worm of his death is also born and sets out to meet him. When you perceive the worm approaching, you must ask why it was created and why you yourself have lived. Odysseus, on his way toward death, grapples with many harsh antinomies and observes many tragic absurdities. He discards one solution after another, and it is only a few months before his death that he understands his life, only in the face of despair that he understands the meaning of hope.

The *Odyssey* of Kazantzakis, therefore, is a spiritual epic. In poetry it belongs to the same class as the *Comedy* of Dante, Goethe's *Faust,* and the poem of the neglected Swiss genius Carl Spitteler called *Olympian Spring*. Mr. Friar says that it owes much to the French philosopher Henri Bergson, and there are clear traces of the thought of that Greek explorer Heraclitus. But its closest ancestor is surely Friedrich Nietzsche. It has more scope and energy than that poor, thin, anxious genius ever had; yet both its truths and its hyperboles spring from the same roots as Nietzsche's *Thus Spake Zarathustra*. They come from a profound loneliness, which can find no real companionship among ordinary human beings— neither in wife nor in children nor in friends—and which trusts no conventional religious or social patterns of thought. They come from a bitter sense of weakness, which makes the soul determined to resist even when resistance is useless. Our body is a mass of bones and blood and cells and electric charges, doomed to last for a few years and capable of a contemptibly few activities. Only our soul—even if it too must disappear—can defy death and laugh at its own despair. That is the meaning of the quest of Kazantzakis's Odysseus, and that is the certainty which he found in the desert and the ice.

Mankiewicz's *Julius Caesar**

Let me have men about me that are fat,
Sleek-headed men, and such as sleep a-nights.
Yond Cassius has a lean and hungry look;
He thinks too much: such men are dangerous.

Wonderful words, whether we call them prose or poetry. Keen psychological observation. Fine drama—for they are spoken by the man who is going to be murdered, about his chief murderer, to the man who is destined to avenge his death. And above all, wonderful words: they settle into the mind's ear like a melody and remain there. That is the final test of good poetry.

They come from Shakespeare's tragedy *Julius Caesar* (1.2.192–95). That is one of the plays everyone ought to reread every year or so, simply because it is so full of profound truths about politics and of superb phrases revealing the depths of the human soul.

The fault, dear Brutus, is not in our stars,
But in ourselves, that we are underlings.

There is a tide in the affairs of men,
Which, taken at the flood, leads on to fortune;
Omitted, all the voyage of their life
Is bound in shallows and in miseries.

Cowards die many times before their deaths;
The valiant never taste of death but once.
Of all the wonders that I yet have heard,
It seems to me most strange that men should fear,
Seeing that death, a necessary end,
Will come when it will come.

These proud and masculine cadences (1.2.140–41, 4.3.215–18, and 2.2.32–37) have rung in our minds for many years, since we first read the play or saw it performed; along with many others, they have become part of the general language of thought and imagination.

The tragedy of *Julius Caesar* was produced in 1599. Over 350 years later (in 1953) it appeared in another new medium, as a

---

*Prepared in 1953 for Highet's radio program (not issued as a *BMCT*).

film, handsomely produced by Joseph L. Mankiewicz,[1] along with a stunning cast of actors and actresses. This is the movie version of *Julius Caesar*. Like every new production of a famous play, it sets up new problems and offers new solutions to some old problems. Poor plays are not so flexible; but this is a tragedy, the first of Shakespeare's deeper tragedies, written when he was in the prime of life—thirty-five years old—and was just assimilating the full power of Plutarch's *Parallel Lives of the Greeks and Romans*. It is a splendid drama.

The actors in the film version are nearly all clever people; they convey the general impression of intelligence. This (I think) is new. The murder of Caesar was not an emotional gesture like the murder of Lincoln, nor part of a vulgar struggle for power like the murder of many later Roman emperors and of other despots since their time. It was a rational operation solemnly and sincerely carried out on a basis of principle, by men who were neither excited nor personally ambitious nor devoted to force as a political solution, who were almost as clever as Caesar himself and far more deeply devoted to the ideal of human freedom. This is well conveyed by one of the stars, James Mason. He plays Brutus. Brutus was a descendant, over five hundred years, of one of the men who had thrown the first monarchs out of Rome and made it into a republic. (Brutus, by the way, means "stupid," and the legend is that the first Brutus pretended to be dull-witted, so as to avoid arrest and execution—like Hamlet in the original Danish story.) This later Brutus is a thoughtful and worried man who likes Julius Caesar and is indebted to him. He hates the idea of killing; and he shrinks from killing Caesar; but he is brought to see that it is his duty.

You know, some of us nowadays do not see why the murder was planned and carried out; we think it unnecessary or crude. We can hardly imagine a situation which might make it inevitable. Our own Republic has lasted for nearly two hundred years. Well the Roman Republic had lasted for nearly five hundred years. To begin with, it had been under foreign kings. It had thrown them off and then grown great as a republic, distrusting any assertion of personal power or class domination. Its pattern of administration resembled our own system of 'checks and balances,' but it went even further. It would not have just one president. It had two, who were called consuls (which means "colleagues") and kept close

---

[1][Actually the 1953 film was directed by Mankiewicz and produced by John Houseman, who reviews at length the making of *Julius Caesar* and the strategies behind it in *Front and Center* (New York, 1979) 382–409. Ed.]

watch on each other throughout their term. And it had a large system of officials who would all keep control over one another's ambitions and work together in times of crisis. And yet, after long generations of growth and war and victory and prosperity, the Republic began to creak at the joints and leak blood at the seams. Class war was growing more and more dangerous; it turned into civil war; it became endemic; and the Romans (rather like the modern French) began to lose faith in their own constitution and their ability to live together. Whenever their constitution was operative, it was almost powerless—as any constitution is if large numbers of citizens do not want to maintain it. Whenever a strong totalitarian arose from the right or the left, he suspended it; and so it grew weaker and more shadowy, like a middle-aged man after a series of major operations.

Finally it was wrecked by Julius Caesar. He trained a private army, by taking it away on a long personally-led expedition to conquer what is now France but was then a dangerous territory full of fighting tribes. After converting his soldiers into a first-rate fighting force and making them not patriotic Romans but his own torpedoes, he marched them back to the frontier, asked the government of the Republic to make a number of impossible concessions to him, and then led his army toward the capital. The government was evacuated, just as though it had been faced by an adventurer with a fleet of bomber-planes. It raised an army, it fought him, it was defeated. Then Caesar became something less traditional than Napoleon and less tactful even than Hitler—neither emperor nor chancellor, but 'perpetual dictator'—an intolerable idea in any country but especially among the Romans, with their tradition of five centuries of republican freedom. Intoxicated by his own success, he was apparently thinking of going further. He was experimenting with the idea of becoming a king—not only a king, but a god-king—like the Pharaohs of Egypt, or Alexander the Great, both king and god.

Shakespeare had no experience with such vulgar blasphemy and such vaulting ambition, but he described it perfectly in the words of Cassius (1.2.115–18):

> And this man
> Is now become a god, and Cassius is
> A wretched creature, and must bend his body
> If Caesar carelessly but nod on him.

No, it was unbearable. If we can imagine in our own country some successful politician and brilliant general challenging the United

States Army with some thirty divisions who had sworn loyalty to himself alone, displacing the judiciary and remolding both houses of Congress, by-passing the Constitution, and toying with plans to declare himself Emperor of the Americas, we can see what the conspirators saw. And yet, in many history books you will find defenses of Caesar or ill-concealed admiration of him. It is sometimes difficult to believe that what succeeds is not necessarily right. And perhaps for the historian, who sits alone in his study writing and wishes he were a man of action, it is still more difficult. Yet what succeeds is not necessarily right. What fails is not necessarily wrong. That is one of the chief problems of *Julius Caesar,* and it is one of the central themes of all tragedy.

As far as I can see, the only important mistake in the production (apart from the inadequate portrayal of Caesar)[2] is the final battle. That was an absolutely vital event—the struggle between the last forces of the Republic and the ruthless energies of dictatorship. The Republic very nearly won. I think it might well have been victorious, if it had not been for the strange phenomenon which we have seen once or twice in our own lifetime—the disunity and mutual distrust of patriots when they are faced by monomaniacs determined on power and conquest. What actually happened was that difficult strategic situation in which one wing of each army attacks and conquers its opponent; so Mark Antony beat Cassius, and Brutus's soldiers stormed the camp of Caesar's heir Octavian. But Brutus did not improve his victory, and Cassius gave up, committing suicide too soon. Shakespeare understood this tactical situation far better than the producer of the movie, who converted it into a Hollywood western, with a small force of Romans marching through a canyon (apparently with no cavalry reconnaissance and no flanking parties—a blunder which the Romans had not committed for about 150 years). Meanwhile, on the skyline above stands Marlon Brando, looking painfully like Sitting Bull, even to the gesture with which he tells his braves to charge (I almost expected to hear a war-whoop).[3] No, the Romans knew more war-

---

[2][See Houseman (above, note 1) 387, who picked Louis Calhern for the role of Caesar and who wanted him (for the purposes of this film) to play the part of "an aging, tired, nervous dictator rather than a triumphant one." Ed.]

[3][See G. Highet, "History on the Silver Screen," in *Talents and Geniuses* (New York, 1957) 191–98, especially 195, where he repeats his criticism of the way in which the film *Julius Caesar* mishandled the Battle of Philippi. See also Houseman (above, note 1) 398–400, for his own critical description of this scene as "an ambush in the best Western style, with Antony's men (in the Indian role) . . . and Brando's grim, impassive Indian profile." Ed.]

fare than that; and the battle was more complex. It was not a surprise but a strategic chess game and a spiritual contest.

But then, after the battle, comes the real tragedy. All the intelligent people die, except for one or perhaps two. Mark Antony lives. Octavian—the future ruler of the world, but we cannot tell that—lives. The last words in Shakespeare's play are spoken by young Octavian (5.5.81), who leads his men off

> To part the glories of this happy day.

It sounds happy, doesn't it? Is there a tragedy at all? Or is the whole play merely a melodrama, like Jean-Paul Sartre's *Dirty Hands*—a struggle for power, in which it is hard to care who wins, and we are interested merely to see how cleverly or how brutally one side will beat the other?

No, there is a tragedy. In fact there are several tragedies, which is a proof that *Julius Caesar* is a powerful, far-reaching drama.

The audience of Shakespeare thought that the death of Caesar made the play a tragedy, because he was a great man killed at the height of his power. I do not see any hint that Shakespeare or his audience knew the suggestion that Brutus was in fact Julius Caesar's own illegitimate son; but they surely knew that Brutus was dear to him, and Shakespeare brought it out in Caesar's dying words.[4] To be killed at the pinnacle of one's hard-won greatness by those whom one has trusted—that is tragic.

And so Caesar is dead. But the play is only half over. The tragedy is not at all complete. Tragedy is the suffering of those who have not fully deserved to suffer. Therefore the central event, the fall of Caesar, involves the further suffering and the deaths of Brutus and Cassius. One of them says so in the depths of misery (5.3.94–96):

> O Julius Caesar, thou art mighty yet!
> Thy spirit walks abroad, and turns our swords
> In our own proper entrails.

Toward the end Brutus and Cassius, once united, quarrel with each other; their faith dies first; and in fact they lose the final battle because Caesar's sword comes between them, and they are less in harmony than the forces of rapine and revenge.

---

[4][Here compare Shakespeare's *et tu, Brute,* "you too, Brutus" (3.1.77) with Suetonius's καὶ σὺ τέκνον, "you too, my son" (*Caesar* 82); and see Plutarch, *Brutus* 5.1–2, on Caesar's youthful affair with Servilia—the origin of the notion that Caesar may have regarded Brutus as his illegitimate son. Ed.]

So the tragedy is the fall of Caesar; and also the fall of those who killed him; but further the fall of the free Roman people, whom Caesar and his successors corrupted. That is shown in the wonderful scene where the citizens of Rome are converted from a group of calm, thoughtful men and women into a raving mob, screaming (3.2.204):

Revenge! About! Seek! Burn! Fire! Kill! Slay!

That scene is balanced by the grim little debate held by the Roman Politburo immediately afterward, where Octavian and Antony and their stooge Lepidus decide who is to be liquidated. Force has succeeded law. The last good Roman citizen dies, and the ideal of freedom dies. Antony says so reluctantly; he calls Brutus what he would not call any other (5.5.68 and 73–75):

This was the noblest Roman of them all . . .
His life was gentle, and the elements
So mixed in him that Nature might stand up
And say to all the world, 'This was a man!'

The tragedy of *Julius Caesar* is therefore not a personal thing but a mighty historical disaster. It is the death of Caesar brought on by himself, the defeat of those who executed him, and the murder of the noble ideal of freedom under law.

Auden's *The Shield of Achilles**

It is difficult to understand the best of modern poetry. I have just been reading a fine new collection edited by Oscar Williams, called *The New Pocket Anthology of American Verse,*[1] and I am excited but bewildered. Perhaps that is the state which modern poets wish to establish in us—bewildered excitement?

There are several difficulties in modern poetry. Three are particularly important: one is the complexity of language; one is the oddity of emotion; one is the remoteness of frames of reference. Or to put it bluntly: sometimes we do not know what the poet is talking about (even if we understand what he is saying); sometimes we do not grasp his emotions; and sometimes we cannot get any meaning out of his words. Each of these obstacles needs different training to get over it. Sometimes it is not worth the effort. But sometimes— when you are sure that the poet is a man who uses his mind and has something like a soul—it is.

Let me make this clear by reading to you a poem by an excellent modern poet—W. H. Auden's *The Shield of Achilles.* Here it is—

No. The difficulty here is the frame of reference. If I read it straight off, you would not know what Auden was talking about, at least not without some effort. What was the 'shield of Achilles'? Who made it? What was on it? Unless you know, and unless you have the artistic and emotional situation in your mind, you will not start hearing the poem; you will rather stumble into it. That would be like going to a famous picture gallery to see the El Greco paintings or the Titians; unless you knew the central subject of each picture, you would look at it merely with external eyes, as a pattern, and miss many of its beauties, all of its significance.

The poem begins:

> She looked over his shoulder
> For vines and olive trees,

---

*Presented in 1955 on Highet's radio program (= *BMCT* 34).
[1][This sizable anthology, published by World Publishing (Cleveland, 1955), contains several poems by W. H. Auden, including *The Shield of Achilles*— a poem reprinted from the volume of Auden's verses published by Random House and itself entitled *The Shield of Achilles* (New York, 1955) 35-37. Ed.]

Marble well-governed cities,
  And ships upon untamed seas,
But there on the shining metal
  His hands had put instead
An artificial wilderness
  And a sky like lead.

Good poetry and—as far as the words go—clear, full of vivid images, with no harsh eccentricities. But who is "She"? Who is the person over whose shoulder she looks? Why should she look over his shoulder for olive trees and cities and "ships upon untamed seas"? The title and the first stanza contain the clue to the riddle. It is not very difficult. Mr. Auden would not perhaps think it was a riddle at all; he might believe that anyone who appreciates poetry ought to know Homer's *Iliad*. And he would therefore expect his readers to recognize the bitter contrast contained in those first short eight lines.

The background of the poem then is one single episode in the *Iliad*. The *Iliad* tells part of the story of the siege of Troy by the Greeks. During the siege the Greek prince Achilles was insulted by his superior officer and left the battle line; his side began to lose; his best friend, in an effort to stop the enemy, borrowed the armor of Achilles, put it on, went out, fought bravely, and was killed. Then Achilles determined to go out and fight once again; but now he had no armor. His mother, the beautiful sea goddess Thetis, asked the god of fire and of craftsmanship to make new armor for him. Of course the armor was strong; but since it was Greek, it was also beautiful. Homer describes it in *Iliad,* Book 18. On the shield there were many sculptures so lively that they seemed to move, showing the whole life of the Homeric world—in peace and war, in conflict and happiness, yet somehow all noble, all beautiful, free from anything common or unclean. It is a famous description and technically a masterpiece of writing, because it is extremely hard to transfer one art to another, to express painting in music or (as here) sculpture in poetry.[2]

---

[2][Homer's description of the shield of Achilles (*Iliad* 18.478–608) greatly inspired Vergil's description of the shield of Aeneas (*Aeneid* 8.626–728), through which Vergil presents his audience with the glory of future Rome and a panorama of Roman leaders culminating in the emperor Augustus. In this regard, see W. H. Auden, *Homage to Clio* (New York, 1960) 26–28, for the poem *Secondary Epic*—Auden's treatment of the fateful, prophetic shield described by Vergil—a poem that Highet read to his students whenever he taught the section of the *Aeneid* involving the shield of Aeneas. Ed.]

All that is summed up in four lines. Auden says that the soldier's mother expected to see one of the scenes of the Homeric world but did not.

> She looked over his shoulder
>   For vines and olive trees,
> Marble well-governed cities,
>   And ships upon untamed seas,
> But there on the shining metal
>   His hands had put instead
> An artificial wilderness
>   And a sky like lead.

An artificial wilderness and a sky like lead. Does that sound like ancient Greece?—or like our own day and our own wars, both hot and cold? Yes, you are right: it is our own day.

Auden goes on to describe in detail what appears on the new version of the soldier's shield:

> A plain without a feature, bare and brown,
>   No blade of grass, no sign of neighborhood,
> Nothing to eat and nowhere to sit down,
>   Yet, congregated on its blankness, stood
>   An unintelligible multitude.
> A million eyes, a million boots in line,
> Without expression, waiting for a sign.
>
> Out of the air a voice without a face
>   Proved by statistics that some cause was just
> In tones as dry and level as the place:
>   No one was cheered and nothing was discussed;
>   Column by column in a cloud of dust
> They marched away enduring a belief
> Whose logic brought them, somewhere else, to grief.

And now the contrast becomes clear. War is always war; it is always the first thing to be reflected in a shield. But in the wars of the *Iliad* there was something noble, there was something passionate, there was much individual heroism on both sides. But now, says Auden, in most wars the aggressor is an inhuman ideology, shouting through a loudspeaker, proclaiming some painfully abstract and quasi-scientific theory, such as the doctrine of *Lebensraum*[3] or the economic interpretation of history:

---

[3][Adopting this doctrine as a fundamental principle of Nazi foreign policy, Hitler believed that he could provide the Germans with additional "living space" by expanding to the east—something that would enable him not only to establish a vast continental empire under German domination but also to secure for the Aryan people its place in the world as a master race. Ed.]

Out of the air a voice without a face
Proved by statistics that some cause was just

Turn back again to the shield which the god is forging. We have seen on it a picture of war, waged by living corpses for the sake of a racial or an economic theory. Now see a picture of religion in the same age, as the soldier's mother saw it carved:

She looked over his shoulder
    For ritual pieties,
White flower-garlanded heifers,
    Libation and sacrifice,
But there on the shining metal
    Where the altar should have been,
She saw by his flickering forge-light
    Quite another scene.

Barbed wire enclosed an arbitrary spot
    Where bored officials lounged (one cracked a joke)
And sentries sweated, for the day was hot:
    A crowd of ordinary decent folk
    Watched from without and neither moved nor spoke
As three pale figures were led forth and bound
To three posts driven upright in the ground.

The mass and majesty of this world, all
    That carries weight and always weighs the same,
Lay in the hands of others; they were small
    And could not hope for help and no help came:
    What their foes liked to do was done, their shame
Was all the worst could wish; they lost their pride
And died as men before their bodies died.

The barbed wire; the bored officials; the helplessness of the ordinary decent folk; the public executions; the displacement of due legal process by governmental power reinforced by army sentries; and the humiliation of the victims, as in a lynching—we have seen this, haven't we? Not, thank God, in our own country but in other countries which have proclaimed that the State is superior to all other values (human and divine); that everything must be done by the government reinforced by its own storm troops, police and army; that the individual is merely a tiny blood corpuscle in the blood stream of the Nation, or History, or one of those cannibalistic abstractions in which all power and all worship have been transferred to a central tyranny.

There must be something else on the shield. The goddess has seen war and religion (or its modern surrogate, politics). Is there no happiness, no sport, no art? Here is the contrast which the goddess sees, between ancient Greece and the modern world:

> She looked over his shoulder
>   For athletes at their games,
> Men and women in a dance
>   Moving their sweet limbs
> Quick, quick, to music,
>   But there on the shining shield
> His hands had set no dancing-floor
>   But a weed-choked field.
>
> A ragged urchin, aimless and alone,
>   Loitered about that vacancy; a bird
> Flew up to safety from his well-aimed stone:
>   That girls are raped, that two boys knife a third,
>   Were axioms to him, who'd never heard
> Of any world were promises were kept
> Or one could weep because another wept.

This is what Auden sees as the result of modern state-worship. When the state or money is everything, when the family is unimportant or casual, young boys and girls simply do not know what to do. They have no code of morals, except the simple cheap enjoyment of power. As Auden says,

> That girls are raped, that two boys knife a third,
> Were axioms to him . . .

Have we seen boys and girls like this? Of course we have. We seem to see more of them every day in every country of the world. We are sorry for them. We want to cure them, if they can be cured. But they make a miserable contrast to their ancestors, who—and this must seem to all of us to be a sinister paradox—were both happier and more strongly controlled.

The shield is finished. The poet draws no moral. He remembers that the soldier who carried that shield was killed. In every war soldiers are killed, whatever shield they carry. From this long distance—over three thousand years—the war between Greece and Troy looks very small, petty, even meaningless. A big war, we think, must have more meaning. Not so, the poet. He knows that even so long a war had ideals and glorious results, because it made men more fully men. Today the poet looks at a war run by state machines—not for individual happiness but for the glorification of a theory, not to free men but to mold them still more ineluctably into instruments of the State and of the few people who control it.

He shows its results on the new shield of a soldier and ends with the sadness of an immortal spirit:

> The thin-lipped armorer,
>   Hephaestos, hobbled away;
> Thetis of the shining breasts
>   Cried out in dismay
> At what the god had wrought
>   To please her son, the strong
> Iron-hearted man-slaying Achilles
>   Who would not live long.

Decipherment of Linear B*

It often amuses me to think that, although every human being in the world can speak (whether he is savage, civilized, or half and half), it is difficult for us to understand one another's languages. Yesterday I had luncheon in a Chinese restaurant and listened to the waiters chatting; it was absolutely impossible for me to tell whether they were talking about communism, or card playing, or cookery. When a language is written down, it is sometimes even more difficult. In our own Roman characters, Spanish looks fairly hard, German quite forbidding, and Finnish bewildering—while in their own scripts Chinese and Arabic and Bengali are apparently quite impenetrable.

Apparently but not really. If you are trained in breaking codes, you can learn to read even a totally strange language—provided you have enough of its written shape to guide you. If in addition you know something about the science of linguistics, your chances will be even better. The professional intelligence officer who analyzes the codes and ciphers of foreign powers is a colleague—and a close colleague—of the student of languages and of lost scripts; some of the best cryptographers during World War II were professional teachers of language who used their own methods and applied them to new material.

One of the finest jobs of breaking an unknown language was done in 1952. I say "one of the finest" because the problem was so difficult, worked out so neatly, and produced such unexpected but important results. Like all cryptanalysis, this discovery was a cooperative effort, pushed on by scholars from several different countries; but the main discoveries were made by a young British enthusiast who was not even a professional scholar. It is a surprising story and (if you like puzzles) fascinating. I should like to give you a short and very simple outline of it. If you want to read a fuller version, you should buy an excellent book, short but meaty, called *The Decipherment of Linear B* by John Chadwick.[1]

---

*Presented in 1958 on Highet's radio program (= *BMCT* 160).
[1][See J. Chadwick, *The Decipherment of Linear B* (Cambridge, 1958[1] and 1967[2]). Ed.]

Now for the story. It begins shortly before 1900. An Englishman called Arthur Evans, who had some money of his own and a passionate interest in digging up the past, was traveling in Greece and the Greek islands. He was hunting for traces of their prehistoric inhabitants. They had suddenly become very real—those distant, half-fabulous men and women, ever since the German amateur Heinrich Schliemann had dug down to find the treasures of Asian Troy and the treasures of Greek Mycenae.[2] Evans wondered what written language they had used, if any. Although no inscriptions or writing of any kind had been found in the palaces of prehistoric Greece, Evans did pick up certain gems which had ancient and unintelligible signs carved upon them; and these he traced to the island of Crete.

In 1900, when Crete was liberated from the Turks, Evans had already bought some important land and now began to dig. He found a huge and sumptuous palace—the palace, as he called it, of King Minos;[3] and in the palace he found many clay tablets inscribed with groups of signs. When he looked over his discoveries, he saw not one single kind of writing but three. The earliest (found on the jewels) was made up of little pictures—a hand, an arrow, a star, and so forth. The other two were different. They were mostly composed not of little pictures but of signs—dashes, curves, lines, squiggles, crosses, hooks; to an unpracticed eye they look a little like Japanese, very much simplified. There were two different sets of these scripts. Since they were both largely composed of lines, Evans called these scripts Linear (Script) A and Linear (Script) B. Linear (Script) B is the subject of the present excitement. Evans himself never read these scripts. He published some reproductions of them but not nearly enough for other scholars to work upon. It was only after he was dead, as late as 1952, that the tablets in Linear B script which he had found in Crete were published in full; and then they were incorrectly transcribed and not deciphered.

In spite of these difficulties, many scholars tried—between 1900 and 1950—to break down these alluring scripts, and they produced some fantastic solutions. I myself—when I was a young, bewildered, and impressionable freshman—attended a lecture in which a sweet old lady from Cambridge University offered her own answer to these riddles. As I recall it now, she was full of gen-

---

[2][See Highet's "Schliemann's Excavations"—a lecture appearing earlier in this volume—for a review of Schliemann's archaeological finds. Ed.]

[3][See A. Evans, *The Palace of Minos*, 4 vols. (London, 1921–35), on Evans's archaeological discoveries on the site of Knossos from 1900 onward. Ed.]

tle enthusiasm and bland conviction; but since she never really told us what the problem was and scarcely even described her own methods, she left most of her audience painfully and paralytically perplexed. In fact I was so discouraged that I thought of giving up the study of the classical languages, since I should obviously never be able to understand what they were about. I honestly did. But look at a dramatic contrast. Only a few years after that, in 1936, Sir Arthur Evans gave a public lecture on Crete and its mysterious writing. It must have been much better than the discourse I heard. In the audience was a fourteen-year-old schoolboy who was already keenly interested in ancient languages and hidden scripts. He vowed to decipher the Cretan writing; and only sixteen years later he succeeded. His name was Michael Ventris; he was not a classicist but an architect; he published his first really impressive results in 1953.[4] Three years later, in a collision of his car with a truck, he was instantly killed.

How did he (and his cooperators) solve the problem? What they had to go on was simply a collection of thin clay blocks with signs incised upon them by something like a darning needle. No one knew what any sign meant. No one knew what language the signs were meant to convey. No one even knew what kind of language they carried. Those who guessed often guessed wrongly: one man thought it was Basque, another Finnish; Ventris himself thought it was Etruscan.

The beginning was made in the simplest way, by copying out all the signs and counting them. Now there are only three main ways of putting language into writing. First, by drawing a picture for each word or concept—as in Chinese; this is the earliest system. Second, by writing a sign, any kind of sign—a dot, a circle, a cross, or what not—for each different syllable of the spoken language. Japanese, for instance, can easily be written in the native kana script, with four signs to show NA-GA-SA-KI or YA-MA-MO-TO. Third, by using a sign for each letter, each single unit of sound, as in English and Hebrew and Russian and Latin and Greek. Now the picture method needs thousands and thousands of different signs. The syllable method needs several scores, something up to a hundred. The letter method needs very few; there are only twenty-six letters in English.

4[For these results and their significance, see M. Ventris and J. Chadwick, "Evidence for Greek Dialect in the Mycenaean Archives," *JHS* 73 (1953) 84–103 and 208–9. Ed.]

Count the signs in the Linear B script, and you will find eighty or
ninety—too few for pictures, too many for an alphabet. Therefore,
each sign represents one syllable. Correction. Some of the signs on
these tablets were obviously pictures—simple pictures like MAN,
WOMAN, WHEEL, CHARIOT, CUP, HORSE. Some were figures
and numerical formulae (a single stroke for 1, a horizontal stroke
for 10, and so on). Some were signs for weights and measures;
these were worked out with great care by the American scholar
Emmett L. Bennett of Yale University.[5] The rest were syllable
signs, usually separated from the rest of the writing by little vertical partitions and joined in groups of two to five; these groups must
be words.

Between 1943 and 1950 another American scholar—Alice E.
Kober, of Columbia University and Brooklyn College—analyzed
the words.[6] Again and again she found that certain words had one
simple form and two longer forms, which were obviously minor
variations of it. (Suppose you saw a picture of a child with a symbol
beside it and then in a nearby list found three variations of the
same symbol; you might easily guess that the first symbol meant
"child" and that the variations were "child's," "children," and
"children's.") Further, she found that some tablets had lists headed
by two different pictures, one of a man and one of a woman; the
totals of these pairs of lists were given in two different forms; obviously one was masculine and one was feminine. Now it was clear what
kind of language the signs were meant to convey—a language
with cases and genders, like Latin or German, and unlike Chinese.

Next, several different scholars produced careful statistical ta-
bles listing all the syllabic signs which were known from the
tablets, and showing how often they occurred, and where in each
word group they were usually found. Dr. Bennett's in particular
was a masterpiece of thoroughness. (Suppose you were trying to
penetrate through a code of the same type to a language which
was in fact English; you would find certain signs which most often
occurred at the ends of words—such as -ing, as in "going" and
"reading"; -ly, as in "slowly" and "quickly"; the plural -es, as in
"houses" and "boxes.")

---

[5][See E. L. Bennett, Jr., "Fractional Quantities in Minoan Bookkeeping,"
AJA 54 (1950) 204–22—Bennett's classic article on the subject of weights
and measures. Ed.]
[6][See A. E. Kober, "The Minoan Scripts: Fact & Theory," *AJA* 52 (1948) 82–
103—Kober's article summarizing the state of knowledge on Minoan writing at that time. Ed.]

Ventris took the next step, which was extremely important. He drew up what he called a grid, breaking the signs down further according to their apparent sound and function. He knew that he had syllables to work with, simple syllables consisting of a vowel and a consonant (or at the beginning of words perhaps only a vowel), so that the possible variations were not unlimited. And he began to do some inspired guessing. He guessed that the masculine endings might all have the same vowel and the feminine endings have another vowel—likewise always the same—as in Latin, where "lord" and "lady" are *dominus* and *domina,* "good" of a man is *bonus* and "good" of a woman is *bona.* From this guess he built up a list of syllables which had the same vowels but different consonants; and by constantly comparing and linking groups of symbols which were alike in most things and different in only one or two, he built up a basic pattern showing five vowels and fifteen consonants. Remember, he still did not know what language he was working on, nor how it sounded; he called these sounds merely VOWEL II, CONSONANT XII, and so on. How could he possibly discover the sounds behind the symbols?

Here he made another brilliant jump. The tablets had been found in Crete and were all lists or inventories, often with headings. Ventris recalled that tablets from an ancient Syrian city contemporary with prehistoric Crete also contained lists with headings and that some of the headings were the names of towns. So he looked among the Cretan lists and found several words which were headings and might be the names of towns. The names of certain towns in ancient Crete were known. One was Amnisos, which—if broken down into syllables—would be A-MI-NI-SO: four syllables, four signs often found together, with minor variations which might be adjectival forms (as an America, American). Ventris found a group of four signs, beginning with a sign which he believed to be a vowel and guessed to be A; with the help of the syllabic language of ancient Cyprus, which had been read long ago, and with a little more guessing, either lucky or inspired, he interpreted the four signs as A-MI-NI-SO. If he was right, he now had three vowels and three consonants. He applied them to another name in the cipher, which was also very common, and he produced the name of the capital of Crete—KO-NO-SO, *Knossos.* The code was broken.

The rest of his work was simply extension of the same principles from proper names to endings and ordinary words; and Ventris worked faster and faster as the material filled itself out and cross-

checked itself. Remember, the grid which Ventris had so laboriously constructed already showed the relationships and the possible natures of many syllables; and each symbol which was solved
helped to solve three or four more of them. Soon Ventris was joined
by a young language expert, John Chadwick, the author of *The
Decipherment of Linear B,* and together the two converted what
had been a mass of unintelligible signs into an intelligible and even
recognizable language.

Confirmation from outside scholars also reached them. The
most dramatic emerged from mainland Greece. Dr. Carl Blegen of
Cincinnati, who discovered the palace of the old Homeric prince
Nestor at Pylos,[7] found in it many tablets bearing the script which
Ventris had deciphered. He tried the interpretation on several
which had just been dug up and had never been published; and at
once he was able to read them. They made sense. What they said
had no poetic value; it contained not a shade of romance and
stirred no wild flights of fancy; it was as dull and prosaic as an in-
surance policy. One of the tablets, among the most famous, was
simply a list of pots: pots with no handles; pots with three handles;
pots with four handles; and—most delightful of all to a philolo-
gist—pots with three legs, described both by a little picture and by
signs which could be translated as TI-RI-PO-DE, *tripods.* But the
historical documents of this kind are always interesting in a secondary way, for they tell us exactly what people thought long ago,
to be important enough to put on record; a lot of them taken together give us a picture of the daily life and social structure of a
distant age, an age unknown from any contemporary historical
record; and they serve as a valuable check on the actual physical
objects which archaeologists dig up and use to reconstruct the past.

TI-RI-PO-DE, *tripods!* Now emerged the point about the tablets
which has astonished nearly all scholars. It astonished Ventris
himself, who deciphered them. Ventris thought that when he
broke the code he would find Etruscan; he might conceivably have
found Hittite, or that lost tongue known to us by only a few fragments and a name, Pelasgian. Sir Arthur Evans had simply assumed that King Minos of Crete and his subjects spoke a strange
language far older than Greek, and that the men of the mainland
were mere parvenus, jabbering the Hellenic language. Most other
historians and linguists had followed him (or suffered for it). It was
not until Ventris had nearly smashed through the sound barrier

---

[7][See C. W. Blegen and M. Rawson, edd., *The Palace of Nestor at Pylos in
Western Messenia,* 3 vols. (Princeton, 1966–1973). Ed.]

that he ventured to hint at the absurd idea that the syllables, expressed by the scratched signs, might be Greek—old-fashioned and queerly spelled, but still Greek. When he had the solution in his hands, he could scarcely credit it; the language was Greek. Now as Mr. Chadwick says toward the end of his excellent book, the discovery "has pushed back some seven centuries the date of the earliest Greek inscriptions, and thus extended our knowledge of the Greek language, which now has a continuous recorded history totaling thirty-three centuries, a record rivaled only by Chinese."[8] But furthermore, as soon as Ventris announced his discovery, half a century of historical reconstructions collapsed with a splintering crash and a choking cloud of dust; and there was a long, low rumbling sound as Sir Arthur Evans turned in his grave.

---

[8][See Chadwick (above, note 1) 133 in 1958 edition and in 1967 edition. Ed.]

Endurance of the Classics*

One of the cleverest men who ever lived made himself both hated and remembered by asking a simple question which (he said) no one could answer; and yet (he said and rightly said) the question itself was of the highest possible importance. He went about a busy, populous, varied, and extremely cultured city, asking people to explain why they did what they did. He wanted to find out why the poets wrote poetry, why the artisans worked, and why the politicians practiced the difficult art of statesmanship. Apparently he never got a satisfactory answer from any single man he interrogated. He concluded that most people live as though they were children, or asleep and dreaming. Toward the very end of his long and dedicated life, he summed up his inquiry in a single sentence, which has been transmitted to us by his greatest pupil (Plato, *Apology* 38a):

ὁ δὲ ἀνεξέταστος βίος οὐ βιωτὸς ἀνθρώπῳ.

An unexamined life is not worth living.

Or put more bluntly—a man should not live without asking himself why.

If this is true, every human being who is more than a child or an animal ought to examine his life, to ask what is his principal purpose in existing, why he does what he does, every day and every year for a long lifetime. Men are patient; men are adaptable; men are brave. But men often, nearly always, shrink from examining the principles in which their lives are rooted. We classical scholars ourselves, although we are in some sense the heirs of Socrates, seldom pose ourselves the simple drastic question that he used to ask; and when we do, we almost shrink from giving a straightforward answer. Indeed, we may feel that there is something indecent about attempting to formulate, in a few sentences or a few minutes, the motives which defined our choice of a career, the ambitions we have been striving to satisfy (and with what scant success!), the benefits we have tried to confer on others, and the re-

---

*Presented in 1956 for the American Philological Association.

wards we hope to attain for ourselves. Yet we should not wish to change our careers. Which of us could even imagine entering another life in which we should never again look at a Greek statue, never again read a page of Homer, never again try to puzzle out any of the numerous enigmas with which classical antiquity is filled, and never again recollect with pleasure the deathless imagery of classical myth and the deathless music of classical poetry? St. Jerome long endeavored to uproot such knowledge and such affections from his soul; and where he failed, who are we to succeed? Therefore, as we should not wish to change our lives, we owe it to ourselves to understand them.

And even more, we owe it to others. There is indeed something ineffably strange, something which cries out for analysis and explanation, in the career of men and women who spend their whole lives on reading books written in two languages which they have never heard spoken and can never hear; on discovering and digging up the cities, the houses, the temples, and the shops of nations which have passed away and been largely forgotten, even by their own descendants, even by those who drive the plow and turn the soil above their burial places; on reconstructing political systems which were destroyed before this continent was discovered; and on analyzing historical events of which there is scarcely a single remaining physical trace on the surface of this planet. It is sometimes difficult for us to explain even to ourselves what we are doing when we study and teach the classics; and yet we indeed strive, or we ought to strive (in Sir Thomas Browne's words) to "behold ourselves by inward opticks and the crystalline of the soul."[1] Even more so it is necessary to explain it to others, to the world which is unlikely to respect what it can neither understand nor consume, and to the ordinary man who, although he is not merely a creature of physical appetite, is still apt to withhold his approval and his support from any system or any profession which refuses to describe the values by which and for which it exists.

That is why, during a long and difficult but rewarding day, we have been discussing and reflecting upon 'the nature of the classical.' Those who have assisted us in this complex task have earned our warm gratitude. The moderators of each session have already expressed our thanks to all the speakers; but may I, on behalf of the audiences who heard them with deep attention, assure them that

---

[1][Highet's adaptation of Browne's statement on self-knowledge: "Behold thy self by inward Opticks and the Crystalline of thy Soul" (*Christian Morals* 3.15). Ed.]

the thought and learning which they put into their addresses will for long continue to work and to germinate in the minds of others? And that germinative force is one of the central elements of everything that is truly classical. If now, under the guidance of these eloquent speakers, we set out to define—for ourselves at least—the nature and the power of classical life and thought and art, and to say why we have chosen to give up our own lives to understanding and interpreting the classics, how shall we begin? Surely the first aspect of that peculiar power is that the best classical achievements are—as far as anything in this world can be—immortal.

In other lands, in different patterns of culture, men have been deeply concerned with death. They have tried with an anguished earnestness to find some assurance that the individual soul would not perish after the death of the body, or even (like the Hindus with their genius for suffering) to attempt to evade the intolerable burden of eternal rebirth. But it was chiefly and supremely the Greek and Roman artists and thinkers who successfully and in large part deliberately strove to create works which should far outlive their own bodies, which would survive the greatest physical changes and political upheavals, and which—although expressed in the frail, almost immaterial medium of written words, and in the even frailer medium of carved stone—should outlive their creators and refuse to admit death. We study the classics first of all not because they are dead but because they are so vividly and permanently alive. There are many other students of the past whose chief concern is to investigate what is very old—so distant that it is virtually unintelligible, and so deeply hidden below the humus of centuries that it is invisible to all but the most patient searcher. Such are the Egyptologists, and the specialists in prehistory, and those who have reconstructed the life of the Mayans and the Inca peoples. Certain important aspects of classical study also deal with that which is dead and gone and very remote from today; they are none the less valuable, for they contribute to human knowledge and in particular to the extension of classical studies. But ever since the partial disappearance of Greco-Roman civilization during the Dark and Middle Ages, one of the most astonishing but widespread facts about it has been the survival, undiminished and almost unimpaired by time, of many of its best works. Through much of their art, their literature, and their thought, the Greeks and Romans are eternal contemporaries.

On a bookcase opposite my desk at home there stands a reproduction of a girl's head dating from the fourth century B.C. It is by a Greek sculptor of some distinction, perhaps Scopas. I have had it for twenty-four years. Not only have I never grown tired of it (although the surrounding wall-pictures and other decorations have often been changed), but it seems to me now—as it seemed to me when I first bought it—neither new nor old, but living. During the daytime, as the sunlight moves across the room, the shadows shift upon the face as though on the face of a young girl breathing and thinking. In the evening the lamplight brings out new curves and subtleties in the features, and both shades and illuminates the eyes, so that often, as I glance up from my work and look at the head twenty-three centuries old, it seems about to turn, to smile, and to speak in terms which I should recognize and understand.[2]

The Greek girl is only a construction in stone; she communicates her life to the eye and the touch. The classical poets and thinkers speak to the ear and through it to the mind. Their wisdom and their sharp critical judgment, their memorable choice of words, and their exquisite sense of rhythm and of melody, make their thoughts perpetually present. Often nowadays, whenever I see the world torn between the extremes of democracy and the extremes of dictatorship, the belief that the majority is necessarily always right and the belief that only an all-powerful despot can solve the problems of humanity, the words of a man who had seen both extremes come effortlessly and somehow reassuringly into my mind (Horace, *Carm.* 3.3.1–4):

Iustum et tenacem propositi virum
non civium ardor prava iubentium,
   non vultus instantis tyranni,
     mente quatit solida . . .

Him who is just, firm, steady in moral will,
no mob of his wrongheaded compatriots,
   no, nor the grim black scowl of despots
     shakes him; his mind is a rock . . .

Thoughts like these and shapes like these cannot die.

They were not intended to die. The Greek and Roman writers and artists designed them for immortality and sometimes (though not always) actually forecast that they would be indestructible. It would be a very curious and interesting task to trace the idea of literary and artistic immortality throughout the ancient world. As

---

2[Highet's son, who has the bust of the young girl in his possession, has informed me that his father carried it back from Germany in 1932 in a knapsack. Ed.]

far as I know, there is no trace of it in Homer; the κλέα ἀνδρῶν ("glories of men") are remembered, but the poems about them are not expected to survive in exactly the same way. And yet, even as early as that, the Muses themselves are deathless. The Homeric poems were created, it would seem, for their own time and for their own hearers; but they survived, they asserted themselves, they became permanent long after their creators had been forgotten and the audience for which they were written had passed away. Surely it was the manifest immortality of the Homeric poems that inspired other Greek writers to think of attaining and sharing that immortality. The tragic poets do not claim that honor for themselves; but the magnificent comedian Aristophanes, at the climax of one of his finest comedies—the *Frogs*—asserted that Aeschylus had not only surmounted physical death but had also deserved and should now enjoy immortality. At about the same time the historian Thucydides was asserting the claim of his own work to be immortal. Without naming his immediate predecessor Herodotus, he criticized him and others bitterly (in a tone which set the pattern for innumerable later critical reviews of one another's work by rival scholars), and then, in a phrase which conveys the strength and the limitations of its author's 'scientific' thought, said that he wished his work to be not just a performance for the moment but a κτῆμά ἐς αἰεί, "a possession for all time" (1.22). A strange but moving utterance, made at a time when the historian's own world was almost visibly crumbling around him.

Now the Greeks, with their independent spirit, their distrust of authority, and their perpetual youth—Ελληνες ἀεὶ παῖδές ἐστε, "you Greeks are always children," said the Egyptian priest to Solon (Plato, *Timaeus* 22B)—were apt to resist the idea that a single poem or book could become immortal. Hence the bitter attacks on Homer, from Homer to Zoilus; hence the rough and ready treatment of the texts of the great poets, and the inventive literary experiments made outside the range of those poets by Callimachus, Theocritus, and others as well. But the pupils of the Greeks—the Romans—produced a new idea of the classics. They had a strong sense of time, and they wished to earn remembrance. Their first great poet, Ennius, not only claimed that Homer was reincarnated in him and his work (*Annales* 1, exordium), but left an epitaph for himself assuring the world that he had not died but lived on the lips of men (Cicero, *Tusculan Disputations* 1.14.34). Thereafter most of the great Roman poets claimed that they had achieved immortality—first, by rivaling in their own language a Greek poet who was already deathless, and second, by creating a work of unchallengeable imagination and of unexceptionable style. So both Horace (*Carm.* 2.20) and Ovid at the end of the *Metamorphoses* (*Met.* 15.871–79) declare that they will never die but will fly victoriously from mouth to mouth throughout mankind; and at the conclusion of Book 3 of his lyric poems, Horace further claims to have created a *monumentum aere perennius*—"a monument more enduring than bronze" (*Carm.* 3.30.1). In the proudest of all these declarations, the modest Vergil describes his own work in the *Georgics* as earning the equivalent of a magnificent Roman triumph and asserts that his next achievement will be to write a poem that will carry the name of Caesar through the years into the fabulous and unforeseeable future (*Georg.* 3.10–48). The concept of immortality for poets had become easier for the Romans to accept than it was for the Greeks of the fifth century B.C., because it had gradually become easier for the world to believe that men could become gods. Horace himself, that suave and balanced realist, speaks in *Epistles* 2.1 of the coming immortality of Octavian Augustus; he parallels it to the immortality, the earned godhead, of Romulus, Bacchus, and Castor and Pollux; and from there he proceeds straight to a discussion of the poetic claims made by himself and his contemporaries not only to fame but to immortality.

In the strange vision of the other world which is vouchsafed to Aeneas at his entry into Italy, he is told that all the souls of the living after their bodily death are purified of all their physical diseases—the corruptions and distortions imprinted on them by their stay in the world—by the cleansing power of mighty winds, by the washing of vast seas, or by purging fire; only after that purification are they truly immortal (Vergil, *Aeneid* 6.703–51). In the same way, nearly all the works of Greco-Roman poetry and art and thought which are truly classical have been cleansed of the unessential, purged of nearly everything casual and unimportant, and stripped down to face the worst of time's weather. A famous sculptor once said that every good statue should be so solidly put together, so ruthlessly freed of the extraneous, that it could be rolled down a hill without injury. So when we look at the best work of the Greeks and Romans, we see that their immortality is related to their spareness, their economy.

The anthologist Meleager, describing the various flowers in his poetic *Garland*, says that the poems of Sappho are βαιὰ μὲν ἀλλὰ ῥόδα—"few, but roses" (*Anth. Pal.* 4.1.6). This is true of many of the great classical writers. They wrote much indeed, but like the gardeners of legend who will destroy fifty buds in order to have one perfect bloom, they allowed only the best to survive. It was not apparently that they had any difficulty in producing creative work; they did not have to wait painfully for inspiration, suffering what the French call "the horror of the white page." On the contrary, their difficulty seems to have been the difficulty of selecting and concentrating the most trenchant and fitting materials from the vast mass of imaginative themes in their minds. One of the most famous of them, a poet filled with ideas, surrounded by stimuli, urged on by friendly admirers and less friendly rivals, confined the whole of his life's work to a total of less than thirteen thousand lines—perhaps a line and a half a day for the whole of his working career. Yet we learn from a valuable contemporary report of his methods that he was not a slow composer. He drafted his most important work in prose, dictated poetic versions of various passages as his interest led him to one or another, and then apparently spent his main effort on compressing the product of his imagination and his eloquence into the form which has weathered nearly twenty centuries. This was Vergil.[3] His friend Horace, who was not at all tongue-tied but gay and rather garrulous, based his entire claim to glory upon eighty-eight short lyric poems. The first great Greek historian produced one single book, together with a special study of a regional problem. (It was Herodotus's history of Assyria,[4] and might rank with the Ph.D. dissertations which later historians reluctantly list among their *opera*.) The second, Thucydides, produced one single book, and even that after a lifetime remained unfinished. Of the two great geniuses who wrote or completed the Homeric poems, each was apparently content to spend a lifetime on one masterpiece.

To write in this way is to be dedicated, to forget oneself. So, many of the most impressive classical works appear to be impersonal. Most of them scarcely mention their author; some of them even lack his signature. A whole shelf of books by one of the most brilliant philosophers of antiquity, dealing almost entirely with people of an earlier generation, never once introduces the author in person. Only twice does he mention his own name: once in a list of

---

[3][See Donatus, *Vita Vergilii* 22–25, on the methods that Vergil used to compose his verses—the contemporary report to which Highet is clearly referring in the above paragraph. Ed.]

[4][A reference to the Ασσύριοι λόγοι, which Herodotus himself mentions in 1.106 and 184—something that he may have written as a separate work, which apparently did not survive. Ed.]

those present at the defense of Socrates (*Apology* 34a); and once again in a description of the most crucial event of his own life, in the remark of a friend about his absence from the last conversations of Socrates—Πλάτων δέ, οἶμαι, ἠσθένει, "Plato, I think, was ill (*Phaedo* 59b). In the same way, many of the greatest works of classical literature are almost wholly anonymous and impersonal. We all know how Thucydides in the first sentence of his history gives his own name as its author; but then, in a later book, when he has to describe the military operation in northern Greece which he personally commanded—an operation which failed so disastrously that he himself was condemned to banishment—he offers no defense but merely says: "Thucydides and his squadron sailed in ταύτῃ τῇ ἡμέρᾳ ὀψὲ, "on the evening of the same day" (4.106.3).

In many of the finest Greek or Roman books, the tradition of anonymity and impersonality is as strong as that or stronger. Of course in certain special types of literature, where personal allusions are not only permitted but expected, we can see many touches of individual character—in elegy, in epigram, in satire, in Athenian Old Comedy, and in oratory, which depends so much on ethos. Even in lyric poetry we frequently find the signature and portrait of the author. But in the higher types of literature and art, the personality of the author is (so far as possible) suppressed. It can never of course be wholly eradicated; it would be a mistake on our part to suppose that the ancients wished to eradicate it. Still, it is surprising how little of themselves the greater writers and thinkers left on the surface. The finest example of this is the earliest. In the two epic poems of early Greek literature, there is scarcely a shred of evidence which would tell us the name, the age, the character, the education, the home, or the interests of the poet or poets who wrote them—or even whether they were written by two men with similar tastes and different natures. We speak of 'the poet' as the Greeks did—'the poet Homer.' But it would be truer to say, as he and his colleagues said, that the Homeric poems were not produced by any one individual but by the impersonal spirit of poetry, the Muse.

One of the main reasons for the apparent impersonality of so many classical artists is that they were deeply concerned with the power of tradition. In art, in thought, and in literature, the dignity of νόμος ("custom"), of the *mos maiorum* ("ancestral tradition"), was as potently felt as in social, political, and religious life. It scarcely even seemed possible to most of the artists of classical antiquity that they should utterly break the molds which had been handed down to them, modified by the achievements of their great predecessors. Nevertheless, we should be mistaken if we suggested that the chief element of the classical is this power of tradition, and implied that it could enforce conformity, crush out originality, deaden the creative genius, and convert aesthetic patterns into formal fetters. The meaning of the classical tradition goes much deeper than that.

To begin with, practically every Greek and Roman artist, when creating, worked within a form, a genus. He knew its purposes. He usually knew its origins (they might be in religious ritual, in folk-poetry, in the social needs and usages of a community), and he always knew the work of those who had preceded him in it. But no artist or painter or poet or thinker who deserved the name of creator ever aimed at preserving the pattern exactly as he had received it. Either he strove to make it more subtle and expressive than it had been—such was the progress of Latin love elegy from Gallus (or Catullus) through Tibullus and Propertius to Ovid—or he introduced new powers into it, made new demands on it, often by borrowing from another genus more or less closely allied, or else by using new types of material and breaking up conventions which he thought to be outworn. Therefore the writers of Greek New Comedy drew much from the tragedies of Euripides; Horace said that his predecessor Lucilius had converted the best of Greek Old Comedy into Roman satire (*Serm.* 1.4.1–13); and Juvenal the satirist endeavored to infuse the genus of satire with something of the power of epic poetry.

Again, the classical writers and artists were certainly not the devoted imitators of those who had gone before. In certain branches of Chinese and Japanese art, a pupil will follow his teacher's style and subjects so closely that he will even adopt his master's name and abandon all claims to an individual independent identity. This, in the classical world of Greece and Rome, was virtually impossible. If we look closely, we can distinguish four relationships between writers and artists working in the same field.

First, a writer may acknowledge his debt to a great predecessor but make it clear that he himself has added much of his own, working in a different medium or with fresh material. The choice of a particular predecessor to be saluted is often very significant. Thus, Aeschylus said that his tragedies were slices from the banquets of Homer (Athenaeus 8.347e). The author of the first great didactic poem in Latin praised Epicurus for his philosophical discoveries (Lucretius 1.62–79) and Ennius for his early exploration of the powers of Latin poetry (Lucretius 1.117–19). Vergil does not mention Catullus or Lucretius by name; but he copies important phrases and lines from Catullus as a tribute to his artistry, and inserts a special evocation of Lucretius—almost in Lucretius's own words—at a high point of the *Georgics* (2.490–92). This charming relationship has continued until our own day: both Dante and Tennyson have signalized their debt to Vergil;[5] and T. S. Eliot has proclaimed himself, indirectly but clearly, a pupil of Dante as well as of Dante's master.

As between the two languages, Greek and Latin, this particular relationship changes significantly. The Greeks had priority. The Greeks invented and developed most of the genera. The Romans, coming so much later, could only follow them—or so it seemed. But in fact the best Roman writers usually managed, when taking over a Greek pattern of literature, to impart to it new powers and beauties which had not been achieved by its original inventors and explorers. The most obvious example is the Roman epics inspired by Homer. Ennius said that he himself was Homer reincarnated (*Annales* 1, exordium). Vergil followed Homer's techniques and patterns with a fidelity which (at first sight) appears slavishly, discouragingly, classically accurate. And yet, the *Annales* of Ennius was a patriotic history, a new departure in epic literature either Greek or Latin. Vergil's *Aeneid* was an intense poem, full of emotions strange to Homer and illuminated by curious lights from worlds which Homer never knew. Therefore, we often find that a Roman writer, while acknowledging the priority of his Greek predecessor, will in fact neglect his predecessor's work. Vergil declares that his *Georgics* is the Roman successor of Hesiod's *Works and Days* by announcing that he sings the song of Ascra through the Roman towns (*Georg.* 2.176). Still, the *Georgics* as a whole has little resemblance to Hesiod's primitive and less eloquent poem, and this particular claim (to be a Roman Hesiod) comes only at the end of a magnificent patriotic evocation of the beauty and nobility of Italy, the evocation which ends on the following superb phrases (*Georg.* 2.173–74):

> Salve, magna parens frugum, Saturnia tellus,
> magna virum!

5[Dante signalized his debt to Vergil in the *Comedy,* by making him his guide through a hell and purgatory inspired by *Aeneid* 6; Tennyson celebrated him in *To Virgil,* "Written at the Request of the Mantuans for the Nineteenth Centenary of Virgil's Death." Ed.]

Hail, earthly paradise, mighty mother of crops,
and mother of men!

That evocation is so sublime and rich that it towers above Hesiod as the cypress towers above the bending osiers (*Bucolics* 1.25).

There is a third possible relationship between classical writers and artists and their predecessors. The latecomer is sometimes critical of the older man. He considers him wrong-headed, clumsy, old-fashioned, and careless. Sometimes he will actually name his forerunner and specifically point out the faults to which he objects. Sometimes, without mentioning a name, he will choose the same themes and handle them differently; or the same pattern, and fill it with new material, pointedly avoiding the elaborations of his elder rival. Thus, at the very beginning of his work, Thucydides explicitly mentions several inaccuracies in the history of Herodotus (1.20–22). And Ennius, when he reached the First Punic War in his epic narrative of Roman history, refused to describe it, saying (*Annales* 7, exordium):

Scripsere alii rem
versibus, quos olim Fauni vatesque canebant.

Others have written the tale
in verses such as Fauns and prophets used to sing.

(This is a half-reverent, half-contemptuous allusion to the *Punic War* of Naevius.) So also Euripides took up the theme of the murder of Clytemnestra by her own son Orestes—already handled by Aeschylus in the *Libation Bearers* and Sophocles in the *Electra*—and deliberately introduced critical references to certain crucial incidents of Sophocles' and Aeschylus's dramas, to show that they were as absurd in their old-fashioned heroism as the unrealistic psychology of the elder dramatists. The two greatest successors of Vergil in heroic poetry were Ovid with his *Metamorphoses* and Lucan with his *Civil War*. Both of these poets avoid every one of the amazing technical improvements in the hexameter for which Vergil is responsible. Lucan chooses theme, machinery, and other effects as different from Vergil's, as violently contrasting with those of the *Aeneid,* as he can well devise. In Book 14 Ovid takes up several of the incidents of the *Aeneid*, alters them and rehandles them (as he had already done in *Heroides* 7 with the story of Dido), and so angles them as to make Vergil seem both unsophisticated and ridiculous. Many other classical writers criticized their predecessors either implicitly or explicitly. The most striking instance of this is perhaps Epicurus, who actually denied his obvious debt to Leucippus and Democritus. The best-known, thanks to the research of Harold Cherniss, is the greatest pupil and shrewdest critic of Plato, Aristotle.[6]

These three relationships between elder and younger writers or artists are all creative, and they are all classical. The fourth alone is usually thought of as most typically classical and provides ammunition for some of the severest attacks on the classical ideal. This is acknowledged, obvious, and subservient tutelage—one step away, or two steps at most, from downright plagiarism. Such was Statius, who, after completing an epic on a subject drawn from Greek myth (and very much in the manner of Vergil), invokes the *Aeneid* and says that his highest ambition will be to follow it at a long distance behind (*Thebeid* 12.810–19). Too many of Vergil's successors have made a similar mistake, producing works in which accurate copying replaced creative imagination; and the elder poet's faults, repeated in his imitator, grew so unbearable as almost to mar his own more original work. But such imitation, apish or devout, is not true to the central spirit of classical art and thought.

But still we have scarcely mentioned one of the supreme values of our classical inheritance. It has been pointed out today by nearly all our speakers. This is aesthetic excellence. The sculpture, the architecture, most of the painting, all the diverse kinds of poetry, the varied types of prose which have survived—these together form a body of work unsurpassed in any of the world's civilizations for range and power and beauty. This excellence depends on many qualities of the classical mind, but on two in particular—a sense of structure, and a minute and subtle control of style.

For scholars interested in the arts, the realization and enjoyment of detail in quite minor Greek and Roman work is a constant satisfaction. Others, who know nothing of Greek and Latin—when they are told of the finesse with which a Greek poet arranges his rhythms and with which a Greek sculptor balances the lines and curves of his figures—are astounded, sometimes frankly incredulous. The average well-informed man today will need very sincere assurances before he will credit what you and I know to be facts— that an important part of the beauty of a Greek temple depends on deliberately calculated optical illusions of extreme delicacy: the

---

[6][In this regard, see H. Cherniss, *Aristotle's Criticism of Plato and the Academy* (Baltimore, 1944)—the culmination of Cherniss's research on Aristotle's criticism of earlier philosophers. Ed.]

columns which appear to be perfectly uniform are not so but swell toward the center by a few fractions of an inch; although they seem vertical, they are not but incline toward one another; and the floor, the platform on which they stand, is not flat but rises in the center in a smooth, imperceptible, exquisitely calculated curve. For teachers of the classics, it is a common experience nowadays to point out and analyze some particular beauty, some refinement of art in an ancient writer, and then to be met with amazed incredulity, which slowly under the weight of evidence collapses into delighted agreement. Tell your pupils that of nearly all the eminent prose-writers of classical Greece and Rome, each has his own distinctive patterns of rhythm; and that these patterns, measured in long and short syllables, can be traced in page after page of his work, so that they identify his writing as unmistakably as the brushwork of a distinguished Renaissance painter identifies his pictures. At first they will tend to disbelieve you; nobody, they think, could possibly have paid such detailed attention to his writing as to count and measure syllables. When it is demonstrated beyond a peradventure, they are filled with genuine amazement. It is as though a new world has opened to them. The same happens when they are told that Plato, as shown by notebooks after his death, wrote and rewrote the opening of the *Republic* many times, simply in order to find the most harmonious order of words in a simple statement (Diogenes Laertius, *Lives of the Philosophers* 3.37).

Since the ears of a modern reader are not trained to catch sound effects, he is usually astonished when you show him how, in seven words of a lyric poem, Catullus is able to echo the roar of the monsoon in the Indian Ocean and the thunder of the breakers on the coast (11.3–4):

> litus ut longe resonante Eoa
>   tunditur unda
>
> where the sea-beach booms to the pounding monsoon's
>   thunderous combers

And he is both surprised and delighted when he is told to listen to the cooing of wood-doves, not only the soft sound but the broken rhythm, in two lines of Vergil (*Buc.* 1.57–58):

> nec tamen interea raucae, tua cura, palumbes,
> nec gemere aëria cessabit turtur ab ulmo.
>
> while your favorite wood-doves woo in melancholy
> and high in the airy elms the mournful pigeons moan.

Yet in fact many of the delicacies of detail in Greek and Roman art and poetry have still to be discovered. Our eyes and ears have been too coarse to see them hitherto. Every culture has its own subtleties. Ours surely are in the realm of science. Our scientists and technologists now habitually do what was always considered impossible, perhaps not even envisaged: they can weigh particles too small to be seen; they can procure absolute clinical and microscopic cleanliness; they can measure one-millionth of an inch. In the Middle Ages the same ingenuity, the same delicate interest in detail was applied to theological discussion; and among the Jews it was such a love for subtlety that concerned itself with the Talmud. It is a peculiar quality of classical culture that this delicacy is applied, not to a received scripture but to the finest details of creative art and literature.

Other nations have displayed equivalent or greater subtlety in artistic detail; I am thinking of Chinese painting in particular. But only the classical peoples have ever possessed and exercised such a mastery of control of the design and symmetry of a large work. Contrast the superb planning, the majestic harmony of parts, which dominates the trilogy of Aeschylus—the *Oresteia*—with the chaotic or indecisive planning of the Book of Job, Goethe's *Faust,* or even its own distant and not unworthy descendant, Shakespeare's *Hamlet.* Contrast the Parthenon or the Pantheon or Hagia Sophia, with the nervous elaboration of the Gothic cathedrals, the proliferating detail of oriental temples. Contrast the clear and noble structure of the *Iliad* or the *Aeneid* with that of the *Ramayana* or any modern poem not written under the influence of classical ideals. Once again, it must be said that this particular aspect of classical art and thought astonishes modern readers who are unaccustomed to looking for structural excellence in contemporary prose or poetry, and would be unlikely to find it if they tried. When they are told, for instance, that the Greeks and Romans had worked out a series of simple patterns to govern the structure of various types of speech, of oratory, they first of all object that such patterns must be arbitrary rules and that creative writing ought to be free, free as the wind. And then, when they are shown that these patterns are not artificial rules, but the result of centuries of experience, methods of assuring effective results, as simple and logical as the modern scientist's rules for laboratory technique—then they are truly astonished, like a colorblind man who has suddenly been given his full perceptions and perceives the world as it is. Then, then, it is one of the rewards of teaching to watch them gradually learn to use their new sense of structure, to see them applying it to more complicated analyses, to such books as the *Republic* of Plato or an ode of Pindar. As well as giving them a new enjoyment of classical literature, this acquisition usually makes them a little distrustful of some of the masterpieces of modern prose and poetry—although whether that is a defect or a benefit, it is not for me to say. Horace (*Epist.* 2.2.128–40) speaks of a man who used to go to the theater when it was empty and applaud imaginary plays; his friends put him under treatment and cured him; but he did not thank them; he said that they had spoiled his life, *cui demptus per vim mentis gratissimus error* ("by the abolition perforce of his very delightful lunacy").

Supreme above aesthetic beauty, supreme above the power of tradition and the comparative impersonality which we have seen as characteristic of classical culture (although no doubt expressing itself through them) stands one ultimate quality which accounts for its permanent vitality. This is the power which Werner Jaeger of Harvard has described and helped to name—for Greek culture at least, although (we must regret) not for all Greek culture and for none of its Roman successor. This is the power to educate, which is παιδεία.[7] The arts of the Greeks and Romans were not conceived merely as decorations or amusements. They were conceived more essentially as factors in spiritual growth and enrichment; they were intended to make men better. Of course the arts differed in their power to educate; and within each art there were important gradations. The minor visual arts were scarcely intended to do more than add grace to an object of common use, a pot or a coin. Sculpture and painting could move the spirit through the contemplation of beautiful bodies, graceful patterns and colors, so that even the statue of a naked goddess could teach the charm and delight of sexual attraction together with the pride of temperance, the grace of restraint. Music, that powerfully emotional art, so intractable to logic, was often felt almost too dangerously exciting; like ourselves, the men of the classical world recognized its powers and wondered how to control and utilize them. At the head of the hierarchy of the arts stood literature, which indeed had the greatest power to educate or (conversely) to corrupt. Within literature again there were gradations of dignity. The minor types, such as

---

[7][See W. Jaeger, *Paideia: The Ideals of Greek Culture,* trans. G. Highet, 3 vols. (New York, 1939–44)—Highet's translation of Jaeger's work from the German, a translation that Jaeger himself regarded not simply as a translation but "a real English book" (vol. 2, p. xv). Ed.]

epigram and mime, were only *lusus* or *nugae* ("trifles"), meant to amuse and not to be estimated by any moral standard. Above them stood comedy and elegy, which were occasionally moral in implication; satire, which was vulgar and violent but aimed at moral instruction; and certain other minor types. Above these were ranged the higher genera of literature—oratory, history, philosophical dialogue, didactic poetry—together with those whose powers were doubtful or irregularly defined, such as lyric poetry. Highest of all stood those types which were the most exacting of all to write, which plunged deepest into the central problems of human life and which furthest transcended the boundaries of prose and of ordinary perception—tragic poetry and epic. It is because the artists and writers of Greece and Rome knew that their highest duty was not to add beauty to the lives of their contemporaries, nor (far less) to express their own personal hopes and fears without reference to others, but to make their fellow men better, that their work is still invaluable. That is one of the chief reasons why we teach it, analyze it, admire it, and (as far as we are able) try to perpetuate it.

The power of παιδεία, of creative education, which is exercised by the Greek and Roman world, is a rare and subtle thing. To analyze it would take several complete books, and they would be worth less than the classical books in which it is exemplified. Yet it is clear that something of that power lies in the extreme aesthetic grace with which the Greek and Roman artists and thinkers transmitted their messages to us; something more of it in the content of these messages—the cool bitter analysis of the destructive results of class war by Thucydides, the gay imaginative versatile optimism which streams out of nearly every page of Aristophanes; and other elements again in the extraordinary power of example, which the Greeks and Romans at their best exerted on one another and in later times on their successors. Classical literature and history are full of glorious *imagines* ("models"), great personalities who by their very existence have added to the sum of nobility in the world—such are Hadrian, Marcus Aurelius, Pericles, Epicurus perhaps, and surely Sophocles; Horace and Scipio the Younger, and that essentially tragic figure Socrates. So also modern history is full of heroic and generous figures who were helped to achieve their own ideals by imitating the great men of old. Dante called Vergil his master and his father (*Inferno* 1.85); Petrarch wanted to be a modern Cicero; Charles XII of Sweden thought of himself as another Alexander of Macedon, slept with Plutarch under his pillow, and with better fortune and stouter followers might have united and civilized the Middle North as Alexander unified and civilized the Middle East.[8] The history of modern European resistance to tyranny is rich with the follies and gallantries of young men who modeled themselves on Brutus and Cassius in order to kill tyrants; and let us hope that this particular example of παιδεία will never be forgotten.

Let us be sure that it will not. Our world is made up of a strange, an inexplicable blend of change and permanence. The individual life of each of us is in constant flux within a framework which we try to keep stable. The spiritual universe which we all inhabit flows like a river, whirls like a galaxy; and yet both the spiritual cosmos and the individual bios have certain fixed poles which keep them from falling into complete chaos. The physical sciences, which dominate so much of our existence, now seem to derive their very meaning from constant change. Their processes are always being revised; their principles are at best provisional, and in less than a generation they are always revised and replaced by new principles, equally provisional. In politics too, how many changes have we seen in twenty years, in forty, in sixty? How many more will we see, if indeed the politicians do not institute one more violent change which may terminate the entire process? In law and in the social sciences, slow though change may be, it is incessant; and so also in economics and other areas of collective life. Within this busy flux of patterns and phenomena, men and women look eagerly, anxiously, pitifully, for some stability, and are perplexed that it is difficult to discover. The truth is that within this mutable life and this realm of change, stability is not to be found—except perhaps in religion and even more certainly in philosophy and in art. It is through these activities alone that we can escape from the constant flux and see something of those ideas, those forms which endure. And much of our most profound philosophy, much of the greatest literature and the noblest art ever created, are the work of the Greeks and Romans. To give up a lifetime to the study of these works is not antiquarianism nor escapism. It is a closer approach to the ultimate truth.

At the end of one of his most thoughtful dialogues, Cicero tells a story which sounds like a Platonic myth, but is Roman in that it is

---

[8][See F. M. A. Voltaire, *History of Charles XII* (Rouen, 1731)—the classic biography on this subject, reprinted and translated numerous times—especially Book 1, for Charles's initial exposure to the career of Alexander the Great via the Latin account of Quintus Curtius. Ed.]

told by a real historical character about an experience of his own. Cicero says that a great Roman of the rising Republic, looking back from the pinnacle of his career, recalled an episode which occurred when he was a young officer on his first foreign campaign. His name was Scipio; he was to be called Africanus the Younger; and the episode was a dream or a vision (*Republic* 6. 9–24).

When the young man reached Africa on his first campaign, he says, he met his father's old friend, the African chief Masinissa. With him he talked for many hours about the character and exploits of the great Scipio, and in a tone which reminds us of the practice of ancient biographers, he says that the old man "had remembered not only all his deeds but also his words"—so that when the young Scipio went at last to rest, he was exhausted, and yet his mind was active and receptive. In his sleep he saw the mighty Scipio Africanus, who said to him: "Be alert, abandon your fears, and remember what I say." As he spoke, he pointed down; and the young man saw that the two of them were high above Carthage, high above the earth in a place full of stars. There, looking downward, young Scipio heard his own future triumph and the glory of his career forecast—just as Aeneas later was to see the future of his enterprise passing like a triumphal procession in the underworld and imaged by a god on his own protecting shield. True patriots, said his adviser, true patriots could never die; and with that he saw his father Paulus approaching. As he embraced his father, he wept. He said: "Why should I not come here at once to join you? Why do I linger on this earth?" His father told him that the law of the Creator ordained that all men should give their lives to serving their fellow mortals and that none should leave his post without his permission. Only after completing their duty, he said (in the accents of a Roman officer), could they enter the assembly of the blessed. And now the young officer saw that he was high above the world, among magnificent stars, invisible from this earth. The planet looked very small and contemptible to him; even (he said) the Roman Empire was pathetic because it covered merely a dot on the small surface of the globe. As he looked at this, his father said to him: "Forget the moment and the place; forget such temporary things as pleasure and pain and glory; think only of your duty and of true virtue and nobility. These virtues, like the soul which they inhabit and inform, are deathless." And with that the vision ceased; the young officer woke from his sleep and entered a career in which, like Aeneas, he met both an obscure and bitter death, and everlasting life.

These are true glories: not only the men, whose characters are exempla to us as the portraits of the ancestors were to a Roman family or the ideally handsome youths and maidens of Greek sculpture to those who admired them; but the powerful and sensitive prose in which Cicero wrote (a product of Greek suppleness mingled with Roman strength); the tradition of the philosophical myth or vision, which he inherited from Plato and which had a far longer ancestry; and the truth, the central truth, that true happiness and fulfillment mean concentration on the permanent powers and values (few as they are) which have been created or at least discerned by man. The true reward of those who give their lives up to the classics is the reward promised to the young Roman by his dead father—that they can rise above time, and above the mists, the distances, and the perplexities of this planet, to see the lights and splendors which are truly deathless, which are symbols and perhaps guarantees of immortality.

Two Cultures: The Arts and Sciences*

Art. Science. Portentous words; vague names for two island universes of thought and experience, both essentially human activities—for how do we distinguish ourselves from the animals with which we share this planet? By only a very few functions which we can call uniquely human, our own creations; and two of these functions are science and art. This they have in common, that they are human in origin; yet they both try, each in its own way, to transcend humanity in their achievements as far as in their origin they transcend the animal and natural realms.

They share (at least in the present time) another quality—expansiveness. All through the twentieth century the works of science have been increasing in vigor, in ambition, and in intensity of individual and cooperative effort. During the same period more works of art have been produced than ever before in history—not necessarily better in quality, but more in sheer volume, more books, more plays (on film, on radio, on television, as well as on the stage), more pictures (including photographs and magazine illustrations), more music in a multitude of different ranges, transmitted and heard through many hitherto unexampled media. At the same time, more works of art produced in earlier epochs have been made visible, audible, and comprehensible to more people through the remarkable spread of museums and libraries and the special type of book-publishing which André Malraux has called the Museum without Walls.[1] As the population of the world has increased, so the realm of science and the realm of art have both been extended.

Yet statistics about massive entities such as 'the world population' can be deceptive. All statistics are misleading; large ones are often pernicious. When we consider how the world population has

---

*Presented in 1966 at Columbia University (= John Jay Associates lecture). [In this lecture Highet presented his views on a subject that teachers and scholars were vigorously discussing in the 1960s following the publication of C. P. Snow's *The Two Cultures and the Scientific Revolution* (New York, 1959) and his *The Two Cultures: And a Second Look* (New York, 1964). Ed.]
[1][See G. Highet, "The Museum without Walls," in *People, Places, and Books* (New York, 1953) 211–18, on André Malraux's *The Psychology of Art*. Ed.]

grown in numbers, and how during the same time the energies of science and art have been expanding, we are apt to assume that the processes have been not only simultaneous but interconnected. In our mind's eye, illuminated by the rosy glow of the ideal future, we see a huge planetary population all equally enlightened by science and uplifted by art. This is a dangerous fallacy. The scientific and artistic achievement of the nineteenth and twentieth centuries has largely been the work of only one single section of the human race. It has chiefly been produced by the nations and peoples who live in the North Temperate Zone, between the Urals on the east and California on the west. In spite of the distrust and hatred which divide them and the dreadful wars which have several times almost ruined them, these nations and peoples have in the last eight or ten generations pushed far beyond the other sections of mankind, both in science and in the arts, so far that an enormous cultural gap has opened between them and their neighbors on what Barbara Ward calls Spaceship Earth.[2]

This cultural gap is not being narrowed by the efforts we make to share our civilization with the others. It is growing wider, particularly in the area of technology. If this process continues for another century or so, the inventive and creative groups will be as far removed from nearly all the other inhabitants of the world as the sophisticated Brazilians of Rio de Janeiro are from the savages of the Amazonian jungles. Before World War II certain propagandists used to divide the world into Have Nations and Have-Not Nations. That was partly an artificial and tendentious distinction. A more real and important one has now emerged and is growing deeper—the division between the Know Nations and the Know-Not Nations. Virtually all modern inventions and techniques and methods of creating and distributing wealth are created by the Know Nations and flow from them to the rest of the world; and all modern ideas have spread out from the Know Nations—political concepts such as nationalism, economic structures, aesthetic and sub-aesthetic forms as diverse as the motion-picture drama and the symphony orchestra. In many (perhaps in most) important respects, the Know-Not Nations are dependent upon the Know Nations—not politically (for most of them proudly proclaim themselves independent) but spiritually; and materially also.

Many of the Know-Not Nations can scarcely feed themselves. Even when they are mainly agricultural and pastoral, they cannot produce enough food for themselves today, and they will not pro-

---

[2][See B. Ward, *Spaceship Earth* (New York, 1966) on this development. Ed.]

duce nearly enough food for themselves tomorrow, when their population has increased beyond the danger limit. As Acock says:[3]

> On the basis of some rather rough statistics and ratios it has been argued that Africa, compared with other parts of the world, has a relative abundance of land, soils, water, forests, cattle and other resources. At the same time it has a relatively small population, mainly composed of farmers. Yet, despite all these farmers well endowed with resources, diets are poor, the continent is a net importer of meat and wood and a growing importer of other foodstuffs and raw materials. The region does not even support itself with its present small population and low levels of living. But population is doubling itself every 30 years; non-farmers in towns are increasing at more than twice this rate.

We are feeding many of them and will be feeding more and more—not only because of our industries, but because of the contrast between their simple, laborious, static methods and our intelligent and versatile and expansive application of technology to farming and the transportation of produce. In Goody's words:[4]

> Africa in 1950 showed greater unevenness of development than Europe in 1850. Technologically it is much more backward. For example, Europe had a metal plough, whereas until the colonial period Ethiopia was the only part of Africa which had even the Mediterranean plough. In large parts of Africa farming is by hoe.

Financially, few of the Know-Not Nations can afford to belong to the twentieth century. Unless they possess large stores of some rare and valuable raw material such as copper or tin or oil, they have to be financed by the Know Nations. This fact is so disagreeable that it forces external observers to use harsh and distorted phraseology to describe it; the disparity is called imperialism, or neo-colonialism, or some other name seething with emotion and bitter with resentment. The emotion comes from the heart, which feels the gulf between the two worlds and hates it. Nowadays it is common for us, watching a newsreel, to see the president of an 'emerging' country either dressed in a Western-styled military uniform, sometimes carrying a British officer's swagger-stick, or else wearing a superbly primitive robe and wielding a ceremonial

---

[3]See A. M. Acock's comments in "Agricultural Potentialities in Africa," in G. Wolstenholme and M. O'Connor, edd., *Man and Africa* (Boston, 1965) 239–57, especially 247.

[4]See J. Goody's comments in the discussion following the paper of A. F. Ewing and S. J. Patel, "Perspectives for Industrialization in Africa," in Wolstenholme and O'Connor (above, note 3) 299–328, especially 324.

fly-whisk, addressing his people through an imported microphone, surrounded by a bodyguard of soldiers uniformed and equipped by Western technology (although not a single man in his army could either design a rifle or make a cartridge for it), and then driving back home to a palace air-conditioned by a West German firm, in an English-made Rolls-Royce or an American Cadillac, fueled by gasoline extracted from a remote desert by Western explorers and refined by Western chemists and then transported by European or Japanese tankers to the Western-constructed storage-tanks in his Western-designed capital city. Every time such a man, both powerful and impotent, picks up a telephone, or hears the clatter of a typewriter, or listens to the radio, or turns over the pages of a printed book, he feels hatefully dependent on the minority of mankind, the Know Nations.

The division between Know and Know-Not Nations is growing wider and deeper. For this there are three main reasons. The technology of the Know Nations—we should not say 'Western' since the group includes Russia and Japan—is advancing more and more rapidly and thus leaving the less developed peoples farther and farther behind. The population of these peoples is increasing faster than their production of food—which means that every year they have less surplus to use for the advancement of ideas and techniques. And their populations are increasing more rapidly than their rates of literacy. (In 1965 the Chairman of the Xerox Corporation pointed out that more than half of the people in Latin America were functionally illiterate, and thus, since the population was doubling every twenty-five years, it was falling backward into barbarism rather than advancing beyond it.)

The gulf is not narrowed but is widened by internationalism. Whenever an advanced nation impinges on a backward group, the backward group is disrupted unless it can adapt to the more sophisticated culture. It rarely can. Association between two disparate peoples always annoys and disquiets the less developed group. The villagers who have left their homes and moved into improvised suburbs on the outskirts of cities—all over the world, from Rio de Janeiro to Leopoldville, from Calcutta to Paris—hate the city folk who have skills and enjoyments which are denied to them. The ostentatious display and waste of possessions and conveniences infuriates the Know-Not Peoples against the Know Peoples—making them insecure, envious, vindictive, sometimes even threatening them with collective insanity. The most pathetic example of this is the natives of Papua, who believe that airplanes are spirit messengers, coming from the home of their own ancestral ghosts and diverted en route by the white men; and who therefore construct imitation airstrips with imitation airplanes parked on them, in the hope that thus they may attract one of the spirit messengers to land and to bring them some of the spirit ancestors' wealth—shoes, canned beer, radios, and guns.

This is the first time in the history of mankind that social, cultural, and political events have been able to affect the entire human race within a few days or weeks or months of their occurrence. Not long ago (as our life should be reckoned) there were two magnificent empires in existence. They were so great that they included and civilized most of the inhabitants of their own domains; and yet they had only the most faint and limited contact with each other, and knew scarcely a single word of each other's language, scarcely a fraction of each other's technical and artistic achievements. These were Rome and China. Within the same era there was an enormous continent which knew nothing of the rest of the world and was unknown to it, a continent nurturing at least three major civilizations which had little or no contact with one another and none with the remainder of humanity—Central and South America. But in recent years, within the last two lifetimes, we have all become interconnected—physically, in the sense that we can quickly and easily visit (or invade) one another's homes throughout the planet, and hear one another's voices through the earth or the sea or the air, and see one another's images on television, and of course attack one another with miraculously rapid and far-ranging weapons. Yet we are still not members one of another. Physically we are neighbors but not spiritually. Therefore we cannot tell in which direction mankind will move.

Let us therefore narrow our focus to science and art within our own sector of the world. In it both science and art have extended their realms—so broadly that no single scientist now even hopes to understand all modern science, and no critic, however young and daring, would claim to comprehend all modern art. This, we feel, is good. We all respect science; we all admire art. We pour a great deal of money into supporting both science and art, into purchasing the results of their activities and rewarding their practitioners. Somehow we think that the ideal human achievement would be a combination of both—a private house designed by Mies van der Rohe, engineered and air-conditioned by General Electric, with an acoustically impeccable high-fidelity system playing Alberto Ginastera and Olivier Messiaen on Angel records through invisible loudspeakers masked behind pictures painted by Pablo Picasso and Salvador Dali.

But apart from such an ideal—the very word *ideal* implies unrealizability, impossibility—what have science and art to do with each other, among us, today? What a question! The mind boggles at it, and starts back, and begins to smother and choke in a miasma of abstract nouns. There is a fine scene in Henrik Ibsen's *Peer Gynt* (2.7), where the hero, after meeting and combating all sorts of concrete physical temptations and opponents with mixed success, at last finds himself embroiled with one antagonist who renders him powerless to fight, powerless to go further, powerless even to understand what is happening to him. This enemy is a thing called the Boyg, which is to all Peer Gynt's senses what fog is to the sense of sight. There is nothing in it on which he can lay hold (like a limb), no body which he can wound, no heart he can stab, no face he can confront, nothing but formless softness into which, the further he advances, the more deeply he is engulfed. Like all good artistic symbols, the Boyg has many meanings. Among others, it signifies the chief danger of thinking in abstract terms—that we may easily addle our brains and waste our efforts by looking for solutions to unreal problems. Any question which contains one or more large abstract nouns—whether hopeful, such as SCIENCE, ART, HUMANITY, CULTURE, RELIGION, and PROGRESS; or depressing, such as WAR, RACE, and REVOLUTION—is likely to be a false question, which may have no sensible answer, or which may have several different and even conflicting answers.

The question about science and art is a false question. The moment we say "art," we think of one particular type of art such as music or sculpture; the moment we say "science," we think of one important branch of science such as nuclear physics—if indeed we do not think rather of applied science, better described as technology. To discuss "art" in general, to ask meaningful questions about it, and to formulate sensible answers to them, is very difficult indeed, all but impossible; and although scientific method is indeed a valuable concept, it is impracticable to use the single abstract noun "science" in any realistic discussion.

So let us rephrase the question. How do the sciences (many as they are) and the arts (diverse as they are) affect one another? The arts scarcely influence the sciences at all. In the romantic nineteenth century it was customary to think of all or most of the arts as activities almost sacred in their idealism and almost superhuman in their potency. Shelley described poets as "the unacknowledged legislators of the world."5 He and some of his compeers actually believed that poetry could lay down principles of conduct and belief with all the solemnity of law, and utter arcane truths with all the assurance of religion. That has all gone now. There are only one or two arts which can still claim to influence belief and conduct. None can aspire to influence the sciences.

Now reverse the question. Do any of the sciences affect the arts? Science (if you define the word loosely enough) influences everything. For anyone who reads a book printed by a machine on paper also made by a machine is (in a crude sense) being indirectly influenced by science. But if we are to discuss the problem more accurately, we must distinguish the sciences from their practical application, technology. And we must ask whether the sciences influence the arts only after we have partitioned off that other question—whether the arts are influenced by technology, and if so, how.

In this latter query there is enough for a long and lively debate. One of the most surprising mass events in our lives—and one of the most unpredictable—has been the spread of technology over a vast section of the world and its invasion of the daily lives of hundreds of millions of people. It has created an era in which plenty has been achieved and has then become superfluity (imagine a civilization which finds it difficult to dispose of old automobiles and refrigerators), and in which change and compulsive adaptation have become uncontrollable mutation and flux. This process has worked upon the arts in some curious ways.

To an extent almost incredible, it has multiplied their products. In this area I am particularly easy to astonish, because one of my concerns is the survival of Greek and Roman art, literature, and thought through the dark ages of barbarism (say 500–1000 A.D.). During those dismal centuries one often finds that a book of the greatest imaginable value, a book for which subsequent generations have expressed reverent admiration, has been able to survive in only one single handwritten copy—because so few people could read it or cared to take the trouble to transcribe it. But today one of my friends, the head of a large publishing house which is exclusively with books of higher learning, tells me that he has under his command one machine which he cannot even afford to start rolling unless he has an order for fifty thousand copies at one run. That is its minimum workload. In the age of technology, books,

---

5[A reference to Shelley's *A Defence of Poetry* (final sentence)—an essay inspired in part by Plato's attack on poetry in the *Republic*. Ed.]

paintings, music, plays (through the medium of film), and ancillary types of art such as decorative fabrics and materials—these have been multiplied into the millions and made accessible to the tens and hundreds of millions.

Some would argue that they have been made cheap in every sense—inexpensive and common and vulgar. I should not agree. It is far too easy to sneer at technology and mass-production and cellophane-packaged art-products, and so forth. Not long ago Alberto Moravia placed all the blame for the present critical state of the arts upon modern industrial civilization (that is, upon technology), "which has of its very nature an incurable tendency to substitute industrial products for artistic products."[6] And yet consider one triumph of technology which I personally bless every day and curse only once or twice a year—the phonograph and its cousin the tape recorder. The first recording of a full orchestra to be made and sold was created well within living memory, in 1909. (It was produced by the Odeon Company, and it was a recording of Tchaikovsky's *Nutcracker Suite.*) Can you think of a single important modern musician who has not welcomed these new machines and worked happily with them? Often and often, as I set the needle delicately on the carefully cleansed record, I have a vision of Arturo Toscanini spending his sleepless nights in front of his phonograph listening with the most intense alertness to his own recordings of great music; and further away, in the lonely land near the Arctic Circle, of Jean Sibelius eagerly reaching out through his radio in the hope of hearing a distant orchestra playing one of his masterpieces. In one of his eloquent and enigmatic poems, W. H. Auden envisaged the advance of music into the future, in terms of technology:[7]

> What next? One can no more imagine how,
> In concert halls two hundred years from now,
> When the Mozartian sound-waves move the air,
> The cognoscenti will be moved, than dare
> Predict how high orchestral pitch will go,
> How many tones will constitute a row,
> The tempo at which regimented feet
> Will march about the Moon, the form of Suite
> For Piano in a Post-Atomic Age,
> Prepared by some contemporary *Cage.*

---

[6]See A. Moravia, *Man As an End: A Defense of Humanism,* trans. B. Wall (New York, 1966) 184.

[7]See W. H. Auden, *Homage to Clio* (New York, 1960) 69–73, especially 70, for the poem *Metalogue to The Magic Flute.*

However, technology is not science. We are asking what the sciences, individually or collectively, have done to some or all of the arts, or what the arts have learned from the sciences during the present century or so. The answer is—very little, almost nothing. Much less, far far less, than in other epochs of human history.

Take one easy instance: the science of biology. Before the modern age the understanding of human anatomy had two remarkable periods of progress in the Western world: in the fifth and fourth centuries before the Christian era and in the fifteenth and sixteenth centuries of the Christian era—the second being in many ways stimulated by the revitalization of the first. In both these times scientists were studying the structure of the human body and learning more and more about it. Concurrently artists were investigating the external appearance of the human body and were learning more and more about how to portray it—in paint or charcoal, in marble or bronze. The explorations of the scientist and the heightened perceptions of the artist were parts of a joint enterprise. But during the last three or four generations, when such remarkable discoveries have been made in many departments of the organic sciences, what effects have they produced on our novelists, our painters, our sculptors, our playwrights, and our musicians? Virtually none.

The inorganic sciences—geology, physics, astronomy, and those other superb adventures of the exploring human mind—how have they influenced our creative artists? Again, very little, at first sight. They have an inhuman or extrahuman character which repels, which seems to freeze the warm currents of the spirit. In Auden's words:[8]

> The order of the macrocosmic spaces,
> The outward calm of their remote occasions,
> Has lost all interest in our confusion;
> Our inner regimen has given way;
> The subatomic gulfs confront our lives
> With the cold stare of their eternal silence.

Yet there is one area in which some modern imaginative writers have set out to explore the new dimensions opened up to them by science, in particular by astronomy. This is 'science fiction,' which now occupies a whole section in most public libraries—although admittedly it is placed close to tales of crime and detection, and ro-

---

[8]See W. H. Auden, *Collected Poetry* (New York, 1945) 11–16, especially 16, for the poem *Kairos and Logos*.

mances of the vanished world of the cowboy. It has a long pedigree, going at least as far back as the Greek Lucian. Distinguished men have practiced it: Johann Kepler, the astronomer of the seventeenth century, and Fred Hoyle, the astronomer of the twentieth;[9] both the polymath Cyrano de Bergerac and the polymath Herbert George Wells. Granted, the general level of style and character-portrayal and plot-construction in science fiction stories is disgustingly low. Granted, the pseudoscientific tricks introduced by their authors (disguised by names as ridiculous as Abracadabra, the "space warp," and the "teleportation formula") are scarcely distinguishable from the magical spells and omnivalent wishes which are the basis of fairy stories and primitive myths. Yet this is an attempt by creative artists to do something with the fresh material and new stimuli provided by one group of scientists.

But have the visual artists of the past three or four generations done as much as they could to use the discoveries of science? As an amateur I dabble in astronomy; and often, when I have spent an hour or two with the telescope studying the amazing spectacle of the planetary and the stellar heavens, I come indoors filled with imaginative tumult. My vision, taking some time to adjust itself to the light of the little electric lamps in my living room, is still full of stars and nebulae and galaxies; so is my mind. And then I occasionally think of the eminent names of modern artists—of Paul Cézanne painting a handful of fruit in a bowl and worrying away at the Montagne Sainte-Victoire, or of Auguste Renoir turning out an endless series of plump pink naked milkmaids as expressionless as their own cows, or of Pablo Picasso compulsively teasing and hacking at the simple elements of the familiar human face and figure; and then I think: "What an abominable, what a damnable waste of time and energy and talent!" And as for our poets . . . It is easy enough to mock 'space fiction,' and indeed I have usually found it impossible to finish any of the 'space fiction' stories which runs beyond half a dozen pages. Yet now and then there appears among them a concept which is worthy to be called poetic, and which—if united with chosen language and sensitive rhythms—

---

[9]Kepler's "Lunar Nightmare," describing a voyage to the moon and the conditions of life there, I have not read, but have learned of it from Arthur Koestler's *The Sleepwalkers* (New York, 1959) 415–19. As for Fred Hoyle, see for instance his *The Black Cloud* (London, 1957), describing the invasion of the solar system by an entity far larger than this earth, which proves to be a living creature of immeasurably higher intelligence than that of any individual man.

would make a good poem.[10] However, I know of only one ambitious modern poem which has tried to deal with the new dimensions and strange possibilities of experience thrust upon mankind by the exploration of space. This is a lyrical narrative by a Swedish poet about an endless, or almost endless, journey on a space vehicle.[11] I cannot call it a success; but at least (like its subjects) it shows the way outward.

There is one field of science which has profoundly affected at least some of the arts. Curiously enough, it is a science which still sadly admits its own imperfection, its own inadequacy. This is psychology—a new exploration of a realm which many poets and prose-writers and some painters and musicians have visited but have never attempted to map out as a whole. Here the artists have preceded the scientists and have shown them the way. More can be learned about the psychology of the adult male and female from great plays, poems, and stories than (so far) from all the work of all the psychologists.

In this area there is one territory, all but unmapped, which fascinates me; and I often wonder when it will acquire its Marco Polo or its Galileo. This involves the psychical composition and behavior of large human groups: armies, mobs, nomadic tribes, colonists, racial and linguistic units, religious confraternities, secret societies, prisoners both civil and military, tightly organized political parties and rigid social classes. (Today it is as difficult to become a member of the Communist party in Russia as it was in eighteenth-century France to become a member of the aristocracy.) Many great novelists have seen how important this theme is and have attempted to treat it. Some have succeeded and some have failed. Charles Dickens wrote two good novels on it: *A Tale of Two Cities,* on the French Revolution; and *Barnaby Rudge,* on a near revolution not many years earlier in London. Victor Hugo showed his masterful grasp of big subjects both in *Les Misérables* and in *Notre-Dame de Paris*—where crowds, mobs, or gangs are prominent characters, not merely background elements as in most Greek tragedy. Jules Romains, with his beguiling theory of 'Unanimism' (which explains how a group can become a higher entity than the individu-

---

[10]I am thinking in particular of Arthur Clarke's magnificently imaginative *Childhood's End* (New York, 1953). Ray Bradbury is a poet in prose, but his brilliant stories should not be thought of as 'science fiction'; rather they are in the direct line of the fantastic visionary tales of E. T. A. Hoffmann and Edgar Allen Poe.

[11]See H. Martinson, *Aniara,* trans. H. MacDiarmid and E. H. Schubert (New York, 1963).

als composing it), approached the theme in several of his novels; but in his chief work *Men of Good Will,* he found it impossible to treat the history of modern Europe in terms of colliding and competing and interlocking groups, and was forced to concentrate on (sometimes symbolic) individuals. In *War and Peace* Leo Tolstoy went to the other extreme, writing a study of conflicting groups led largely by unconscious forces and not really influenced by their ostensible leaders. (Is some disciple of Tolstoy now writing a novel to prove that in the 1941–44 invasion of Russia Hitler really had no decisive power over the destinies of millions of men and women, any more than Napoleon had in 1812?)

All the sciences are explorations. All the arts can be explorations, if the artists are strong and bold enough. Mere size, mere dimensions, have nothing to do with it. A two-page fugue by Bach is a penetration of a recondite world, which can be compared in intensity to the mathematical investigations of his contemporary Leonhard Euler and which surely springs from a similar impulse. Sometimes I think that the men of the future will look back upon our scientists with interest and sympathy and some admiration, but upon most of our artists with contempt, despising them for working on such a pitifully small scale in a universe rapidly expanding both physically and spiritually. They will rank our playwrights with puppet masters, our painters with interior decorators, our sculptors with designers of toys, our architects far below the engineers who build bridges and dams, and our novelists with newspaper hacks. I hope I am wrong. Every now and then a new vision emerges, such as the sculpture of Richard Lippold,[12] and my hopes revive. Perhaps we are at the beginning of a long period of search and experiment, during which many thousands of mistakes must be made before new territory can be invaded and occupied. Perhaps none of us will see more than two or three important works of art worthy to take their place beside the splendid discoveries of the scientists; but our grandchildren may witness a new age in which the arts will at last begin to overtake the sciences, not only in subtlety but in grandeur and audacity.

---

[12][See "Richard Lippold," *Current Biography* 17 (New York, 1956) 379–81, on the career of this American sculptor, still cited in art history books and best known for his intricately arranged and engineered space cages, wire constructions, and suspension bridges. Ed.]

Classical Influences on Today's World*

"We cannot escape history," said one of the wisest of American leaders.[1] It is a great saying. Like many great sayings, it is true in several different senses. One of these senses is that we cannot cut ourselves loose from the past. We may try to forget the past; we may (through sheer ignorance) fail to understand the continuous power it exercises; we may distort or minimize its significance; but it is always with us. It is not our physical but our spiritual heredity.

We have taken millions of years to evolve into the unique beings which we are—animals with minds, and with something else—is it the soul? Several good books have recently been written to show how that long process has instilled in us, both as individuals and as groups, many patterns of unconscious behavior which we may either adapt or sublimate, but can never completely uproot. (Such are Robert Ardrey's *The Territorial Imperative* [1966], Konrad Lorenz's *On Aggression* [1966], and Desmond Morris's *The Naked Ape* [1967].) These patterns come from our animal part and our precivilized experiences. But it is more important to understand how our thinking minds, our imaginative activities, our political attitudes, our philosophical principles, our religious concepts, and many other essential parts of our lives have been shaped by the civilizations which, only eighty or ninety generations ago, our forefathers created and maintained. Of course we have not taken over all that these civilizations produced. What we took we have often changed. We are changing it constantly and constantly adding to it, particularly in the universe of science and technology—a universe which looks increasingly, terrifyingly, inhuman and even antihuman. Yet we have retained much that is valuable, often without being fully conscious of its extent or its value.

Here is one small example. The words you are now reading are printed in slightly adapted Carolingian letters. The shapes of these letters were developed by the scribes working for the Holy Roman Emperor Charlemagne around the year 800 A.D., under the di-

---

*Prepared in 1968 for a special volume of the National Geographic Society, but not published since a publishing agreement was never concluded.
[1] See Lincoln's *Second Annual Message,* delivered on December 1, 1862.

rection of the English scholar Alcuin, in order to copy both the Scriptures and the pagan classics in Latin. (The capital letters were those used by the Romans; the small or 'minuscule' letters were modifications of the capitals.) Later, when printing was invented in the West, some of the first printers and the scholars who were editing the classics for publication revived these fine clear letter-forms. That is why you are not reading Germanic script based on late medieval handwriting but lucid Roman letters. (Russian is printed in Greek letters—ΠΡΑΒΔΑ—with a few additional signs, because the Russians were converted to Christianity by the Greek-speaking missionaries Cyril and Methodius, who invented a script based on Greek for their converts.)

And here is a more important instance. In the United States we live in a federal republic and try to practice a social and political system called democracy. The word *republic* and the word *federal* are both Roman words; the word *democracy* is Greek. Our democratically governed republic is a polity invented independently by the Greeks and Romans, and then—after many centuries of abandonment—deliberately and consciously revived and improved by the Founding Fathers of this nation. Perhaps it is not necessary for us to know that we write and read Roman letters, as reshaped by the Renaissance of the eighth century and by the Renaissance of the fifteenth century—although it is interesting. But surely it is valuable for us to know that the new nation brought forth in 1776 and established by constitution in 1789 was intended to live largely by principles which embodied many of the ideals of the Greek and Roman republican societies.

A basic human fact is language. A language shapes the thought of those who speak it and attaches them to their cultural ancestors. (Not necessarily to their physical ancestors. I have had an African student whose mother-tongue was a tribal dialect with small distribution and no written literature, but who had attached himself to an older and broader cultural system by speaking and writing perfect Latin[2] and perfect English.) All the languages of western Europe and the Americas are enriched by Latin and colored by Greek—except Basque, Maltese, and the indigenous Amerindian tongues. Our own language is a plain strong Germanic structure, reinforced by Latin buttresses and elaborated with Latin refine-

---

[2][Here Highet is referring to *academic* Latin, a form of neo-Latin that is still practiced in some of our own schools and colleges—not to be confused with the Latin spoken and written in classical antiquity, for which we no longer have any native speakers or writers. Ed.]

ments and decorated by Greek elegances. Ever since the Anglo-Saxon invaders of Roman Britain were converted to Christianity, and perhaps before, Latin and Greek words have been entering and enlarging their language: first, simple words like the Greek *church* and the Latin *street;* later, partly through French, abstract words like *act, cause, matter, position;* and then in the Renaissance and later, words too many to count or classify, many imported by men who knew Greek and Latin as well as they knew English and wished to improve the language, some even invented—*actuary, alimony, alphabet, amnesty, angle, antenna, antique, apparatus*—there are thousands. And they are still being added. The Germans say *far-speaker* and *far-seer;* we say *telephone* and *television,* and feel the words more natural. We could say *star-sailors;* we prefer *astronauts. Space-capsule* is better to our ears than *room-box. Atoms* and *atmosphere, psychic* and *physical*—these pure Greek words are part of our language.

Not only that. Most of the building elements we use to make new words are not Germanic (notice that *-ic?* it is the Greek -ικός) but Greek and Latin. The *de-* of *debunk* and *decoction* and *dehydrate* and *demobilize* is pure Latin. The *hyper-* of *hypersensitive* and *hypertension* is pure Greek. Much of the yeast in our language is a mass of little active Greek and Roman particles which exist to fertilize larger units: some tailless, such as *anti-, auto-, con-, dis-, dys-, post-, re-, sub-,* and *super-;* others headless, such as *-al, -an, -crat, -ic, -ile, -ist, -ma, -matic, -ment, -tion, -ture,* and *-yl.* The Germanic leaven is far thinner: *a-, for-, -dom, -ly, -wise, -y,* and not many more. The French, Italians, Spaniards, and Rumanians are aware that they are speaking languages which were once offshoots of Latin and have since been enriched and subtilized and are still growing from a Roman trunk. Our rootstock is Germanic, but the grafts on it which have produced most blossom and fruit are Latin and Greek.

Language leads to literature. Most of the forms of Western literature were created by the Greeks and handed on to us by the Romans. Not all. The novel? They had long romantic prose fictions, which are still (with effort) readable, but nothing even approaching the best of modern times. Their great artists preferred more concentration and would have found *Moby Dick* and *Crime and Punishment* rambling and uneconomical. Therefore there were no great Greek or Roman novels; and the modern novel is largely a modern creation. Good folksong of course always comes from the heart of a people; although the singer may borrow from earlier and sometimes from foreign patterns, he usually pays little attention to books and to literary tradition; and so most European lyrics, apart from the great odes, owe little to the classics. Satire also; there is much Roman poetic satire, and there are modern poems written in the same style, by John Dryden and Nicolas Boileau and Alexander Pope; but most of the striking modern satires are unorthodox and unclassical.

Yet the great literary patterns apart from the above were first worked out in the Greco-Roman world, and then were recovered and revivified during the Renaissance. Shakespeare's tragedies descend not from medieval morality plays but from the Roman Seneca, and Seneca from the Greek Euripides. And Shakespeare's comedies descend not from medieval farces but from the Roman Plautus, and Plautus from the Greeks Menander and Diphilus and others. (*The Comedy of Errors* by William Shakespeare—play adapted from T. Maccius Plautus's *Menaechmi* and *Amphitruo;* original book by Anonymus Graecus.) Opera was created in the Renaissance by men who knew that Greek plays incorporated music and dancing and spectacle as well as plot and dialogue, and who wished to achieve a drama that would contain all these appeals to the emotions of the audience; the very word *chorus* is, like the concept, Greek.

It was not only the patterns that were reborn in the Renaissance; it was the spirit as well. Shakespeare's *King Lear* and Racine's *Phaedra,* Ben Johnson's *Volpone* and Molière's *Miser* go to the heart of the tragic and the comic views of life. In recent years, perhaps because playwrights no longer know their classics, many European and American plays have lost that penetration. We have some flat trivial tragedies and some cruel unfunny comedies—interesting as experiments, perhaps valuable as psychical outlets—but unlikely to be permanent works of art. Great drama is central.

Epic poetry is now scarcely ever attempted—although something of the epic impulse can be felt in big historical novels like Pasternak's *Dr. Zhivago;* and Joyce's *Ulysses,* based on Homer's *Odyssey,* is an antiheroic epic of little men in a trivial world. But Dante's *Comedy,* Tasso's *Jerusalem,* and Milton's *Paradise Lost* were composed to emulate the best of Greco-Roman epic and are full of resonances from classical heroic chords. So also, until three or four generations ago, oratory was written and delivered by men who worked in the Greek and Roman tradition and used Greek and Roman devices of style. These devices and something of the inspiration behind them they handed on to later speakers who knew no classical literature. Thus, when Lincoln says "of the people, by the people, for the people,"[3] and when Roosevelt says "ill-housed, ill-clad, ill-nourished,"[4] and when Churchill says "never was so much owed by so many to so few,"[5] they are all using the triple link called *tricolon* and the repeated hammer-blow called *anaphora*— two of the many stylistic devices which the Greeks invented and which Cicero perfected, and which are now naturalized in modern oratory.

These writers were not simply imitating the classics. Close imitation may produce good art in China and Japan, but not in the West. They were endeavoring to emulate them and to outdo them in their own fields. When Richard Wagner was writing the *Ring of the Nibelung*—a tragic prelude and trilogy about a powerful Germanic myth, interweaving music, words, and spectacle—he composed all morning; and in the afternoon he read the noblest of the Greek tragedies. He did not think of himself as an imitator of Aeschylus but as his rival.

In architecture and sculpture Europe and America owe much to the Greeks and Romans; in painting, something; in music, little.

St. Peter's in Rome and the Capitol in Washington are both domed and pillared Roman buildings, not by accident or by convention, but because they house institutions derived from Rome. The Madeleine in Paris, and the Jefferson and Lincoln Memorials in Washington, and many Greek-revival churches in the United States are Hellenic temples, stressing purity and aesthetic simplicity rather than grandeur and power. The Washington Monument is an obelisk. Its designers thought not of Egyptian pharaohs and of sun-worship, but of the obelisks erected in Rome by the successors of Augustus and of the uniqueness of George Washington—which needed no pompous and long-winded inscription on the pillar. In a hundred cities from Leningrad to Buenos Aires there stand noble theaters and palaces, arches and monuments, governmental offices and even railway stations, which were built in styles borrowed from Greece and Rome, not because of lack of imagination, but in order to recall history, to be decorative, and to stress the hope of continuity and permanence. Nowadays architectural fashion has changed, and every Megalopolis is becoming a glass-fronted

---

3[See Lincoln's *Gettysburg Address,* delivered on November 19, 1863. Ed.]
4[See Roosevelt's *Second Inaugural Address,* delivered on January 20, 1937. Ed.]
5[See Churchill's *Tribute to the Royal Air Force,* delivered on August 20, 1940. Ed.]

Slabsville. But these cold flat rectilinear hives designed by engineers are both nonhuman and (fortunately) impermanent. They are disposable architecture: the Greeks and Romans and their modern pupils built to last, not only in material but in form.

Greek and Roman painting was virtually lost in the Dark Ages, and modern painting in the West had to start again with Giovanni Cimabue. Thereafter it developed into a superb independent art. And yet many modern painters have used Greek sculpture and thought as their inspiration. Botticelli's lovely *Spring* contains a group of the three Graces, more delicately portrayed in his paint than in Greek stone. Titian's dead martyr St. Sebastian follows the pose of one of the Greek Laocoon's dying sons. The pretty naked girl in Manet's *Picnic* may be a Parisian artist's model, but her pose is inspired by Raphael's *Judgment of Paris,* and that in turn by a sculptural group on a Greek sarcophagus. In modern sculpture, after the Gothic style produced its masterpieces, most artists chose to learn from the Greeks, even the most boldly original such as Michelangelo and Rodin. Aristide Maillol not only carved nudes of Greek frankness and purity but left their heads or limbs off, so that they should have the simple pathos of a torso found mutilated in the ruins of antiquity.

Classicizing art of that type has been going out of fashion—although Picasso has depicted several Minotaurs and a series of piping and dancing fauns and nymphs, while Jacques Lipchitz has created an impressive bronze Prometheus. These artists were not interested in the form, however, but in the myth. And it is remarkable that in the twentieth century nothing of the classical world has captivated creative artists and writers more than the myths— those strange multivalent stories and concepts which go back to the late Stone Age and which were put into beautiful and memorable shapes by the Greeks. Oedipus, doomed by his unconscious sin; Odysseus the wanderer with his many lovers and his one true love; Antigone defying tyranny in the name of the unwritten law; and Medea hunted through suffering to vengeful insanity, burning her rival and butchering her own sons—these and other archetypes have been inspiring important poems and plays and novels in many Western languages. Few authors now draw on Jewish and Christian mythological lore; none, since Yeats, on Celtic; none on Germanic; many, very many, on ancient Greek. The chief character in T. S. Eliot's *Waste Land* is the ancient seer Tiresias. Ezra Pound's *Cantos* begin by evoking the voyage of Odysseus to the world of death. In his *The Myth of Sisyphus* Albert Camus makes

Sisyphus the symbol of the existential man, accepting the absurd cruelty of his doom and thus transcending it.[6] In his *Mourning Becomes Electra* Eugene O'Neill transfers the family curse and inbred hatreds of the house of Agamemnon to America darkened by the tragic shadow of civil war. Scarcely a single one of these and other modern treatments of Greek myth is logical. That is why the myths appeal to us. They go far beneath the sunlit levels of reason, into the rayless ocean of the subconscious—a realm peopled by thousands of mysterious beings who, although they inhabit our minds, are strange to us, and when they appear, prove to be temptingly beautiful, and often disturbing, and sometimes messengers of terror and madness and death.

Much rubbish has been written about the cool serenity of Greek life by simple admirers, who saw only the structural balance and not the agonizing moral strain of Greek tragedy, who ignored the coarse violence and lewdness of Aristophanes' comedies, and who concentrated on the placid arts like vase-painting, and who forgot the fierce and cruel conflicts of cities, of classes, and of individual statesmen which disfigure many centuries of Greek history. The life of Greece was not pure. It was not calm. Its sculpture and the expressions of its thought in literature were beautifully shaped and balanced. But beneath the poetry and philosophy and history lay passionate discords and almost unendurable tensions. John Keats understood this well when he wrote his *Ode on a Grecian Urn*. The Greek vase which he evokes shows not one picture of Greece but two; and those discordant. There is a procession of white-clad citizens led by a priest to a peaceful and reverent sacrifice. There is also a wild bacchanalian revel with ecstatic drunkenness and rapturous passion, an orgy which is dominated by Dionysus and Eros. Two such disparate scenes never appeared on any classical Greek vase; but the conflict of lucid sanity and riotous energy which Keats imagines is typical of Greek art and Greek thought.[7] The early Greek philosopher Heraclitus taught this in his oracular style. He said:[8]

---

[6][For Highet's further thoughts on this subject, expressed in an article published after his death, see his "The Myth of Sisyphus," in R. J. Ball, ed., *The Classical Papers of Gilbert Highet* (New York, 1983) 326–31. Ed.]

[7][See G. Highet, "The Poet and the Urn," in *The Powers of Poetry* (New York, 1960) 236–43, for his analysis of Keats's poem, which he admired for its conflicting utterances. Ed.]

[8]See H. Diels, ed., *Die Fragmente der Vorsokratiker,* 3 vols. (Berlin, 1954) vol. 1, p. 162.

πόλεμος πάντων μὲν πατήρ ἐστι.

War is the father of everything.

Existence he compared to a bent bow and to a lyre with strings tuned and taut. The energy of the bow comes from the pull of the string against the resistance of the curving wood. The lyre can make no music unless its strings are tense. The vital forces of mankind emerge from the struggle of opposing powers. Life is not tranquillity but effortful equilibrium. Harmony is tension.

In Greece and Rome there were many such tensions. Some of them have been inherited by modern man. One—perhaps the most acute—is between myth and reason, between religion and philosophy. This conflict may for a time be reconciled in painting, sculpture, and poetry, in drama and ritual; but when the music has come to an end, and the sacrifice is over, and the light fades on the picture, the quiet voice of philosophy is heard again, asking the insistent questions. Myth and religion assert; philosophy analyzes, examines, inquires, and sometimes (although not always) finds an answer to its inquiries. It was the Greeks who first in the West posed the great problems of rational thought, endeavored to solve them, and worked out methods for doing so. Not all these problems concern religious matters—for instance, the relation of language to things, or the meaning of causation, or the connection of matter and form. But some do, and some of the most important.

Among the *Epistles* of St. Paul there is none addressed to the Athenians. Paul did preach in Athens, but his mission was a comparative failure. The story is told (a little tendentiously) in Acts 17. Paul had been in Athens for some time, holding discussions of Christianity with Jews in the synagogue and with Greeks in the agora, the marketplace. Then some trained philosophers heard of him and asked him to give a public lecture—which he did, at a spot which we may still see, on the Areopagus. Most of his lectures expounded the doctrines that the divine power is one and not many, that human beings are wholly dependent on it, and that it cannot be visually represented in painting or sculpture. Now these ideas were far from new, at least to the philosophers in his audience. Several centuries had passed since Plato and Aristotle had declared that the godhead is a unity—since Aristotle had asserted the dependence, not only of mankind but of all that exists, upon the Unmoved Mover; and since the Stoics had worked out a system of their own, making God the spirit which infuses all the universe, and our human souls sparks temporarily detached from that divine fire, but none the less immortal, fiery particles within a transient mortal body. Paul knew some of this, since he was born in Tarsus, where Greek philosophy flourished; and he acknowledged it in his lecture by quoting a line from the Stoic poet Aratus—"for we are also his offspring" (Acts 17.28). Then, after this general discussion, Paul went on to preach that mankind should repent of its sins and expect the Last Judgment; and he concluded by declaring the resurrection of the dead. With this declaration he lost his audience. We are explicitly told that "some mocked: and others said, we will hear thee again of this matter" (Acts 17.32)—which was a polite dismissal. It is not difficult to conjecture that those who mocked were the Epicureans, who held that the soul was merely a function of the body, which ceased at death, while the body was a complicated physical system, which after death was dissolved into its original atomic components; while those who dismissed Paul politely were the Stoics, who held the soul to be immortal, indeed to be divine, and despised the body as a hindrance to pure intellectual existence. "So Paul departed from among them" (Acts 17.33).

This little incident is the second example of the conflict between the religion of Christianity and the inquiring spirit of Greek philosophy. The first is the exchange between Jesus and the Roman governor Pontius Pilate, as told in John 18.37–38. Pilate asked Jesus about his mission. Jesus replied: "To this end was I born, and for this cause came I into the world, that I should bear witness unto the truth." Not with contempt, but in the very tones of Greek philosophy (we seem to hear a distant echo of the questioning voice of Socrates), Pilate answered: "What is truth?"

As Christianity over the following four centuries established itself and grew stronger, it sought to convert not only the poor and the lowly but the rich and cultured Greeks and Romans. Some of its most powerful apologists were well-educated men—Tertullian, Augustine, Jerome, and Basil. These men had supple and highly trained minds. When addressing their intellectual equals, they and their successors felt bound to interpret Christian doctrine through Greek rational methods. (Philo of Alexandria had already expounded Judaism in this way and had endeavored to reconcile the Torah with Platonism and Stoicism.) Much of the intellectual history of Europe in the next thousand years or so can be best understood as the interpenetration of Christian dogma and Greek philosophical thought. When St. Thomas Aquinas in the thirteenth century used Aristotle's method and principles to resolve many of the problems of the universe, he was both a believing medieval Christian and an inquiring ancient Greek.

Not only were analytical methods taken over from the Greeks by Christianity, but some spiritual doctrines as well. For example, nothing is said in the New Testament about purgatory. But there are memorable descriptions of purgatory in Plato's *Gorgias,* in Plato's *Republic,* in Vergil's *Aeneid,* and other pagan books. Since most men seem not bad enough for eternal damnation or good enough for eternal salvation, it was natural for the church gradually to take over the idea of purgatory, and cutting out the pagan theory that the soul once purified would be reborn an indefinite number of times, to incorporate it in Christian teaching.

There is a more important philosophical theory which was formulated by Plato and centuries later adopted by the Christians. This is the idea that there are two worlds, not one, and that the two are unlike, and even hostile. Plato reasoned that since we inhabit a world filled with change and imperfection, true knowledge is impossible to achieve; yet in the realm of mathematics and pure science and philosophy, knowledge is attainable. Therefore all that exists in this world (he concluded) is unreal and illusionary. The other world is the habitation of the external Forms, of which particular entities here are only imperfect shadows or copies. It is our duty and our hope to escape from this world—where we are imprisoned in our bodies and blinded by our senses and stupefied by our emotions—to that other world of changeless perfection. This Platonic concept was easily assimilated to an original Christian doctrine—the doctrine that "this world," meaning the materialistic pagan society of Greece and Rome, whose ruler is the devil (John 12.31), must be destroyed and succeeded by the world of pure eternal life; and that the duty of the good man is to withdraw himself from this world. So just as Plato and his pupils separated themselves from the world of politics and moneymaking to study the eternal verities, so (and for comparable reasons) innumerable Christian monks, nuns, and hermits turned their backs on human society to concentrate on communion with the One in whom there is no "shadow of turning" (James 1.17).

Apart from religion, many important philosophical and moral ideas which the Greeks first formulated are still active in our minds. One of these is humanism—the notion that man is something more than a miserable wretch, corrupt from birth by reason of the sins of his ancestors, and doomed (unless by a divine and miraculous mark of favor) to eternal condemnation. Man is more than an animal and less than the divine. He need not therefore—if he acts honestly and worthily—be ashamed and feel himself an exile in this world, bearing a heavy load of guilt. It was the Greek Protagoras who declared:[9]

πάντων χρημάτων μέτρον ἐστὶν ἄνθρωπος.

Man is the measure of all things.

And he was followed by many Greeks and Romans who believed without arrogance that man's highest duty was to develop his own capacities to the full, while service to God did not in any way mean self-abasement and self-degradation. This creed was revived in the Renaissance and has not since died. It is exemplified in François Rabelais's ideal institute of learning and social life, the Abbey of Thelema (= Will = Good Will); personified in Leonardo da Vinci; and nobly expressed by Shakespeare's Prince Hamlet (2.2.311–15):

> What a piece of work is a man, how noble in reason, how infinite in faculties, in form and moving how express and admirable, in action how like an angel, in apprehension how like a god!

At the beginning of this paper we noticed the concepts of 'republic' and 'democracy' as being Roman and Greek inventions taken over by the Founding Fathers. They were proud of this. And they placed on the Great Seal of the United States (shown on every dollar bill) the eagle of Zeus, holding his thunderbolts and the olive branches of peace, accompanied by three Latin quotations adapted from Vergil—ANNUIT COEPTIS ("he has favored our enterprise"), NOVUS ORDO SECLORUM ("a new order of the ages"), and E PLURIBUS UNUM ("one out of many").[10] However, they made the United States more of a Roman than a Greek political structure—because they distrusted the mob which often threw Greek states into anarchy, and because they aimed at a durable system such as that which kept the Roman Republic viable and prosperous for five centuries. I speak as an immigrant who nearly twenty years ago studied the American Constitution in preparation for attaining American citizenship, when I say that to foreigners the most impressive thing about the American system is the

---

[9]See Diels (above, note 8) vol. 2, p. 263.
[10][See Highet's "America's Classical Heritage"—a lecture appearing earlier in this volume—for a more detailed look at the quotations appearing on the Great Seal. Ed.]

principle behind it—that every state power must be limited and must be checked and balanced by other powers. Now this was the theory behind the Roman republican constitution. They were pessimists, those old Romans—like our own Founding Fathers. They trusted no one with unlimited power (unless during a grave emergency, for a strictly defined time and purpose—a dictator). They had not one but two presidents at the same time, the consuls, sitting as equal colleagues. All their other magistracies were collegial. Of the three branches of American government, each has its own function, and each serves as a check on the others. In the same way Rome was governed by "the Senate *and* the Roman People" through legally elected magistrates, and each group checked and balanced the others. It sounds clumsy. Yet it was effective. Writing about 150 B.C., the Greek historian and statesman Polybius described with admiration the working of this system. Eighteenth-century students of history, who looked with disgust on the absolute power of kings and thought with horror about the unlimited despotism of the people, took up this theme. Chief among them was Montesquieu, who in *The Spirit of Laws* pointed to a similar separation of powers in the England of his day. Montesquieu's work was read with care by the men who framed our Constitution, and the central principle of checks and balances was adopted from the practice of contemporary England and from the system of ancient Rome.

It is a curious relationship, the link between our world and the civilization of Greece and Rome. Different eras have interpreted it in different ways. Different men interpret it differently today. Some wise and sensitive classical scholars simply refuse to discuss it. And if pressed to explain why they spend their lives studying Homer's poems or the philosophy of the Stoics, they would merely say that they found these things worth studying for their own sake. A musician will dedicate his entire life to playing Bach, or an art historian to understanding the Flemish painters. Such fields of study are their own justification.

In earlier periods men believed that the Greeks and Romans were valuable because they provided noble ideals to imitate. Many a pious Christian in the Middle Ages would choose a particular saint on whom to pattern his conduct. So at other times many a young poet dreamed of rivaling Pindar or Horace; a patron of literature took Maecenas as a model of generosity; thinkers founded Academies, which were named after the school of Plato; and the British Grenadiers stepped out to a martial song beginning: "Some talk of Alexander, and some of Hercules, of Hector and Lysander, and such great names as these."

Both these beliefs are valid. The professional scholar studies poetry and philosophy and the history of great nations because they enlarge his mind and enable him to realize more of the endless versatility and energy of the human spirit. Outside the scholarly world, Greek and Latin books are read in translation, Greek and Roman works of art are admired, Greek and Roman myths are revived and reshaped—as stimuli, as food for the endlessly hungry intellect and imagination. The two concepts are complementary; they are parts of one activity, which is education. Anything permanently beautiful and noble educates, whether it is relevant to contemporary life or not. Anything wise and moving educates, because it enlarges our small time-bound souls.

Material civilization can be torn down every thirty years or so and rebuilt. Spiritual culture grows out of the past and cannot be uprooted without mutilating or killing it; and it takes many centuries to replace it, once destroyed. Machines change, and technology develops, and new scientific discoveries are made; but the human soul does not change in its essentials. It is indescribably strange, even after thirty years of teaching, to discuss Homer's poems with keenly interested students in the twentieth century A.D., when they were composed about the eighth century B.C. on the basis of legends and poems going back five hundred years earlier. It is stranger still, and even more encouraging, to watch the stimulating power of Greek thought and Greek art sending geysers of energy into Western civilization, not once but again and again.

First, the Greeks educated themselves by studying their past. The men of Plato's time found Homer very nearly as difficult as we do; but they read his poetry carefully and thought about it and profited from it, as Jews and Christians have profited from reading the Bible.

Next, after the conquests of Alexander, Greek culture spread to many new nations which had known little of it before; the civilization of Egypt, of Asia Minor, of lands once almost fabulously distant, became Greek. A magnificent center of intellectual and aesthetic research was established in the Shrine of the Muses (= the Museum + Library) of Alexandria. There the great books were edited and commented on: Eratosthenes calculated the circumference of the earth to within fifty miles; Euclid systematized geometry and investigated the theory of numbers. Although not Greek by blood, the Greek-speaking nations now shared in this achievement.

Then, from about 200 B.C. onward, the Greeks began to educate the Romans—sometimes reluctant, sometimes eager pupils. They taught them philosophy and poetry, oratory and drama, and the principles of artistic form; they helped them to refine their coarse and clumsy language. Roman literature surged upward in a rolling wave of creation impelled by Greece. Lucretius turned the philosophy of Epicurus, cold and dry in the original texts, into magnificent poetry. Although not an original thinker, Cicero developed the thought-patterns and the vocabulary which were to be the vehicles of philosophy in western Europe for a thousand years. (For example, Cicero needed a Latin word to express the fact that an object possesses certain characteristics, that it has a 'what-kindness'; on the model of Plato's ποιότης he coined *qualitas*—an invention which now seems quite natural, as our *quality*.) Horace wrote a hundred subtly various odes to rival the Greek lyrics of Alcaeus and Sappho. Vergil emulated Theocritus's idylls of herdsmen's life in his *Bucolics,* the *Works and Days* of Hesiod in his *Georgics,* and Homer's *Iliad* and *Odyssey*—interfused with deeper religious and ethical thought—in his *Aeneid.* Thus, under Greek stimulus, the Romans created a second world literature.[11]

Then came the Dark Ages of barbarism, poverty, and illiteracy. The few men in the West who could read and write, read and wrote Latin, and under unimaginable difficulties, kept both the Scriptures and the pagan classics alive. In the East (centering on Byzantium) devoted scholars did the same for the Bible and the classics in Greek.

And then, after some dismal centuries, the light reappeared. A small but potent outspreading of culture occurred around the emperor Charlemagne in the West; and still another, more powerful, around the emperor Constantine Porphyrogenitus in the East. The pagan classical books which had managed to survive the Dark Ages were now recopied, and it is to the diligent scribes and schoolmen of this little Renaissance that we owe the treasures we now possess.

A second and more widespread Renaissance in the West began in the twelfth century. This meant a deeper penetration of Greek and Roman thought and a far wider distribution of the great books,

---

[11][For further information about the Greeks as teachers of the Romans, see G. Highet, *Man's Unconquerable Mind* (New York, 1954) 20–23, and *The Migration of Ideas* (New York, 1954) 18–21. Ed.]

through the newly founded universities which were springing up in many countries. Homer was still unknown, and Plato, and most of the other Greek singers and thinkers. But St. Thomas Aquinas assimilated and converted to Christian purposes the thought of Aristotle; and Dante, choosing Vergil as his guide and inspiration, produced the first great poem in any modern language.

Another epoch of confusion and despair, war and waste, ensued; but it did not last long. By the year 1333 Petrarch had started to search for forgotten manuscripts of Cicero and other classical writers; he often found them; and he copied them and circulated them among his friends.[12] Others did the same, searching for lost books and transcribing inscriptions. And soon the third and the richest Renaissance was spreading from central Italy to France and Spain and England and Germany like the sun's rays over the earth after an eclipse. From that radiance we are still drawing light and life.

---

[12][See J. E. Sandys, *A History of Classical Scholarship,* 3 vols. (Cambridge, 1903–8) vol. 2, pp. 3–11, especially 6–7, for Petrarch's ardent interest in Cicero, which culminated in the two epistles that he addressed in Latin to Cicero himself in his *Letters to Dead Authors.* Ed.]

Classical Influences on Modern Literature*

The classical tradition—the spiritual world which was created by the Greeks and developed by the Romans—is still alive in modern literature and in the contemporary imagination of Europe and America. It has never died since its creation. Like its own temples, it has often been half-buried in the debris of disaster, converted to strange purposes, robbed and mutilated by invaders; but it has never been wholly destroyed. Its very ruins have gained, from their imperfections and scars, and their inexpressible pathos and charm. After the drums and tramplings of twenty centuries, it still lives; it still gives birth to new manifestations which are vital, unpredictable, and appealing; in the words of the first Greek who deliberately wrote a classic, it has become a κτῆμά ἐς αἰεὶ—"a possession for all time" (Thucydides 1.22).[1]

But what does it mean for the writers of the twentieth century? It varies greatly. To some eminent authors it means nothing, absolutely nothing whatever. To some it is completely absorbing; it feeds their minds as oxygen in our blood feeds our brain. To others it is important and stimulating but not dominant. So the Greek and Roman world might never have existed, so far as we can tell from the poetry of Dylan Thomas, from the novels of Marcel Proust and Ernest Hemingway and William Faulkner, and from the dramas of Tennessee Williams. On the other hand, without the Greek and Roman themes and patterns, it is hardly possible to conceive the masterworks of James Joyce, Paul Valéry, Constantine Cavafy, and other brilliant moderns.

In the third group, classical influences vary greatly from man to man, and often within the life of a single man, at different times. They are one of the essences—although only one—in the work of

---

*Presented in 1970 for the Classical Association of the Atlantic States. [In several places in this lecture, I have inserted passages from the 1967 version of the manuscript—passages that Highet suppressed in the 1970 version in order to shorten his presentation and that I decided to reintroduce for their literary value and for their enhancement of his arguments. Ed.]
[1][See G. Highet, *The Classical Tradition* (New York, 1949), for Highet's classic study of Greek and Roman influences on the literatures of western Europe and the United States. Ed.]

T. S. Eliot and Ezra Pound and Robinson Jeffers and Rainer Maria Rilke. They have a limited and intermittent power over W. B. Yeats and Robert Lowell. And to some curious and interesting writers, they are something like a seduction which is to be resisted, a paternal domination to be overcome—something Given, which almost inhibits creation. I remember hearing W. H. Auden cry out: "I hate the Greeks," and I know what he meant; yet he has written several fine poems on classical inspirations. In the life of A. E. Housman, one of the more fertile conflicts was his struggle *not* to write Greek or Latin poetry in English.

Upon those modern writers who do feel and use the power of the Greek and Roman world, what are its effects? What does it mean to them?

Seven or eight generations ago this question would have evoked a quick answer. The classics (we should have been told) were the masters of form and of structure; and what the writer gains from studying them is, first of all, the ability to shape his thoughts architecturally and symphonically. But today scarcely anyone thinks of copying classical meters, and most poets shrink from classical symmetry of form, even when it might seem acceptable. For instance, the first of Ezra Pound's *Cantos* is a paraphrase, a deliberate echo, of part of Homer's *Odyssey,* Book 11. One of the chief strengths of Homer is the steady balanced pace of his long hexameter lines: they are like big Atlantic billows rolling in to shore from a storm at sea, all straight and matched and massive, yet each with its individual curves and colors. Now Pound admires Homer deeply and tries in this very poem to rival Homer's vocabulary; so you would expect him to try to write regular powerful but disciplined verse. But no. To represent *Odyssey* 11.13–22, he produces this (*Cantos* 1.11–18):

> Came we then to the bounds of deepest water,
> To the Kimmerian lands, and peopled cities
> Covered with close-webbed mist, unpierced ever
> With glitter of sun-rays
> Nor with stars stretched, nor looking back from heaven
> Swartest night stretched over wretched men there.
> The ocean flowing backward, came we then to the place
> Aforesaid by Circe.

Six rambling pentameters—a little too much like the rhythm of Longfellow's *Song of Hiawatha,* with two half-lines; impressionistic syntax; a jerky asyndetic succession of phrases; a sketchy offhand throwaway tone. That is not the form of Homer. Regularity for many modern poets implies discipline, and discipline is imposed from outside, and so intolerable.[2]

Nor do the actual words, the language, of the classics mean much to writers of the twentieth century. No one nowadays knows the texts of Greek and Latin literature so intimately as to be penetrated by them in the same way as Milton and Pope and Shelley and Swinburne, from childhood through maturity to death. Many poets nowadays are monoglots. Some of them scarcely even know the full scope of their own language—for instance, Allen Ginsberg. Polyglots like T. S. Eliot are uncommon and untypical.

Perhaps, then, our writers ignore the externals of form and language, and pierce through to the thought within? The Greeks were superb thinkers and devised many great philosophical systems; the Romans were severely efficient at historical and psychological analysis. Is that what our authors prefer to take from the classics?

No. On the whole, modern literature is opposed to systematic thought. Logic it finds repugnant. The calm regular movement of reason is alien to its deepest purposes and its most typical utterances. Therefore it rarely mentions or employs the philosophies and histories of antiquity. W. B. Yeats, it is true, was at one time deeply concerned with Greek thinkers. "It seems," he once said (*The Tower* 11–15),

> that I must bid the Muse go pack,
> Choose Plato and Plotinus for a friend
> Until imagination, ear and eye,
> Can be content with argument and deal
> In abstract things.

But in fact what Yeats enjoyed in Plato and Plotinus was not their philosophical argumentation but their poetry; and not their logic but their mysticism—doctrines such as reminiscence of truths learned before birth, and the Great Year which will bring history back full circle, and the ascent of the soul to the inexpressible truth, and symbols such as the cosmic spindle from Plato's *Republic* (10.616–17), which, although profoundly suggestive, will not endure examination by rigorous logic.

Logic, no. This is not an era in which logic has much honor, except in the realm of science; not always even there. Ours is an epoch of irrationality, of mysticism, and of myth. It is the myths,

---

[2][For Highet's criticism of Pound's use / abuse of the classics, see his "Beer-Bottle on the Pediment," *Horizon* 3.3 (January 1961) 116–18—reprinted in *Explorations* (New York, 1971) 244–56. Ed.]

the myths made by Greek imagination and polished by Greek art and poetry, which are the chief classical influence upon the writers of the twentieth century. Illogical, graceful, sometimes delightful and sometimes terrible, but seldom bestial or trivial or sordid or ridiculous, the Greek myths have, like the Greek statues, a marvelous and almost inexplicable power to enter our minds, although proceeding from a far different world, and to inhabit us as though they were creatures of our own fancy—or perhaps as though we had already been shaped to receive them. It is possible that C. G. Jung may have begun to explain that power, by describing myths as patterns built into our imagination by hundreds of generations of dreaming; they are, he says, archetypes of the collective unconscious.[3] But no one has yet fully explored the mysterious labyrinthine corridors which connect the minds of a twentieth-century painter, a seventeenth-century sculptor, and a fourteenth-century poet, with the heroic illiterates of the Bronze Age. It is strange. It is, so far, inexplicable. Poetry is made with words, but it is made out of visions.

Yes, it is the myths, fashioned by Greeks of the New Stone Age and the Bronze Age, and sometimes transmitted to us through the Romans, that carry the greatest power from classical antiquity into our literature today. What do they mean for our writers? How are they used? In many different ways. They change like Proteus. They assume disguises like Odysseus. They travel and travail like Hercules. They refuse to be killed and classified. They change with us who experience them, and as they change each new artist or poet, so he changes them.

But speaking crudely, we can see three ways in which Greek and Roman myths invade the modern imagination.

First, they are examples, models, forms into which writers can fit themselves, paradigms which they can copy, parallels to assist them in understanding themselves and realizing their powers. The myths provide *personae* ("masks"), from which the poet can speak—masks which are not utterly false, as the face of a demon or an animal might be, but which allow the passage of the poet's own voice and in certain contours resemble his own features, and which nevertheless are not the poet as he is but rather as he imagines himself or wishes to appear.

---

[3][See B. Forryan and J. M. Glover, comps., *General Index to the Collected Works of C. G. Jung* (Princeton, 1979) 469–71, for citations listed under the heading 'myth(s)/mythology'—especially under the subheadings 'collective dreams' and 'collective unconscious.' Ed.]

Thus, there is an important and intricate poem by Paul Valéry called *The Young Fate (La Jeune Parque)*—a monologue in which a Greek mythical figure, a young Destiny, meditates on the birth and self-realization of her spirit, its dialogues with itself, its temptations and self-judgments. It might be a poetic account of a girl's passage from unreflective childhood through awakening adolescence into eager yet anxious womanhood; the person who speaks is feminine and is haunted by a serpent, symbol of masculine otherness. No doubt it is such an account. A poem is as many things as it can be. But for Valéry it was, in spite of its name, an act of autobiography; so he called it in a letter to a friend.[4] And if the title had not been pre-empted by one of his best friends, Valéry would have called the poem by a name also classical but more revealing— *Psyché, The Soul.*[5] The Young Parca or Destiny whose birth Valéry described was in fact his own power as a poet, suppressed for nearly twenty years, and his character as an individual detached from Society (most of the poem came out of him in 1915 and 1916 while France was being both the butcher and the victim at Verdun); conceivably also it was a gradually developing sexual activity and attitude. The quiet little self-absorbed poet, what has he in common with the terrible *Parcae,* the spirits who mete out life to mankind—one spinning the thread, one measuring it, and one slitting it with the abhorred shears? Little externally; but within every man's soul is a pressure which he feels as his destiny; and therefore Paul Valéry at the age of forty-four, beset outwardly by war and inwardly by the long suppressed urge to poetry, felt his undiscovered self, the *mystérieuse Moi,* to be a Young Fate.

T. S. Eliot's *Waste Land,* written during the same period as Paul Valéry's *Young Fate,* is a far more disorderly poem, almost chaotic. Valéry describes a soul realizing itself. Eliot describes a soul passing through a phase of almost total disintegration and emerging from it into a painfully precarious equilibrium, in which its shattered frame is sustained only by thoughts of an exotic religion and a few exquisite poetic fancies (429–31):

> *Quando fiam uti chelidon*—O swallow swallow
> *Le Prince d'Aquitaine à la tour abolie*
> These fragments I have shored against my ruins . . .

---

[4]See J. Hytier, ed., *Oeuvres de Paul Valéry,* 2 vols. (Paris, 1957–60) vol. 1, p. 1622, for the letter to André Fontainas.
[5]See Hytier (above, note 4) vol. 1, p. 1617, for the letter to Pierre Louÿs.

The Waste Land is almost wholly modern, emphatically modern, and personal, almost inexplicably personal. Its elaborate temporal and local allusions, its sophisticated polyglot language, its thread-like but electrically alive connections with Eliot's earlier poems—all these make the poem one of those works which (although it radiates other significances too) is a sort of autobiography, a confession, a purge. Yet its central figure is the Greek prophet Tiresias. You and I would perhaps not realize this at first from reading the poem, but Eliot (in his note on line 218) explicitly warns us that "Tiresias is . . . the most important personage in the poem, uniting all the rest . . . What Tiresias *sees* . . . is the substance of the poem." He adds that "the two sexes meet in Tiresias," and then quotes a passage from Ovid (*Metamorphoses* 3.320–38), showing that this mythical Theban was born male, and in maturity miraculously became a woman, and then after seven years changed back into a man again.

Three aspects of Tiresias's character are clearly meant to stand out. He is bisexual, having experienced love both as a man and as a woman. He is blind, yet a seer. He is old and weak, yet preternaturally wise. These compounds of antithetical qualities are what Eliot considers important in him. The historical or mythical career of Tiresias is quite neglected. Eliot does not speak of him anywhere as the warner of Oedipus, "revolving inly / The doom of Thebes,"[6] or as the adviser of Odysseus among the dead. On the contrary, he makes him an inhabitant of modern London. What he sees is life in western Europe and in London, dated exactly by allusions just after World War I—the time and the place where Eliot was living and writing and evidently suffering. If we put these facts together with the rest of the poem and with certain significant hints given in his earlier poems, the conclusion is probable. Tiresias is a mask through which Eliot can confess and yet half-conceal certain truths about himself—in particular, certain painful discoveries affecting his sexual life. These discoveries, the poem tells us, induced an almost total collapse, mental and spiritual, which exhausted him, reducing him to impotence (physical and emotional) and to premature old age, and from which his recovery was slow, dubious, and incomplete.

In fact, *The Waste Land,* which has so often been called a poem symbolizing the spiritual aridity of Europe after World War I, is

---

[6][A reference to Matthew Arnold's *The Strayed Reveller* 141–42, where the poet refers to Tiresias as the soothsayer who witnessed the fate of Oedipus and Oedipus's children. Ed.]

not in the first instance intended to convey any such message. It entirely omits most of the chief problems which then occupied men's minds—poverty, and the threat of war, and the spread of revolution, and the disruption of social structures everywhere. Tiresias, the "old man with wrinkled dugs" (line 228), has no connection with any of these mass phenomena. Through his eyes the poet looks at a world of private afflictions; and although they are the torments of a living man, the key to understanding them is the figure of an antique Greek so old that even for Homer he is remote and all but fabulous.[7]

There is another way of using classical myths—not to mark resemblances but to stress contrasts.

The greatest modern example of this is James Joyce's *Ulysses,* which, set in twentieth-century Dublin, faithfully follows the lines of nearly every episode in Homer's *Odyssey*—and why? In order to substitute for every noble or graceful Homeric theme and figure a comic or sordid modern parallel, and thus to demonstrate the full vulgarity and absurdity of the modern world, and particularly of the city of Dublin. Thus, the wandering hero Odysseus, cast away on the shore of an island, is graciously welcomed by its young princess Nausicaa: he treats her with charming courtesy and respect; she thinks of him as a possible husband. In *Ulysses,* at the end of the corresponding episode, the wanderer Leopold Bloom, on the shore of the Irish Sea, gazes at Gerty MacDowell from a distance and commits an act of the meanest and vilest indecency, while she swings back and forward to let him see her underwear. (To make this particular episode even more repellent, specialists in Joyce should ask themselves whether it is not a foul parody of the exquisite revelation of the profane angel to Stephen Dedalus, the girl wading silently in the water at the end of chapter 4 of *Portrait of the Artist As a Young Man.*)[8]

This device, that of emphatic contrast between ancient myth and modern reality, is used with great skill by T. S. Eliot, in a poem which is worth analyzing because it has (like so much else) been misunderstood by Robert Graves. This is *Sweeney Erect.* It is in eleven stanzas of simple ballad meter. Two form an introduction. The others tell (with sourly witty irony) a story about Sweeney, the

---

[7][See G. Highet, *"The Waste Land,"* in *The Powers of Poetry* (New York, 1960) 323–29, for his analysis of the themes of Eliot's poem, apart from the characterization of Tiresias. Ed.]

[8][See Highet's "Joyce's *Ulysses*"—a lecture appearing earlier in this volume—for a more detailed examination of Joyce's novel. Ed.]

crude Irish-American who occurs in other Eliot poems; or rather, they describe a single episode in his career. We see Sweeney rising in the morning and preparing to shave, while an unnamed woman with whom he has been sleeping screams with dangerous hysteria in his bed and has to be calmed by another woman with smelling-salts and brandy.[9] The scene—for those who have eyes to see—is a brothel. (It is politely called "the house," as in the phrase made famous by the late Polly Adler, "a house is not a home.")[10] The madam is Mrs. Turner (a colleague of Mrs. Porter, whom Sweeney visits in *The Waste Land*); the other women, "the ladies of the corridor," are prostitutes living there and working for her. Here is the poem:

Paint me a cavernous waste shore
    Cast in the unstilled Cyclades,
Paint me the bold anfractuous rocks
    Faced by the snarled and yelping seas.

Display me Aeolus above
    Reviewing the insurgent gales
Which tangle Ariadne's hair
    And swell with haste the perjured sails.

Morning stirs the feet and hands
    (Nausicaa and Polypheme).
Gesture of orang-outang
    Rises from the sheets in steam.

This withered root of knots of hair
    Slitted below and gashed with eyes,
This oval O cropped out with teeth:
    The sickle motion from the thighs

Jackknifes upward at the knees
    Then straightens out from heel to hip
Pushing the framework of the bed
    And clawing at the pillow slip.

Sweeney addressed full length to shave
    Broadbottomed, pink from nape to base,
Knows the female temperament
    And wipes the suds around his face.

---

[9]See R. Graves, *Food for Centaurs* (New York, 1960) 112, where the author refers to the unnamed woman with Sweeney as "his hysterical wife in the adjacent bedroom."

[10][See P. Adler, *A House Is Not a Home* (New York, 1953)—written by an American brothel-keeper, who practiced her profession in the United States for over twenty-five years. Ed.]

(The lengthened shadow of a man
   Is history, said Emerson
Who had not seen the silhouette
   Of Sweeney straddled in the sun.)

Tests the razor on his leg
   Waiting until the shriek subsides.
The epileptic on the bed
   Curves backward, clutching at her sides.

The ladies of the corridor
   Find themselves involved, disgraced,
Call witness to their principles
   And deprecate the lack of taste

Observing that hysteria
   Might easily be misunderstood;
Mrs. Turner intimates
   It does the house no sort of good.

But Doris, towelled from the bath,
   Enters padding on broad feet,
Bringing sal volatile
   And a glass of brandy neat.

The characters and the setting are clear. But what is the point of the poem? And why is Sweeney's girl having hysterics early in the morning? The other girls are calm enough and (although disapproving) quite relaxed. The question is answered by the myth to which (although cryptically) the first two stanzas allude. They describe a desert island in the Greek seas, and the Mediterranean wind rising to blow

              insurgent gales
   Which tangle Ariadne's hair
   And swell with haste the perjured sails.

Ariadne was a princess of Crete. She helped Theseus to escape after he killed the Minotaur; she became his mistress and sailed with him toward his home in Athens; but on the way he set her ashore sleeping, on the island of Naxos among the Cyclades, and so deserted her. When she awakened, she suffered agonies of grief and shame.

In the same way, Sweeney is now abandoning his girl. Having seduced her, he is leaving her in a brothel; evidently he has just told her that she can work henceforward as a prostitute. She responds with hysterical screams and epileptic convulsions. The final stanza contains a particularly cruel and subtle detail.

> But Doris, towelled from the bath,
>   Enters padding on broad feet,
> Bringing sal volatile
> And a glass of brandy neat.

In the original legend, Ariadne, deserted on Naxos, was discovered by Dionysus, the wine-god, and became his consort. Sweeney's girl is consoled by brandy and will drink herself to death.

Both Theseus and Sweeney are hard-hearted perjurers, cruel betrayers of women who trusted them. So far, myth and modernity are parallel. The difference, the essential difference, is that the world of legend, although cruel, has a certain majesty, a romantic intensity, whereas the world of today is purely mean and sordid. Ezra Pound put the contrast in a single sentence (*Cantos* 7.51–52):

> Beer-bottle on the statue's pediment!
> That, Fritz, is the era, today against the past.

There is an equally explicit contrast between the ancient and the modern world in a poem by W. H. Auden, called *The Shield of Achilles.* You notice that unless you know the myth of Ariadne and Theseus, you will certainly fail to get the point of *Sweeney Erect.* In the same way, unless you know Homer's *Iliad,* Book 18, you will fail to get the point of Auden's poem. In this book Homer describes a splendid shield made for the hero Achilles by the god Hephaestus, covered with designs showing the Greek world of Homer's time just as it was—men and animals, war and peace, weddings and lawsuits, death and rejoicing. Auden describes the forging of a new shield of Achilles, suitable for today. Homer was on the whole an optimist; he did not see this world as a vale of tears; his shield has the calm happiness of the young men and women, the gods and goddesses, who inhabit the frieze of the Parthenon. Auden is a pessimist, and of our life he sees mainly the sordid and the brutal. Therefore he suggests that an Achilles of today would carry on his arm not a picture of beauty and simplicity and charm, but portrayals of the dreary, impersonal, degrading routine of the one-party, all-enslaving dictatorial state.[11]

There is a third way of using the Greek myths, which is more truly Greek. This is to do as the Greeks and Romans did themselves and to retell the stories for their own sake, giving them new psychological developments and new twists of plot, altering their

---

[11][See Highet's "Auden's *The Shield of Achilles*"—a lecture appearing earlier in this volume—for a more detailed examination of Auden's poem. Ed.]

salient lines and emphasizing neglected aspects of strength and beauty.

Thus, the entire work of the modern Greek poet Constantine Cavafy is (apart from some personal lyrics dealing with the ardors and despairs of homosexual love) composed of meditations upon the history and legend of the ancient world.[12] Although Cavafy lived and died in the Egyptian city of Alexandria, he only once even mentions the Arab world, or the mosques, or Islam, or the native Egyptians (in the early poem *Sham-el-Nessim*). He dwelt in and was nourished by the Hellenic past. Its myth and history meant to him a time when greatness and heroism, always difficult and often dangerous, were possible as they are not possible today. His poems contain a long gallery of portraits of monarchs, whose frail grandeur is tinged with a melancholy that makes them more admirable than any triumphant conquerors. Such is Mark Antony abandoned by his guardian divinity (*The God Forsakes Antony* 1–6 and 17–19):

> When suddenly at midnight there is heard
> invisible a procession moving away
> with marvelous music, with voices—
> your fortune that is collapsing, your labor
> that is lost, the plans of your life
> that have all gone—do not mourn in vain . . .
> Now for the last time enjoy these sounds,
> the marvelous instruments of the mysterious procession,
> And say farewell to her, the Alexandria you are losing.

Such are the Byzantine monarchs in a declining and impoverished court, wearing at their coronation instead of jewels (*Of Colored Glass* 6–7 and 10–12):

> a lot of bits of glass,
> red, green, or blue . . . Yet they seem to me
> like a plaintive protest
> against the unjust misery of those crowned heads.

The Swiss poet Carl Spitteler, who won the Nobel Prize for literature in 1919, wrote an entire epic on the birth, growth, deeds, and destinies of the Olympian deities—*Olympian Spring* (1910). It is in my view one of the greatest unrecognized poetic masterpieces of our century. The verse (a long swinging six-beat rhythm), the

---

12[See Highet's translation of Cavafy's *Waiting for the Barbarians*—a translation appearing earlier in this volume—on the love-hate relationship between two contrasting cultures. Ed.]

vocabulary (full of bright new coinages and Homeric compounds), the superb architecture (developing a number of difficult themes in fine balance through hundreds of pages to a grand climax)—these alone would justify it. But the imagination: that is really superb. To read the adventures of the Olympian divinities just as they were conceived and related by the Greeks (for instance in Hesiod's *Theogony*) would be intensely boring. Therefore, what Spitteler does is to take their characters as given—Zeus the ruler, Apollo the deity of light, Aphrodite the laughter-loving spirit of beauty—and then to imagine for them an entirely new origin, new adventures, and a new collective mission. They are not, as the Greek gods were, born on Mount Ida and the isle of Delos and so forth. They have no physical birth but are called forth when their time comes, from an endless sleep in the dark underworld, to ascend Olympus, to become themselves, and to learn to rule the world. (As they climb up, slowly realizing their identities, they pass the dethroned dynasty of Kronos riding sullenly down.) Their relations with one another are more sinister than those of the Greek deities, for Spitteler was a pessimist. Thus, Apollo the spirit of light and reason was meant to be their ruler, but Zeus the tyrant seized power from him by a degrading trick and held it fast. And they are not the rulers of the universe; they govern only mankind in this world. Far above them, supremely powerful and supremely cruel (for power and cruelty go together), not enthroned upon Olympus in our petty planet but dwelling far away in outer space and whirling the mechanical mill of creation, is the eternal ruler who called the Olympians into life and who will in time depose them—the monstrous tiger-headed Ananké ("Necessity"), who hates life and will whenever possible destroy it. Of all twentieth-century authors, it seems to me that Carl Spitteler had the truest understanding both of epic poetry and of tragedy.[13]

In prose fiction and in drama, many modern authors have been retelling tales from classical myth and history. Here we can trace two main methods—rationalization and reinterpretation. Those who like history and comparative religion and anthropology usually rationalize the old stories. Those who prefer psychical analysis usually reinterpret and reshape them.

Take the story of Theseus, which we have already glimpsed at in one of Eliot's Sweeney poems. It is, in its original shape, full of problems. Although brave and shrewd and kingly, much admired in

---

[13][See G. Highet, *"Olympian Spring,"* in *The Powers of Poetry* (New York, 1960) 251–63, for a more detailed analysis of Spitteler's poem. Ed.]

his lifetime and after his death, Theseus still seems to be treacherous, malicious, cruel, and mean; he inaugurates his monarchy by causing the death of his father Aegeus and virtually closes it by causing the death of his son Hippolytus. And he is recorded as doing deeds which can scarcely be understood as normal history—such as killing a half-human monster with the head of a bull, the Minotaur. He even deserted the princess Ariadne who helped him in his adventure.

Mary Renault, in two novels presented as the autobiography of Theseus—*The King Must Die* (1958) and *The Bull from the Sea* (1962)—spends most of her imaginative energies on giving comprehensible explanations of the mythistorical oddities. Thus, the monster was a monarch who reigned in Crete and who for rituals wore a bull's-head mask. And the desertion of Ariadne—how could Theseus do such a thing? How can he explain it in telling his own life story? Mary Renault remembers that Ariadne was consoled by Dionysus and became his consort. Therefore, in her version the princess and Theseus are both drawn away into the revels of the Bacchanalia in Naxos. She is maddened with wine and lust, and leads the hideous human sacrifice in which the Wine King is torn to pieces and eaten. When Theseus sees her again after the revel, still unconscious, there is dried blood on her lips, and in one closed hand, a fragment of the Wine King's mutilated body. Theseus could never love her again; she had found her own fulfillment; he left her and sailed away. This then is a historical rationalization of the story.

André Gide, who also wrote an autobiography of Theseus in 1946, virtually ignored archaeology and anthropology to concentrate on psychical reinterpretation. He has little interest in the truly heroic deeds of the young prince, and deliberately wrecks the climactic scene of his career by making him say that he cannot remember how he killed the Minotaur and that he forbids himself from inventing a story about it.[14] But he makes Theseus explain himself as a cold clever young man who outwitted and dominated all those whom he met through his entire and devoted selfishness. Theseus in Gide's book glories in his own cruelty, because it is his, and because it expresses his revolt against convention, and against control, and against the rights of others and the chains of love and duty. Perhaps, after all, we may take this kind of rewriting as another example of the mythical persona. Gide himself inflicted upon

---

[14]See A. Gide, *Thésée* (New York, 1946) 85, especially for the words *je me défends d'inventer*.

the unfortunate lady whom he married many complex and carefully devised humiliations and torments, ending—after many protestations of his preference for homosexuality—by begetting a child in adultery with a younger woman. When we read his recreation of Theseus, deserting Ariadne on the island because she loved him too much—and complaining about her intolerable protestations of eternal love and about the tender little names with which she smothered him[15]—then we wonder whether, for such an introspective writer as Gide, mythical narrative may not be another method of self-exposure and self-justification.

Few modern playwrights choose a modern setting to dramatize an ancient myth. None who does, succeeds. I wonder why. Partly, I imagine, because we do not believe in personal immanent plural gods; partly because we do not believe in inherited nobility, whether of family or of destiny.

T. S. Eliot's *Family Reunion* is a modern drama of life among the English nobility. It is a mixture of gloom, refinement, and tedium, all perfectly in character and all loftily insular—except that the Greek Furies, the Eumenides, appear on stage, haunting one of the characters. No member of the English upper class believes in the Eumenides; most do not even know who they were; and to put them visibly on the stage, in the alcove of an English drawing room, is as ridiculous as making the floor open to disclose a medieval devil with horns and tail and pitchfork.

Eugene O'Neill's *Mourning Becomes Electra* was a gallant attempt to transfer the problem of love and jealousy and hate within a proud ambitious Greek monarch's family to a setting in middle-class America. Since New England's tradition of verbal and spiritual economy and repression is inimical to dramatic eloquence and heroic gesture, the drama—although it contains some moving scenes—is a failure. As for Jean Anouilh's *Eurydice,* whose characters are strolling actors and cheap musicians, it sinks far, far below the poignant beauty of the original myth and merely degrades its model.

Therefore, most modern dramatists who use a Greek or Roman legendary theme keep it in ancient settings. Jean Giraudoux's Greeks and Trojans carry spears, and their women wear the lovely dress of antiquity. Albert Camus's Caligula is a first-century Roman emperor with the appropriate costume and retinue. In Jean Cocteau's *Infernal Machine* young Oedipus meets a beauti-

---

[15]See Gide (above, note 14) 52, especially for the statement *j'ai l'horreur des diminutifs.*

ful girl, who changes into the Sphinx with its terrible eyes and claws. But the characters of these modern dramas are not usually men and women of the Bronze Age, not even of the Athens of a thousand years later. Their language is far less formal. Their manners are less controlled. Their motives are usually a good deal more complicated. (For example, the attempt of Camus to dramatize the insanity of the emperor Caligula is so subtle that it is almost unintelligible; and the amorous intrigues of Giraudoux's *Amphitryon 38* are more ingenious and sophisticated than any of the earlier versions, ancient or modern.)

Robinson Jeffers, in *The Tower beyond Tragedy,* retold the tragic tale of Agamemnon, Clytemnestra, and Orestes, and was not afraid to compete with the Greek tragedians by bringing in his own interpretations. Three of these are especially striking on the stage, and I wonder how old Aeschylus would have viewed them. In one of them Electra proposes an incestuous union to her own brother Orestes after his triumph; that, I think, would have disgusted Aeschylus. In another, Clytemnestra does a striptease to delay the bodyguard of Agamemnon until her lover Aegisthus can arrive with his troops; that would have amused him. But the third, a scene in which the murdered king speaks—after his death, in his own voice, like a dybbuk, through the mouth of his slave-concubine the prophetess Cassandra—would perhaps have aroused the old Greek's admiration.

In particular, our dramatists emphasize sexual love as a dominating theme, far more than did the Greeks and Romans; and they stress the lust for power considerably less, or play it down. There is scarcely anything in modern mythical drama like the tyrannical Zeus of Aeschylus, the revenge-maddened tyrants of Seneca, or even the arrogant Oedipus of Sophocles, who spits metrical venom at old Tiresias in an immortal line (*Oedipus the King* 371):

τυφλὸς τά τ᾽ ὦτα τόν τε νοῦν τά τ᾽ ὄμματ᾽ εἶ.

You are blind in your ears, in your mind, and in your eyes.

It seems strange to me that, in an epoch which has seen the recrudescence of personal tyranny more ruthless and efficient than anything which has existed for some centuries, our playwrights have mostly been reluctant to portray it, even in mythical terms. For example, the arrogant Roman general Coriolanus was treated by Shakespeare as a bitter scorner of democracy, the enemy of the people. As they banish him for (alleged) treason, he shouts in their faces (3.3.121–28):

> You common cry of curs, whose breath I hate
> As reek o' th' rotten fens, whose loves I prize
> As the dead carcasses of unburied men
> That do corrupt my air, *I* banish *you!*
> And here remain with your uncertainty!
> Let every feeble rumor shake your hearts!
> Your enemies, with nodding of their plumes,
> Fan you into despair!

And so he leaves his home forever, calling the sovereign people "the beast with many heads" that "butts him away" (4.1.1–2).

During the 1930s T. S. Eliot published *Coriolan*, consisting of two interesting fragments of an unfinished drama on the same theme. Neither of the scenes deals with the banishment of Coriolanus; but one is a monologue which transforms him completely from the arrogant Roman general of Livy and Shakespeare into a modern administrator—impersonal, efficient, and almost insane with boredom and fatigue.

> The first thing to do is to form the committees:
> The consultative councils, the standing committees, select committees and sub-committees.
> One secretary will do for several committees . . .
> A commission is appointed
> To confer with a Volscian commission
> About perpetual peace: the fletchers and javelin-makers and smiths
> Have appointed a joint committee to protest against the reduction of orders.
> Meanwhile the guards shake dice on the marshes
> And the frogs (O Mantuan) croak in the marshes.
> Fireflies flare against the faint sheet lightning
> What shall I cry?
> Mother mother
> Here is the row of family portraits, dingy busts, all looking remarkably Roman,
> Remarkably like each other, lit up successively by the flare
> Of a sweaty torchbearer, yawning . . .
> O mother (not among these busts, all correctly inscribed)
> I a tired head among these heads
> Necks strong to bear them
> Noses strong to break the wind
> Mother
> May we not be some time, almost now, together,
> If the mactations, immolations, oblations, impetrations,
> Are now observed
> May we not be

O hidden
Hidden in the stillness of noon, in the silent croaking night . . .
O mother
What shall I cry?
We demand a committee, a representative committee, a committee of investigation
RESIGN RESIGN RESIGN

Exhausted not with frustration and opposition, and wounded not by the enemy's spears but by the infinite pettiness of detail, Eliot's Coriolanus is less like a Roman Coriolanus than a modern administrator who is too tired even to enjoy the prizes of his power.[16]

Now we have looked at several aspects of the interplay of Greco-Roman legend and twentieth-century literature. Sometimes our authors take mythical figures and identify them with contemporary characters, including themselves. Sometimes they use such figures and the stories about them to make a striking contrast with our own world. Sometimes they retell the ancient stories in order to extract new insights from them. (So did many of their predecessors, even in antiquity; both the lyric poet Stesichorus [in his *Palinode*] and the dramatist Euripides [in his *Helen*] said that Helen never really went to Troy at all.) Sometimes again they meditate simply on figures projected in stone by the Greek artists.

But the world of Greece and Rome appears in still other ways, less definite, harder to explain and exemplify. Valéry says that every man belongs to two eras.[17] Some modern writers belong to their own time and find their real spiritual home in the age of classical antiquity. To them sometimes Greece and Rome mean opposition to Christianity. The conflict between the spiritual world of paganism and the Christian church has continued for nearly two thousand years, and shows no signs of ending. It has often produced valuable and fruitful tensions, and has sometimes subjected individual poets and thinkers to agonies of doubt or made them half-hysterical with the violence of its pressure. Some contemporaries, therefore, use Greek myths in order to attack Christianity, either by reducing it to only one among many possible religious experiences or by opposing it as a spiritual enemy.

This is the real meaning of Jean-Paul Sartre's only play on a classical theme, *The Flies*. Because it was produced in Paris during the German occupation in 1943 and dealt with an ancient Greek

---

[16][See G. Highet, "An Unfinished Poem," in *The Powers of Poetry* (New York, 1960) 293–300, for his analysis of *Coriolan* and his theory as to why Eliot never completed it. Ed.]

[17]See Hytier (abcve, note 4) vol. 1, p. 1063, for this statement from *Variété*.

city filled with swarms of bloodsucking flies which tormented its citizens without killing them, many critics assumed that it was somehow an allegory about political tyranny and about the duty of resistance. That it may be; but its main theme is opposition to Christianity. This is made clear by two important emphases in the drama: first, the complete deformation of the Hellenic religion and its ideals; second, the final confrontation between God and man. The Greeks, as we know, believed in gods who were grand and powerful, but issued no Ten Commandments, punished only the greatest offenders, and maintained happy harmony in the universe. But as we see it in *The Flies,* the city of Argos is haunted by the Christian concept of original sin. There is a public confession of guilt every year; small children suffer from the consciousness of their inborn evil; ghosts return to taunt the living with remorse; and the god called Zeus loves all this—he feeds upon it. This, I need hardly tell you, is not Greek at all; it is a caricature of Christianity. Finally, God attempts to intimidate Orestes, addressing him in a mighty voice like the Divinity who addresses Job out of the whirlwind. Orestes replies that God may be the ruler of the universe, but he is not the ruler of man. And at this Zeus—no, he does not blast Orestes with his lightning; he shrinks down to the size of an idol built by human hands. Orestes leaves, having freed his own citizens; but with him he takes the bloodsucking flies, who represent the sorrow and loneliness which the redeemer must endure. Only a human redeemer can truly suffer.

But perhaps it may not be necessary for a human being to suffer passively, even if he opposes a transcendent God and asserts humanity? This clearly is the message of the modern *Odyssey* by Nikos Kazantzakis, in which we see the old Homeric hero, even more indestructible and more versatile, passing through thousands of years of history back to the caves, and thousands of miles of pilgrimage to the remotest place on this globe, still refusing to lose his courage and his confidence. This extraordinary poem, a modern Greek *Faust,* has a strange and a seldom-read classical Greek counterpart—the tale by Nonnus of the victorious journey of Dionysus from Asia into Europe, achieving his godhead. Difficult to read as it is, because of its apparent planlessness and its constant exaggeration, it is strengthening to the heart because it is so full of energy. It can be called, like the original *Odyssey,* an epic of non-Christian humanism and unquenchable optimism.[18]

18[See Highet's "Kazantzakis's *Odyssey*"—a lecture appearing earlier in this volume—for a more detailed examination of Kazantzakis's poem. Ed.]

A few twentieth-century authors, however, have felt both the power of Christianity and that of the classical world, and have responded to both. Thus, Rilke wrote not only *Sonnets to Orpheus* but a *Life of Mary,* evoked not only Leda and Sappho, but Joshua and the risen Christ. In one or two of his most famous and difficult poems, Yeats suggested that the crucifixion of Jesus was a new enactment of an ancient mythical event, the mutilation and slaying of the god; and that the coming of Jesus, like that of his predecessor Dionysus, was to inaugurate a new era of chaos and disaster (*Two Songs from a Play* 1.1–8 and 13–16):

> I saw a staring virgin stand
> Where holy Dionysus died,
> And tear the heart out of his side,
> And lay the heart upon her hand
> And bear that beating heart away;
> And then did all the Muses sing
> Of Magnus Annus at the spring,
> As though God's death were but a play . . .
> The Roman Empire stood appalled:
> It dropped the reins of peace and war
> When that fierce virgin and her Star
> Out of the fabulous darkness called.

Surely it is most strange, this confrontation of the modern world with that vanished realm which seems to be both far remote and eternally compresent. One of its strangest aspects is that we do not choose to take from the Greeks and Romans what they themselves took the greatest trouble to create and considered their principal contributions to civilization: philosophical theories; political and administrative systems; principles of aesthetic structure; and laws of thought and conceptions of history. These gifts our forefathers accepted and passed on to us. Some we have neglected. Others we think of as entirely our own. From some, particularly in art and philosophy, we are deliberately turning away. But we most admire the products of that curious Greece of the New Stone Age and the Bronze Age—a Greece which could not think logically but which had, more eminently than any other people, the soul of a poet. That soul created the beautiful monsters whom we still admire—the nymphs of the watersprings, the satyrs of the woodland, Aphrodite born of the sea foam, the Furies snuffing the scent of blood, Priam kissing the hands of the man who killed his son, Oedipus the king turned into a blind beggar, Apollo with his choir of Muses, and Orpheus with his lute enthralling the sentinels of death. They are all irrational, and they inhabit our imagination as though born there. Perhaps we love the Greek myths not only because they are lovely and noble, but because they express essential forces in our minds, which, if forced to find other media, would issue in far more hideous and dangerous shapes.

In our century the man who has best comprehended this possibility is C. G. Jung. In order to explain it, he turned to one of the earliest Greek philosophers, who was also a mystic and a poet—Heraclitus—who[19]

> discovered the most extraordinary of all psychological laws, namely, the regulating function of the opposites . . . The rational attitude of culture necessarily goes over into its opposite, the irrational devastation of culture. One must not identify oneself with reason, because man is not and cannot be wholly rational, nor will he ever become so. This is a fact which should be noted by all pedants of culture. The irrational cannot and must not be wiped out. The gods cannot and must not die.

The same has been said in poetic terms by Auden, in a splendid sonnet (*In Time of War* XII):

> And the age ended, and the last deliverer died
> In bed, grown idle and unhappy; they were safe:
> The sudden shadow of the giant's enormous calf
> Would fall no more at dusk across the lawn outside.
>
> They slept in peace: in marshes here and there no doubt
> A sterile dragon lingered to a natural death,
> But in a year the spoor had vanished from the heath;
> The kobold's knocking in the mountain petered out.
>
> Only the sculptors and the poets were half sad,
> And the pert retinue from the magician's house
> Grumbled and went elsewhere. The vanquished powers were glad
>
> To be invisible and free: without remorse
> Struck down the sons who strayed into their course,
> And ravished the daughters, and drove the fathers mad.

---

[19]See Jung's *Psychology of the Unconscious,* chapter 5, for this passage—quoted from J. Jacobi, ed., *Psychological Reflections: An Anthology of the Writings of C. G. Jung* (New York, 1953) 229.

Advice to a Barnard Freshman*

Decipit, heu, miseras audax Martini puellas;

Canada Dry potior Cocave Cola tibi.[1]

---

*A 1973 'textual emendation' fully entitled: "Advice to a Barnard Freshman Invited to a Party *(Fragmentum Pseudovidianum Post Versum 3.766 Artis Amatoriae Ponendum)*."

[1][The following translation, by Professor J. D. Ellsworth, is provided here for the general reader:

> A dry martini clouds a young girl's head;
> It's better that you have a Coke instead.

See Highet's "A Dissertation on Roast Pig," *CW* 67 (1973) 14–15, for another amusing emendation. Ed.]

Then and Now: The Classics Profession[*]

Let me begin by greeting all my colleagues as friends. Friends we must be, since we love the same things—the world of ancient Greece and Rome, and hate the same things[1]—ignorance (we are pledged to remove it, or at least to diminish it), barbarism (which threatens us as it threatened our spiritual ancestors), and materialism (against which we support and defend some of the noblest ideals of humanity). So I greet you all as friends; I felicitate you on helping the New York Classical Club to attain not a ripe old age but an honorable and vigorous maturity; and I wish you all a long-continuing happiness, illuminated by the perpetual radiance that streams upon us from Rome and Greece.

On an occasion such as this it is natural to look backward as well as forward. I started to learn Greek and Latin in grade school at the age of eleven; I shall be sixty-nine next month—so that I have been thinking about the classics more or less continuously for more than fifty years. (Frankly, I am still perplexed by the fact that I know so little about the classics. And I don't even know whether this should be discouraging, "the life so short, the craft so long to learn,"[2] or delightful, in that there is still so much left to discover and to enjoy.) With you, my friends, I wish to discuss some of the experiences which classicists have gone through during that half-century.

First comes a fact, a highly important fact, of which I was only dimly aware for the first few years or so. This is that classical studies—like many other intellectual and aesthetic pursuits—were injured, almost paralyzed, and nearly wrecked, by World War I and by the social and economic upheavals that followed it. Certainly American classicists had done some sterling work before that war, and the United States was not grievously afflicted by its

---

*Presented in 1975 for the New York Classical Club.
[1][An echo of the Latin idiom *idem velle atque idem nolle*—found in Sallust (*Catiline* 20.4) and Seneca (*Epist.* 109.16)—the two sources noted by Highet in the margin of his manuscript. Ed.]
[2][A reference to Chaucer's *Parliament of Fowls* 1—as Highet noted in the margin of his manuscript—but originating with Hippocrates' *Aphorisms* 1.1 (ὁ βίος βραχύς, ἡ δὲ τέχνη μακρή). Ed.]

disasters. Nevertheless, the strategic center of classical studies had been western and central Europe; and World War I, followed by an appalling depression, arrested most of that outflow of intellectual energy in Germany, in the Austro-Hungarian Empire, in France, in Great Britain, and in Italy. It is painful to look over the books, the periodicals, and the large far-sighted enterprises of scholarship which were being produced in Europe with increasing vitality and ever widening range through the years from 1880 through 1900 to 1910 to 1914, and then to see how—abruptly and irresistibly— they were cut down. Many young scholars were killed. Many others were impoverished. State subsidies were cut back. University presses ran out of money. And publishers could not even get decent paper. In 1923 Wilhelm Kroll published an admirable edition of Catullus, which only a few years later was apt to come to pieces in the hand and to crumble away even on the library shelf.[3] Many important series of texts—the Teubners, the Budés, the Oxfords— dwindled down to a trickle. Many valuable books went out of print and were not republished.

Compared with the massive human suffering that devastated a whole generation and more, all this was unimportant. Still, for students, it did have all sorts of discouraging and damaging effects. As I grew up after the war and became deeply interested in studying the classics, I—like thousands of others—found it very difficult to obtain a wide range of texts and commentaries. Again and again there was only one single copy of an important edition available; and again and again that belonged to the university library, had been taken out by a senior professor six months earlier, and was unattainable. Or else it had been returned to the library but was instantly withdrawn for rebinding; and after rebinding it was in such a parlous condition that it could not be taken out, but had to be consulted within the library building (SIX O'CLOCK, CLOSING TIME, SIX O'CLOCK). I used to haunt secondhand bookstores. You would laugh if you went through my bookshelves today and saw some survivors of that era—battered old books dated 1910, bearing the names of three or four previous owners, carefully repaired and rebound by my father and myself.

This is one of the great changes, one of the splendid improvements, which have marked classical studies in our era. Reprints— or photographic reproductions—of important books, long long out of print, are now readily available. God bless (in particular) Georg Olms of Hildesheim; he has given us (at not too great a cost) fresh

---

[3]See W. Kroll, ed., *C. Valerius Catullus* (Leipzig, 1923).

clean copies of many works which I never expected to see except
on a reserved shelf, far less to own and use regularly. Between ourselves, I am sometimes shocked when I visit certain large libraries
and find that—even in these days of strict budgeting and penny-
pinching—the Department of Acquisitions has been lavishly buying up reprints of collections of nineteenth-century classical essays, eighteenth-century translations of dubious value, and commentaries long ago superseded. But then I remember the old days,
when the note VERGRIFFEN or OUT-OF-PRINT appeared opposite every title one wanted in the booksellers' catalogues, accompanied by a price hike of 500%; and I revel in the luxury of having
too many books.

That war—World War I—did a great deal of spiritual damage.
The European nations had never been really friendly (except perhaps when fighting against Napoleon); but as 1914 grew into 1915
and 1916 and 1917, toward the desperate exhaustion of 1918, they
came to hate and to detest one another. One result of all this was
that many young British and French and Italian students never
thought of learning German, or did so with great reluctance—although (as they were later to discover) many of the basic tools for
classical study are in German. I mention only the great encyclo-
pedia of classical learning edited by A. Pauly and G. Wissowa. It is
essential. Its eighty-some stately if ill-printed volumes have long
adorned the shelves of my personal library; but I don't think I had
ever heard of it, and certainly I had never been advised to use it
until I was approaching graduation. This was in Great Britain,
which had suffered much from the Germans. Similar feelings of
revulsion and hostility were at work elsewhere. Even now, this
particularism or chauvinism still appears from time to time and
still injures the study of our discipline. In 1968 Albin Lesky published a magnificent survey of modern Homeric research in
Pauly-Wissowa's *Real-Encyclopädie,* in which he discusses the
discovery made by the American Milman Parry, that much of
Homer's poetry is based on traditional phrases handed down from
generations of earlier poets, and then adds: "Research on Homer
was not helped by the fact that on the continent of Europe, scholars
for long closed their minds to all that could be learned from Parry
and his school."[4] The study of Greece and Rome is indeed an inter-

---

4[See A. Lesky, "Homeros," in *RE, Supplementband* 11 (1968) 687–846, especially 702, for the words *es ist der Homerforschung nicht zugute gekom-
men, dass man sich auf dem Kontinent lange allem verschloss, was von
Parry und seiner Schule zu lernen war.* Ed.]

national enterprise. It cannot be carried on by the descendants of only one or two of the semi-barbarian tribes to whom the Greeks and Romans taught civilization.

Forty or fifty years ago classical studies suffered from another defect, which still continues to afflict them. I know about this partly because I had to fight hard against it in my own mind. The professor of Latin at the first university I attended, J. S. Phillimore, embodied it personally and impressed it on his students by the power of example. He expressed it in a famous epigram, in which he contemptuously dismissed archaeological research. "One line of Propertius," he said, "is worth more than all the pots and pans in the Peloponnese." So when I studied Greek and Latin, and later when I started to teach these subjects, I had never been to Italy or Greece. I had never spent more than a couple of hours in a museum devoted to Greek and Roman things—although (as an aesthete of that period) I had passed many days looking at great Renaissance and modern paintings in art galleries. I had never closely examined an ancient inscription; I had never handled a papyrus. And more fundamentally, I had never realized—and many of my colleagues had never realized—that the texts, the whole corpus of Greek and Latin literature, did not represent nearly the whole of the life of the classical world; that the texts themselves could not be truly understood without the supplementary data provided by archaeological studies, by epigraphy, and by papyrology; and that for all their liveliness and charm, the texts were sometimes even a little artificial, a little unreal, as compared with visible and tangible records of the past. We were taught to make a sharp distinction between philology (the study of language and literature) and archaeology, and to consider philology far superior. This was wrong; but it was widespread.

Sometimes it worked the other way also, so that archaeologists, who were constantly discovering something new, assumed a patronizing attitude to the philologists, sitting in their studies going back and forward over the same old texts. Sometimes the hostility between these two methods of exploring the ancient world, within the minds of classical scholars, was subconscious rather than rational. T. W. Allen, editor of the Oxford text of Homer and author of *Homer: The Origins and the Transmission,* refused to visit Greece, saying that the modern Greeks did not know how to cook.[5] Werner

---

[5]For this anecdote, see the review of Geoffrey Trease's autobiography, *A Whiff of Burnt Boats,* which appeared in the *Times Literary Supplement* (April 16, 1971) 438.

Jaeger of Harvard, the author of a famous three-volume analysis of Greek culture called *Paideia,* having once climbed up to the Acropolis of Athens and having spent some time there, absolutely refused to repeat the experience.[6] Those who tried to bridge the gap between the two disciplines were, during those early years, only a few in number and not at first influential. One of them was Alan Blakeway. Not long before his premature death he said to me (and I wrote it down in my diary for 1934): "If you were to tell our colleagues that Aeschylus produced the *Oresteia* in the same year that the pediments at Olympia were completed, they would pay no attention." But J. D. Beazley knew how important this was and said so.[7]

But in recent years this situation has greatly improved. As you know, the American Philological Association and the American Institute of Archaeology hold their meetings in conjunction, at the same times and places, and some of our most notable philologists have been equally eminent in archaeology. For instance, Henry Rowell, who edited the *American Journal of Philology* for many years and had fine literary taste (he was one of the few men I ever knew who could make a fluent speech in Latin, literally extempore), was also President of the American Institute of Archaeology (1953–56), and he combined both activities as President of the American Academy in Rome. One could also mention Margarete Bieber and the late T. B. L. Webster; there are many more who combine the activities.

As well as individual teachers, books now address themselves to a wider audience and demand a broader spread of interest. Here is one example. Two of the most startling classical discoveries made in recent years have both affected the study of Homer's epics—Milman Parry's conception of Homer as 'oral poetry' and Michael Ventris's decipherment of Linear B.[8] These and other investigations are all embodied in a huge companion to Homer.[9] Agreed, the

---

[6][Here Highet noted that he obtained this information from someone named Doro Levi. Ed.]

[7]See J. D. Beazley, "Early Classical Sculpture," in J. B. Bury, S. A. Cook, and F. E. Adcock, edd., *The Cambridge Ancient History* (New York, 1927) vol. 5, chap. 15, sect. 3, pp. 426–32, especially 430.

[8][See Highet's "Decipherment of Linear B"—a lecture appearing earlier in this volume—for a more detailed examination of Ventris's achievement in this area. Ed.]

[9]Here see A. J. Wace and F. H. Stubbings, edd., *A Companion to Homer* (London, 1962).

book has its defects of emphasis.[10] But I look at it and think how, when I was first making my laborious way through Homer's poetry fifty-five years ago, I was not only puzzled by dozens of the questions which this book examines but also in despair of ever finding a book which would discuss them clearly and point toward solutions. Then I remember that, both for the ancient Greeks and for us modern classicists, the study of Homer is one of the central delights of literature; and yet once again I realize that in the world of classical study, within one lifetime, much has improved—greatly improved.

Talking of books, here is another fact which must be, from our point of view, an advance. There are more translations of classical literature available today than ever before. Some are good. A few are truly distinguished. Many are pretty poor. Yet even the poor ones are not bad in the same way as the bad translations which I saw in my youth. They were sometimes dreadfully pompous, even to the point of being unintelligible. For instance, the eminent poet Robert Browning, translating the *Agamemnon* of Aeschylus, gives us this rendering of part of the dialogue between Cassandra and the Chorus (1246–49):

CASSANDRA
  I say, thou Agamemnon's fate shalt look on.
CHORUS
  Speak good words, O unhappy! Set mouth sleeping!
CASSANDRA
  But Paian stands in no stead to the speech here.
CHORUS
  Nay, if the thing be near: but never be it!

If they were not turgid, the translations of those days were sometimes literal in the grossest degree. I remember deciding (aged thirteen or so) that Horace must be a crude and vulgar lyric poet if he wrote (as the Bohn translator made him say for *Carm.* 1.13.3–4) "alas, my inflamed liver swells with bile difficult to be repressed." Nowadays even the poor translations strive to talk a language that sounds contemporary (not that this is always appropriate); and even if their technique—like the free verse which most of them use—abandons much of the subtlety and grandeur of classical poetry, at least they are like monochrome photographs of

---

[10]H. Lloyd-Jones, reviewing it in *The Listener* (September 27, 1962) 484, objected that it still tends to mix up the world of Homer's poems and the world of Mycenae. See the strictures of E. R. Dodds in "Appendix to Chapter 1" of *Fifty Years (and Twelve) of Classical Scholarship* (New York, 1968) 38–42.

Greek sculpture or Roman architecture; they make the remote accessible.

Sometimes even the mistakes of modern translations are instructive and make good thinking-points or at least good talking-points for teachers. Half an hour spent with Robert Graves will always throw up some marvelous misinterpretations. A simpler one is the translation of Caesar by Rex Warner (1960), which puts the whole *Commentarii* into the first person singular, so that *Caesari nuntiatum est* becomes "I received reports." This of course destroys the whole elaborate camouflage of objective reporting which Julius took so much trouble to create and which permits us to see through what the French historian Rambaud called "the art of historical deformation."[11]

Translations make the remote accessible—accessible to both classicists and nonclassicists. Classical language students must learn to read the original languages. Yes, but there are many books scarcely worth reading through in the original, unless by specialists. Very early in my own life I made a rule never to look at a translation of any Greek or Roman work—unless it had its own special aesthetic merit or unless I was desperately puzzled by a difficult sentence. But recently I have been breaking this rule in order to read rapidly some author whom I should not wish to work through line by line—for instance, Appian's *Roman History* and Josephus's *Jewish Wars*—although even there, whenever I see a particularly striking paragraph, or whenever I suspect that the translation may be inaccurate, I go straight to the original. The great thing is to get plenty of reading done in the classics, not only intensively but extensively also. Therefore I believe it is legitimate for all but the most advanced students to read some part of the important classics in translation and the rest in the original, in order that they may get a view of the whole as a whole.

One note on translation. All translations are imperfect and all translations are inadequate. The more of any language you know, the more you realize how imperfect all attempts to translate its great books must be. (Here is a parallel from another art. Arturo Toscanini very rarely heard a performance of any great musical work which satisfied him, even when he himself had rehearsed and conducted it. Once an admirer brought him a phonograph record which reproduced one of Toscanini's favorite pieces, done by his own orchestra under his own baton. He listened with ner-

---

[11][For the arguments employed, see M. Rambaud, *L'Art de la déformation historique dans les "Commentaires" de César* (Paris, 1952[1] and 1966[2]). Ed.]

vous intensity. When it was over, he heaved a big sigh and said: "Yes, almost as good as reading the score!") Virtually all translations are smaller, thinner, less variegated, less full of strange words and striking figures of speech and subtle rhythmic patterns than their originals. Therefore we ourselves, and still more our pupils, should never use one single translation—always several, side by side, to remind us that we looking at jejune reproductions and faded photographs, not the solid sun-warmed marble or the living breathing body.

So then, as compared with fifty years ago, there are far more translations of the classics readily available, in modern style, often with useful notes. If we look carefully, we can even discover the watershed between modern and antique, in translation. It was an attack on the translations of Gilbert Murray, published by the arrogant young critic T. S. Eliot, which appeared in a collection of essays called *The Sacred Wood*.[12] Murray's versions of Greek drama had been often staged, and even during the hard times of World War I they had been highly successful. Even after Eliot's attack they continued to be successful, for a time. But Eliot's strictures, and the new style which he and his contemporaries were developing, were soon to make Gilbert Murray's rhyming couplets and Swinburnian phraseology hopelessly out-of-date. Indeed, Eliot himself was later to produce several plays with Greek themes, only partly concealed behind modern situations, and to write them in a new style closer to prose than to verse. The old glamour has gone; but the dramatic power has increased.

There are far more translations today. There are also far more books of reference: atlases of the classical world; histories of classical literature; surveys of ancient history; albums of photographs showing rare works of art, famous places seen from the air, coins twenty times magnified; dictionaries of biography, of mythology, of literature, of the classical world in general; specialist collections— for instance, the *Bibliography of Classical Imagery* sponsored by Viktor Pöschl in more than 600 pages;[13] and—more important than all—bibliographical reference-books which show us everything that has been published in a given year on a given subject. All such books are far more frequent, far more attainable, and far more comprehensive than they were during my youth. *L'Année*

---

[12]See T. S. Eliot, "Euripides and Professor Murray," in his book *The Sacred Wood: Essays on Poetry and Criticism* (London, 1920) 71–77.
[13]See V. Pöschl, ed., *Bibliographie zur Antiken Bildersprache* (Heidelberg, 1964).

Philologique, that indispensable French bibliographical annual on which American and German scholars are now collaborating, was just being born in the 1920s; but how it has grown! In 1929 it was three years old, and the volume published then, covering the year 1928, had 287 pages (including a mention of Margarete Bieber's *Greek Clothing,* on p. 217). The latest volume I have is volume 42, covering the year 1971, which contains 856 pages (including a mention of the new edition of Bieber's *Greek Clothing,* on p. 502). It takes me about a month of evenings to go through it.

Most of the entries in *L'Année Philologique* concern not books, but articles which have appeared in magazines, specialist and even some nonspecialist articles dealing with classical subjects. The list of periodicals surveyed each year now covers seventeen closely printed pages and must run to something like 800 items. (The corresponding list for 1928 covers eight pages, perhaps 550 items—of which many were small local antiquarian bulletins now superseded.) It is tempting to look at today's parade of periodicals, row upon row, and say that there are too many, that too many articles are being published, that nobody can possibly read even a quarter of the material that keeps pouring out, that much of it is a waste of time and paper and energy, both spiritual and electrical. But this temptation we must resist. One essential stimulus for the growth of knowledge is lively discussion, the exploration of many new fields and unfamiliar points of view. That stimulus is given to us by the multiplicity of periodicals. It is difficult everywhere nowadays to get hardcover books published; and once published, it is not easy to have them kept in print. Rather than fail of publication altogether, it is useful to have articles brought out in serious magazines. Indeed, I can think of several distinguished classical scholars who have published only two books or one or none, but who are widely respected and powerfully influential because of the magisterial studies which they have brought out in periodicals.

And there is a marvelous feeling of encouragement in reading a new periodical every week or so. The deadly, discouraging thing for some young students nowadays—for instance in small towns without a good library, or in foreign lands where new books and new magazines are not readily available—is to feel that their subject is static, that nothing new is being thought or discovered about it, and that nothing ever will; so that all they can do is laboriously to learn off the essentials and then to sink back into repetition and repose. But this feeling can be cured by constant exposure to new discoveries, new ideas, and new interpretations. I remember once in a moderately advanced class I handed out a reading-list giving the essential books to be studied and discussed; and then a second list of recently published articles in periodicals, which could and really should be looked through. One of the more impulsive students could not restrain himself. "Gosh," he cried, looking at the second list, "gosh, I never realized there was so much going on!"

There is another field in which enormous advances have been made, particularly since World War II. Important classical texts have been discovered, and sometimes in the most peculiar places. (Fragments of a comedy—Menander's *Man from Sikyon*—were found inside a mummy-case in the storage room of the Sorbonne, where they had reposed undisturbed for many years.) And modern scholars have been scanning manuscripts with greater care and with more sensitive critical standards than their predecessors. Two or three generations ago it was not uncommon to read in the preface to a new text that the editor had been unable to inspect manuscripts A, B, and C for himself, and had relied on collations made by his colleagues or by earlier critics. But now scholars such as Ulrich Knoche (editor of Juvenal) and R. D. Dawe (who specializes in Aeschylus), and L. D. Reynolds (editor of Seneca's letters) insist on reading all the important manuscripts personally, and often construct a more complicated but more trustworthy picture of their relation to the original—and so a more acceptable text. We are truly fortunate to be working at a time when *there is so much going on*. It is pathetic to look far back into an age of real barbarism, into the Dark Ages when so many of our good manuscripts were being laboriously copied out, and to see there that some books were so rare and precious that a librarian would write to his colleague hundreds of miles away, begging him to lend a text to be copied and promising faithfully to return it, while others were virtually unobtainable.[14] At the beginning of his book on education, Cassiodorus tells his pupils (the monks) that he has searched for one particular book in vain (St. Ambrose on the Psalms) and that after he is gone they must do their best to discover it—*quae vobis magno studio quaerenda derelinquo* (*Institutiones* 1.3.6). From an era eight hundred years later, we may also think of the Clerk of

---

[14][At this point Highet noted in the margin of his manuscript the words "chained books in Laurentian library"—a reference to a practice followed by certain European libraries for hundreds of years in order to prevent theft. Regarding this practice as it existed in the Laurentian library in Florence, consult B. H. Streeter, *The Chained Library: A Survey of Four Centuries in the Evolution of the English Library* (London, 1931) 24–25 and 295–97. Ed.]

Oxenford in Chaucer's *Canterbury Tales*. His most prized possession, we are told (*General Prologue* 294-95), would be

> Twenty books, clad in black or red,
> Of Aristotle and his philosophy.

Very praiseworthy; but do you know what these books would cost
him? I learn from a Chaucer expert that they would cost as much
as three good citizens' houses in a large town.[15]

The discovery of new Greek texts on papyrus is an intriguing
story. I know nothing about the inner workings of this particular
type of treasure-hunting, but I gather from occasional hints in
footnotes and in conversation that it is full of—shall I say skull-
duggery? No, clandestine, or at least unacknowledged activity. We
have been told in a fine book by Edmund Wilson, who was both a
good amateur scholar and a skilled journalist, how the Dead Sea
Scrolls were discovered and offered for sale and huckstered and
broken up and haggled over in a way which no one could call scientific.[16] They are not papyri; but papyri are almost as tricky. Eric
Turner, the English papyrologist, has written that after World
War II no expedition went to Egypt specifically to dig for papyri
until 1965.[17] Twenty years. Experts will correct me if I am wrong;
but I imagine this is a manifestation of the impulse to national self-
assertion which is growing stronger all over the world (and which
Karl Marx, in his analysis of the coming struggle for power, almost wholly neglected). An expert in this field told me that he personally knew a dozen sites; he was sure they were full of papyri,
but in the present political—what is the opposite of a detente? a
crunch?—he did not dare to visit them, far less to negotiate for official permission to dig there.

In spite of such difficulties, many new texts have recently been
revealed to us on papyri—fine, if fragmentary. Most important
are some of Menander's plays, the fragments of dramas by the
three great tragedians, and new work by the Greek lyric poets.
Now these are all fine reading in themselves. But almost equally
important is the way they are changing our thinking about the
classics. Unconsciously, for many generations, many scholars assumed that the classics were simply what we had, what had sur-

---

[15]See G. G. Coulton, *Chaucer and His England* (New York, 1957) 99.

[16][See E. Wilson, *The Dead Sea Scrolls (1947–1969)* (New York, 1969)—probably the best general work that had appeared on this subject at the time that
Highet gave this lecture. Ed.]

[17]See E. Turner, *Greek Papyri: An Introduction* (Oxford, 1968) 40.

vived the Dark Ages in the East (where Wilamowitz called that period "the catastrophe of the seventh and eighth centuries")[18] and in the West, to reach the late Middle Ages, the Renaissance, and the printers. Sophocles wrote seven plays, also some fragments, less often studied. The same for Aeschylus. Euripides wrote eighteen tragedies, but that made him terribly difficult, so that people wrote books called *Euripides the Rationalist* and *Euripides the Irrationalist* and *Euripides the Surrealist* and so on, while lecturers lamented the fact that he could not be classified. Outside these three, no other Greek dramatists existed—except in jokes by Aristophanes and as names in reference books. This was the background of conventional thought about Greek tragedy. Therefore it was possible to write whole books about Greek tragedy based only on these thirty-two plays as though no others had ever existed, and to write whole books on each of the three tragedians analyzing their individual styles and ethical attitudes on the basis of the few plays which had survived. At the back of the scholar's mind, when he reads or writes such a book, is the image of the iceberg and its tip. The seven plays of Sophocles are the tip; the lost plays are further down beneath the surface—all the same sort of structure and composition, all the same ice.

But this is mistaken. The discovery of new texts in papyri and the renewed study of the fragments of Greek tragedy show that it is mistaken. The image should not be that of an iceberg with its tip showing. We should think rather of a mountain range marked by varied stratification and violent distortion and occasional volcanic upheavals. What we see is not the tip of a berg but an outcrop of ore revealed by earlier prospectors. Beneath the outcrop—if we could only penetrate down to the invisible strata—there are twists and distortions in the rock, some of them perhaps holding new precious minerals, perhaps even—if we ever find some more Euripides—a huge reservoir of natural gas. This we know, because the new texts revealed by papyrus discoveries have been so unexpected. Besides that, the other writers are going to be given their due. We are always a little surprised when reading histories of Greek drama to see that Sophocles won only the second prize for a wonderful play which has survived, and that Euripides got only the third prize for

---

[18][Here (as related to me by Professor William M. Calder III) Highet is very likely quoting U. von Wilamowitz-Moellendorff's *Geschichte der Philologie* (Leipzig, 1927³ = 1959⁴) 3, where Wilamowitz uses the word *Zussamenbruch* ("collapse")—paraphrased by Highet as "catastrophe"—to characterize the demise of learning in Byzantium during the Dark Ages in the East. Ed.]

his famous drama, still being performed. We do not think much about A and B and C, the poets who beat them. Yet they were part of the wonderful poetic activity which was going on in Athens during the fifth century B.C., and without which the three great survivors would scarcely have been so great as they are. A fragment of a hitherto unknown tragedy on a historical theme—the adventures of Gyges, the early king of Lydia—has turned up on papyrus. It is very striking, although the specialists are not yet sure whether it belongs to the fifth century or the third. In any case, the point is that it is pretty good poetry on an original theme. There are more such anonymous fragments in recent collections. When we read them, we do not lose respect for the great geniuses but rather gain respect for the versatility and energy of the many talents who surrounded, stimulated, challenged, and sometimes conquered the geniuses. Horace says there were brave men before Agamemnon, but they are forgotten because they had no Homer to commemorate them—*carent quia vate sacro* (*Carm.* 4.9.25–28). So it has been, until recently, with the many brilliant writers of Greece; recent discoveries are bringing them back to life.

Books are the most important element in any branch of learning. The other two factors you know: they are the students and the teachers.[19]

I wish that I were able to say something both original and true—or if not that, striking and epigrammatic—about our students. But I cannot. I do not know enough about the schools—although I read statistics which are gloomy, or at least anxious-making, about the numbers of high-school students studying the classics both in this country and in other countries overseas. The one thing I feel sure of is that teaching in a high school nowadays is a dangerous profession—less like being a lawyer or a clergyman than like being a fireman or a policeman, or an attendant in an institution for the mentally disturbed. Why this should be so, I can only conjecture; I do not know. Nor do I see any solution to the problem. A subcommittee of the United States Senate recently issued the appalling statement that violence and vandalism in schools cost the nation $500,000,000 every year.[20] You and I read the statement. We read

---

[19][See Highet's *The Art of Teaching* (New York, 1950), for an analysis of the methods of teaching (a book translated into many languages), and his *The Immortal Profession* (New York, 1976), for a forty-year perspective on the joys of teaching and learning (his final book, written from retirement). Ed.]

[20]See E. B. Fiske, "Rising College Costs Bode Restructuring of Teaching," *New York Times* (April 23, 1975) 39.

and heard many comments upon it filled with disgust, dismay, and horror. But I at least did not see any comment which embodied a comprehensive and reasonable policy to solve this problem.

Did I say "teaching in a high school"? Teaching on all levels is becoming hazardous. The Senate of Vassar College has just declared that vandalism cost the college almost $100,000 last year and has reached a crisis level.[21] This is not only an American phenomenon. We also read of pint-sized gangsters, scarcely into their teens, terrorizing and blackmailing their classmates in English schools. A pen pal of mine in one of the great Japanese universities writes me that he finds it hard to concentrate when two rival student gangs of thugs are fighting a regular battle beneath his office window. Not long ago the president of one of the most prestigious educational institutions of France, the Ecole Normale Supérieure in Paris, asked for permission to resign, on the ground that he could no longer guarantee the safety of the property of the French Republic. The boys had invited street people inside and had broken into the wine cellars. His own students, one of the really superior elites of France, were wrecking the buildings.[22]

Is this not part of a widely spread psychical epidemic? Only a few generations ago (before 1883), when cholera broke out in a city, doctors knew what it was; but they could not cure it; and until certain radical discoveries were made, they could not prevent it from spreading. Nowadays we can combat many infections invading the human body. But pandemics attacking the human mind spread rapidly and irresistibly from country to country, from continent to continent, and are very difficult to control. They lay waste an enormous amount of valuable property and an even greater amount of intellectual and moral capital, human potential, and human souls. These pandemics have not yet been accurately diagnosed or described—although any physician will tell you that to describe a disease, to classify its symptoms, and to explain its incidence and its dangers, is the first step toward curing it. Surely the disorders of our schools and colleges are symptoms of a dangerous pandemic. There are other symptoms. Rioting at sports events (at a recent game between Manchester and Oxford in England, the seats were covered with blood; and this winter in Italy I saw on

---

[21]See Fiske (above, note 20).

[22][At this point Highet noted the name 'R. Flacelière' in the margin of his manuscript—a reference to the French classicist who served as President of the Ecole Normale Supérieure from 1963 to 1971 and who wrote *Normale en péril* (Paris, 1971), on the student disorders in his elite institution. Ed.]

television several footballers severely injured by dangerous mis-
siles thrown from the stands). Violent disorders at popular music
festivals, sometimes encouraged by the outrageous and the half-
insane costumes and gestures of the stars. Recourse to immediate
mob action in a political crisis, bypassing the slower but more reasonable methods of representative government. And of course the
most dangerous symptom of all—the widespread cult of mind-
blowing, mind-destroying drugs. This psychical pandemic is especially distressing because it chiefly attacks the young. How can we
diagnose it? How can we cure it? We do not know. We are in the
same situation as doctors were when dealing with yellow fever
until 1900, when a small team of devoted researchers discovered
its etiology. Of one thing I am sure. We as teachers cannot cure it.
At best we can (I hope) prevent it from spreading further and from
injuring still more of the young people whom we pity and sometimes love.

I can say little, then, about our students. How about the teachers
of the classics? Over the last fifty years have they got better or
worse? Going chiefly on my own experience, I declare that they
have grown much better. Their level of scholarship has risen and
continues to rise; that is, they are working harder and using more
of their gray matter. A couple of generations ago, some teachers
were dedicated. Others were deadbeats. My colleague and friend
Moses Hadas told me that at college he actually attended a course
of lectures given by a man who had written them out years and
years before. Apparently he never updated them—which of course
means that he ignored all the new articles and books on the subject
which were coming out year after year. But what was almost as
bad, he read them instead of talking them; and he never altered
them or adapted them or inserted a little spontaneity—because
(Hadas said) he had a tick in the margin telling him exactly when
he had reached the fifty-minute mark and could stop reading.
There were others like that man, far too many of them.

But there is one factor which we nowadays might forget in ap-
praising our predecessors. This is that many of them were poor.
Many were miserably badly paid—worse, I believe, in colleges and
universities than in schools. Because they were poor, they were
tired and discouraged. As Juvenal says, *paenituit multos vanae
sterilisque cathedrae*, "many professors regretted their useless and
barren careers" (7.203). And they were part of a pyramid, which
was very steep. A few near the top of the pyramid could afford to
buy lots of books and have a second home in the country and visit

Europe in the summers. Beneath these favored few, there were
multitudes of professors in smaller colleges, layers and layers of
assistant professors and instructors and 'associates,' who lived in a
state which might be called genteel indigence. And it was thought
to be indecent to complain about academic salaries (after all, "we
are not in this profession to make money"); and it came as a small
revolutionary shock when—I think it was in the 1940s—Jacques
Barzun pointed out that by accepting tiny salaries and enduring
the privations that went with them, the teachers were actually
subsidizing the education of the students.[23]

There was in those days rather a gulf between rich classicists
and poor classicists. Some well-known figures had large private
incomes—W. W. Tarn, the historian of Alexander; Arthur Evans,
the excavator of Knossos. Others had rich wives. Gilbert Murray
married the daughter of the Earl of Carlisle, who had an allow-
ance and who inherited more after her parents died—so that, as
Murray himself declares in his unfinished autobiography: "I have
never since the age of twenty-three . . . had much anxiety about
money."[24] These were the lucky ones. But many were not so lucky.
Only last week I was reading a biography of C. S. Lewis, author of
The Screwtape Letters and the *Perelandra* trilogy. He was eight
years older than I and began teaching English literature in 1924.
The biographers say that his "long years of grinding self-inflicted
poverty . . . made it second nature to him never to buy a book if he
could master its contents without doing so" and that his "meagerly
populated shelves looked as if they had been stocked entirely from
'the Fourpenny Box'"—that is, the cheapest section of a secondhand bookstall, where everything is marked down to a dime.[25] A
little later, in a description of his working habits, we see him writing not with a fountain pen but with "wooden penholder and steel
nib."[26] In most European countries things were much worse.
Eduard Fraenkel, who later became Professor of Latin at Oxford,

---

[23][See J. Barzun, *Teacher in America* (New York, 1945) 283–97, especially
289–97, for the views of this Columbia University professor on teachers'
salaries during the 1940s and for his suggestions as to the kinds of things
teachers might do to improve their conditions. Ed.]

[24]See G. Murray, *An Unfinished Autobiography* (London, 1960) 99. [See also
G. Highet, "Gilbert Murray," in *The Immortal Profession* (above, note 19)
145–74, for Highet's tribute to one of the three great teachers under whom
he studied at Oxford—Gilbert Murray, Cyril Bailey, and C. M. Bowra. Ed.]

[25]See R. L. Green and W. Hooper, *C. S. Lewis: A Biography* (London, 1974)
144.

[26]See Green and Hooper (above, note 25) 146.

told me he still remembered journeying to his first professorial post at Kiel. He and his wife were transporting a small baby and could not afford a thermos flask; and so at all the chief stops the young professor would run forward and get hot water from the engine driver to warm up the baby's formula.

In the United States this anomaly, the poverty of the teacher, was particularly painful during the boom years following World War I. Several of my colleagues told me how galling it was for them in the 1920s to be making four or five thousand a year when their stupider classmates, who had chosen to go into Wall Street as 'customers' men,' were making twenty or thirty thousand. (Such was Nick Carraway in F. Scott Fitzgerald's *The Great Gatsby*.) But then, one of them added with a reflective grin, came the Great Depression: "In the 1930s I was still making five thousand a year, and prices had fallen very low, while the customers' men had all been forced out of Wall Street and were living with their wives' parents."

Since then we have seen another boom or two. Now we are in the middle of—what shall I call it? A retrenchment. How much our economic situation as teachers has improved, I cannot tell. The problem has grown more complicated because new factors have intruded—such as the growing disparity between salaries in private schools and private universities, and salaries paid by the taxpayers in state-supported institutions. No, I cannot tell; but I feel confident that during the past forty or fifty years, it has got better. We are still not nearly as well-rewarded as we ought to be. We never were. Juvenal at the end of *Satire* 7 notes that teachers have a heavy moral and intellectual responsibility, and then adds that they make less in a year than a racing driver in one match (7.242–43). That certainly has not changed. In fact, it has got worse. Which of us can hope in half a lifetime to equal the year's prize-money of the tennis player Jimmy Connors, or the golfer Jack Nicklaus, or the boxer Muhammed Ali?

Looking back, then, over fifty or sixty years, we see that in our field, our demanding but rewarding field of study, some things have grown worse, but others have grown better.

It is more difficult to teach the young now than it used to be. But for that fact we *as teachers* are not responsible. We are rather more earnest, and dedicated, and keen on our subject, and eager to help our pupils than some of our predecessors early in the century. And we are not responsible *as Americans:* for (as I pointed out) student disorders which would have been unthinkable a generation or so ago are now widespread, all over the world. In fact, it is far more difficult to be parent than it once was; and teaching is a kind of parenthood.

Nowadays, though, it is easier to be a classicist. Not that the subject itself—or the whole range of subjects which we call the classics—has grown simpler. On the contrary, it has broadened out and deepened down so enormously that it is now beyond the scope of any single human mind. However, access to it has become much simpler and more inviting that I remember it. There are more and better texts, commentaries, and reference-books, more national and international discussions where new ideas are generated by spiritual contact, and in general a sense of optimism and expansion which is solidly based on a real and growing achievement.

To that achievement we have contributed our small share by our work as teachers and as friends of ancient Greece and Rome. Our greatest and truest repayment is the work itself. When we are threatened and almost overwhelmed with tidal waves of aesthetic garbage and with strangling clouds of intellectual smog, we can be proud that we have always concerned ourselves with much of the finest in literature and art and thought, and are still upholding that primacy. We may felicitate ourselves as members of this Club, dedicated to such ideals. We can look forward with hope and with confidence to the future. For the next twenty-five years—which will take us to the year 2000—I offer the New York Classical Club, and all its members present and future, my most sincere and warm good wishes.

INDEX